Artificial Intelligence and Copyright

AIPPI Law Series

VOLUME 10

Series Editors

AIPPI

Introduction & Contents/Subjects

Books in this series are developed within the framework of the International Association for the Protection of Intellectual Property (AIPPI), a non-affiliated non-profit organization dedicated to the development and improvement of legal regimes for the protection of intellectual property at both national and international levels.

Objective & Readership

The aim is to publish innovative work appealing to practitioners, other users of IP systems and academics.

The titles in this series are listed at the back of this volume.

Artificial Intelligence and Copyright

Edited by

Guillaume Henry

and

Sanna Wolk

Wolters Kluwer

Published by:
Kluwer Law International B.V.
PO Box 316
2400 AH Alphen aan den Rijn
The Netherlands
E-mail: lrs-sales@wolterskluwer.com
Website: www.wolterskluwer.com/en/solutions/kluwerlawinternational

Sold and distributed by:
Wolters Kluwer Legal & Regulatory U.S.
920 Links Avenue
Landisville, PA 17538
United States of America
E-mail: customer.service@wolterskluwer.com

Printed on acid-free paper.

ISBN: 978-94-035-4278-2

e-ISBN: 978-94-035-4288-1
Web PDF ISBN: 978-94-035-4298-0

AIPPI Law Series ISBN 98-888-8020-8

About the Contributors

Luiza Alkaim is a senior associate at Souto Correa Advogados, specializing in Intellectual Property and Media & Entertainment Law. She advises clients in transactions related to trademark, copyright, advertising, marketing, software, and unfair competition. Luiza holds a law degree from IBMEC and a postgraduate degree in Intellectual Property Law from PUC-Rio.

Hailey Bureau, PhD, specializes in preparing and prosecuting patent applications in the fields of chemistry and biotechnology. Hailey utilizes her scientific background to develop strategic approaches for patent prosecution. She has experience working alongside international law firms and in-house counsel, and she frequently lectures on various patent-related subjects. Her expertise encompasses a variety of areas, including batteries, polymers, antibodies, cell culturing, resins, rubbers, diagnostics, medical devices, food and beverage additives, and nanomaterials.

Gao Cheng is an attorney at Beijing TA Law Firm, specializing in intellectual property (IP), entertainment and media, and AI-related legal services. GAO Cheng has provided comprehensive professional legal support to leading film/television companies, online audiovisual platforms, industry associations, artists, writers, and creators, including dispute resolution, IP transactions, and diverse and complex legal affairs. Additionally, GAO Cheng has also co-authored the book *General Knowledge on Personal Information Protection*.

Martyna Czapska is an attorney-at-law and Senior Associate at Baker McKenzie. She has been practicing the law of new technologies and intellectual property law since 2016. As a technology enthusiast and a gamer herself, she also specializes in artificial intelligence law and video games law.

Malin Ekstrand is a counsel/advokat at Ström Law Firm in Sweden, specializing in intellectual property law, with a strong focus on the music and entertainment industries. With a deep understanding of the creative sector and its legal landscape,

Malin regularly assists clients in navigating complex IP issues in an evolving digital environment, advising on transactions of creative assets, and negotiating contracts in cross-border matters.

Brian W. Gray is an arbitrator and mediator and works in all aspects of intellectual property technology and media matters. He is a member of the panel of arbitrators of the World intellectual Property Organization and the Canadian International Internet Dispute Resolution Centre. Brian is also a fellow of the Chartered Institute of Arbitrators and a member of the ADR Institute of Canada and IP Neutrals of Canada.

Guillaume Henry, PhD, is an IP litigator. He is first Deputy Reporter General and co-editor of this volume.

Sarmad Hasan Manto is a seasoned legal professional with nearly twenty-five years of experience across the Middle East, Asia, and Africa. Sarmad has deep expertise in advising rights holders on portfolio development, management, prosecution, franchising, licensing, data protection, and enforcement matters. Sarmad is the Managing Partner at Audiri Vox, an IP boutique firm headquartered in the United Arab Emirates.

Maarten Herbosch is an AI consultant at Liedekerke and an assistant professor of AI and law at KU Leuven in Belgium. His research focuses on the legal implications of AI development and deployment, as well as on AI regulation and its interaction with traditional legal frameworks.

Elisa Huusko is a partner and a licensed legal counsel in a European full-service IP law firm Berggren Oy. Elisa is a technology lawyer who specializes in licensing and contracts, IP related disputes and securing intellectual assets. Elisa assists small, midcap, and large clients in data and AI related matters, compliance, and licensing agreements. Elisa Huusko has been working with intellectual property matters for more than fifteen years. Elisa is a member of the AIPPI copyright standing committee.

Ellen Keenan-O'Malley is a solicitor at EIP, a law firm specialising in intellectual property, new and emerging technology and data protection. She has extensive experience handling litigation, advisory and transactional work with respect to patents, copyrights, and trademarks. Ellen works with clients on a wide range of commercial matters including IP licencing arrangements, FRAND licences, AI and software matters, R&D contracts, disputes involving copyright and patent infringement and breaches of licensing.

Linda Lecomte is a US Patent & Copyright Attorney, practising for more than twenty-five years in the electrical, telecommunications, robotics, IOT, fintech, aerospace, and AI industries. She has served on the AIPPI Reporter General Team and Trade Secret Standing Committee.

Ian Liu is a partner in Deacons' Intellectual Property Department, dual-qualified as a solicitor and patent attorney with a background in electrical engineering, computer science and fintech. He specializes in advising on technology-focused intellectual property matters, including complex copyright protection for software, digital content, and generative AI issues as well as cross-border patent litigations, hi-tech transactions,

IP due diligence, licensing, acquisitions and outsourcing. Ian is a member of the AIPPI IT and Internet committee.

Neel Mason is the Managing Partner of Mason & Associates. He is presently Vice President of the India Group of Aippi. Neel is a litigator in the field of Intellectual Property and Information Technology regularly acts for entities in the Media and Entertainment Industry, Publishing and Intermediaries in relation to conflicts in India. He regularly advises entities in the music industry in relation to licensing of content and has previously authored the India chapter for *Law of Raw Data*, published as part of the AIPPI Law Series.

Aldo Fabrizio Modica is an attorney-at-law in Intellectual Property and professor at the Universidad Católica de Asunción in Paraguay. He is also President of the Asociación Paraguaya de Agentes de la Propiedad Intelectual (APAPI) and partner at Bareiro Modica Abogados.

Stefan Naumann is a partner of the law firm Szleper Henry Naumann. Stefan handles litigation, arbitration, advisory and transactional work with respect to patents, trademarks, trade dress, copyrights, neighbouring rights, and image rights. He acts for well-known entertainment, medical device, financial and manufacturing companies and for a government on IT infrastructure projects. His patent litigation practice covers additional industries. His media work includes motion picture production, distribution and merchandising, film financing, talent contract negotiation and collective bargaining, anti-piracy, enforcement, and French media regulations. He is vice-chairman of the AIPPI Copyright committee and chairman of the AIPPI French national group Copyright committee.

Leticia Provedel is a senior partner of Souto Correa Advogados in Brazil, a general practice firm with a large IP practice. With almost thirty years' experience in the field of Intellectual Property and Entertainment, Leticia regularly assists national and international clients in judicial disputes, prosecution, contracts and business transactions involving Intellectual Property rights.

Sofia Sars is a lawyer and associate at Ström Law Firm in Sweden who frequently advises internationally acclaimed artists, music producers, songwriters, labels and other entities within the music industry, as well as production companies and directors within the film and TV industries. She is specialized in disputes and litigation and has worked thoroughly within artificial intelligence and copyright.

Athina Theodoridis is a Doctor of Law and attorney at the German boutique law firm Preu Bohlig in Munich. She advises national and international clients on intellectual property and competition law. She also specializes in advising on trade secrets and providing legal support to companies on IT and data protection issues.

Bernard Vanbrabant is professor at the University of Liège and member of the JurisLab. His research is focussed on intellectual property law, in particular the interactions thereof with unfair competition and civil law (property, contracts, and torts). Bernard is also a lawyer at the Brussels bar, assisting clients in contentious and non-contentious matters for twenty-five years.

Sarah van den Brande is a partner in Liedekerke's IP/IT/Data team and a seasoned litigator in IP, tech, and data law. She advises on copyright, data compliance, and tech contracts across key sectors. She often works for clients in media, entertainment, tech, and new industries. Sarah is a Brussels Bar member and active in IP associations including AIPPI, BMM, and ABA.

Divyendu Verma is an advocate and a registered Patent, Design, and Trademark Attorney in India and the UAE. He is the Partner and Global Head of Patents & Designs Practice at Audiri Vox, UAE. With over twenty years of experience, Divyendu has advised a wide array of national and international clients on IP strategy, prosecution, and litigation. His expertise spans multiple industries, with a particular focus on high-tech sectors, where he has handled complex matters involving computer-related inventions, standard-essential patents (SEPs), technology standards, and IP infringement indemnification.

Alexandra Wachtel is a Doctor of Law German attorney at the boutique law firm Preu Bohlig & Partner in Munich. Alexandra's practice focuses on copyright and trademark law, design rights, and IT-related matters. Her in-depth expertise in copyright law is rooted in her doctoral thesis and further reinforced by publications in the field since then, reflecting her deep academic and professional engagement with the subject.

Allen (Jun) Wang is a managing partner of Beijing TA Law Firm, chairman of Copyright Committee of AIPPI China, chairman of Copyright Licensing Committee of LES China. He has been deeply involved in TMT and entertainment law, including IP management, Artificial Intelligence, film co-production and international distribution, talent representation, gaming, music, trademarks and creative arts.

Sanna Wolk is Professor, arbitrator and Union President of the Swedish Association of University Teachers and Researchers (SULF) as well President of the United Nations Association of Sweden. She has written a number of academic publications and worked with government inquiries. Sanna is the initiative taker so the AIPPI Law Series and also co-author of the first book in the series, namely *Employees' Intellectual Property Rights*.

Raphael Zingg is a partner and attorney-at-law at IPrime, a boutique law firm for intellectual property and technology law. Previously, he was an Assistant Professor at Waseda University in Tokyo and has worked as a visiting scholar or professor at a number of foreign institutions, notably the University of California in Berkeley, the University of Hong Kong, Singapore Management University, and the Max Planck Institute for Innovation and Competition in Munich.

Table of Contents

About the Contributors v

Foreword xix

Lorenza Ferrari Hofer, President of AIPPI

A Comparative Global Overview 1

Sanna Wolk and Guillaume Henry

1. AI and Copyright Around the World 1
2. Legal Similarities and Differences Across Jurisdictions 2
   2.1 Shared Legal Principles 2
   2.2 Points of Divergence 3
3. Case Law Developments and Trends 3
   3.1 Developments in Europe 3
   3.2 Developments in North America 4
   3.3 Developments in Asia and the Middle East 4
4. Summary and Legal Trajectory 5

Chapter 1

Belgium 7

Maarten Herbosch, Sarah van den Brande and Bernard Vanbrabant

1. Introduction 7
2. Training AI Models 8
   2.1 Training AI with Copyright-Protected Works 8
   2.2 Exceptions/Limitations Allowing Training of AI 10
   2.3 Remedies and Enforcement 11
   2.4 Summary 12
3. Use of AI Systems 12
   3.1 Permission to Reproduce and Make Available to the Public 12
   3.2 Exception/Limitations Allowing AI Use 13
   3.3 Remedies and Enforcement 13
   3.4 Summary 13
4. AI-Generated Output 14
   4.1 Protection of AI-Generated Content 14
      4.1.1 Copyright Protection of AI Output 14
      4.1.2 Neighbouring Rights Protection of AI Output 15
   4.2 AI-Generated Output Infringes Existing Copyright 16
   4.3 Remedies and Enforcement 17

4.4 Summary 17
5. Conclusions 18

Chapter 2
Brazil 19
Leticia Provedel and Luiza Alkaim

1. Introduction 19
2. Training AI Models 20
2.1 Training AI with Copyright Protected Works 20
2.2 Exceptions/Limitations Allowing Training of AI 21
3. Use of AI Systems 21
3.1 Permission to Reproduce and Make Available to the Public 21
3.2 Exception/Limitations Allowing AI Training 21
3.3 Remedies and Enforcement 22
4. AI-Generated Output 22
4.1 Protection of AI-Generated Content 22
4.1.1 Copyright Protection of AI Output 22
4.1.2 Neighbouring Rights Protection of AI Output 23
4.2 AI-Generated Output Infringes Existing Copyright 23
4.3 Remedies and Enforcement 24
4.4 Summary 25
5. Conclusion 25

Chapter 3
Canada 27
Brian W. Gray

1. Introduction 27
2. Training AI Models 30
2.1 Training AI with Copyright Protected Works 30
2.2 Exceptions/Limitations Allowing Training of AI 35
2.3 Fair Dealing 36
3. Use of AI Systems 37
4. AI-Generated Output 38
5. Conclusions 41

Chapter 4
China 43
Allen (Jun) Wang and Gao Cheng

1. Introduction 43
1.1 Development Status of Generative Artificial Intelligence in China 43
1.2 Attitudes of the Chinese Artificial Intelligence Industry Towards Ownership of Generated Content Rights 44
1.2.1 Model One: Self-Maintenance of Copyright by Users 45
1.2.2 Model Two: Service Providers of Generative Artificial Intelligence Do Not Claim Rights to Generated Content 45
1.2.3 Model Three: No Agreement on Ownership of Generated Content 46

1.3 Legal Provisions Related to Generative Artificial Intelligence 46
1.4 Judicial Practices Regarding Copyright Issues Related to Generative Artificial Intelligence 47
1.4.1 Judicial Determination of Copyright Issues in AI Model Training Process 47
1.4.1.1 Spring Breeze Case [Trial Court: Beijing Internet Court, Case No.: (2023) Jing 0491 Min Chu 11279 / (2023)京0491民初11279号] 48
1.4.1.2 The Ultraman Case in Guangzhou [Trial Court: Guangzhou Internet Court, Case No.: (2024) Yue 0192 Min Chu 113 / (2023)粤0192民初113号] 48
1.4.1.3 Virtual Human Case [Trial Court: Hangzhou Intermediate People's Court, Case No.: (2023) Zhe 01 Min Zhong 4722 / (2023)浙01民终4722号] 49
1.4.1.4 The Ultraman Case in Hangzhou [Trial Court: Hangzhou Internet Court; Hangzhou Intermediate People's Court] 49
1.4.2 Judicial Determination of Copyright Issues Related to AI Model Output Content 51
1.4.2.1 Dreamwriter Case [Trial Court: Nanshan District People's Court of Shenzhen City, Guangdong Province; Case No.: (2019) Yue 0305 Min Chu 14010 / (2019)粤0305民初14010号] 51
1.4.2.2 The Wolters Kluwer Database Case [Trial Court: Beijing Intellectual Property Court, Case No.: (2019) Jing 73 Min Zhong 2030 / (2019)京73民终2030号] 54
1.4.2.3 Spring Breeze Case [Trial Court: Beijing Internet Court, Case No.: (2023) Jing 491 Min Chu 11279 / (2023)京0491民初11279号] 55
1.4.2.4 The Ultraman Case in Hangzhou [Trial Court: Hangzhou Internet Court; Hangzhou Intermediate People's Court] 59
2. Training AI Models 60
2.1 Training AI with Copyright Protected Works 60
2.1.1 Reproduction Rights 61
2.1.2 Adaptation Rights and Translation Rights 61
2.1.3 Other Rights 62
2.2 Exceptions/Limitations Allowing Training of AI 62
2.2.1 No Permission Required 63
2.2.1.1 Fair Use System 63
2.2.1.2 Statutory Licensing System 64
2.2.2 Differentiation of Scenarios 65
2.3 Remedies and Enforcement 65
2.4 Summary 66
3. Use of AI Systems 66
3.1 Permission to Reproduce and Make Available to the Public 66

3.2 Exception/Limitations Allowing AI Training 66
3.3 Remedies and Enforcement 67
3.4 Summary 67
4. AI-Generated Output 67
4.1 Protection of AI-Generated Content 67
4.1.1 Copyright Protection of AI Output 68
4.1.1.1 Justification of Authorization 68
4.1.1.2 Attribution of Rights 70
4.1.2 Neighbouring Rights Protection of AI Output 72
4.1.2.1 Justification of Authorization 72
4.1.2.2 Attribution of Rights 73
4.1.3 Negative Perspective 74
4.2 AI-Generated Output Infringes Existing Copyright 77
4.3 Remedies and Enforcement 78
4.4 Summary 79
5. Conclusions 80

Chapter 5
Finland 81
Elisa Huusko

1. Introduction 81
2. Training AI Models 84
2.1 Training AI with Copyright Protected Works 84
2.2 Exceptions and Limitations Allowing Training of AI 86
2.2.1 Temporary Reproduction 86
2.2.2 Text and Data Mining 87
2.3 Remedies and Enforcement 91
3. Use of AI Systems 92
4. Output of AI and Copyright Issues 96
4.1 Copyright Protection of AI-Generated Content 96
4.2 Protection of AI-Generated Content Through Neighbouring Rights 97
4.3 Remedies and Enforcement 99
5. Conclusions 99

Chapter 6
France 101
Stefan Naumann

1. Introduction 101
1.1 EU Regulation of Artificial intelligence – the AI Act 101
1.2 Text and Data Mining 105
1.3 AI and Copyright Law 105
2. Training AI Models 106
2.1 Training AI with Copyright Protected Works 106
2.2 Exceptions/Limitations Allowing Training of AI 106
2.3 Remedies and Enforcement 109
3. Use of AI Systems 109
3.1 Permission to Reproduce and Make Available to the Public 109

3.2 Exceptions/Limitations Allowing Use of AI Systems 110
3.3 Remedies and Enforcement 110
4. AI-Generated Output 110
4.1 Protection of AI-Generated Output 111
4.1.1 Copyright Protection of AI Output 111
4.1.2 Potential Additional Authors of Works Created with Generative AI 112
4.1.3 Neighbouring Rights Protection of AI Output 113
4.2 AI-Generated Output Infringes Existing Copyright 113
4.3 Remedies and Enforcement 115

Chapter 7
Germany 117
Alexandra Wachtel and Athina Theodoridis

1. Introduction 117
2. Training AI Models 118
2.1 The Training of AI with Protected Works 118
2.2 The Intervention of Limitation Provisions 119
2.3 Hamburg Regional Court 120
2.4 Other Current Developments in This Context 122
3. Use of AI Systems 123
4. AI-Generated Results 125
4.1 Protection of AI-Generated Content 125
4.1.1 Copyright Protection of AI-Generated Results 125
4.1.2 Protection of AI-Generated Results by Other Rights 128
4.2 AI-Generated Results Infringes Existing Copyright 129
4.2.1 Infringement of Rights 129
4.2.2 The Intervention of Limitation Provisions 130
4.3 Legal Remedies and Enforcement 131
5. Conclusions 131

Chapter 8
Hong Kong 133
Ian Liu

1. Introduction 133
2. Training AI Models 133
2.1 Training AI with Copyright Protected Works 133
2.2 Exceptions/Limitations Allowing Training of AI 134
2.3 Summary 135
3. User of AI Systems 136
3.1 Permission to Reproduce and Make Available to the Public 136
3.2 Exception/Limitations 137
3.3 Summary 137
4. AI-Generated Output 137
4.1 Authorship of AI-Generated Literary, Dramatic, Musical or Artistic Work 137
4.2 Protection of AI-Generated Content 138

4.3 AI-Generated Output Infringing Existing Copyright 138
4.4 Remedies and Enforcement 138
4.5 Summary 138
5. Conclusions 139
5.1 Areas for Further Development 139
5.2 Recommendations for AI Users 139

Chapter 9
India **141**
Neel Mason

1. Introduction 141
2. Training AI Models 142
2.1 Training AI with Copyright Protected Works 142
2.2 Exceptions/Limitations Allowing Training of AI 144
3. Use of AI Systems 145
3.1 Permission to Reproduce and Make Available to the Public 145
3.2 Exception/Limitations Allowing AI Training 145
4. AI-Generated Output 146
4.1 Protection of AI-Generated Content 146
4.1.1 Copyright Protection of AI Output 146
4.1.1.1 What Would Constitute Works That Would Qualify Within the Copyright Act? 146
4.1.1.2 Authorship 146
4.1.1.3 Can AI be an Author? 147
4.1.1.4 Infringement by AI-Generated Output 148
4.1.2 Neighbouring Rights Protection of AI Output 149
5. Remedies and Enforcement 151
5.1 Civil Remedies 151
5.2 Criminal Remedies 151
5.3 Jurisdiction 152
6. Conclusion 152

Chapter 10
Paraguay **153**
Aldo Fabrizio Modica

1. Introduction 153
2. Training AI Models 153
2.1 Training AI with Copyright-Protected Works 153
2.2 Exceptions/Limitations Allowing Training of AI 154
2.3 Remedies and Enforcement 154
2.4 Summary 154
3. Use of AI Systems 154
3.1 Permission to Reproduce and Make Available to the Public 154
3.2 Exceptions/Limitations Allowing AI Training 155
3.3 Remedies and Enforcement 155
3.4 Summary 155
4. AI-Generated Output 155

4.1 Protection of AI-Generated Content 155
4.1.1 Copyright Protection of AI Output 155
4.1.2 Neighbouring Rights Protection of AI Output 156
4.2 AI-Generated Output Infringing Existing Copyright 156
4.3 Remedies and Enforcement 156
4.4 Summary 156
5. Conclusions 157

Chapter 11
Poland 159
Martyna Czapska

1. Introduction 159
2. Training AI Models 160
2.1 Training AI with Copyright Protected Works 160
2.2 Exceptions/Limitations Allowing Training of AI 162
2.3 Remedies and Enforcement 163
2.4 Summary 166
3. Use of AI Systems 166
3.1 Permission to Reproduce and Make Available to the Public 166
3.2 Exception/Limitations Allowing AI Training 166
3.3 Remedies and Enforcement 166
3.4 Summary 166
4. AI-Generated Output 167
4.1 Protection of AI-Generated Content 167
4.2 AI-Generated Output Infringes Existing Copyright 169
4.3 Remedies and Enforcement 170
4.4 Summary 170
5. Conclusions 171

Chapter 12
Sweden 173
Malin Ekstrand and Sofia Sars

1. Introduction 173
2. Training AI Models 174
2.1 Training AI with Copyright Protected Works 174
2.2 Exceptions/Limitations Allowing Training of AI 175
2.2.1 Temporary Reproductions 175
2.2.2 Text and Data Mining 176
2.3 Remedies and Enforcement 177
2.4 Summary 178
3. Use of AI Systems 179
3.1 Permission to Reproduce and Make Available to the Public 179
3.2 Exception/Limitations Allowing AI Training 179
3.3 Remedies and Enforcement 179
3.4 Summary 180
4. AI-Generated Output 180
4.1 Protection of AI-Generated Content 180

4.1.1 Copyright Protection of AI Output 180
4.1.2 Neighbouring Rights Protection of AI Output 181
4.2 AI-Generated Output Infringes Existing Copyright 182
4.3 Remedies and Enforcement 183
4.4 Summary 183
5. Conclusions 183

Chapter 13
Switzerland 187
Raphael Zingg

1. Introduction 187
2. Training AI Models 187
2.1 Training AI with Copyright Protected Works 188
2.2 Exceptions/Limitations Allowing Training of AI 188
2.3 Remedies and Enforcement 189
2.4 Summary 189
3. Use of AI Systems 190
3.1 Permission to Reproduce and Make Available to the Public 190
3.2 Exception/Limitations Allowing AI Training 190
3.3 Remedies and Enforcement 190
3.4 Summary 190
4. AI-Generated outputs 191
4.1 Protection of AI-Generated Content 191
4.1.1 Copyright Protection of AI Output 191
4.1.2 Neighbouring Rights Protection of AI Output 192
4.2 AI-Generated Output Infringes Existing Copyright 193
4.3 Remedies and Enforcement 194
4.4 Summary 195
5. Conclusions 195

Chapter 14
United Arab Emirates 197
Divyendu Verma and Sarmad Hasan Manto

1. Introduction 197
2. Training AI Models 197
2.1 Training AI with Copyright-Protected Works 198
2.2 Exceptions/Limitations Allowing Training of AI 198
2.3 Remedies and Enforcement 199
2.4 Summary 199
3. Use of AI Systems 199
3.1 Permission to Reproduce and Make Available to the Public 200
3.2 Exception/Limitations Allowing AI Training 200
3.3 Remedies and Enforcement 201
3.4 Summary 202
4. AI-Generated Output 202
4.1 Protection of AI-Generated Content 202
4.1.1 Copyright Protection of AI Output 203

4.1.2 Can AI-Generated Content Be Protected Under UAE Copyright Law? 203
4.1.3 Defining 'Authorship' in the Context of AI: Human versus Machine Authorship 203
4.1.4 Neighbouring Rights Protection of AI Output 204
4.1.5 Legal Challenges in Recognizing AI Outputs as Eligible for Protection 204
4.1.6 International Approaches to Neighbouring Rights for AI Content 204
4.2 AI-Generated Output Infringing Existing Copyright 204
4.2.1 AI-Generated Works and the Risk of Infringing Artistic Styles 204
4.2.2 Identifying 'Substantial Similarity' in AI Outputs 205
4.2.3 Liability for Copyright Infringement: AI Developers versus Users 205
4.3 Remedies and Enforcement 205
4.4 Summary 205
5. Conclusions 206

Chapter 15
United Kingdom **209**
Ellen Keenan O'Malley

1. Introduction 209
1.1 Creative Works Dilemma 209
1.2 Copyright Designs and Patents Act 1988 210
1.2.1 Categories of Work and Authorship 211
1.2.2 Originality 212
1.2.3 Ownership 212
2. Training AI Models 212
2.1 Training AI with Copyright Protected Works 212
2.2 Location of the Training and/or Development of a Model 213
2.3 Exceptions/Limitations Allowing Training of AI 214
2.3.1 Section 28A - Making Temporary Copies 214
2.3.2 Section 29 - Research and Private Study 214
2.3.3 Section 29A - Text and Data Mining Exception 214
2.3.4 Section 30 - Criticism, Review, Quotation and News Reporting 215
2.3.5 Section 30A - Caricature, Parody and Pastiche 215
2.4 Remedies and Enforcement 216
2.5 Summary 216
3. Use of AI Systems 217
3.1 General Use of AI Systems 217
3.2 Exception/Limitations on the Use of AI-Generated Works 217
3.3 Remedies and Enforcement 217
3.4 Summary 217
4. AI-Generated Output 218
4.1 Protection of AI-Generated Content 218
4.2 AI-Generated Output Infringes Existing Copyright 219
4.2.1 Permission to Reproduce and Make Available to the Public 219

4.2.2 Importing Copyright-Protected 'Articles' into the UK 220
4.2.3 Knowledge 220
4.3 Remedies and Enforcement 221
4.4 Summary 221
5. Conclusions 221

Chapter 16
United States of America **223**
Linda Lecomte and Hailey Bureau

1. Introduction 223
2. Training AI Models 224
2.1 Training AI with Copyright Protected Works 224
2.2 Exceptions/Limitations Allowing Training of AI 230
2.3 Remedies and Enforcement 235
3. Use of AI Systems 236
3.1 Permission to Use and Make Available to the Public 236
3.2 Exceptions/limitations allowing AI training 236
3.3 Remedies and Enforcement 237
4. AI-Generated Output 237
4.1 Protection of AI-Generated Content 237
4.1.1 Copyright Protection of AI Output 245
4.1.2 Neighbouring Rights Protection of AI Output 246
4.2 AI-Generated Output Infringes Existing Copyright 246
4.3 Remedies and Enforcement 248
4.4 Summary 251
5. Conclusion 253

Foreword

Lorenza Ferrari Hofer, President of AIPPI

AIPPI – The International Association for the Protection of Intellectual Property – has been improving and promoting the protection of intellectual property (IP) since being founded in 1897. Today, AIPPI is a truly global association with 68 national and regional groups and over 9000 members from more than 125 countries and regions in Europe, the Americas, Asia, Oceania and Africa. AIPPI promotes the value of all types of IP through its comprehensive analyses of existing and proposed IP laws and policies; working with government and non-government organisations to develop and improve international and regional treaties and agreements, as well as national laws; and hosting conferences and seminars.

The now traditional yearly 'AIPPI Law Series' is part of AIPPI's objective to conduct comparative law studies at the highest level. The first book in the series was published ten years ago. This year's book is focused on artificial intelligence and copyright. The present book is inspired by the AIPPI extensive scientific work on artificial intelligence and copyright that has been conducted since 2019. The first Resolution was adopted at the 2019 London Congress on 'AI and Copyright'. This resolution addresses the issue of copyright protection for creations made by or through AI systems. This first resolution has been supplemented by the resolution adopted in Yokohama in 2025, also on the subject of 'AI and Copyright', but focusing on the issue of training AI systems with copyright-protected works, as well as the conditions under which creations generated by an AI system (outputs) should be qualified as copyright infringement. This book is the perfect complement to these two resolutions, as it deals with the state of the law (legislation and case law) on these two issues.

AIPPI expresses its sincere thanks to Wolters Kluwer for its continued cooperation to promote the protection and harmonisation of IP. AIPPI also thanks all AIPPI chapter authors for their excellent work which has produced this valuable resource. In particular, AIPPI, gives special thanks to this year's Volume Editors, Sanna Wolk and Guillaume Henry. Sanna Wolk is chair of the AIPPI Standing Committee on Copyright. She was the one who initiated the book series with

Wolters Kluwer, and she was leading successfully the first Wolters Kluwer book in 2015. Guillaume Henry is first Deputy Reporter General and has supported the work of several AIPPI-Kluwer books.

Lorenza Ferrari Hofer
July 2025

A Comparative Global Overview

Sanna Wolk and Guillaume Henry

1. AI AND COPYRIGHT AROUND THE WORLD

The emergence of artificial intelligence (AI) as a creative and analytical tool has sparked profound debates in legal communities around the world. As AI systems become more capable of generating images, text, music, and other forms of media, governments and legal scholars are forced to reconsider the traditional foundations of copyright law.

In jurisdictions where copyright has long been grounded in the principle of human authorship, the notion that a machine could be considered an author presents a fundamental challenge. The core legal questions revolve around two major themes: the legality of using protected content to train AI models, and the protectability of AI-generated content.

In the **European Union (EU)**, the legal framework is guided by harmonizing directives such as the InfoSoc Directive[1] and the DSM Directive.[2] Member states, including **France**, **Germany**, **Sweden**, **Poland**, **Finland**, and **Belgium**, have adopted these directives into national law. A key development is the recognition of text and data mining (TDM) as a lawful exception under certain conditions – most notably when rightsholders do not opt out. However, the implementation and enforcement of these directives vary, and further harmonization is needed to ensure legal certainty across the internal market.

The **United Kingdom**, while no longer part of the EU, still mirrors many aspects of EU copyright law. UK law is somewhat unique in explicitly recognizing

---

1. Directive 2001/29/EC of the European Parliament and of the Council of 22 May 2001 on the harmonisation of certain aspects of copyright and related rights in the information society.
2. Directive (EU) 2019/790 of the European Parliament and of the Council of 17 April 2019 on copyright and related rights in the Digital Single Market and amending Directives 96/9/EC and 2001/29/EC.

computer-generated works, attributing authorship to the person who made the arrangements necessary for their creation. The UK is actively reviewing its Copyright Designs and Patents Act to clarify these rules in light of contemporary AI use. Future proposals are expected to address the licensing of training data and mechanisms for opting out of TDM.

In **China**, a country renowned for rapid technological advancement, courts have taken the lead in developing legal interpretations. Several high-profile decisions have begun to form a judicial framework around AI-generated works and the unauthorized use of data for AI training. However, while China's case law is advancing, statutory reforms have not kept pace, leading to some legal uncertainty.

In **India**, **Brazil**, **Paraguay**, and the **United Arab Emirates**, AI-related copyright regulation is still emerging. These nations primarily rely on legacy copyright statutes that were not designed to account for non-human creativity. The United Arab Emirates' updated Copyright Law from 2021, for instance, still lacks explicit provisions addressing AI-generated content. In these jurisdictions, legal scholars and government consultations are increasingly focused on developing frameworks that promote innovation while respecting authors' rights.

Canada, **Hong Kong**, and the **United States** also lean on existing statutes, but with varying levels of adaptability. The United States benefits from a flexible fair use doctrine, which courts are now testing in multiple AI-related cases. Canada, meanwhile, maintains a firm stance on human authorship but is exploring how AI-assisted works might be accommodated under current registration systems. In Hong Kong, while no case law yet exists, proposed guidelines suggest a cautious approach that emphasizes minimal human contribution for eligibility.

Thus, as AI technology continues to evolve, so too must the legal frameworks designed to regulate it. The coming years are likely to see major shifts, both legislatively and judicially, in how AI and copyright are reconciled. International cooperation and harmonization efforts may become increasingly necessary to ensure consistency and fairness in the global digital economy.

2. LEGAL SIMILARITIES AND DIFFERENCES ACROSS JURISDICTIONS

As AI technologies are increasingly integrated into content creation and data processing, countries across the globe are grappling with the legal implications for copyright law. Although a universal consensus remains elusive, many jurisdictions display striking similarities in their legal approaches, as well as notable divergences.

2.1 Shared Legal Principles

One of the most consistent principles found across numerous countries is the emphasis on human authorship. Copyright laws in jurisdictions such as **Canada**, **Finland**, **India**, **Germany**, **Sweden**, **Switzerland**, **United Arab Emirates**, and the **United States** emphasize that copyright protection is granted only to works that reflect human creativity. Purely machine-generated content, absent human input, is widely excluded from protection.

Another point of convergence lies in the treatment of AI training. The act of using protected works to train AI systems is generally viewed as a form of reproduction, thus necessitating authorization from rights holders unless a specific statutory exception applies. This is particularly crucial in the context of large language models and other generative AI systems that depend on vast corpuses of text, images, and other media.

Further harmonization can be observed in the approach to fair use or its equivalents. While the United States employs a broad fair use doctrine – evaluated case-by-case under a flexible four-factor test – most other jurisdictions, such as those in **Europe**, **India**, **United Arab Emirates**, and **Hong Kong**, rely on narrow, enumerated exceptions. This difference creates a significant legal divide in how permissible AI training activities are assessed.

Finally, the concept of TDM is gaining traction internationally, particularly within the EU. Countries including **France**, **Germany**, **Sweden**, **Finland**, and **Belgium** have enacted TDM exceptions following EU directives, with the **UK** actively considering similar reforms post-Brexit.

2.2 Points of Divergence

Despite these shared foundations, national approaches diverge considerably in implementation. Legislative progress on AI and copyright varies widely. Countries such as **France**, **Germany**, and the **United Kingdom** are taking a proactive role in drafting and updating legal frameworks to accommodate AI innovations. By contrast, **Brazil**, **Paraguay**, **India**, and the **United Arab Emirates** are still in the early stages of this legislative journey.

Judicial engagement with AI-related copyright issues also differs. **China**, **Germany**, the **United Kingdom**, and the **United States** have witnessed significant legal proceedings shaping the future of AI and copyright. Meanwhile, courts in **India**, **Paraguay**, and the **United Arab Emirates** have yet to weigh in substantially, leaving many questions unresolved.

Licensing mechanisms further highlight differences in national policy. Some countries, such as **Belgium**, **Germany**, **United Arab Emirates**, and the **United Kingdom**, stress the importance of written licenses and well-defined contractual terms. Others, including **Switzerland** and **Sweden**, support licensing but prefer EU-aligned models that provide broader structural guidance without rigid formalities.

These similarities and differences reflect the dynamic evolution of copyright law in the AI era, underscoring the need for both global cooperation and jurisdiction-specific strategies.

3. CASE LAW DEVELOPMENTS AND TRENDS

Case law plays a pivotal role in shaping how AI and copyright intersect. While legislation often lags technological advancements, judicial decisions have begun to provide a clearer framework – albeit varied – across regions.

3.1 Developments in Europe

In **Germany**, courts have begun to recognize the permissibility of TDM under specific exceptions. German jurisprudence accepts TDM for both commercial and scientific purposes, provided that rights holders have not explicitly opted out. This interpretation aligns with the EU's Digital Single Market (DSM) Directive and positions Germany as a key player in balancing innovation with rights protection.

In addition, the **United Kingdom** has been actively evaluating the Copyright, Designs and Patents Act (CDPA) in light of AI developments. Recent cases reveal judicial concern about the attribution of authorship and the extent to which TDM should be permitted. Government consultations suggest the UK is preparing more explicit guidance to reduce legal uncertainty for developers and rights holders alike.

3.2 Developments in North America

Canada is beginning to see litigation around AI-generated and AI-assisted works. In particular, the case of *Toronto Star Newspapers et al. v. OpenAI. Inc.*[3] has brought to the fore questions of authorship, originality, and liability. Preliminary decisions suggest that only the human-authored components of AI-assisted outputs are eligible for copyright protection.

In the **United States**, the landscape is more dynamic. The case of *Thomson Reuters v. Ross Intelligence*[4] has had significant ramifications. The court ruled that training an AI system using proprietary legal annotations without permission constitutes copyright infringement. The ruling explicitly rejected fair use in this context, setting a critical precedent. Other cases, including *Getty Images v. Stability AI,*[5] continue to test the boundaries of copyright in generative AI systems, particularly regarding large-scale data scraping.

3.3 Developments in Asia and the Middle East

China has taken a proactive judicial approach. Notable cases like *Dreamwriter*[6] and *Ultraman*[7] have addressed the extent to which AI-generated works may be protected and what constitutes unlawful use of copyrighted content in training datasets. Chinese courts focus heavily on the reproduction and adaptation rights inherent in copyright law.

In **India**, the legal system has yet to produce landmark decisions, though pending cases such as *ANI v. OpenAI*[8] are poised to clarify key questions around training liability and authorship. As Indian courts begin to address these issues, they are likely to draw on comparative jurisprudence from other common law countries.

The **United Arab Emirates** remains in a nascent phase. While no major case law has yet emerged, regulatory authorities are actively assessing the legal

3. Ontario Superior Court of Justice CV-24-00732231-00CL. Statement of Claim filed 28 November 2024.
4. U.S. District Court, No. 1:20-cv-613, (D. Del., Feb. 11, 2025).
5. *Getty Images, Inc. v. Stability AI Inc.*, No. 1:23-cv-00135 (D. Del., June 9, 2025).
6. *Dreamwriter* case [Trial Court: Nanshan District People's Court of Shenzhen City, Guangdong Province; Case No.: (2019) Yue 0305 Min Chu 14010 / (2019)粤0305民初14010号].
7. *Ultraman* case in Guangzhou [Trial Court: Guangzhou Internet Court, Case No.: (2024) Yue 0192 Min Chu 113 / (2023)粤0192民初113号].
8. *ANI Media Pvt. Ltd. v. OpenAI Inc & Anr.*, CS(COMM) 1028/2024.

landscape. Anticipated judicial decisions and regulatory reforms are expected to bring much-needed clarity to questions surrounding data sourcing and AI outputs.

4. SUMMARY AND LEGAL TRAJECTORY

The legal discourse around AI and copyright is undergoing rapid transformation, driven by the technology's unprecedented capabilities and broad adoption. Across global jurisdictions, common themes are emerging that offer insight into the likely trajectory of future legal developments.

One of the most prominent trends is the continued insistence on human authorship as a prerequisite for copyright protection. Despite AI's increasing autonomy and creative capacity, nearly all jurisdictions maintain that works must involve human creativity to qualify for protection. This consensus is evident in jurisdictions as diverse as **Canada**, **Germany**, **Switzerland**, **India**, **China**, **the United States** and the **United Arab Emirates**. However, few countries have proposed specific statutory language to define 'sufficient human input', which may become an important area for reform.

Closely related is the growing need to develop legal frameworks around TDM. **EU** member states, led by the DSM Directive, have embraced a model that allows TDM with an opt-out mechanism for rights holders. The **United Kingdom** appears poised to follow suit with similar provisions under consideration. Countries such as **Brazil**, **Paraguay**, and the **United Arab Emirates** are beginning to explore how to incorporate TDM into their copyright regimes, though progress remains limited and dependent on broader copyright reform initiatives.

Judicial bodies are increasingly becoming the arenas where these issues are debated. In **China**, **Germany**, **the United Kingdom**, **Canada**, and the **United States**, courts are actively shaping the rules through landmark decisions. These cases are not only clarifying the limits of fair use, licensing obligations, and authorship but are also prompting legislators to update outdated laws. Still, inconsistency in rulings across different jurisdictions may create barriers to international AI development and deployment.

Another shared focus is the importance of licensing transparency and data provenance. Many jurisdictions are implementing – or at least discussing – requirements for developers of AI systems to disclose the sources of their training data and to obtain the appropriate permissions. These efforts aim to prevent hidden exploitation of copyrighted materials and to ensure equitable compensation for rights holders. There is also a growing call for industry standards or government-led repositories of pre-cleared data sources to reduce litigation risk.

Overall, the global legal system stands at the threshold of a significant reconfiguration. The path forward will require a careful balance between encouraging innovation in AI and upholding the core values of intellectual property protection. While some countries are moving swiftly with reforms and jurisprudence, others are only beginning the journey. Regardless of pace, the direction is clear: AI and copyright are on an irreversible collision course that demands urgent and thoughtful legal adaptation.

Chapter 1

Belgium

Maarten Herbosch, Sarah van den Brande and Bernard Vanbrabant

1. INTRODUCTION

Copyright law in Belgium, like in many jurisdictions, faces significant challenges in adapting to the rise of artificial intelligence (AI). High-profile examples, such as the case introduced by the *New York Times* against OpenAI,[1] illustrate the growing tensions between the use of copyright-protected material and AI deployment. The legal landscape remains unclear, and Belgium is no exception. A core difficulty lies in the unpredictability[2] and lack of explainability[3] of AI systems, which complicates the attribution of AI-generated output to the individuals behind the technology. Similarly, it is not immediately evident whether and under what circumstances the use of copyright-protected data for AI training is permissible. This includes literary works, software and databases. As AI agents – systems that operate largely autonomously – become more prevalent, these challenges may be exacerbated, potentially to the point where humans are no longer directly involved in selecting training data.

1. Michael M. Grynbaum and Ryan Mac, *The New York Times Sues OpenAI and Microsoft for Copyright Infringement*, The New York Times (27 December 2023) https://www.nytimes.com/2023/12/27/business/media/new-york-times-open-ai-microsoft-lawsuit.html. For the actual complaint, see https://storage.courtlistener.com/recap/gov.uscourts.nysd.612697/gov.uscourts.nysd.612697.1.0.pdf (accessed 17 March 2025).
2. Ronald Yu and Gabriele Ali, *What's Inside the Black Box? AI Challenges for Lawyers and Researchers*, 19 Legal Information Management 2, 5.
3. Yavar Bathaee, *The Artificial Intelligence Black Box and the Failure of Intent and Causation*, 31 Harvard Journal of Law & Technology 889, 897; Michael Hatfield, *Professionally Responsible Artificial Intelligence*, 51 Arizona State Law Journal 1057, 1118; Yu and Ali, *supra* n. 2, 5.

Under Belgian law, these issues arise in various respects, three of which we will discuss in more detail in this chapter: the legality of using copyrighted data for AI training, the extent to which inputting copyrighted material into AI tools constitutes a copyright violation even if it does not contribute to model training, and the copyrightability of AI-generated output. Each of these aspects presents unique legal and practical challenges, which we will explore in detail below.

Additionally, it should be emphasized that this topic is very much the subject of ongoing debate. As a result, there are various national[4] and European[5] guidance and study initiatives that help provide clarity for the actors concerned. Furthermore, depending on the data concerned, the General Data Protection Regulation (GDPR) may play a crucial role that we will not discuss here.

2. TRAINING AI MODELS

2.1 Training AI with Copyright-Protected Works

The Belgian legal framework for copyright protection in the digital context is largely shaped by European regulatory initiatives, particularly Directive 2001/29/EC (the InfoSoc Directive) and Directive 2019/790/EU (the DSM Directive). These directives have been transposed into the Belgian Code of Economic Law (BCEL), specifically in Articles XI.165 and following, which define authors' rights, the scope of their protection, and the measures available to them against infringement.

Articles XI.165, §1, XI.186 and XI.295 BCEL grant authors exclusive rights over their works, including the rights to reproduce, distribute, and communicate them to the public for works of literature or art, databases and software respectively. Each of these protected acts requires the author's authorization unless a legal exception applies.[6] Additionally, Articles XI.165, §2 and XI.297 BCEL recognize authors' moral rights, including the right to attribution and the right to integrity[7] of the work, though these will not be discussed in detail here.[8]

When a work is protected by copyright, its use in AI training likely constitutes an act of reproduction, governed by Article XI.165, §1 BCEL. The author's rights

4. E.g. Knowledge Centre Data & Society, *brAInfood: Belangrijke auteursrechtelijke overwegingen met betrekking tot tekst-naar-x generatoren* (November 2022) brAInfood, https://data-en-maatschappij.ai/publicaties/brainfood-auteursrechtelijke-overwegingen-tekst-naar-x-generatoren.
5. See e.g. the ongoing development of the General-Purpose AI Code of Practice, https://digital-strategy.ec.europa.eu/en/policies/ai-code-practice.
6. See similarly Victoria Hendrickx and Lorenzo Gugliotta, *Chatbots op basis van 'generative pre-trained transformers'*, NJW 2, 17.
7. This moral right could, for example, be at issue when an AI system is used to adapt content, rendering it discriminatory, invasive or racist, for example. This moral right is given a broad interpretation in Belgian law, see e.g., Brussels 5 May 2011, A&M 2012, 202, annotated.
8. They, too, could be violated in case of AI training or deployment, however. This might be the case when the author did not consent to make the content available to the public, but when it nevertheless used for AI system training, discussed below in the context of text and data mining exceptions.

with regard to reproduction include digital copies, temporary copies in RAM, and partial excerpts.[9] Similarly, adaptations and transformations, such as translations or reformatting, are also covered.[10] Belgian law - much like EU law - does not require the copy to be permanent[11] and applies irrespectively of whether it is part of an automated procedure.[12]

Some Belgian authors express uncertainty with regard to this question,[13] but we would argue that they are too focused on the representation of the training data in the system parameters - which, in a way, forms a compressed version of the training data[14] - rather than on the acts of reproduction needed to train the system initially, which includes creation copies to initially compute those parameters.

AI training typically involves creating (temporary) copies of large volumes of training data, including copyrighted material. This applies both to the potential preliminary step of copying data into a centralized environment for future training and to the actual training process, where the algorithm iterates over the data. At each stage, reproductions of the work are made, which may constitute copyright infringement unless covered by an exception, as discussed below, or authorized by the author.[15]

To invoke authorization by the author or rights holder, the conditions of Article XI.167, §1 BCEL must be met. First, to prove such authorization against the author, written permission is required.[16] Secondly, contracts granting authorization are subject to a restrictive interpretation in favour of the author.[17] Thirdly, the written agreement with the author must explicitly specify each type of use, its duration and scope, as well as the corresponding compensation.[18] This implies - and the law explicitly confirms - that any use unforeseeable at the time of contracting is not covered by a pre-existing authorization for exploitation.[19] This aspect may be particularly relevant for agreements concluded before AI systems and their training became as prevalent as they are today.

Such authorization exists, for instance, for various databases and data sources that provide open-access licences, such as the Creative Commons CC BY 4.0.[20]

---

9. See similarly Frank Gotzen and Marie-Christine Janssen, *Kunstmatige Kunst. Bedenkingen bij de toepassing van het auteursrecht op Artificiële Intelligentie*, A&M 323, 336.
10. Article XI. 165 §1 second part BCEL.
11. Article XI. 165 §1 first part BCEL.
12. CJEU Case C-5/08 *Infopaq International A/S v. Danske Dagblades Forening* [2009] ECR I-6569; Hendrickx and Gugliotta, *supra* n. 6, 18.
13. See Hendrickx and Gugliotta, *supra* n. 6, 17.
14. See Andres Guadamuz, *A Scanner Darkly: Copyright Liability and Exceptions in Artificial Intelligence Inputs and Outputs*, 73 GRUR International 111, 117.
15. See similarly Gotzen and Janssen, *supra* n. 9, 336; Hendrickx and Gugliotta, *supra* n. 6, 18.
16. Article XI.167 §1 BCEL, second part.
17. Article XI.167 §1 BCEL, third part.
18. Article XI.167 §1 BCEL, fourth part.
19. Article XI.167 §1 BCEL, sixth part.
20. https://creativecommons.org/licenses/by/4.0/

Examples include the Belgian Statbel[21] and the European Eurostat Database.[22] Commercially available databases are another example, as they may grant access to relevant data for a fee.

On a related note – though not a true exception to this principle – certain data may not be subject to copyright protection for the purpose of AI training. This applies, for example, to government documents[23] or speeches delivered in meetings of representative bodies, public court hearings, and political gatherings.[24] It similarly applies to content that is no longer protected by copyright, for example, because its author passed away over seventy years ago (Article XI.166 §1 BCEL).[25]

2.2 Exceptions/Limitations Allowing Training of AI

Unlike some common law systems, Belgian law does not recognize a broad, general fair-use exception. Instead, it follows a closed system of specific, narrowly defined exceptions to the general copyright protection rules outlined above.[26] These exceptions are codified in Articles XI.189 and following BCEL.

In the context of (future) AI training, certain text and data mining exceptions may allow parties to collect data for use in AI system training. One key exception, derived from Article 4 of the DSM Directive and implemented in Article XI.190, 20° BCEL, permits the reproduction of copyrighted content unless the rights holder has opted out.[27] Rights holders can opt out through licensing terms or technical measures, such as robots.txt files or API restrictions. However, if the content is publicly accessible online, the second part of Article XI.190, 20° BCEL requires that the opt-out be in a machine-readable format.

Similarly, a broader exception exists for scientific research.[28] Articles XI.191/1, 7° and XI.191/2, 3° BCEL, implementing Article 3 of the DSM Directive, permit text and data mining without prior authorization from the copyright holder, provided the party conducting text and data mining has legitimate access to the content and the purpose is scientific research. This exception is mandatory, meaning copyright holders cannot opt out. It applies to research organizations, publicly accessible libraries, museums, archives, and institutions dedicated to cinematographic or audio(visual) heritage.

21. https://statbel.fgov.be/en/open-data#: ~ :text = How%20to%20use%20open%20data%3F.
22. https://ec.europa.eu/eurostat/help/copyright-notice#: ~ :text = 2,information%20on%20the%20individual%20documents.
23. Article XI.172 §2 BCEL.
24. Article XI.172 §1 BCEL, second part.
25. Hendrickx and Gugliotta, *supra* n. 6, 18.
26. Hendrickx and Gugliotta, *supra* n. 6, 18.
27. Alexandra Bensamoun, *(Ré)concilier l'intelligence artificielle et le droit d'auteur en Europe et au-delà*, A&M 155, 156; Hendrickx and Gugliotta, *supra* n. 6, 19; Thomas Margoni, *[Text and Data Mining] TDM and generative AI: Lawful access and opt-outs*, A&M 172, 178 ff.
28. Bensamoun, *supra* n. 27, 156; Hendrickx and Gugliotta, *supra* n. 6, 19; Margoni, *supra* n. 27, 178 ff.

For purely private and non-commercial use, a general exception applies, as codified in Article XI.190 9° BCEL.[29] Here too, lawful access to the data remains a fundamental prerequisite.[30]

In addition, also on a general level, Article XI.189 §3 BCEL provides that copyright holders cannot oppose temporary acts of reproduction of a transient and incidental nature that form an integral and essential part of a technical process applied solely for the purpose of the transmission in a network or a lawful use of a protected work, provided that these acts have no independent economic significance.[31] There is no consensus that this would provide an additional exception permitting the training on more data than those discussed earlier, as these conditions are usually not met in the case of AI training.[32]

2.3 Remedies and Enforcement

Violations of the rules set out above can give rise to civil and criminal sanctions. On a civil level, Article XI.334 BCEL allows rights holders to seek an injunction to stop ongoing copyright infringements. Courts may correspondingly order the cessation of those activities and impose additional measures, including the seizure of the infringing goods. Article XI.335 BCEL allows rights holders to claim damages for losses incurred due to the infringement. This may cover both actual damages and lost profits. While courts will try to assess those as accurately as possible, they may turn to a lump sum in case that quantification is impossible.[33] Punitive damages may not be awarded under Belgian law.[34]

Criminal sanctions may also be imposed for violations of copyright law if they are committed intentionally or fraudulently.[35]

Indirectly, compliance for general-purpose AI system training is also enforced by the European AI Act.[36] This Act mandates that providers of general-purpose AI models implement policies ensuring compliance with copyright,[37] specifically the

29. Also see M-C Janssens, *Art XI.189 WER/CDE* in *Hommage à Jan Corbet Huldeboek – Het Belgische Auteursrecht. Artikelsgewijze commentaar/Le droit d'auteur belge. Commentaire par article* (F. Brison and H. Vanhees eds, Larcier 2018) 201 ff.
30. This implies that the copyright holder should have consented to making the data available to the public, see CJEU C-463/12 *Copydan Båndkopi v. Nokia Danmark A/S* [2015] ECLI:EU:C:2015:144, paras 75–79.
31. Gotzen and Janssen, *supra* n. 9, 336; Hendrickx and Gugliotta, *supra* n. 6, 18.
32. See Marie-Christine Janssens and Hendrik Vanhees, *Aanpassing van het Belgische auteursrecht aan de (Richtlijn inzake de) digitale eengemaakte markt*, RW 1442, 1445; Gotzen and Janssen, *supra* n. 9, 336; Hendrickx and Gugliotta, *supra* n. 6, 18 (critical of the application of this exception in this context).
33. Article XI.335 §2 BCEL.
34. See B. Michaux, *Art XI.335 WER/CDE*, in *Hommage à Jan Corbet Huldeboek – Het Belgische Auteursrecht. Artikelsgewijze commentaar/Le droit d'auteur belge. Commentaire par article* ((F. Brison and H. Vanhees eds, Larcier 2018) 1059–1060.
35. Article XI.293 BCEL.
36. Also see Bensamoun, *supra* n. 27, 158; Margoni, *supra* n. 27, 172 ff.
37. Article 53 1 (c) European AI Act; Bensamoun, *supra* n. 27, 158–159.

opt-out option for text and data mining.[38] Additionally, they must be transparent about the content used to train these models.[39]

2.4 Summary

In summary, Belgian copyright law seems restrictive regarding AI system training. In the absence of a general fair use doctrine that would permit such training, AI developers and deployers must first obtain consent from rights holders to use their works. This can be done at scale using open-access databases or other commercially available training datasets. Without such authorization, they must rely on general exceptions such as the private use one or specific exceptions, notably text and data mining exceptions – one of which applies mandatorily for scientific research if the relevant data is publicly accessible.

For commercial purposes, a similar text and data mining exception may apply. However, this exception allows rights holders to opt out and prevent their content from being used for AI training. The significance of such opt-outs, and copyright restrictions more broadly, is highlighted by the sanctions and damages applicable for breaches of copyright provisions. As a result, the current regime appears to significantly favour copyright protection over AI innovation. While defensible, further developments and calls for AI competitiveness may warrant a reconsideration of this balance.

3. USE OF AI SYSTEMS

3.1 Permission to Reproduce and Make Available to the Public

The aforementioned scope of authors' copyright protection similarly applies to the use of copyrighted material in the context of AI deployment. Using AI on or in relation to copyright-protected material typically involves uploading a copy of the material to the server hosting the AI tool. This results in the creation of a digital copy, which clearly constitutes a reproduction under copyright law (*supra* section 2.1) – thus infringing the rights of the rights holder. Belgian copyright law acknowledges the existence of a reproduction irrespective of the copy's temporary nature (*supra* section 2.1). At a minimum, using an AI tool on certain material requires the creation of a copy in the AI server's memory – which likewise qualifies as a reproduction.

The question of whether the use of copyrighted material in conjunction with an AI tool constitutes a communication to the public under Article XI.165, §1 BCEL is less clear and likely context-dependent. If this occurs in a confidential setting – where the AI system provider guarantees and observes confidentiality regarding the material – this could not qualify as communication to the public, as no other party – except possibly the AI system provider – would gain access to the work. The situation becomes more complex if the system uses uploaded materials to improve its training. The case initiated by the *New York Times* against OpenAI[40] – the company

38. Article 53 1 (c) European AI Act; Bensamoun, *supra* n. 27, 158–159.
39. Article 53 1 (d) European AI Act; Bensamoun, *supra* n. 27, 158–159.
40. Grynbaum and Mac, *supra* n. 1.

behind ChatGPT – illustrates this complexity. The *New York Times* was able to prompt ChatGPT to reproduce an entire article of theirs, despite the article being hidden behind a paywall and inaccessible to the public. In other instances, the AI's output may closely resemble the original work without proper attribution. In such cases, uploading protected material to an AI tool could effectively resemble uploading it to a publicly accessible repository, thereby constituting a communication to the public.

3.2 Exception/Limitations Allowing AI Use

There are no specific exceptions that apply to AI use in the context of uploading copyright-protected works to an AI system. In the context of an AI system that is run privately, e.g. offline on a local device, the party using the system may qualify for the private copy exception found in Article 190 9° BCEL meaning that there is no direct or indirect economic use.

More generally, in cases of system training, the above discussion applies in full.

3.3 Remedies and Enforcement

The enforcement regime mirrors that of the use of copyrighted material for AI training. Here too, violations can trigger civil and criminal penalties. Article XI.334 BCEL enables rights holders to seek injunctions to halt infringements and authorize the seizure of infringing goods. Article XI.335 BCEL allows them to claim damages for actual losses and lost profits or a lump sum if precise quantification is unfeasible.

3.4 Summary

Much like for AI training, the Belgian copyright regime is not adapted to AI deployment. In its current form, it rigidly prioritizes traditional copyright without offering specific exceptions to accommodate potential AI benefits.

The reproduction regime fully applies to temporary copies created during AI processing. It remains unclear whether communications of copyrighted material to AI systems are permissible as they can likely constitute communications to the public, particularly if user inputs are used for further training. No specific exceptions exist for AI training, apart from a limited private copy exception. Enforcement mechanisms are stringent, enabling rights holders to seek, among other things, injunctions, seize infringing goods, and claim damages – putting a strong emphasis on traditional copyright protection, potentially at the expense of AI innovation.

4. AI-GENERATED OUTPUT

4.1 Protection of AI-Generated Content

4.1.1 Copyright Protection of AI Output

An intriguing question – which has received a lot of attention in legal scholarship – is whether AI output can qualify for copyright protection under Belgian law.[41] For this to be the case, the relevant output[42] – such as a text, an image or a video – must constitute a concrete[43] and original expression by its author(s).[44] Furthermore, it is crucial to underscore that copyright does not allow the system itself to be the copyright holder under Belgian copyright law, as the law explicitly states that the author has to be a natural person (Article XI.170 BCEL).[45]

These requirements pose crucial challenges in the AI context. On one end of the spectrum,[46] modern AI systems allow users to avoid making specific or concrete choices while still generating specific output. On the other end, a generic prompt ('Write me a poem') can yield highly detailed results. In such cases, it is difficult to maintain that the role of the system is limited to that of a mere tool the author used to express themselves[47] – like a pencil or a painting brush. The output cannot genuinely be considered to constitute an original expression by the author-prompter.[48] As a result, if the output is too largely based on the system's autonomy rather than constituting an expression of the author's originality, that output will not be copyright protected,[49] and instead be part of the public domain.[50]

For a work to qualify for copyright protection, Belgium follows the CJEU case law according to which it must reflect the author's personality and be an expression of their free and creative choices.[51] In cases where users provide minimal input to

41. See e.g., Hendrickx and Gugliotta, *supra* n. 6, 15.
42. See Paulien Wymeersch, *De toepassing van het auteursrecht op AI-output*, RW 1562, 1564; Hendrickx and Gugliotta, *supra* n. 6, 16.
43. The 'concreteness' criterion serves to distinguish protected expressions from mere ideas, which are not covered by Belgian copyright law, also see Jozefien Vanherpe, *AI and IP: Great Expectations*, in *Artificial Intelligence and the Law* (J. De Bruyne and Cedric Vanleenhove eds, Intersentia 2023) 244; Hendrickx and Gugliotta, *supra* n. 6, 16.
44. See Vanherpe, *supra* n. 43, 244; Wymeersch, *supra* n. 42, 1564–1566; Hendrickx and Gugliotta, *supra* n. 6, 16. Also see CJEU Case C-5/08 *Infopaq International A/S v. Danske Dagblades Forening* [2009] ECR I-6569; Case C-145/10 *Painer v. Standard Verlags GmbH* [2011] ECR I-12533, nos. 88–89; CJEU Case C-683/17 *Cofemel – Sociedade de Vestuário SA v. G-Star Raw CV* [2019] ECLI:EU:C:2019:721, no. 30. See e.g. Kh. Brussels 6 February 2018, *IRDI* 2018, 54.
45. In this sense, see Wymeersch, *supra* n. 42, 1563; Hendrickx and Gugliotta, *supra* n. 6, 16.
46. See for a similar dichotomy: Gotzen and Janssen, *supra* n. 9, 327.
47. See e.g., Hendrickx and Gugliotta, *supra* n. 6, 15.
48. See similarly Wymeersch, *supra* n. 42, 1564 ff; Hendrickx and Gugliotta, *supra* n. 6, 16–17.
49. See similarly Gotzen and Janssen, *supra* n. 9, 329; Vanherpe, *supra* n. 43, 249.
50. Wymeersch, *supra* n. 42, 1568–1569.
51. CJEU Case C-5/08 *Infopaq International A/S v. Danske Dagblades Forening* [2009] ECR I-6569; CJEU Case C-393/09 *BSA v. Ministerstvo kultury* [2010] ECLI:EU:C:2010:816; CJEU

AI systems, this criterion is not met.[52] However, on the other end of the spectrum, where an author provides highly detailed prompts, users might leverage AI as a tool to express their originality, potentially bringing the output within the scope of copyright protection.[53]

A core challenge here, compared to traditional expressions of originality, is that AI use obscures whether the author genuinely expressed themselves, based solely on the output. AI deployment underscores the importance of the *process* for copyright law. Moreover, the exact boundary between what constitutes an expression of human originality and what results from the system's autonomy remains unclear.

Lastly, AI users should carefully review the terms and conditions of AI tool providers to ensure they do not restrict the intended use of the AI output. In some cases, providers may limit their tools to recreational or non-commercial purposes.

4.1.2 Neighbouring Rights Protection of AI Output

Some authors highlight the potential value of neighbouring rights to address certain undesirable consequences of applying existing copyright law in AI contexts.[54] However, Belgian copyright law does not, in general, recognize a broad neighbouring right for parties deploying AI systems.

This is not to say that certain neighbouring rights may not apply. Traditionally, these rights aim to protect investments rather than the expression of originality itself. Consequently, they are less closely tied to the requirement of originality and could potentially apply in situations where expressions of human originality are absent - due to AI-generated content - but where a human investment is substantial. For instance, the producer's rights to phonograms and audiovisual fixations, as set out in Article XI.209 BCEL, do not explicitly require the recorded material to result from a human author. [55]

Similarly, neighbouring rights for broadcasting organizations (Article XI.215 BCEL) may apply even when AI is used to generate content. The same holds for press publishers' rights (Article XI.216/1 BCEL), regardless of whether AI was involved in content creation, and for database rights (Article XI.305 ff BCEL), where the use of AI in creating the database is irrelevant. In each case, the relevant conditions must still be met, but these are not necessarily obstructed by the involvement of an AI system, unlike the requirements for copyright protection itself - as discussed earlier.

Case C-145/10 *Painer v. Standard Verlags GmbH* [2011] ECR I-12533. Also see Vanherpe, *supra* n. 43, 244.

52. See similarly Gotzen and Janssen, *supra* n. 9, 331–332.
53. See similarly Gotzen and Janssen, *supra* n. 9, 329; Vanherpe, *supra* n. 43, 250.
54. See, for example, Vanherpe, *supra* n. 43, 252.
55. In a more traditional context, this right may apply in the context of a recording of birdsong or natural sounds.

4.2 AI-Generated Output Infringes Existing Copyright

The relevance of the question of whether AI-generated outputs can violate copyright is beautifully illustrated by the *New York Times* case[56] briefly mentioned earlier. AI systems may, given sufficiently precise prompting, be able to reproduce documents that were used during system training, resulting in outputs that are akin to reproductions of the original document.

It is not entirely clear how to apply Belgian copyright law to such instances. In some cases, an underlying issue may be that copyright, as discussed earlier, may have been violated during system training.

Whether the output also constitutes a copyright violation is, more generally, difficult to assess. First, Belgian copyright law does not grant protection to 'styles' – allowing content creators to draw inspiration from a style used in some copyrighted work.[57] This could be relevant if the AI output only incorporates the same style as some copyright-protected work.

In case the output goes further than to mimic the style of some copyrighted work, the rule that reproductions and adaptations are, generally, not allowed plays out in full (*supra* section 2.1).[58] To determine whether there is an adaptation or reproduction, the general impression of the average viewer is decisive,[59] with similarities weighing more heavily than differences.[60] Additionally, the 'thinner' the originality of the original, copyrighted work, the stronger the output has to resemble that original work for there to be an infringement.[61]

The application of these principles is inherently difficult in AI cases where the person using the system is unaware of the fact that they created a reproduction/adaptation. It could be argued that they did not violate copyright if the AI output is the genuine result of an expression of their creativity. That situation is likely akin to a situation where someone independently comes up with some work that happens to be very similar to an existing work, without having used the latter as a basis – i.e. an 'independent creation'.[62]

In many instances of AI use, however, the system does not truly 'independently' arrive at similar output to the original copyrighted content, but rather because that content was included in the system training. This may be due to an explicit prompt of the user – asking the system to generate something similar to some specific work.[63] The user of the system, however, may also be unaware of the original content or its use in system training. From their perspective, the resemblance of the original copyrighted content may appear coincidental.

56. Grynbaum and Mac, *supra* n. 1.
57. See, e.g., Cass. 17 February 2017, C.15.0144.N; Antwerp 24 March 2021, *IRDI* 2021, 95; Brussels 23 September 2024, *IRDI* 2024, 289.
58. See in more traditional contexts Brussels 13 June 2024, *IRDI* 2024, 170.
59. Antwerp 18 November 2020, *IRDI* 2021, 81; Pres. Antwerp 31 March 2015, *IRDI* 2018, 111, annotated by K. Lauwers.
60. Antwerp 18 November 2020, *IRDI* 2021, 81.
61. Antwerp 18 November 2020, *IRDI* 2021, 81.
62. Hendrickx and Gugliotta, *supra* n. 6, 20.
63. Hendrickx and Gugliotta, *supra* n. 6, 20.

It is not entirely clear how the Belgian copyright regime applies to the user of an AI system in such scenarios. It is clear, however, that Belgian copyright law allows the 'independent creation' defence rather strictly,[64] applying a presumption that some later work was not truly independent but was rather inspired by earlier copyright-protected work.[65]

Additionally, these challenges also raise the question of the potential accountability of the system developer – who is uniquely positioned to be (more) aware of the content used for system training. This adds emphasis to the European AI Act's requirement that providers of general-purpose AI systems should develop a copyright policy concerning the data the system was trained on.[66]

It is, in any case, clear that this will lead to very tricky assessments and a complicated burden of proof, as the process is inherently more challenging to assess.[67] This applies in particular given the unexplainable and unpredictable nature of many AI systems (*supra* section 1).

4.3 Remedies and Enforcement

Remedies for copyright infringement by AI output or the protection of AI-generated output, mirrors the enforcement regime in more traditional contexts as described in more detail above for the use of copyrighted material for AI system training. Violations of copyright protection can thus trigger civil and criminal penalties, and Article XI.334 BCEL enables rights holders to seek injunctions to halt infringements and authorize the seizure of infringing goods. Additionally, Article XI.335 BCEL allows them to claim damages.

4.4 Summary

In summary, Belgian copyright law requires human authorship. Most AI-generated content, generated based on rather minimalistic or general prompts by a human user, lacks human originality and resultingly falls into the public domain. The threshold of originality may be met if the system user has written more detailed prompts, but the precise delineation is unclear.

Some neighbouring rights – although out of the scope of this contribution – protect investments regardless of an underlying right of authorship – such as for phonograms or databases. In such instances, the use of an AI system in the creation of relevant content that is protected by that neighbouring right does not necessarily obstruct that protection.

64. Brussels 4 September 2007, IRDI 2008, annotated by A. Hallemans; Kh. Brussels 6 February 2018, *IRDI* 2018, 54; Alexis Hallemans, *De rechtsfiguur van de onafhankelijke creatie in het auteursrecht: Was Michael Jackson toch alleen?*, IRDI 106, 107 ff; Hendrickx and Gugliotta, *supra* n. 6, 20.
65. Cass. 3 September 2009, *IRDI* 2009, 411; Antwerp 2 October 2019, *IRDI* 2019, 206; A. Berenboom, *Le nouveau droit d'auteur* (Larcier 2022) 72.
66. Article 53 1 (c) AI Act.
67. See similarly Wymeersch, *supra* n. 42, 1569.

Furthermore, AI output can infringe copyright if it reproduces training data, or if it is otherwise used to adapt copyrighted content without the consent of the right holders. While the precise delineation with independent creations may be unclear, accountability for developers is a concern.

This copyright protection – as well as similar protection in the case of neighbouring rights – is enforced in the same way as in traditional AI contexts. Rights holders can thus seek injunctions and damages for AI-related or -based infringements.

5. CONCLUSIONS

An analysis of Belgian copyright law reveals that the current framework is not particularly tailored to address the widespread training and deployment of AI systems. Notably, Belgian law does not contain a general fair use exception that could facilitate AI training. Instead, parties seeking to train AI systems must rely on narrowly defined and restrictive exceptions. In most cases, this necessitates obtaining explicit consent from copyright holders to use their content.

Some limited exceptions relevant to AI training do exist. In particular, the general exception of private use, the text and data mining exceptions for scientific research, and, more generally, for commercial purposes – provided the copyright holder has not opted out – offer some flexibility. However, these exceptions remain constrained and do not broadly accommodate AI innovation.

Regarding AI-generated content, such output is generally not eligible for copyright protection under Belgian law. An exception may arise if the user of the AI system invests substantial effort in optimizing prompts, thereby reducing the AI system to a mere tool used to express the author's originality. However, the threshold for such protection remains unclear and is likely to exclude most AI-generated works from copyright protection.

In contrast, certain neighbouring rights offer more potential for protection. Rights related to databases and producers' contributions, for example, do not explicitly require human authorship of the underlying content, making them potentially applicable to AI-generated content, provided other relevant conditions are met.

The use of AI systems to generate content also poses a risk of infringing existing copyrights. AI-generated outputs may closely resemble the training data used, raising complex liability issues. Even if the user is unaware of the prior use of such content in AI training, a defence based on 'independent creation' is, in general, not very likely to succeed under Belgian copyright law.

Overall, Belgian copyright law reflects traditional copyright principles and lacks specific exceptions to accommodate AI innovation and development. While it remains uncertain whether the current balance adequately supports AI progress, one clear short-term need is greater legal clarity. The unique characteristics of AI systems make the application of existing copyright rules and exceptions challenging, underscoring the need for more comprehensive guidance for judges and legal advisors handling AI-related copyright claims.

Chapter 2

Brazil

Leticia Provedel and Luiza Alkaim

1. INTRODUCTION

The regulation of artificial intelligence (AI) in Brazil is a relatively recent topic, but one that has been gaining increasing attention, especially with the advancement of technologies and the growing use of automated systems across various sectors. Although the country has important legislative frameworks in the areas of innovation and technology, such as the *Marco Civil da Internet* (Civil Framework for the Internet), the *Marco Legal da Ciência, Tecnologia e Inovação* (Legal Framework for Science, Technology, and Innovation), and the *Lei Geral de Proteção de Dados* (General Data Protection Law), until recently, the National Congress had not addressed AI regulation in a structured manner.

It was only in 2019, with the introduction of Bill 5,051/2019 proposed in the Federal Senate, that regulatory movement on the subject began, and only in 2020 did the correlation between AI and copyright start to be addressed with the inclusion of Article 5, VIII, in Bill 21/2020, which established the legal possibility of accessing and using content from databases without it constituting a violation of copyright.

In 2022, the Commission of Jurists Responsible for Supporting the Drafting of a Substitute on Artificial Intelligence in Brazil (CJUSBIA) was created to consolidate the AI-related Bills under discussion (5,051/2019, 21/2020, and 872/2021), resulting in the creation of Bill 2,338/2023. This Bill establishes general national standards for the development, implementation, and responsible use of AI systems in Brazil, aiming to protect fundamental rights and ensure the implementation of safe and reliable systems. The Bill has already been approved by the Senate but is still awaiting approval by the Chamber of Deputies.

As noted, Brazil is still in the process of legislative evolution on the subject, often requiring the analogical application of existing legal provisions, as will be further explored in the following sections.

2. TRAINING AI MODELS

2.1 Training AI with Copyright Protected Works

As previously indicated, there is no specific regulation in force in Brazil regarding the use of copyright-protected works in the training of AIs. Additionally, case law is scarce, and there is no doctrinal consensus on the issue. In this regard, the prevailing understanding is the analogical application of the provisions of the *Lei de Direitos Autorais* (Copyright Law, Law No. 9,610/1998).

In this context, Articles 28 and 29 of the Copyright Law establish that authors hold the exclusive right to use, enjoy, and dispose of their work, requiring prior and express authorization for any form of use of the work:

> **Article 28**. The author holds the exclusive right to use, enjoy, and dispose of the literary, artistic, or scientific work.
>
> **Article 29**. The use of the work, in any form, depends on prior and express authorization from the author, including:
> I partial or full reproduction;
> II editing;
> III adaptation, musical arrangement, and any other transformations;
> IV translation into any language;
> V inclusion in a phonogram or audiovisual production;
> VI distribution, when not inherent in a contract between the author and third parties for the use or exploitation of the work;
> VII distribution for offering works or productions via cable, optical fiber, satellite, waves, or any other system that allows the user to select the work or production for viewing at a time and place predetermined by the one making the request, and in cases where access to the works or productions requires payment by the user;
> VIII direct or indirect use of the literary, artistic, or scientific work, through: [...].

Based on these provisions, it is understood that the use of protected works is the exclusive right of their author, and the indiscriminate use of such works for AI training constitutes a legal violation.

AI training with protected works can be carried out when authorization is obtained, whereby copyright holders grant permission for the use of their works, even establishing the terms and conditions for the use of the work in training.

The use of works in public databases may also be feasible, provided that these works are available for reuse or adaptation, which may be subject to specific conditions, such as open licences or explicit permissions.

If AI training is carried out without the proper authorization, the developer of the AI model, as well as the user who utilizes the model, may be held liable for legal violations, depending on the context and circumstances.

2.2 Exceptions/Limitations Allowing Training of AI

The limitations on the use of protected works in AI training are also provided in the Copyright Law in Articles 46, 47, and 48, which establish the conditions under which the use of such works does not constitute a legal offence.

Article 46, for example, specifies that reproducing news or informative articles in the press, public speeches, commissioned portraits, works for visually impaired individuals, and small reproductions for private use without the intention of profit are not considered an infringement. It also permits the citation of excerpts for study, criticism, or controversy, provided the author and the source of the work are properly credited. Article 47 addresses paraphrasing and parodies, allowing their use as long as they do not constitute an exact reproduction of the original work or discredit it. Article 48 allows for the reproduction of works located in public spaces through paintings, drawings, photographs, and other audiovisual means.

It is important to clarify that in Brazil, fair use is not recognized, and the only legally allowed exceptions are those mentioned above.

If the Bill 2,338/2023 is approved, the exceptions will be modified. According to Article 61 of the draft, the automated use of protected content in text and data mining processes for research or the development of AI systems by research organizations, institutions, journalism, museums, archives, libraries, and educational entities will not constitute a violation of copyright. The exceptions will only apply if: I) access to the content was lawful; II) there are no commercial purposes; III) the activity does not primarily aim to reproduce, display, or disseminate the original work itself; and IV) the use is limited to what is necessary, without harming the economic interests of the work's owners or competing with the normal exploitation of the works.

3. USE OF AI SYSTEMS

3.1 Permission to Reproduce and Make Available to the Public

In the Brazilian context, any reproduction and/or making available to the public of a work protected by copyright without the authorization of the rights holder, in principle, constitutes an infringement. Making the work available to the public is also included within this scope, as it involves the distribution of the work in a manner that allows others to access it.

Similarly, in the case of AI training, to reproduce and/or make available a protected work, such as a book, it is necessary to obtain permission from the copyright holder, which generally involves acquiring a usage licence.

The responsibility for obtaining such permission lies with the party using the work, namely, the developer or the platform utilizing the AI system.

3.2 Exception/Limitations Allowing AI Training

A legal violation will only not occur if this reproduction and/or making available is expressly stated in the limitations outlined in Articles 46, 47, and 48 of the Copyright Law, which, as discussed in the previous chapter, address the use of works for specific purposes, such as research, study, or criticism, provided there are no commercial purposes and the use does not harm the economic interests of the rights holders.

3.3 Remedies and Enforcement

See below, section 4.3.

4. AI-GENERATED OUTPUT

4.1 Protection of AI-Generated Content

4.1.1 Copyright Protection of AI Output

The Copyright Law, in its Article 11, clearly states that 'author' refers to a natural person who creates a literary, artistic, or scientific work, and this protection can be granted to legal entities in the cases provided for by this Law.

Therefore, an AI, as a computer program, could never, by itself, be considered an author, nor could it be granted the protection given to legal entities, as it does not possess legal personality. Thus, even if an AI is considered capable of producing intellectual works autonomously, in light of the current legislation, it could not, in any way, be classified as an author or holder of copyright.

This understanding was reinforced by the Brazilian Federal Justice Council, which, in its IX Civil Law Journey, approved Enunciation 670, affirming that 'regardless of the degree of autonomy of an artificial intelligence system, the status of author is exclusively reserved for human beings'.

As a consequence of exclusion of authorship from AI, as a general rule, it is understood that content generated solely by AI systems would automatically fall into the public domain, since, with the possibility of authorship excluded, it would be considered a work of an unknown author, falling under the provision of item II of Article 45 of the Copyright Law:

> **Article 45**. In addition to works for which the term of protection of economic rights has expired, the following belong to the public domain:
> [...]
> II works of unknown authorship, except for the legal protection of ethnic and traditional knowledge.

However, it is important to note that this issue is controversial, and there is significant debate surrounding it.

The view that all original works by AI fall into the public domain has several consequences, the main one being the legality of their dissemination, which can be seen as something positive for society, but may also be viewed as demotivating to the author or the person responsible for the material.

Considering that AI is a computer program that operates by reproducing codes previously programmed its developer, some believe that, in fact, all the intellectual output from its autonomous actions should be attributed to the person who created the AI, instead of falling into the public domain.

Another aspect for consideration is the level of human intervention in the creation of the content. Many researchers on this subject argue that works created without direct human involvement should be the only ones to fall into the public domain. In cases where AI is merely a tool or extension of a human's creative activity, without playing a significant role in the creation of the work, the user would be considered the author and would be protected by the Copyright Law.

Therefore, it is evident that in Brazil, there is a significant gap on this subject, with the case often being analysed on an individual basis in order to determine the authorship and protection of a work generated by AI.

4.1.2 Neighbouring Rights Protection of AI Output

Regarding the protection of neighbouring rights, the discussion remains similar: if content generated by AI do not have copyright, they also would not have neighbouring rights.

This is a sensitive issue, especially when considering the collection of public performance rights, which is carried out in Brazil by the Central Office of Collection and Distribution (ECAD), an entity authorized by the Copyright Law to collect and distribute the rights related to the public performance of music.

In summary, the collection of copyright fees is required from commercial establishments that use music in public spaces, such as radio and TV stations, concerts, events, streaming platforms, among others. ECAD collects these fees based on objective criteria and distributes the amounts related to public performance to the copyright holders.

In the case of music created by AI, since there is no recognized authorship, collection by ECAD would not be possible, which would harm both the entity and the agents in the music market.

Moreover, similar to the authorship issue, some argue that, in the case of an AI-generated production involving, for example, a producer or a company responsible for creating and exploiting the AI system, the producer's rights could be attributed to the entity responsible for the creation or investment in the technology.

Therefore, the protection of neighbouring rights regarding AI-generated works would also depend on the involvement of a human in the creation or development of the work.

4.2 AI-Generated Output Infringes Existing Copyright

If content generated by AI is considered a substantial reproduction or a copy of an existing work, or if it presents significant similarities to a protected work, especially regarding elements that characterize the original creation, such as composition, design, narrative, among others, it will be understood that an infringement has occurred, in accordance with Articles 28 and 29 of the Copyright Law, which, as previously discussed, ensure that the rights to use and reproduce works are exclusive to the author, and any use without the necessary authorization from the rights holder constitutes a violation of copyright.

In these situations, the responsibility for the infringement may fall on the party using the AI to generate the content. This may include the developer of the

AI system, the platform providing the system, and/or the end user who created the content, depending on the specific circumstances.

4.3 Remedies and Enforcement

The emergence of AI technologies has steered a new era of innovation, raising significant questions regarding the enforcement of intellectual property rights, particularly in the realm of copyright. In Brazil, where the legal landscape for copyright protection is established by the Copyright Law, understanding the nuances of copyright enforcement for AI innovations has become increasingly vital. This is especially important because AI often relies on software, algorithms, and creative outputs that challenge traditional notions of authorship and originality.

In Brazil, software and algorithms, including those used in AI, are considered literary works under the Copyright Law. This classification grants them protection against unauthorized reproduction, distribution, and public performance. Importantly, copyright protection extends to the specific expressions of ideas (the source code, for example) but does not extend to the underlying ideas, methods, or processes that the software might employ. This means that while the code of an AI algorithm may be protected, the general principles or functionalities that the AI operates on remain in the public domain.

One of the key challenges in enforcing copyright for AI innovations in Brazil is the determination of authorship. In traditional copyright regimes, the author is typically a human creator. However, with the increasing sophistication of AI, questions arise regarding whether an AI system can be deemed an author of its outputs. Currently, Brazilian law does not explicitly recognize AI as a legal author, placing the onus of copyright ownership on the human developers or organizations that created the AI. This complicates enforcement when multiple parties may claim rights to AI-generated outputs.

When it comes to enforcing copyright for AI-related works in Brazil, the law provides several remedies for infringement. In cases of copyright violations, rights holders have the legal right to seek:

1. Injunctive Relief: copyright holders can request a court-issued injunction to stop the unauthorized use or distribution of their protected work. This swift remedy is crucial in preventing further infringement and mitigating harm.
2. Damages: victims of copyright infringement can claim damages for losses incurred due to unauthorized use. Brazilian law allows for both actual damages and potential profits that the infringer might have gained from the unauthorized use. For creators reliant on income from their works, this remedy is essential for ensuring financial compensation.
3. Statutory Damages: in certain cases, Brazilian copyright law permits the pursuit of statutory damages, predetermined by the courts, which can simplify the process of addressing infringement without the need to demonstrate specific losses.
4. Seizure of Infringing Goods: courts can order the seizure and destruction of infringing materials, which serves both as a punitive action against the

infringer and as a preventive measure against the further distribution of unauthorized works.

5. Legal Costs: in successful infringement cases, courts may order the infringer to pay the legal costs of the copyright holder, including attorney fees, thereby reducing the financial burden of pursuing legal action.

Despite this robust framework for enforcement, several challenges hinder the effective application of copyright laws in relation to AI in Brazil. One significant hurdle is the backlog in the judiciary, which can delay justice for copyright holders seeking remedies. Additionally, the nature of AI technologies – particularly the ability to replicate and distribute software digitally – exacerbates the potential for widespread copyright infringement.

Moreover, proving copyright infringement in the case of AI systems can be complex. In many instances, code can be easily altered to evade detection, and the intricate nature of AI algorithms makes it challenging to demonstrate a direct infringement without detailed technical analysis.

Furthermore, as AI-generated works become more prevalent, the legal ambiguities surrounding authorship and ownership may lead to disputes among creators, developers, and organizations about who holds the copyright to AI outputs. Clarity in the law and judicial interpretation will be essential for navigating these challenges.

To bolster the enforcement of copyright for AI innovations in Brazil, certain measures can be taken to address these challenges effectively. Legislative reforms aimed at clarifying copyright ownership regarding AI-generated works could significantly enhance legal certainty. Specialized training for legal professionals on the intricacies of AI technologies could also improve the efficacy of copyright enforcement.

Moreover, promoting awareness among creators about their rights and the mechanisms available for enforcing those rights can empower them to take protective actions. Collaboration between private entities, the government, and academic institutions can foster an environment conducive to innovation while safeguarding intellectual property rights.

4.4 Summary

In Brazil, the intersection of copyright and AI is an evolving area of law as traditional copyright frameworks begin to address the challenges posed by AI technologies. The Brazilian Copyright Law currently recognizes copyright for works created by human authors, leading to ambiguity regarding the legal status of works generated solely by AI. As the law does not explicitly state whether AI can be considered an author, the prevailing view is that if an AI tool generates a creative work, the copyright would likely need to be attributed to the human overseeing or directing the AI's output.

5. CONCLUSION

Under Brazilian law, copyright is inherently tied to human authorship, which raises questions about the ownership and rights to works created with significant AI involvement. Moreover, the use of copyrighted materials for training AI models can lead to potential copyright infringement issues, especially if the training data is not properly licensed. As of now, Brazil's legal framework does not provide clear guidelines on using copyrighted works for AI training. Nevertheless, Brazilian statutory law provides several remedies and instruments for enforcement which can be applied on a case by case basis.

With rapid developments in AI technology, Brazilian lawmakers, legal scholars, and industry stakeholders are increasingly discussing the need for potential reforms or new legislation to address these issues more clearly. Additionally, the country is engaged with international forums to adapt copyright laws to better accommodate and regulate innovations in AI while respecting the rights of creators. Overall, while Brazilian copyright law does not provide explicit provisions for AI-generated works, ongoing discussions indicate a recognition of the necessity to adapt legal frameworks to the implications of AI on copyright.

In conclusion, as Brazil embraces the transformative potential of AI technologies, the country is refining its legal framework, increasing awareness, and strengthening enforcement mechanisms, to ensure that the creative and technological industries navigate in an environment of respect for intellectual property, thereby fostering greater innovation and economic development.

Chapter 3

Canada

Brian W. Gray

1. INTRODUCTION

In Canada there are now (as of February 2025) two cases relating to use of copyrighted works to train artificial intelligence (AI) engines and the use of such engines to reproduce infringing copies: *Toronto Star Newspapers et al v. OpenAI.Inc.*[1] and *CanII v. CasewayAI.*[2] These cases mirror similar litigation ongoing in the United States. As in the United States, with a few exceptions,[3] no decisions have been reached about liability or the merits of any of the main defences raised. However, we can see from cases developing in the United States and elsewhere[4] the kinds of scenarios that are leading to disputes. We can then apply general Canadian copyright concepts to discuss the issues that will likely arise under Canadian law. However, before discussing infringement, it is useful to discuss certain principles relevant to the creation and protection of AI generated works.

> AI is software that does fancy data processing. It generates predictions, recommendations, or decisions based on statistical reasoning (precisely, this is true of machine learning types of AI). Evidence-based statistical policy making

---

1. Ontario Superior Court of Justice CV-24-00732231-00CL. Statement of Claim filed 28 November 2024.
2. *Canadian Legal Information Institute v. 1345750 B.C. Ltd. et al., dba doing business as CASEWAY AI*. Supreme Court of British Columbia 4 November 2024.
3. *Thomson Reuters v. Ross Intelligence Inc.* D.C. Delaware No. 1:20-cv-613-SB 11 February 2025, and partial summary judgments on fair use *Kadrey v. Meta Platforms* NDCA 23-cv-03417-VC, 25 June 2025; *Bartz et al. v. Anthropic PBC*, NDCA 24-cv-05417-WHA 23 June 2025.
4. A similar case is on-going in the UK as well, *Getty Images (US) Inc. et al. v. Stability AI Ltd. et al.* UK High Court of Justice Case No: IL-2023-000007 (2023). And there is a large language model case in India: *Asian News International v. OpenAI.*

> or statistical reasoning is a powerful tool for improving human lives.... If AI software automates aspects of the human process of science, that makes it very powerful, but it remains software all the same.[5]

Similarly, an AI model that digests literary works and that can produce literary works (so called large language models or LLMs) or that digests music to produce artificially created music, is still a computer program. Since at least 1985, computer programs have been protected in Canada as literary works.[6] A computer program is defined as a 'set of instructions or statements, expressed, fixed, embodied or stored in any manner, that is to be used directly or indirectly in a computer in order to bring about a specific result.'[7]

Copyright is granted to works that are authored by humans. The Act does not explicitly define the term 'author' or whether an AI application can be an author of a work, but the Copyright Act ties the term of protection to the life and death of an author,[8] from which it follows that the author must be a living person. Recognizing an AI model as a sole author is not consistent with the current scheme of the Canadian Copyright Act.

Nevertheless, in December 2021, the Canadian Intellectual Property Office (CIPO) registered a copyright for a *Starry* Night-inspired painting titled *Suryest*. The copyright registration listed two co-authors – Mr. Ankit Sahni and RAGHAV Artificial Intelligence Painting app (RAGHAV). This appears to be the first-ever Canadian copyright registration with an AI author.[9] However in July 2024, the Samuelson-Glusko Clinic applied to the Federal Court to correct the copyright register to remove the AI Painting app on the basis that only a human can be an author.[10] The case however has proceeded slowly with no hearing date in sight.

AI-assisted works, in contrast to AI-generated works, may qualify for copyright protection and registration where humans are involved in generating the work, but it seems problematic that AI assistance should make it possible to name an AI model as a co-author. A more satisfactory approach may be to limit the copyright protection to the portion of the work that is the product of human creativity, where that can be ascertained. Such an approach was adopted by the US copyright office in the *Zarya of the Dawn* case where the copyright registration covered only the human created works in the illustrated story and not the images that were generated by an AI model in response to prompts.[11]

As pointed out by the American Intellectual Property Law Association in its response to the US Copyright Office request for comments:

---

5. *Software Must Be Secure by Design, and Artificial Intelligence Is No Exception*, https://www.cisa.gov/news-events/news/software-must-be-secure-design-and-artificial-intelligence-no-exception.
6. Copyright Act. R.S.C. 1985, c. C-42 Sections 2 and 5.
7. Copyright Act Section 2.
8. See for example Copyright Act Sections 6–9 and *Setana Sport Limited v. 2049630 Ontario Inc. (Verde Minho Tapas & Lounge)*, 2007 FC 899, at para. 4.
9. Copyright Registration No. 1188619.
10. *Samuelson-Glusk Canadian Internet Policy Public Interest Clinic v. Ankit Sahni*, Federal Court T-1717-24.
11. Copyright.gov, https://www.copyright.gov/docs/zarya-of-the-dawn.pdf.

> the term 'AI-generated works' … encompasses works whose genesis involves varying degrees of AI contribution. We suggest that this framework should be understood as encompassing three distinct categories of 'works generated by or using AI'. These are:
>
> > Category A: Works created by a human author with the assistance of an AI technology (AI as mere tool of human creativity);
> > Category B: Works created by a human in collaboration with AI, wherein the activity of the human, would be considered sufficiently original and creative to merit copyright protection (AI as co-author with a human author); and
> > Category C: Works created by an AI that, if created by a human, would be considered sufficiently original and creative to merit copyright protection, but under circumstances in which there is no human creativity or originality sufficient to meet the legal standard for copyright protection (AI as sole author).[12]
>
> It is submitted that under current Canadian law, only works in category A or possibly B would be subject to copyright protection.
>
> But what about Category C? The Copyright Act provides that copyright exists for 'every original literary, dramatic, musical and artistic work'.[13]

The meaning of the word 'original' in Section 5 of the Copyright Act was considered by the Supreme Court in *CCH Canadian Ltd. v. Law Society of Upper Canada*:[14]

> For a work to be 'original' within the meaning of the Copyright Act, it must be more than a mere copy of another work. At the same time, it need not be creative, in the sense of being novel or unique. What is required to attract copyright protection in the expression of an idea is an exercise of skill and judgment. By skill, I mean the use of one's knowledge, developed aptitude or practised ability in producing the work. By judgment, I mean the use of one's capacity for discernment or ability to form an opinion or evaluation by comparing different possible options in producing the work. This exercise of skill and judgment will necessarily involve intellectual effort. The exercise of skill and judgment required to produce the work must not be so trivial that it could be characterized as a purely mechanical exercise. For example, any skill and judgment that might be involved in simply changing the font of a work to produce 'another' work would be too trivial to merit copyright protection as an 'original' work.

The *CCH* case considered originality well before AI generated works were known or considered. However, by phrases such as 'an exercise of skill and judgment' which 'will necessarily involve intellectual effort' it would seem that entry of prompts to an AI model where the AI model then produces a work whose output is not controlled by the human prompter will not generally have the necessary skill and judgment to

---

12. AIPLA Comments Submitted to US Copyright Office pursuant to Notice of Inquiry and Request for Comments, 88 Fed. Reg. 59942 (30 August 2023).
13. Copyright Act, RSC 1985, c. C-42 Section 5.
14. *CCH Canadian Ltd. v. Law Society of Upper Canada*, (2004 SCC 13 [CCH]).

qualify as a copyrightable work, no matter how 'original' it may seem. However, no Canadian court has had to consider this.

On 29 January 2025, the US Copyright Office released Part 2 of its guidance on originality and copyrightability with respect to works which have been generated in whole or part by an AI engine.[15] The Office reiterated that the use of AI to assist in the process of creation or the inclusion of AI-generated material in a larger human-generated work does not bar copyrightability. However, the Office also confirmed the centrality of human creativity for copyright protection. A work created entirely by an AI engine with no human original input is not protectable by copyright. The report still leaves many unanswered questions as to the level of human involvement that would be necessary for copyright protection. However, it would seem that a text prompt to an AI engine alone, however detailed, may not be enough to provide sufficient human originality, at least from the US Copyright Office point of view.

In February 2025, the Canadian Government issued its observations following extensive consultations under the title *What We Heard: Consultations on Copyright in the Age of Artificial Intelligence*.[16] The report concluded that, generally, participants in the consultation expressed support for keeping human authorship central to copyright protection. Many submitted that only AI-generated content with sufficient human contributions should be protected. However, again, the observations left unanswered the extent of the originality of the human contribution that would be required to obtain protection. [17]

2. TRAINING AI MODELS

2.1 Training AI with Copyright Protected Works

AI uses a variety of inputs for training. Arguably much of it falls under the category of data. However, we see that some of the training is done on copyright protected artistic or literary works. The extent to which these works are copied and digitalized and viewed as 'data' will have a bearing on whether the training itself is a copyright infringement.

Data may be protectable under copyright as a 'compilation' but only if the database is 'original' and the result of skill and judgment in the selection and arrangement of the data, and the act of compilation is not a mere mechanical exercise. This is likely to be the case with some databases but almost certainly is not the case with unstructured data. If the data is being collected as a result of machine learning, i.e. a car or robot receiving 'sensory' input, this is most likely unstructured data. There is a long standing principle that 'there can be no copyright in facts'.[18]

---

15. US Copyright Office release 1060 https://www.copyright.gov/newsnet/2025/1060.html 29 January 2025,
16. https://ised-isde.canada.ca/site/strategic-policy-sector/en/marketplace-framework-policy/consultation-copyright-age-generative-artificial-intelligence-what-we-heard-report.
17. *Op cit.*, Observation 4.
18. See *CCH Canadian Ltd. v. Law Society of Upper Canada*, 2002 FCA 187 at para. 212, [2002] 4 FC 213; also see *Deeks v. Wells*, 1931 CanLII 157 (ON CA), [1931] 4 DLR 533, 1931 CarswellOnt 247 (CA), per Orde, J.A.

As previously pointed out, the Copyright Act provides that copyright exists for 'every original literary, dramatic, musical and artistic work'.[19] This phrase is defined in the Copyright Act section 2 to include compilations, which is in turn defined to include works 'resulting from the selection or arrangement of data'. In *Toronto Real Estate Board v. Commissioner of Competition*[20] the classification of the database of house prices as a compilation was not contested by either party on appeal. However, the Court found that the evidence of the Toronto Real Estate Board did not speak to skill and judgment in compiling the database, but rather the evidence showed that the collection was a mechanical exercise and that therefore copyright did not attach to that database.[21]

However, in *Geophysical Service Inc. v. Encana Corp*,[22] the Alberta Court of Queen's Bench held that copyright can subsist in seismic data of the following kind, namely:

(i) raw seismic field data, or raw seismic, magnetic, and gravity data;
(ii) seismic related navigation data;
(iii) processed and reprocessed seismic data;
(iv) selections, arrangement and compilations of raw, processed and reprocessed seismic data;
(v) productions and reproductions of seismic data in various forms and media including physical, electronic, magnetic and digital works;
(vi) interpretations, derivations and translations of the seismic data; and
(vii) related seismic data materials.[23]

In *Distrimedic Inc. v. Dispill Inc.*,[24] the Federal Court held that 'when the content and layout of a form is largely dictated by utility and/or legislative requirements, it is not to be considered original' (at para. 324). Indeed, the Copyright Act specifically provides that it is not an infringement of copyright to apply to a useful article features that are dictated by a utilitarian function or using any method or principle or construction.[25]

That copyright need not extend to mere data is also a result of the TRIPS Agreement (Article 10(2)) which does not require extending copyright protection to the data or subject matter itself:

> 10(2) Compilations of data or other material, whether in machine readable or other form, which by reason of the selection or arrangement constitute

19. Copyright Act, Sections 2 and 5.
20. 2017 FCA 236.
21. Subsequent interlocutory proceedings have cast some doubt on the general applicability of that decision outside of the context of the competition proceeding. See *Toronto Regional Real Estate Board v. R E Stats Inc. (ReDatum)* 2021 FC 1193 and see *IMS Incorporated v. Toronto Regional Real Estate Board*, 2023 FCA 7 where the Federal Court of Appeal found that its earlier 2017 decision was *obiter* and in any event related to at least some different works.
22. (2016) ABQB 230.
23. *Geophysical Service Inc. v. Encana Corp.* (2016), 2016 CarswellAlta 742, 2016 ABQB 230, [2016] 10 W.W.R. 111, 38 Alta. L.R. (6th) 48.
24. (2013 FC 1043).
25. Copyright Act, Section 64.1.

> intellectual creations shall be protected as such. Such protection, which shall not extend to the data or material itself, shall be without prejudice to any copyright subsisting in the data or material itself.[26]

So there is question for some AI training engines as to whether they are using unstructured and uncopyrightable data or data of which the selection or arrangement constitutes an 'intellectual creation'. There will also be a question as to whether the works have copyright individually and also as a compilation or collection of works.

There seems to be no question that some AI training is done on works that are subject to copyright, for example photographs (such as collected by Getty Images) or words (for example *New York Times* articles), and if may also be that the collection as a whole is protected as a compilation. In many cases, the whole of the database of photographs or collection of articles is scanned, digested, or digitized to train the AI model.

The process of training seems to involve in general tokenization, embedding, contextualization and prediction with the result that the whole of the works used for training are digested in bits and apparently can be recreated on demand.[27]

It is not an infringement in Canada to use a copyrighted work if it does not involve copying or dealing with a work that has been copied without authorization. In addition, not all copying is an infringement if the work has not been copied in whole or substantial part or if the copying is fair dealing according to Section 29 Copyright Act. What is substantial is judged by the quantity and quality of the amount taken.

The following quotes from *Cinar Corporation v. Robinson*,[28] the leading Supreme Court of Canada case on substantial copying are illustrative:

> [25] However, the Act does not protect every 'particle' of an original work, 'any little piece the taking of which cannot affect the value of [the] work as a whole': Vaver, at p. 182. Section 3 of the Copyright Act provides that the copyright owner has the sole right to reproduce 'the work or any substantial part thereof'.
>
> [26] A substantial part of a work is a flexible notion. It is a matter of fact and degree. 'Whether a part is substantial must be decided by its quality rather than its quantity': Ladbroke (Football), Ltd. v. William Hill (Football), Ltd., [1964] 1 All E.R. 465 (H.L.), at p. 481, per Lord Pearce. What constitutes a substantial part is determined in relation to the originality of the work that warrants the protection of the Copyright Act. As a general proposition, a substantial part of a work is a part of the work that represents a substantial portion of the author's skill and judgment expressed therein.
>
> [27] A substantial part of a work is not limited to the words on the page or the brushstrokes on the canvas. The Act protects authors against both literal and

26. Agreement on Trade-Related Aspects of Intellectual Property Rights, https://www.wto.org/english/docs_e/legal_e/27-trips_04_e.htm.
27. For a discussion of the process involved in training an AI model in the context of whether there is a reproduction, see Daniel J. Gervais, Noam Shemtov, Haralambos Marmanis & Catherine Zaller Rowland, *The Heart of the Matter: Copyright, AI Training, and LLMs* (21 September 2024). Available at SSRN: https://ssrn.com/abstract=4963711 or http://dx.doi.org/10.2139/ssrn.4963711.
28. 2013 SCC 73 (CanLII), [2013] 3 SCR 1168.

> non-literal copying, so long as the copied material forms a substantial part of the infringed work.
>
> ...
>
> [36] The cumulative effect of the features copied from the work must be considered, to determine whether those features amount to a substantial part of Robinson's skill and judgment expressed in his work as a whole.
>
> ...
>
> [39] The question of whether there has been substantial copying focuses on whether the copied features constitute a substantial part of the plaintiff's work – not whether they amount to a substantial part of the defendant's work: Vaver, at p. 186; E. F. Judge and D. J. Gervais, Intellectual Property: The Law in Canada (2nd ed. 2011), at p. 211. The alteration of copied features or their integration into a work that is notably different from the plaintiff's work does not necessarily preclude a claim that a substantial part of a work has been copied. Infringement includes 'any colourable imitation' of a work.[29].

This last quote from paragraph 39 of *Cinar* is particularly relevant because the works or part of works copied by the AI model may not be a substantial part of its training opus but seems like it may well be a substantial part of the individual materials used for training, particularly in the case of image databases or literary works.

Copyright infringement therefore is established when the defendant has produced a substantial copy, including a colourable imitation of the plaintiff's work. Infringement is not limited to an exact copy.[30]

Can expressive works be turned into uncopyrightable data and absorbed by the AI engine in that way?

Does this involve copying in whole or substantial part?

How are the works assimilated or digested by the AI model? Are they being absorbed by direct copying? Are they being split into digitalized bits and then reassembled? In most cases, except in the case of unstructured data, we can assume that there is copyright in the works used for training, but does that mean the works have been copied in whole or substantial part? In some cases, such as LLMs, the material is not reproduced in the training process for its expressive content, *per se* but is reproduced in order to understand the structure of, for example, the English language. Is it being copied as a whole or are selective bits 'copied' and then re-assembled to create a natural language answer? It seems possible that in this training, some of the expressive content of the training material will be reproduced, but is it copied in substantial part if is not used by the AI model for expressive content? How the AI model uses or absorbs the material for training may be relevant as to whether the material has been copied in whole or substantial part or whether it is fair dealing (to be discussed below).

29. Copyright Act, Section 2, definition of 'infringing', *Cinar op. cit.* paragraph 39.
30. *Rains v. Molea*, 2013 ONSC 5016 (CanLII), https://canlii.ca/t/g03f7.

Thus, in *Andersen v. Stability AI Ltd*,[31] in a series of interlocutory decisions in 2023 and 2024 in the Southern District of California, the Court struck part of the original complaint with leave to amend because it was not clear that there had been direct copying in some instances by the storing of 'compressed images' on the facts pleaded. Although images had allegedly been used for training, the court found that plaintiffs' complaint did not adequately explain how Stable Diffusion actually stores and makes use of training images. Specifically, the complaint was unclear as to whether Stable Diffusion created copies of copyrighted works or whether it used 'statistical and mathematical methods' to capture concepts from the training images.

The AI model may learn from individual insubstantial or uncopyrightable parts of a dataset to make predictions about future inputs. The result of training can be correlations and patterns that neither compete with, nor are a substitute, for the original works.

Similarly in *Concord Music v. Anthropic PBC*,[32] the plaintiff alleges that Anthropic copied a massive corpus of previously copied text into computer memory and processed this data in multiple ways to train the Claude AI models, or establish the values of billions of parameters that form the model. That includes copying, dividing, and converting the collected text into units known as 'tokens', which are words or parts of words and punctuation, for storage. This process is referred to as 'encoding' the text into tokens. For Claude, the average token is about 3.5 characters long.

In response, the creators of the AI model assert that the copyrighted works will be used in the synthesis and collection of bits of information and copyright material without necessarily copying a substantial part of the work. However, there will be unanswered questions as to whether the use of a whole work in different parts in training the AI model, where no part of the whole work is used at any one time, would be a copy of a substantial part.

Anthropic states that its Generative AI tools are built on LLMs. LLMs which in turn are built using a computer program called a 'neural network' showing to it trillions of data 'tokens', from which the program derives unfathomably complex statistical correlations among the constitutive elements of the texts it has seen, to approximate an understanding of human language.

Anthropic asserts that the purpose of including instances of those genres in the training dataset is not to ultimately replicate the particular way any original author expressed the idea embodied in the text—which is what copyright law protects.

> It is to expose the model to the full range of types of texts that exist, encompassing as broad an array of facts as possible, so that the model can synthesize the information embodied in the texts into new and different outputs. In the service of achieving that goal, Claude does not use its training texts as a database from which pre-existing outputs are selected in response to user prompts. Instead,

31. Case No. 23-cv-00201-WHO.
32. Case 3:23-cv-01092, in the United States District Court for the Middle District of Tennessee Nashville Division, Case 3:23-cv-01092 Document 67 Filed 01/16/24 Page 9 of 40 PageID #: 3013 pleadings and motion materials available at https://www.bakerlaw.com/concord-music-group-inc-v-anthropic-pbc/.

> it uses the statistical correlations gleaned from analyzing texts to construct a 'model' of how language operates and what it means.[33]

> The model represents those correlations in a series of numerical parameters (sometimes called 'weights' and 'biases') that enable software to generate sensible-seeming responses to requests from end users. *Id.* ¶¶ 15–16. Those parameters are what the model stores—not the texts of the training data.[34]

At this stage there are fact issues that a Canadian court would need to know in order to decide if there was substantial copying of the works used for training. In cases like *Concord v. Anthropic* and *Andersen v. Stability AI Ltd*, the parties disagree about what is going on within the AI model. Once these facts are determined, a Canadian court may still need to determine what it means to make a copy in whole or substantial part when a work is digested 'piece meal' or for its statistical correlations and not for its expressive content.

In addition to direct reproduction, '[i]t is an infringement for anyone to do, without the consent of the copyright owner, "anything that, by this Act, only the owner of the copyright has the right to do" (s. 27(1)), including, ... the right "to *communicate* the work to the public by telecommunication ... and to *authorize* any such acts" (s. 3(1)(*f*)...)' (emphasis in original).[35]

While it is likely that many acts of making available of a work by telecommunication will also involve a reproduction, nevertheless this is a separate right which, for example, will be infringed without a reproduction, *per se*, if hardware or software is sold which makes the works available to the public. Similarly providing such hardware or software may amount to authorizing such reproduction in infringement of copyright. [36]

No AI case has yet to consider this separate right of making available by telecommunication but it is at least theoretically possible that an additional infringement occurs when works or input into an AI engine and made available to the public on the internet. This should perhaps be more relevant to the discussion of output (see section 4).

2.2 Exceptions/Limitations Allowing Training of AI

Section 30.71 was introduced into the Act by the Copyright Modernization Act of 2012. It reads as follows:

> 30.71 It is not an infringement of copyright to make a reproduction of a work or other subject-matter if

33. Defendant's response Case 3:23-cv-01092, in the United States District Court for the Middle District of Tennessee Nashville Division Document 67 Filed 01/16/24 Page 13 of 40 PageID #: 3017.
34. References are to the response pf Anthropic to the motion for an interlocutory injunction in *Concord v. Anthopic PBC*, page 13 see footnotes 32 and 33.
35. *Society of Composers, Authors and Music Publishers of Canada v. Canadian Assn. of Internet Providers*, 2004 SCC 45 at para. 42.
36. *Bell Canada v. L3D Distributing Inc.* (INL3D), 2021 FC 832 (CanLII), < https://canlii.ca/t/jhgbg > .

(a) the reproduction forms an essential part of a technological process;
(b) the reproduction's only purpose is to facilitate a use that is not an infringement of copyright; and
(c) the reproduction exists only for the duration of the technological process.

This section has not been interpreted by any Canadian court to date but it has been considered in a number of Copyright Board decisions particularly *SOCAN, Re:Sound, CSI, Connect/SOPROQ, Artisti – Tariff for Commercial Radio*.[37] In this decision the Copyright Board concluded that reproductions made in the course of certain streaming services were reproductions that formed an essential part of a technological process and that the purpose was not to facilitate a use that is an infringement.

Although 'technological process' is not defined, the Board concluded that it did not extend to every business process or economic activity, which consists of one or more steps involving technology. The Board concluded that this provision was intended to capture copies that happen automatically, or without the direct control of the user. The Board also noted that the process must be temporary and that reproductions that fall under Section 30.71 of the Act are those that are useless or non-usable, but for the technology that causes them to be created in the first place. They have no other independent purpose or use than to allow the technological process to run its course.

How this Section would be interpreted by a court in the context of AI is not known but certain aspects of the AI training input referred to above may qualify for the exemption insofar as the scanning for training may be automatic, no copy of the original scanned work may be kept. This would assume that the ultimate product itself was not infringing once the material has been scanned and incorporated into the AI model.

While this Section was introduced at a time when AI was not known, it will be intriguing to see how it would be interpreted if a question concerning Section 30.71 ever reaches a court.

2.3 Fair Dealing

If the works or data have copyright (see sections 1–3) and are copied in whole or substantial part (see sections 4–5), there remains the question of whether the use for training is fair dealing. Training is a specific type of use by the AI engine, which then uses the trained data to create an output.

It is not an infringement in Canada if the copying amounts to fair dealing.

Fair dealing is limited to certain purposes: criticism or review, news reporting, research, private study, education, parody or satire. Unless the use falls under one of these purposes fair dealing cannot provide a defence to copying. Unlike the United States, this is a closed set of purposes.

However fair dealing has been liberally interpreted as a user right and if the copying does fall under one of the allowed purposes, the fairness of the dealing

37. 2011–2017, 2016 CanLII 156141 (CA CB)

would be decided under the six factors articulated by the Supreme Court in the *CCH* case mentioned above. [38]

These factors are:

1. the purpose of the dealing;
2. the character of the dealing;
3. the amount of the dealing;
4. alternatives to the dealing;
5. the nature of the dealing;
6. the effect of the dealing on the work.

As McLachlin C.J.C. stated in *CCH* at para. 48:

> Aside from those attribution obligations, the test for fair dealing requires the defendant to prove that (a) the dealing was for one of the allowable purposes listed in Copyright Act, and (b) the dealing was fair: *CCH*, at para. 50. [...] In considering the purposes, the court must give them 'a large and liberal interpretation in order to ensure that users' rights are not unduly constrained,' and even 'research is not limited to non-commercial or private contexts:' *CCH*, at para. 51. Further, the Supreme Court observed in in 2012 in SOCAN, at para. 27, 'CCH created a relatively low threshold for the first step so that the analytical heavy-hitting is done in determining whether the dealing was fair.[39]

The mostly likely purposes that would apply to an AI model are research, private study and education. Research is not restricted to non- commercial purposes. It is not known how broadly research might be interpreted when works are used for training.

3. USE OF AI SYSTEMS

As discussed previously, it is likely a reproduction to 'use' a work for training an AI model but no Canadian case has so ruled. Where the work is not reproduced *per se* but digitized or digested into tokens for use in training and not for its expressive content, there are still questions as to whether this is a reproduction.

If the output of the AI system is a copy of a book or a reproduction in whole or substantial part, then there would seem to be little question but that this is an infringement, subject to considerations of fair dealing discussed previously (or the other exceptions previously covered).

Canada also has a making available right. In *Society of Composers, Authors and Music Publishers of Canada v. Entertainment Software Association*,[40] the Supreme Court interpreted Canada's making available right as applying to on-demand technologies, and to works performed as soon as they are made available for online streaming. According to the Court, Canada fulfils its obligations under Article 8 through a combination of the performance, reproduction, and authorization rights. If a work is streamed or made available for on-demand streaming, the author's performance right is engaged. If a work is downloaded, the author's reproduction

38. *CCH Canadian Ltd. v. Law Society of Upper Canada*, (2004 SCC 13 [CCH]).
39. See *SOCAN* n. 37 above.
40. 2022 SCC 30.

right is engaged. If a work is made available for downloading, the author's right to authorize reproductions is engaged. There are no gaps in protection.

Thus the Copyright Act grants authors three rights: (1) a reproduction right, (2) a performance right and (3) a first publication right. Every other right is merely illustrative of the reproduction, performance or first publication right. A single activity may only engage one of these three copyright interests. Any activity that does not engage a reproduction, performance or first publication right is not protected by copyright.

The implications of this are that an AI system that makes available on the internet a copy of a work on request or demand would likely infringe the making available rights as one of the Court's three enumerated rights. This may also be the case whether or not anyone chooses to access the work.

Canada does not have any express provisions allowing AI training, although as discussed previously, certain fair dealing for research private study or other limited purposes may allow the use of works for these purposes. It is an infringement to scrape non-public domain works off of the internet, unless protected by fair dealing. Unlike in the European Union, there are no requirements to notify restrictions to access to works posted on the internet to maintain protection against copying, but fair dealing and implicit licence exemptions may still apply. At least one case has suggested that it is a violation of the Copyright Act technical protection measures to circumvent a paywall to get access to a work, and in such circumstances fair dealing exemptions may not apply.[41]

Canada has all the usual remedies for copyright infringement, including damages, statutory damages and injunctive relief, accounting of profits, and delivery up of infringing articles. Canada also has broad ranging moral rights. However moral rights will only apply if the work results in prejudice to the author's or performer's honour or reputation. It is thought that this would be unlikely to be the case where the work is not identifiable in the output of the AI engine. In relation to paternity, the right is limited to where it is 'reasonable in the circumstances' to be associated with the work. Again, it is likely that the work used for training will no longer be identifiable and that the question of association will not arise.

A 'wide' injunction is also available to further enjoin a defendant from infringing the copyright in any other work if the court is satisfied that the defendant will likely infringe the copyright in other works of the plaintiff. There are also provisions to prevent the circumvention of technological protection measures and to protect rights management information.

None of the remedies referred to above are peculiar to AI-generated or trained works or to output generated by an AI system.

4. AI-GENERATED OUTPUT

We have examined above how copyright may or may not be infringed when an AI model copies or uses material for training. Is the material copyrightable data, is it

41. *1395804 Ontario Limited (Blacklock's Reporter) v. Canadian Vinters Association* 2015 CanLII 65885 (ON SCSM).

original, is the material copied in whole or substantial part, is it fair dealing? Similar considerations apply with respect to the output from an AI model.

As previously discussed, Section 27(1) of the Act prohibits infringement of copyright: 'It is an infringement of copyright for any person to do, without the consent of the owner of the copyright, anything that by this Act only the owner of the copyright has the right to do.'[42]

> [26] Section 2(a) of the Act defines "infringement" to include:
>
> (a) in relation to a work in which copyright subsists, any copy, including any colourable imitation, made or dealt with in contravention of this Act.
>
> [27] Section 3(1) of the Act defines the rights that vest in a copyright holder to include:
>
> For the purposes of this Act, "copyright", in relation to a work, means the sole right to produce or reproduce the work or any substantial part thereof in any material form whatever, to perform the work or any substantial part thereof in public or, if the work is unpublished, to publish the work or any substantial part thereof.
>
> [28] Copyright infringement therefore is established when the defendant has produced a substantial copy, including a colourable imitation of the plaintiff's work. Infringement is not limited to an exact copy.

As with training discussed above, copyright infringement in the output requires the same analysis. However, unlike training where the processes undertaken by the AI engine are opaque and difficult to understand, the output may be more easily compared with an existing work using recognized copyright principles, as set out above.

One of the more interesting questions concerns whether an AI engine imitating the style of an author or artist would infringe copyright. In this connection the case of *Rains v. Molea* is illustrative. [43]

In this case there was a claim that one artist had copied the others style although none of the alleged infringer's works were found to be substantially similar. Copyright protection does not necessarily extend to an artist's 'look' or 'style'. As stated by the court:

> Further, in my view it would be unwise to extend copyright protection to the visual perception of an artistic work, which is intangible and subjective. Copyright subsists in the expression of an idea in a fixed material form: *CCH*, at para. 8. There is good reason for this. The scale would be tipped in favour of the creator's rights if copyright were to protect an undefined and unarticulated feeling emoted from artistic works. There would be little room for the public domain to flourish. Others would be unable to produce new artistic works without fear of infringing a creator's self-imposed or critically-bequeathed imprecise evocation of his work's feeling or expression. Moreover, the protection would often extend to works not yet created. This would be a perverse result considering the purpose of the Act as set out above.[44]

42. Copyright Act, R.S.C. 1985,C-42 Section 27(1).
43. *Rains v. Molea*, footnote 30.
44. *Rains v. Molea*, footnote 30, paragraph 15.

> As set out above, copyright law does not require novelty in order to find a work original. However, Rains cannot establish infringement by relying on his use of the noted unoriginal, commonplace, historical painting techniques. This would be akin to Shakespeare relying on his use of iambic pentameter in his writing or Drake relying on his use of 16 bars to a verse in his music. Commonly used techniques must remain available to all artists creating literary, dramatic, musical, and artistic works. If the compilation of these techniques is original, as defined above, the work enjoys copyright protection. If, after disregarding the commonplace techniques, there remain sufficient similarities between one work and a preceding original, substantial copying will likely be established. Because Rains relies on unoriginal elements, other than shape, to demonstrate similarity, these elements do not establish substantial copying.[45]

One wonders what a court would make of an AI engine imitating an artist's or author's style. Do the same principles espoused about relating to the public domain and allowing the production of new artistic works apply to those created by an AI model.

Defendants, for example in the *Concord Music Group, Inc v, Anthropic PBC* case,[46] argue that:

> the purpose of including instances of those genres in the training dataset is not to ultimately replicate the particular way any original author expressed the idea embodied in the text—which is what copyright law protects. It is to expose the model to the full range of types of texts that exist, encompassing as broad an array of facts as possible, so that the model can synthesize the information embodied in the texts into new and different outputs.

They argue that the Claude AI model does not use its training texts as a database from which pre-existing outputs are selected in response to user prompts. 'Instead, it uses the statistical correlations gleaned from analyzing texts to construct a "model" of how language operates and what it means.' ... 'The model represents those correlations in a series of numerical parameters (sometimes called "weights" and "biases") that enable software to generate sensible-seeming responses to requests from end users.... Those parameters are what the model stores – not the texts of the training data.'[47] The training process encodes the patterns and relationships derived from the training data into the model's architecture.

While this may or may not be true, it is unlikely that a court will be concerned how the model managed to make a copy, if the result of the output is a copy in whole or substantially part. However, it might be relevant as to whether the making of the copy amounts to fair dealing. Although fair dealing in Canada is restricted to a closed end set of purposes, among which are 'research' or 'private study', if these purposes are met, the copied work does not have to be transformative to be fair dealing. Nevertheless, an AI model which operates such as the AI model in the *New York Times v. Chat GPT* case[48] to produce copies of *New York Times* articles is unlikely to be fair dealing in Canada.

---

45. *Rains v. Molea*, footnote 30, paragraph 40.
46. See n. 32 above.
47. See n. 33 above.
48. *The New York Times Company v. Microsoft Corporation*, 1:23-cv-11195, (S.D.N.Y.)

However here the question may be who is doing the dealing if the copies are intentionally and knowingly created by requests designed to elicit copies. In that case perhaps the user of the model is infringing and not the creator of the AI model. This may also be the case if the user is making the work available by communicating the work to the public by telecommunication or authorizing the reproduction of the work.

It is worth noting that those who would scrape content off of the internet may be in violation of provisions relating to technical protection measures. The Copyright Act prohibits the circumvention of such measures which are defined generally as those measures that control access to a work.[49]

Similarly scraping may violate terms of use which will likely be binding on those who access content on the internet that is protected by a paywall or other provisions which require an agreement to access. These contractual provisions are likely to be enforceable in Canada and are not subject to the pre-emption issues that seem to be arising in the United States.

5. CONCLUSIONS

There may be important social and technical reasons why scraping of copyrighted material from the internet should be allowed to train AI models.[50] However there are equally important considerations with respect to the rights of authors and creators to control the use of their works. No case in Canada has ruled on these considerations and while traditional copyright principles will provide some guidance, they do not point to a conclusive result in all of the circumstances of AI training and AI output that might arise.

49. Copyright Act, Section 41 and 41.1.
50. See C. Craig for an argument in favour of allowing copyrighted works to be used for training: Carys J. Craig, *The AI-Copyright Trap* (15 July 2024), Osgoode Legal Studies Research Paper No. 4905118, Available at SSRN: https://ssrn.com/abstract=4905118 or http://dx.doi.org/10.2139/ssrn.4905118.

Chapter 4

China

Allen (Jun) Wang and Gao Cheng

1. INTRODUCTION

1.1 Development Status of Generative Artificial Intelligence in China

In November 2022, the chatbot ChatGPT developed by OpenAI was publicly released. Unlike some AI products before it, ChatGPT not only can simulate human language very naturally and engage in real-time conversations with users but also can complete tasks such as translation, proofreading, and even code writing under user instructions. It can even create something from nothing, generating imaginative and unexpected content. Upon its release, the product garnered widespread attention and discussion. Its immense potential in language understanding, text generation, logical reasoning, and its general ability to deal with complex problems not only caused a sensation in the industry but also gradually brought generative artificial intelligence (AI) into the public's daily life.

Subsequently, various countries began actively exploring the application possibilities of generative AI in multiple scenarios, and Chinese companies were no exception. Major players, including Huawei, Alibaba, Bytedance, Tencent, Baidu, JD, 360, SenseTime, and iFlytek, along with leading universities such as Tsinghua University and Fudan University, have actively conducted research and developed products related to generative AI. These products have sprung up like mushrooms, presenting a flourishing situation.

Based on the '2023 AI Large Model Application Research Report' released by Sullivan Consulting and LeadLeo Research Institute, in just over half a year after the public release of ChatGPT, nearly 80 Chinese large models with billions of parameters or more emerged. Some influential products include Baidu's ERNIE Bot, SenseTime's SenseNova, Alibaba's Qwen, iFlytek's Spark, Moonshot's Kimi, Fudan University's MOSS, and Tsinghua University's GLM, among others.

Today, generative AI products are no longer scarce but are gradually becoming integrated into the daily lives of ordinary people. According to the 'China AI-Generated Content Text-to-image Industry White Paper 2023', jointly released by the China AI-Generated Content Industry Alliance and the Unbounded AI in 2023, 5–10% of the content on China's most popular short video platform Douyin or the youth social e-commerce platform Xiaohongshu may have been generated by AI, and this percentage is expected to increase further.

According to the 'AI-Generated Content Series Report-China AI-Generated Content Industry Panorama Report' released by iResearch, the industrial scale of generative AI in China reached about CNY 14.3 billion (approximately USD 2.04 billion) in 2023. This figure is predicted to grow to CNY 720.2 billion (approximately USD 102.88 billion) by 2028 and exceed CNY 1,000 billion by 2030, reaching CNY 1,144.1 billion (approximately USD 163.44 billion). This indicates the tremendous potential of generative AI in the Chinese market.

The development of generative AI has brought infinite possibilities to the content industry but has also raised some new legal and regulatory issues. In particular, because generative AI extensively uses existing works during model training and its output content fully resembles the characteristics of works, it naturally intersects with the Copyright Law. This article discusses issues related to generative AI from the perspective of Chinese Copyright Law, regulations, departmental rules, and regulatory policies. In the thriving development of generative AI, such discussions undoubtedly have significant practical significance.

1.2 Attitudes of the Chinese Artificial Intelligence Industry Towards Ownership of Generated Content Rights

On 3 April 2024, the Cyberspace Administration of China issued a notice on the release of information on registered generative AI services. As of March 2024, China had registered 117 generative AI services. The notice also stipulates that the online generative AI applications or functions should prominently display or detail the registered generative AI services used, including the model name and registration number.

As mentioned earlier, in the absence of clear legal systems, to address whether the content generated by AI constitutes a work under copyright law, and issues such as the ownership of copyright for generated content, providers and users of generative AI services enter into service agreements to handle the rights and obligations of the parties involved in providing and using generative AI services in a negotiated manner. This includes issues such as the ownership of intellectual property rights involved in the input and generation process of generative AI services and liability. Therefore, examining and analysing the service agreements of AI products can explore the industry's attitudes and positions on the copyrightability of artificially generated content.

1.2.1 *Model One: Self-Maintenance of Copyright by Users*

The user agreement of Zidong Taichu Large Model[1] states:

> The copyright of the content generated by you based on the Zidong Taichu Large Model open platform shall be maintained by you and used independently after your independent judgment. Any intellectual property issues arising from the creation and use of content generated by the Zidong Taichu Large Model open platform shall be handled by you, and Wuhan Artificial Intelligence Research Institute shall not be responsible for any losses caused thereby. Wuhan Artificial Intelligence Research Institute has the right to recover losses from you caused by such losses.

The user agreement of Kimi Intelligent Assistant[2] states:

> The copyright of the content generated by you based on Kimi Intelligent Assistant shall be maintained by you and used independently after your independent judgment. Any intellectual property issues arising from the creation and use of content generated by Kimi Intelligent Assistant shall be handled by you, and Beijing Yuezhianmian Technology Co., Ltd. shall not be responsible for any losses caused thereby. Beijing Yuezhianmian Technology Co., Ltd. has the right to recover losses from you caused by such losses.

The service agreement of Pangu Large Model[3] states:

> The 'reasoning' function of this service generates 'output content' based on the 'prompt words' input by you or 'your users'. You agree and acknowledge that you or 'your users' are the right holders of the above 'output content' and grant Huawei Cloud a permanent, irrevocable, free, non-exclusive licence to use, modify, distribute, etc. the above 'output content'. The 'output content' refers to the results calculated based on the 'prompt words' input by you or 'your users'. You or 'your users' can decide how to use the above 'output content' by laws and regulations and shall be responsible for the use of the above 'output content'. Huawei Cloud will not bear any responsibility for your or 'your users' use of the above content.

1.2.2 *Model Two: Service Providers of Generative Artificial Intelligence Do Not Claim Rights to Generated Content*

The user agreement of Bean Software[4] states:

> During your use of this software and related services, you may submit text, audio, or other content or information to this software and related services (referred to as 'input'), and receive content generated in response to your input ('output', 'generation'). During the period between you and the company, within the scope

1. https://docs.wair.ac.cn/taichu/UserAgreement.html.
2. https://kimi.moonshot.cn/user/agreement/modelUse.
3. https://www.huaweicloud.com/declaration/tsa-pglm.html.
4. https://www.doubao.com/legal/terms.

> permitted by applicable laws, the intellectual property rights of the input you provide shall belong to you or the right holder who enjoys these intellectual property rights according to law. The company does not assert ownership of the output content.

1.2.3 Model Three: No Agreement on Ownership of Generated Content

The user agreement of ERNIE Bot[5] states:

> You understand, acknowledge, and agree that if you have the right to your input (including all content you upload and publish during your use of this service) and/or output according to the law (including but not limited to intellectual property rights and portrait rights), your use of this service will not result in the transfer or reduction of the aforementioned legal rights unless we have made other agreements with you. At the same time, you understand and agree that Baidu will store and use the content you upload and publish within the scope permitted by law to achieve the purpose of this service (including but not limited to copying, distributing, transmitting, publicly displaying, and editing).

Through the rights attribution clauses in the service agreements of generative AI services, it can be understood that, regardless of the model, it is generally clear that the providers of generative AI services are unlikely to contest the rights of the generated content. Moreover, in the current uncertain legal environment regarding the regulation of generated content, providers of generative AI services tend to adopt broader statements regarding the types of rights or ownership of generated content. For example, in the Pangu Large Model, users are referred to as the 'right holders' of the generated content, while in the Bean Software agreement, the company explicitly states that it does not claim ownership of the output content. Additionally, the agreement of ERNIE Bot indirectly applies statutory attribution. It can be seen that, at the present stage, in China, the AI industry is in a state of observation regarding issues such as whether to grant rights to generated content, the types of rights related to generated content, and how to attribute related rights.

1.3 Legal Provisions Related to Generative Artificial Intelligence

As the AI industry develops, various levels of legislation have been promulgated in China. Currently, laws and regulations, as well as policy documents related to AI in China, have been successively issued and implemented to meet the needs of industry development. These include the Interim Measures for the Management of Generative Artificial Intelligence Services, Regulations on the Management of Internet Information Services for Deep Synthesis, and the Network Security Standard Practice Guide – Method of Indicating Content of Generative Artificial Intelligence Services. The Draft Artificial Intelligence Law also appeared in the 2023 Annual Legislative Work Plan of the State Council of China. Additionally, China plans to establish a

5. https://yiyan.baidu.com/agreement.

more comprehensive legal and regulatory system, ethical standards, and policy framework for AI by 2030.[6]

However, at present, there is no specialized legislation or policy guidance on the issue of AI copyright in China. Judicial practice and academic research mainly apply existing copyright laws to solve new problems arising from technological development and social change. Regarding intellectual property issues involved in the training of generative AI, Article 7 of the Interim Measures for the Management of Generative Artificial Intelligence Services stipulates that generative AI service providers shall conduct training data processing activities such as pre-training and optimization training by the law and comply with the following provisions: involving intellectual property rights, they shall not infringe upon the intellectual property rights enjoyed by others by the law. While this regulation outlines the basic principle of respecting intellectual property rights in the development of AI, it does not provide clear and referenceable behavioural norms. The lack of legislation and regulations to some extent also reflects the characteristic of legal lag.

1.4 Judicial Practices Regarding Copyright Issues Related to Generative Artificial Intelligence

1.4.1 Judicial Determination of Copyright Issues in AI Model Training Process

As previously mentioned, the training process of AI models involves feeding a large amount of corpus and data materials, which include, to a certain extent, primarily pre-existing works created by others (depending on the different functionalities of AI products, these works may include literature, music, photos, paintings, etc.). Therefore, during the AI model training process, there may be legal issues related to whether the data feeding behaviour constitutes a reproduction under copyright law and whether the data feeding materials infringe upon the pre-existing copyrights of others.

To date, regarding whether AI model training constitutes infringement, apart from the case of Ultraman in 2024, where the Hangzhou Intermediate People's Court held that the act of users uploading images and other content to train AI models constituted fair use, other existing judicial precedents in China have not demonstrated many judicial opinions on this issue. This is mainly because the controversies in relevant cases have not specifically targeted the AI model training stage; rather, the courts have focused more on the legal nature of AI-generated works, rights attribution, etc. The information reflected in the judgments of these cases regarding the facts related to AI model training is not very detailed. For example:

6. *New Generation Artificial Intelligence Development Plan*, issued by the State Council with the document number [2017] No. 35.

1.4.1.1 *Spring Breeze Case [Trial Court: Beijing Internet Court, Case No.: (2023) Jing 0491 Min Chu 11279 / (2023)京0491民初11279号]*

In the *Spring Breeze* case handled by the Beijing Internet Court, the court found that the painting principle of the involved AI product 'Stable Diffusion' software was to:

> *interpret and create highly blurred mosaic images based on the model and the user's input prompt words. The model can determine the usable materials of the image and affect the overall artistic type and style of the work.* Currently, tens of thousands of models provided by open-source authors are freely available for download on the internet, and users are free to choose the model they rely on for creation based on their aesthetic preferences [emphasis added].

Given the previous research on existing technologies in the Chinese AI industry, the court found that the 'Stable Diffusion' software was trained by feeding a large amount of training material data (pre-existing artistic works). The technology type used should be diffusion models. These pre-existing artistic works are fed into the software as training data and are internalized and learned by the 'Stable Diffusion' software as pixel points (referred to as 'highly blurred mosaic images' in the judgment). In the output process, they are combined with the user's input prompt words to interpret the internalized image pixel points and generate output results. However, since the controversy in this case was brought by a user of the involved AI software as the plaintiff, alleging that the defendant had used his work of fine art generated by the AI without permission, it did not involve discussions on ownership or infringement issues during the AI model training process. The final judgment did not elaborate much on the identification and description of the data training process.

1.4.1.2 *The Ultraman Case in Guangzhou [Trial Court: Guangzhou Internet Court, Case No.: (2024) Yue 0192 Min Chu 113 / (2023)粤0192民初113号]*

In the Ultraman case handled by the Guangzhou Internet Court, the dispute between the parties involved whether the involved AI product infringed the copyright of others' pre-existing works during the model training process. In this case, the plaintiff was the copyright holder of the well-known artwork 'Ultraman'. It discovered that when using the AI product provided by the defendant's website and inputting descriptions such as 'Ultraman', the product could generate images substantially similar to its copyrighted artwork 'Ultraman'. The plaintiff claimed that the defendant's actions infringed its reproduction right, adaptation right, and the right of communication to the public on information networks. However, based on the factual reasons stated in the plaintiff's lawsuit, there was no actual infringing party using the AI product to generate infringing 'Ultraman' images (the images used by the plaintiff to prove and compared with the copyrighted work were generated by the plaintiff's own test using the involved AI product). Based on these facts, it can be inferred that the actual infringement claimed by the plaintiff should not be the specific use of the AI product to generate infringing 'Ultraman' images (because the plaintiff did not prove that this behaviour occurred objectively), but rather that the involved AI used the plaintiff's copyrighted work 'Ultraman' artwork during the data feeding and model training process. This is also consistent with the plaintiff's first lawsuit request, which asked the defendant to 'remove the Ultraman materials involved from its [involved AI product] training dataset'. Unfortunately, the defendant's website used the involved AI product through a third-party service provider: the defendant signed an 'Order Agreement' with the third-party service provider, and the third-party service provider opened the AI model's open interface to the defendant's website based on this agreement. Therefore, the court did not make factual findings regarding the model training process of the involved AI product in this case but used the images generated by the plaintiff's own test using the involved AI product as the infringing works, compared them with the plaintiff's copyrighted works, and thus determined the infringement of reproduction right and adaptation right. This also led to the final determination of infringement of reproduction rights, which was not the 'reproduction behaviour occurring during the model training process of the AI due to data feeding' claimed by the plaintiff.

1.4.1.3 *Virtual Human Case [Trial Court: Hangzhou Intermediate People's Court, Case No.: (2023) Zhe 01 Min Zhong 4722 / (2023)浙01民终4722号]*

In the Virtual Human case handled by the Hangzhou Intermediate People's Court, the involved AI object was a digital virtual human, which belonged to the collective product of the AI industry in the derivative field. Although the form and functional roles of virtual digital humans differ from more common types of generative AI, they can also produce other forms of intellectual achievements, such as performances, and thus can be classified as generative AI. The first-instance court determined that 'the virtual digital human is a visual representation of a virtual character created through modelling, intelligent synthesis, motion capture, and other digital technologies, with features and behavioural patterns in appearance, sound, etc'. However, in this case, the involved virtual digital human belonged to the type driven by real people, that is, it was created through real-time voice generation and motion capture using intelligent wearable devices by a 'person inside' named Xu. It borrowed from the physical form of 'the person inside' Xu and exhibited highly restored 'performances' such as voice, expressions, and movements related to 'the person inside' Xu. Therefore, in this case, the involved virtual digital human did not involve the situation of others' pre-existing works and copyright interests during the modelling, intelligent synthesis, and other training processes but was more related to various personality rights of 'the person inside'.

1.4.1.4 *The Ultraman Case in Hangzhou [Trial Court: Hangzhou Internet Court; Hangzhou Intermediate People's Court]*

In the Ultraman Case before the Hangzhou Internet Court, the plaintiff was the exclusive licensee of the Ultraman series of works, while the defendant was the operator of an AI platform. Users could upload images and other materials to train and share AI models of Ultraman through the platform, and further utilize these models to generate works that were substantially similar to the plaintiff's Ultraman characters. The plaintiff argued that the defendant's statement in the user service agreement, which disclaimed any review of user-uploaded materials and generated content, and the defendant's active encouragement of users to publish such content, infringed upon the plaintiff's right of communication to the public on information networks and constituted an act of unfair competition. As a result, the plaintiff filed the lawsuit with the Hangzhou Internet Court. During the trial, one of the key issues in dispute was whether the act of users uploading images from their computers or mobile phones to the defendant's website and training fine-tuned models using third-party foundational models accessed through the website constituted copyright infringement. The court held in its judgment that, in the absence of evidence showing that the generative AI was used for the purpose of exploiting the original expression of the copyrighted works, or that it had affected the normal use of the copyrighted works or unreasonably harmed the legitimate interests of the copyright holders, the act could be considered as fair use. This case set a precedent for determining whether data training activities constitute fair use. However, the court's reasoning regarding why the data training of fine-tuned models by users constituted fair use and which specific statutory exception under China's Copyright Law it fell under was somewhat simplistic. This may raise questions about whether it overstepped the boundaries of the statutory exceptions for fair use under China's Copyright Law.

The table below consolidates the factual findings related to the AI model training processes as determined by the court in the aforementioned four cases:

No.	Case Name and Number	Name/ Type of AI Involved	The Court's Findings on the Relevant Factual Circumstances Pertaining to the AI Model Training Process
1.	*Spring Breeze* case adjudicated by the Beijing Internet Court; Case Number: (2023) Jing 0491 Min Chu 11279.	Stable Diffusion: Drawing AI	The court found that the painting principle of the involved AI product 'Stable Diffusion' software involves '*interpreting and creating highly blurred mosaic images based on models and user input prompt words. The model can determine the usable materials of the image and influence the overall artistic type and picture style of the work.* Currently, there are tens of thousands of models freely provided by open-source authors on the internet, all of which can be downloaded publicly via the internet. Therefore, the model relied upon for creation is freely chosen by the user, and the specific model used depends on the user's aesthetic preferences' [emphasis added].
2.	*Ultraman* case adjudicated by the Guangzhou Internet Court; case number: (2024) Yue 0192 Min Chu 113.	Tab (alias): Drawing AI	Since the AI product and drawing service used by the defendant's website were actually implemented through interfaces provided by third-party service providers, and the defendant did not personally conduct the model training process, the court did not ascertain the relevant facts of this process.

3.	*Virtual Digital Human* case adjudicated by the Hangzhou Intermediate People's Court; case number: (2023) Zhe 01 Min Zhong 4722.	Ada: Digital Virtual Human	'The virtual digital human is a visual representation created through *modelling, intelligent synthesis, motion capture, and other digital techniques*, possessing characteristics and behavioural patterns in terms of appearance, sound, and other aspects' [emphasis added].
4.	The *Ultraman* case in Hangzhou	Chushou AI: Model Training AI	'In the absence of evidence showing that the generative AI was used for the purpose of exploiting the original expression of the copyrighted works, or that it had affected the normal use of the copyrighted works or unreasonably harmed the legitimate interests of the copyright holders, the act could be considered as fair use'

As can be observed from the aforementioned case judgments, there is currently *no definitive* judicial stance revealed in judicial practice regarding the legal issues that may arise in the training process of AI models.

1.4.2 *Judicial Determination of Copyright Issues Related to AI Model Output Content*

1.4.2.1 *Dreamwriter Case [Trial Court: Nanshan District People's Court of Shenzhen City, Guangdong Province; Case No.: (2019) Yue 0305 Min Chu 14010 / (2019)粤0305民初14010号]*

Basic Case Details:

The involved AI product, Dreamwriter, is computer software developed independently by Tencent in August 2015. It is an intelligent writing assistance system based on data and algorithms. Since 2015, Tencent has enabled creators using Dreamwriter to complete approximately 300,000 works per year.

In 2018, Tencent used Dreamwriter to write a financial news article entitled 'Noon Evaluation: Shanghai Composite Index Slightly Up by 0.11% to 2671.93 Points, with Communications and Oil Exploitation Sectors Leading' (referred to as the 'involved article'). The article was published on Tencent's securities website on 20 August, with a note at the end stating, 'This article is automatically written by Tencent's robot Dreamwriter'.

Later, Tencent found that Shanghai Yingxun Technology Co., Ltd. (referred to as the 'defendant') had copied the involved article without permission and published it on the 'P2P Home' website operated by the defendant for online dissemination. Tencent believed that the defendant's actions infringed its right of communication to the public on information networks. Furthermore, Tencent asserted that the defendant, by directly copying the plaintiff's work without intellectual labour, used it to gain traffic and competitive advantages on the defendant's website, violating principles of good faith and recognized commercial ethics, and disturbing the fair competition order in the financial media market, thus constituting unfair competition. Based on these claims, Tencent filed this lawsuit.

Court Findings on the Process of Generating the Involved Article:

During the trial, the court made findings on the process of generating the involved article by Dreamwriter.

Tencent stated that the creation process of the involved article mainly involved four steps: data service, triggering and writing, intelligent verification, and intelligent distribution. First, the data service module of Dreamwriter software collects multidimensional data and analyses valuable data through learning algorithms, combining historical statistical data and other content dimensions to form a database for detection. Secondly, the trigger module of Dreamwriter software sets up rule engines and trigger conditions to intelligently judge whether the content in the database for detection meets the requirements for article generation. Once the trigger conditions are met, it enters the writing engine module to write the article. Thirdly, the Dreamwriter software inputs the data generated by the data service module into the writing engine. The writing engine first verifies the data and then writes the involved article using templates. Fourthly, after the involved article is generated, the intelligent verification module conducts review and proofreading, and after proofreading, it is intelligently distributed to platforms such as Tencent's website. In the above process, the selection and arrangement of data types, data format processing, trigger condition setting, template selection, corpus style setting, and intelligent verification algorithm model training were all arranged and selected by the relevant personnel of the plaintiff's creative team.

Key Points of the Court's Judgment:

a. Whether the Involved Article Constitutes a Literary Work:

The court believed that the involved article possessed originality.

First, the involved article, generated by Dreamwriter and published externally, conforms to the form of a literary work. Its content reflects the selection, analysis, and judgment of relevant stock market information and data for that morning, with a reasonable structure and clear logical expression, showing a certain degree of originality.

Secondly, the process of generating the involved article reflects the personalized selection, judgment, and skills of the creators. In the steps of Dreamwriter generating the involved article, the arrangement and selection of data types, data format processing, trigger condition setting, template selection, corpus style setting, and intelligent verification algorithm model training were all arranged and selected by relevant personnel of the plaintiff's creative team. The court emphasized the relationship between the creative behaviour of the plaintiff's creative team members and the generation of the involved article by Dreamwriter:

> The lack of synchronicity of the involved article is determined by the technical path or the characteristics of the tools used by the plaintiff themselves. The arrangement and selection of the above choices made by the plaintiff's creative team members are directly related to the specific expression form of the involved article's intellectual activities. From the perspective of the entire generation process, if only the two minutes when Dreamwriter software automatically generated the involved article are considered as the creation process, indeed, there was no human participation, and it was only the result of the computer software running established rules, algorithms, and templates. However, the automatic operation of Dreamwriter software is not without reason or self-consciousness. Its automatic operation method reflects the choices made by the plaintiff, and it is also determined by the characteristics of Dreamwriter software itself. If only the process of Dreamwriter software's automatic operation is considered as the creation process, it is, in a sense, treating computer software as the subject of creation, which is inconsistent with the objective situation and unfair.

Therefore, the court concluded that the authors of the involved article were the relevant personnel of the plaintiff's creative team, who carried out specific creative acts.

b. Ownership of Copyright in the Involved Article:

The court believed that it constituted a legal entity work, and its copyright should be enjoyed by the plaintiff, Tencent.

The court believed that the involved article was a work completed by multiple teams and individuals under the leadership of the plaintiff Tencent, which overall reflected the plaintiff's intention and demand for publishing stock evaluation summary articles. Moreover, the plaintiff published the involved article on its own operated website, and the article also indicated 'This article is automatically written by Tencent's robot Dreamwriter'. The 'Tencent' sign should be understood as referring to the plaintiff Tencent Company, indicating that the involved article was produced by Tencent for external responsibility. Therefore, the court determined that the involved article was a legal entity work created under the leadership of the plaintiff Tencent Company.

Judicial Result:

As the infringement facts of this case were relatively obvious, and the legal relationship was simple, the court, while determining whether the involved article constitutes a literary work and its copyright attribution, ruled that the defendant constituted infringement of the right to disseminate information networks. Since the plaintiff had been remedied according to the specific provisions of the Copyright Law for this infringement, it no longer met the conditions for the application of the Anti-Unfair Competition Law. Therefore, the court dismissed the plaintiff's claims regarding unfair competition

1.4.2.2 *The Wolters Kluwer Database Case [Trial Court: Beijing Intellectual Property Court, Case No.: (2019) Jing 73 Min Zhong 2030 / (2019)京73民终2030号]*

Basic Case Details:

In September 2018, a law firm in Beijing published an article entitled 'Judicial Big Data Analysis Report on the Film and Entertainment Industry' on its public account. The article was subsequently reposted on Baidu's content platform 'Baijiahao' by a user, with the removal of the author's name and the concluding paragraph. The law firm alleged that Baidu's reposting constituted copyright infringement.

After the court trial, it was found that the plaintiff, when creating the article in question, used the Wolters Kluwer Database System (referred to as the 'Wolters Kluwer Database') for assistance. Specifically, the article in question includes both charts and text. The text portion was further developed based on the analysis report generated by Filin Law Firm using the Wolters Kluwer Database.

According to the court investigation, Wolters Kluwer is a professional legal information search tool that provides services such as laws and regulations, judgments, common legal document templates, practice guides, legal English translations, and other legal information. The plaintiff set search criteria in the *Wolters Kluwer* case by entering the keyword 'movie', setting the court as Courts in Beijing, and setting the trial date between 1 January 1995, and 31 December 2017. After searching and clicking on 'visualization', a chart and analysis report of the relevant articles were generated.

Key Points of the Court's Judgment:

a. Regarding the Claim of Graphs Constituting Graphic Works:

Both trial courts concluded that the graphs did not constitute graphic works.

The rationale behind this decision was that the graphs were created by the law firm using data collected and processed through the Wolters Kluwer Database software. While the shapes of the graphs varied with changes in data, such variations were based on data differences rather than creative expression. Therefore, the graphs did not meet the originality requirement for graphic works.

b. Regarding Whether Automatically Generated Analysis Reports Constitute Works:

The courts determined that although the process of generating the analysis reports demonstrated a certain level of creativity in selecting, judging, and analysing relevant data, possessing creativity was not sufficient to qualify as a work under copyright law. Works must be created by natural persons, which is a prerequisite for copyright protection. In this case, the analysis report did not convey the creative expression of the software developers. Moreover, the law firm, as a user of the software, only inputted keywords for the search and utilized the Wolters Kluwer Database's visualization function to generate the output. Therefore, the analysis report could not be considered as authored by the law firm. Instead, it was deemed to be 'created' by the Wolters Kluwer Database through the combination of input keywords, algorithms, rules, and templates. Consequently, the courts ruled that the analysis report did not qualify as a work under copyright law.

As the court found that the plaintiff created the textual part of the article based on the analysis report generated by Wolters Kluwer Database, it naturally confirmed that it constituted a written work. However, this part of the judgment is not relevant to the issues addressed in this report, so it will not be elaborated on here.

c. Regarding the Rights Attribution and Signature of Analysis Reports:

Although the courts determined that the automatically generated analysis reports did not qualify as works under copyright law, they recognized that such reports still possessed certain rights that should be protected by law. Failing to protect the rights of contributors would hinder the dissemination of their contributions (i.e., analysis reports) and undermine their utility.

Therefore, the courts held that these rights should be vested in the users of the software rather than the software developers. The courts suggested that the law firm, as the user of the software, should indicate its ownership of the relevant rights in a reasonable manner to protect the public's right to information and maintain social honesty and credibility.

Additionally, the courts recommended adding a label in the analysis report to indicate that it was generated by the software, thereby ensuring transparency and honesty.

Judicial Result:

The court ruled that the automated analysis reports generated by the Wolters Kluwer Database did not constitute works under copyright law.

Nevertheless, the court recognized that users had certain rights to these reports and upheld their right to attribution.

The court recommended that the reports include a notation indicating their automated generation to inform the public and maintain transparency.

In summary, while the Wolters Kluwer Database-generated analysis reports were not deemed copyrightable works, the court acknowledged the rights of users to these reports and upheld their right to attribution, emphasizing the importance of clarity in legal frameworks surrounding AI-generated content.

1.4.2.3 Spring Breeze Case [Trial Court: Beijing Internet Court, Case No.: (2023) Jing 491 Min Chu 11279 / (2023)京0491民初11279号]

Basic Case Details:

On 24 February 2023, the plaintiff used the open-source software Stable Diffusion to generate the disputed image by entering prompt words, and subsequently published it on the Xiaohongshu platform under the title 'Spring breeze brings tenderness'.

Later, on 2 March 2023, the WeChat public account 'I am Cloud Sunrise' published an article titled 'Love in March, Among Peach Blossoms', using the disputed image as an illustration. The plaintiff alleged that the defendant, without permission, used the image, cropped out the plaintiff's watermark, and misled users on the Xiaohongshu platform to believe that the defendant was the author of the work, thus severely infringing the plaintiff's right of authorship and the right of communication to the public on information networks of the disputed image.

During the trial, the court investigated the facts of the output process of the AI product involved in the case:

Upon opening the AI drawing product Stable Diffusion, the plaintiff entered the following prompt words in the input box:

> (Super realistic photo 1:3), ultra-high-quality detailed original image data processing format color photo, outdoor scene, Japanese idol, highly detailed and symmetrical face, perfectly smooth skin, skin pores, dreamy black eyes, reddish-brown braids, even, long legs, knee-high socks, soft focus, (film texture, vivid colors, film simulation, Kodak Gold Portrait 100.35mm, Canon 50f1.2), lens flare, golden hour, high-definition, movie, beautiful dynamic lighting.

In addition, the plaintiff entered the following negative prompt words:

> (3d, rendering, for example: painting, sketching, cartoon, animation, comic 1.2), poor anatomical structure, poor hands, text, errors, missing fingers, excess numbers, fewer numbers, cropping, worst quality, signature, watermark, username, blur, artist's name, (elongated body), poor anatomical structure, liquid, deformity, mutation, poor proportions, inconsistent body, unnatural body, destruction, ugliness, exaggerated proportions, mutation, destruction, deformation, (mutation), (child: 1.2), black and white, fat, extra nipples, minimalism, not suitable for workplace, low resolution, poor anatomical structure, poor hands, text, errors, missing fingers, excess numbers, fewer numbers, cropping, worst quality, low quality, normal quality, jpeg artifacts, signature, watermark, username, blur, disfigurement, kitsch, ugliness, oversaturation, texture, low resolution, deformation, disfigurement, poorly drawn faces, mutation, mutation, excess limbs, ugliness, poorly drawn hands, missing limbs, floating limbs, detached limbs, deformed hands, blur, defocus, long necks, long bodies, ugliness, nausea, poorly drawn, childish, incomplete, fragmented, old-looking. Surreal, text. Black and white monochrome, conjoined twins, multiple heads, extra legs, extra arms, meme, elongation, distortion, fingers, strabismus, heterochromia, closed eyes, blur, watermark, wedding, group, dark skin, dark-skinned women, tattoos, nudity, low resolution, poor anatomical structure, poor hands, text, errors, missing fingers, excess numbers, fewer numbers, cropping, worst quality, low quality, normal quality, jpeg artifacts, signature, watermark, username, blur.

Only a small part of the above negative prompt words were edited by the plaintiff, while the rest were directly copied from the content shared by users on a forum.

Subsequently, the plaintiff adjusted some parameter values and added prompt words such as 'shy, elegant, cute, sensual, cool pose, teenager, preview, masterpiece, best quality' in the positive prompt words. The AI product involved in the case generated the disputed image accordingly.

During the on-site inspection, when the plaintiff changed certain prompt words or parameters, the resulting images differed.

According to publicly available information and related research, the Stable Diffusion model is trained on a large number of images and their corresponding textual descriptions from the internet. The model can generate images matching the text by utilizing the semantic information contained in the text and the pixels in the images. The image is not retrieved from existing images through a search engine nor is it a combination of preset elements by the software designer.

Moreover, according to the evidence in the case, the designer of the AI model involved stated in the licence provided:

> Unless otherwise specified in this licence, the licensor does not claim any rights to the output generated by your use of the model. You are responsible for the subsequent use of the output. The use of the output must not violate any provisions of the licence.

Key Points of the Judgment:

a. Whether the Disputed Image Constitutes a Work and What Kind of Type of Work:

The court ruled that the disputed image constitutes a work of fine art. The court focused on whether the image reflects the plaintiff's intellectual efforts and whether it enjoys originality.

First, the court acknowledged that the plaintiff demonstrated a certain intellectual input in using the AI product to generate the image, such as designing the presentation of characters, selecting prompt words, arranging the order of prompt words, setting relevant parameters, and selecting the desired image. The image reflected the plaintiff's intellectual input and fulfilled the requirement of 'intellectual effort'.

Secondly, the court believed that users' requests for generating images with AI varied in specificity and clarity, reflecting individualized expression. Despite not physically drawing specific lines or fully instructing the Stable Diffusion model on how to draw specific lines and colours, the plaintiff 'designed the presentation of characters and other visual elements through prompt words, and arranged the layout and composition of the image through parameters, reflecting the plaintiff's choices and arrangements'.

Furthermore, the plaintiff's subsequent adjustments and revisions in obtaining the image also demonstrated aesthetic choices and personal judgments, ultimately resulting in the disputed image. During the on-site inspection, by changing certain prompt words or parameters, the plaintiff generated different images. Therefore, the creation using this model is not a 'mechanical intellectual output' but demonstrates individualized expression, meeting the requirement of 'originality'.

Additionally, the court emphasized the widespread application of generative AI technology in the current era and the intellectual expression and originality reflected in the generated works by human users. The judgment stated:

> Generative artificial intelligence technology has changed the way people create, similar to the impact of many technological advancements in history. The development of technology gradually outsources human work to machines. Before the invention of the camera, people needed advanced painting skills to reproduce objective objects, and the invention of the camera made it easier to record objective objects. Now, the camera function of smartphones is becoming more powerful and easier to use. However, as long as the photos taken with smartphones reflect the photographer's creative intellectual input, they still constitute photographic works protected by copyright law. Therefore, as technology advances and tools become smarter, human involvement decreases,

> but this does not affect our continued application of the copyright system to encourage the creation of works.

Additionally, regarding the distinction between AI-generated works and commissioned works, the court believed that:

> the commissioned artist has his own will, and when completing the painting commissioned by the client, he will incorporate his own choices and judgments into the painting. At the current stage, generative artificial intelligence models do not have free will and are not legal subjects. Therefore, when people use generative artificial intelligence models to generate images, there is no question of determining who the author is between two subjects... fundamentally, it is still humans creating with tools... In this context and technological reality, when artificial intelligence generates images, as long as it reflects human creative intellectual input, it should be recognized as a work.

However, it should be noted that the judgment explicitly states that its determinations are based on the current stage of AI technology and the technical development level of the AI model involved, i.e., 'At the current stage, generative artificial intelligence models do not have free will'. According to the premise that 'generative artificial intelligence models do not have free will and are not legal subjects', it can only be concluded that AI does not constitute an author. However, it cannot be automatically inferred from this that AI users can constitute authors. If AI users have less control over the aesthetic and expressive aspects of the generated works due to their technological capabilities, their creative space may be reduced accordingly; if the intellectual input contributed by AI users to the generated works is lower than what can be considered as 'creation' in the sense of copyright law, then AI users cannot be considered as the authors of the generated works, but the reasoning differs from that of AI due to the user's lack of creation activity.

b. Whether the Plaintiff Holds Copyright of the Disputed Image:

First, the court determined that since the AI model does not meet the requirements of the Copyright Law for the identity of the author (limited to natural persons, legal persons, or unincorporated organizations), although the disputed image was 'drawn' by the AI model involved, the model cannot be the author of the disputed image.

Secondly, the designer of the AI model involved 'neither had the intention to create the disputed image nor predetermined the subsequent generated content', so they are not the author of the disputed image.

Finally, the court believed that the disputed image was created based on the plaintiff's intellectual input, reflecting the plaintiff's personal expression. Therefore, the plaintiff was ultimately determined to be the author of the disputed image and holds the copyright in it.

c. The Obligation to Indicate that the Disputed Image was Generated by Artificial Intelligence:

The judgment stated that although the plaintiff was recognized as the author of the disputed work and holds the copyright, 'according to the principle of good faith and the need to protect the public's right to information, the plaintiff should prominently indicate the use of artificial intelligence technology or models'. The court also gave full affirmation to the plaintiff's behaviour of marking 'AI illustration' as a way of indication.

Judicial Result:

The court determined that the plaintiff's disputed image generated using the AI model possesses originality, constitutes a work of fine art, and the plaintiff holds the copyright. The defendant's actions constitute infringement of the plaintiff's right of authorship and the right of communication to the public on information networks.

1.4.2.4 The Ultraman Case in Hangzhou [Trial Court: Hangzhou Internet Court; Hangzhou Intermediate People's Court]

Basic Case Details:

The plaintiff is the exclusive licensee of the copyright in the Ultraman series of works, having obtained exclusive authorization from the copyright owner of the Ultraman series. The defendant, a certain Intelligent Technology Company in Hangzhou, is the operator of the 'Chushou AI' platform. This platform offers a wide range of functionalities, allowing users to upload images and other materials to train and share Ultraman AI models. Furthermore, users can utilize these Ultraman AI models to generate works that are substantially similar to the plaintiff's Ultraman characters.

As a provider of generative AI services, the defendant charges fees for certain services. However, in its user service agreement, the defendant declares that it does not review the materials uploaded by users or the content generated through its platform. Moreover, the defendant actively encourages users to publish the generated content.The plaintiff alleges that the defendant's actions infringe upon its exclusive right of communication to the public on information networks and violate the principle of good faith under the Anti-Unfair Competition Law. These actions have caused serious damage to the plaintiff's lawful rights and interests. Consequently, the plaintiff has filed a lawsuit with the Hangzhou Internet Court.

Key Points of the Judgment:

a. Whether the Plaintiff Has the Right to Initiate the Lawsuit

The court held that the Ultraman animated character in question is a work of fine art, and the copyright therein is owned by Tsuburaya Productions. Tsuburaya Productions has duly authorized the plaintiff to exercise relevant rights. Therefore, the plaintiff has the right to initiate the lawsuit.

b. Whether the Defendant Bears Joint Liability for User Infringement

In this case, internet users have engaged in the act of publicly disseminating the output content of lightweight fine-tuning models on the Touch Hand AI platform. The court determined that the infringing content in this case consists of the cover images, example images, and generated images of the lightweight fine-tuning models disseminated by the users. Therefore, the users are the providers of the infringing content and have directly infringed upon the right of communication to the public on information networks. Consequently, the output content of the AI model has infringed upon the legitimate copyright interests of others. Furthermore, taking into account the specific circumstances of the case, the court concluded that the platform should have been aware that the network users were utilizing its network services to infringe upon the right of communication through information networks for the involved works but failed to take necessary measures. The platform did not fulfil its reasonable duty of care and thus bears joint liability for compensation.

Judicial Result:

On 25 September 2024, the Hangzhou Internet Court held that the defendant had failed to take necessary measures in line with the technological level at the time of the infringement to prevent the infringement and had not fulfilled its reasonable duty of care, thereby constituting contributory infringement. Meanwhile, the court determined that the personalized services provided by the defendant constituted technological neutrality, which did not disrupt the market competition order and therefore did not constitute unfair competition. On 30 December 2024, the Hangzhou Intermediate People's Court dismissed the appeal in the second instance and upheld the original judgment.

Based on the precedent of AI-generated content cases in China where judgments have been rendered and become effective, it can be observed that there has been a shift in the attitude towards the copyrightability of AI-generated content and the qualitative standards thereof in Chinese judicial adjudication. Moreover, the controversies and discussions surrounding relevant cases have also become hot topics in both the Chinese AI industry and the intellectual property law academia.

2. TRAINING AI MODELS

During the training phase of AI models, there are two main behaviours: one is the extensive acquisition of various types of data, and the other is the 'training' of the acquired data, enabling AI to simulate human thinking abilities. Therefore, the copyright issues in the training process also focus on these two aspects: whether obtaining permission from the copyright owner is required during the data acquisition stage of AI, and whether there may be infringement issues during the data training stage of AI. This section primarily introduces the views of the Chinese academic community on these two issues.

2.1 Training AI with Copyright Protected Works

During the data training stage, scholars mainly discuss the potential infringements of copyright and further explore whether such infringement can be defended through the current fair use system. Currently, most Chinese scholars advocate that generative AI may infringe on the reproduction rights of authors during the training process. Others also argue that the training process may infringe on other rights of authors, such as adaptation rights and translation rights. Apart from the rights of copyright holders, some scholars argue that behaviour during the training stage may also infringe personality rights, including but not limited to privacy rights and portrait rights.

2.1.1 Reproduction Rights

Some perspectives indicate that there are two stages of reproduction involved in the operation of AI models: one is the acquisition stage of existing works, and the other is the output stage of generated content. During the acquisition stage, if the works being acquired are public domain works without copyright, there is no dispute. However, if the works are copyrighted and unauthorized by the author, the acquisition behaviour carries risks, especially if AI subsequently engages in a series of operations such as copying, storing, and learning with the ultimate purpose of commercial profit, then such behaviour constitutes infringement.[7]

Scholars holding similar views also point out that, generally, before AI engages in deep autonomous learning, existing works need to be digitized and converted into a standard data format suitable for 'machine reading'. The behaviour in this stage constitutes complete reproduction and faithful representation of existing works without altering the content, which falls under the category of 'reproduction' in copyright law and carries the risk of infringing reproduction rights.[8]

Some scholars categorize copying during machine learning into temporary and permanent copying behaviours. For temporary copying, current Chinese law does not consider it as infringement; however, for permanent copying, unless it can be interpreted within the fair use system during the AI machine learning process, thus obtaining a defence against infringement, such copying constitutes copyright infringement.[9]

2.1.2 Adaptation Rights and Translation Rights

Some scholars argue that the main technical process involved in AI learning is text and data mining, which involves analysing large amounts of data to extract specific features, trends, and other information. The primary process of text and data mining includes: (1) data collection, (2) cleaning and appropriately formatting the data for computer recognition, (3) analysing the data using algorithms, (4) archiving the data for subsequent result verification activities. During the data cleaning stage, personnel need to translate and mark the data, and these actions may infringe on the adaptation and translation rights of works.[10]

---

7. Ye Zhaochi, *Tort Liability and Resolution Pathways of AI Model Output Content*, Journal of South-Central Minzu University (Humanities and Social Sciences) 6 (11 January 2024).
8. Jiao Heping, *Copyright Risks and Resolutions in Data Acquisition and Utilization within AI Creation*, 4 Contemporary Law Science 132 (2022).
9. You Kaijie, *Study on Copyright Legal Issues of AI-Generated Content: A Humanistic Perspective* 271 (Intellectual Property Publishing House, 1st ed. 2024).
10. Wang Changzheng, *Copyright Risks and Mitigation Strategies in the Development of Generative Artificial Intelligence: A Case Study of ChatGPT*, 2 Journal of Huaiyin Teachers College (Philosophy and Social Sciences Edition) 140 (2024).

2.1.3 *Other Rights*

Some perspectives argue that generative AI may lead to large-scale privacy or personal information leakage issues. Large-scale generative AI requires a vast amount of data as parameters, and providers of AI products may unlawfully collect a large amount of personal information during the training of AI products or use a large amount of information from non-legal sources for training AI products. This may lead to new forms of privacy and personal information infringements,[11] such as service providers failing to meet the requirements of informed consent and illegally collecting user information as parameters for training. The failure of service providers to act may also constitute infringement, such as not taking reasonable measures, resulting in system vulnerabilities or hacker attacks and causing data leakage issues.[12]

Some scholars point out through investigations that disputes involving personality rights have already emerged in the field of AI painting, especially regarding infringements on individual portrait rights and privacy rights. First, AI painting may infringe on individual portrait rights. Many AI painting apps in China have the function of transforming real photos into cartoon images, and the premise of such functions is that users must first submit their real photos to AI. At this time, it becomes very uncontrollable how the submitted images will be used, which poses a severe threat to users' portrait rights. The most severe case that has occurred before is that, under the malicious inducement of other users, a user's photos were spliced into obscene and pornographic images, which were then widely disseminated after being sent to other users, constituting an infringement of the user's portrait rights and reputation rights. Secondly, if users do not handle the photos uploaded to AI carefully, they may easily expose their private information. Under the processing of AI, this privacy information may appear in the output images in fragmentary form, which may also constitute an infringement of users' privacy rights.[13]

2.2 Exceptions/Limitations Allowing Training of AI

Regarding the possibility of defence through the fair use system under China's current law, Chinese scholars have reached the basic consensus on this issue that it is difficult to provide a defence against copyright infringement during the training phase of AI through the fair use system stipulated by current Chinese copyright laws. The reason is that AI creation does not conform to the specific types enumerated by the fair use system. Some scholars have advocated that the behaviour of AI using works during the training stage does not fall within the scope of 'personal learning or research', 'scientific research', 'proper citation' or other types specified by the fair use system. Therefore, the use of data in AI creation still carries the risk

11. Wang Liming, *Legal Responses to Infringements by Generative Artificial Intelligence*, 5 Chinese Journal of Applied Jurisprudence 28 (2023).
12. Wang Liming, *Legal Responses to Infringements by Generative Artificial Intelligence*, 5 Chinese Journal of Applied Jurisprudence 30 (2023).
13. Ye Zhaochi, *Tort Liability and Resolution Pathways of AI Model Output Content*, Journal of South-Central Minzu University (Humanities and Social Sciences) 7 (11 January 2024).

of copyright infringement.[14] Scholars holding the same view also point out that the content generation mode of 'text mining + conversion output' does not fall within the scope of fair use under the current Chinese copyright law system. The reason is that the current Chinese copyright law system adopts a closed mode of regulation for fair use, and during the revision of the Chinese Copyright Law in 2020, it still follows the 'three-step test' to define the circumstances of fair use and delineates thirteen categories of fair use from the perspective of legal texts, with text mining not falling under any of the statutory fair use circumstances.[15]

Regarding the possible protection pathways for future AI data training, Chinese scholars have formed two main perspectives regarding this issue. One group believes that no permission is required and that exemptions from copyright licences can be obtained through the fair use or statutory licensing system, while the other group advocates for differentiating between scenarios to determine whether permission from the copyright holder is necessary.

2.2.1 *No Permission Required*

Scholars in this category argue that although, according to current copyright laws, obtaining permission from the copyright holder is necessary if the data acquired contains the works of others, this requirement should be exempted through the fair use or statutory licensing system.

2.2.1.1 *Fair Use System*

Scholars advocating for exemptions through the fair use system primarily argue based on the *high cost of obtaining permission*. They point out that requiring permission as a prerequisite for using works imposes a heavy burden on text and data mining activities, and the development of the AI industry will incur even higher acquisition costs. Therefore, they suggest adding provisions within the framework of the fair use system to address this issue. Some believe that the fair use system, as one of the statutory systems limiting the scope of copyright, embodies fairness and public welfare goals and can reconcile the relationships between creators, disseminators, and users, aligning with the current values of encouraging technological development while protecting authors' rights. The transformative use theory implied by this provision can serve as a path to resolve machine learning infringement issues. Therefore, it is further suggested that a provision be added under the fair use system to exempt behaviour such as 'The act of using data or text analysis by artificial intelligence for creation, reproducing, compiling, or providing works obtained legally from others to the public for free use, may not obtain permission from or pay the remuneration

14. Jiao Heping, *Copyright Risks and Resolutions in Data Acquisition and Utilization within AI Creation*, 4 Contemporary Law Science 135 (2022).
15. Mei Yizhe & Dong Xinyi, *Copyright Law Risks and Regulatory Frameworks for Strong Artificial Intelligence: A Case Study of ChatGPT*, Science and Management 3-4 (29 March 2024).

to the copyright holder'.[16] Scholars with similar views also propose that if generative AI obtains and utilizes works for the purpose of machine learning and does not substantially affect the market value of the relevant works, it can obtain an exemption from copyright infringement under fair use.[17]

Scholars have also detailed the design of new provisions within the fair use system from three aspects: the purpose of use, the behaviour of use, and the result of use. They suggest that, in terms of the purpose of use, the scope of using works for mining activities should be limited to non-commercial purposes; regarding the behaviour of use, it should not be limited to copying behaviour but also include distribution, broadcasting, and information network dissemination; and concerning the result of use, it should be clarified that the information extracted after mining does not include specific expressions from the original works.[18]

2.2.1.2 Statutory Licensing System

Scholars advocating for exemptions through the statutory licensing system assert that applying the fair use system is not reasonable and that the statutory licensing system should be applied to exempt the behaviour of obtaining data. Some propose that there are difficulties in exempting data acquisition behaviour through the fair use system: first, China's current copyright law stipulates specific situations of fair use in a closed manner, none of which correspond to the situations of using works for machine learning; secondly, although there are fallback provisions, there are currently no other laws or regulations governing the fair use system; thirdly, machine learning of original works does not meet the requirements of the 'three-step test' of fair use in copyright law. They argue that machine learning may threaten copyright law and the potential market in original works, conflicting with their normal use and unreasonably harming copyright owners' rights and interests.[19]

Based on the inability to apply the fair use system, some scholars further propose that applying the statutory licensing system can achieve both justice and efficiency. Specifically, the statutory licensing system can adjust the justice of social relations in machine learning issues and balance the conflicts between the exclusive rights of copyright holders and the rights of users to use. From the perspective of efficiency value, applying the statutory licensing system can fully enhance the efficiency of dissemination and use of works, reduce negotiation costs between copyright holders and users, and, in terms of designing the statutory licensing system, a provision such as 'artificial intelligence technology companies reproducing works already published by others for training machine learning technology can be exempt from obtaining

16. Chen Zengbao, *Regulation of Copyright Law for Generative Artificial Intelligence*, 6 Digital Governance 23 (2023).
17. Feng Xiaoqing & Shen Yun, *Research on Copyright Issues of Generative Artificial Intelligence*, 2 Journal of Copyright Law and Governance 22(2023).
18. Wang Changzheng, *Copyright Risks and Mitigation Strategies in the Development of Generative Artificial Intelligence: A Case Study of ChatGPT*, 2 Journal of Huaiyin Teachers College (Philosophy and Social Sciences Edition) 142–143 (2024).
19. Gao Yang & Hu Danyang, *Challenges and Responses to the Fair Use Doctrine Posed by Machine Learning*, 10 Journal of Electronic Intellectual Property 21(2020).

permission from the copyright holder but should pay remuneration' can be added within the existing legal framework.[20]

2.2.2 *Differentiation of Scenarios*

Some scholars point out that addressing whether permission from the copyright holder is required during the data acquisition stage solely through the fair use system to mitigate the copyright liability of machine learning works is a simple treatment of complex issues. They suggest that distinctions should be made based on the manner of machine learning. According to this viewpoint, machine learning can be categorized into 'expressive machine learning' and 'non-expressive machine learning' based on whether there is output of expressive content. 'Expressive machine learning' can be further divided into 'ordinary expressive machine learning' and 'special expressive machine learning'.[21]

Within this framework, scholars note that non-expressive machine learning, as it does not output expressive content, uses works that fall within non-copyright law terms and, therefore, does not constitute copyright infringement. For ordinary expressive machine learning, the output expressive content is a reorganization and alteration of the expressive content of the learned works but does not include the original expressive content of the learned works, so this type of machine learning does not substantially affect the market of the learned works. Even if it objectively affects the market of the learned works, it is not because of appropriating original expressive content but because the works created by the machine have new value distinct from the original works. This type of machine learning can constitute fair use and be exempt from copyright infringement. However, special expressive machine learning is considered an infringement because it specifically learns works of specific authors to output similar expressive content. In this case, before using works for machine learning, permission from the rights holder should be actively sought and remuneration paid.[22]

2.3 Remedies and Enforcement

Infringements occurring during the data training phase are generally attributable to the data trainers, who are typically AI service providers. However, in practice, there are also platforms that enable users to conduct Lora (Low-Rank Adaptation of Large Language Models) training by integrating third-party foundational models. In such cases, users can independently train lightweight AI models with a small amount of data to generate specific content. If the generated content infringes upon others' rights and is subsequently published, the user generally constitutes direct infringement. The platform, on the other hand, will be assessed based on its fault

20. Gao Yang & Hu Danyang, *Challenges and Responses to the Fair Use Doctrine Posed by Machine Learning*, 10 Journal of Electronic Intellectual Property 24(2020).
21. Li An, *Copyright Law Analysis of Machine Learning Works – Non-Work Use, Fair Use, and Infringement Use*, 6 Journal of Electronic Intellectual Property 67 (2020).
22. Li An, *Copyright Law Analysis of Machine Learning Works – Non-Work Use, Fair Use, and Infringement Use*, 6 Journal of Electronic Intellectual Property 68 (2020).

to determine whether it has fulfilled its reasonable duty of care and whether it constitutes contributory infringement (as seen in the *Ultraman* case in the Hangzhou Intermediate People's Court).

2.4 Summary

In the exploration of copyright infringement issues and legal defence paths during the data training phase of generative AI, numerous scholars have pointed out that during the AI training process, there is a potential infringement of the right of reproduction, right of adaptation, and right of translation under copyright law. Additionally, there is a risk of infringement on personality rights (including the right to privacy and the right to portrait). The current fair use system, due to its closed nature and incompatibility with AI training activities, is difficult to effectively exempt such infringing acts.

Regarding future legal protection paths, the academic community has formed two main viewpoints: one advocates exempting permissions through the fair use system or statutory licensing system to reduce the cost of obtaining authorization and promote technological development; the other suggests differentiating based on the output type of machine learning, arguing that non-expressive machine learning does not constitute infringement, while special expressive machine learning requires authorization and payment of remuneration.

In terms of liability determination for infringement, there is a view in the academic community that the liability for infringement during the AI training phase is generally borne by the data trainer. Meanwhile, in scenarios where users train lightweight AI models on their own, users may constitute direct infringement, and the platform may be determined to bear corresponding contributory liability based on its fault.

3. USE OF AI SYSTEMS

3.1 Permission to Reproduce and Make Available to the Public

Generally, AI systems do not make the data within their systems available to the public. Therefore, even if users input or upload infringing materials into the AI system (to obtain output results), it does not enable other users to directly access such data. Additionally, some scholars argue that the act of users uploading data constitutes the creation of temporary copies in cyberspace, which is a form of temporary reproduction and does not amount to infringement. Thus, no permission is required.

3.2 Exception/Limitations Allowing AI Training

Under the current Copyright Law of China, the circumstances of fair use include 'use of a published work of another for purposes of personal study, research, or appreciation' 'translation or reproduction in a small quantity of copies of a published work for use by teachers or scientific researchers in classroom teaching or scientific research, provided that the translation or reproduction shall not be published or distributed' and 'appropriate quotation from a published work of others in one's work for the purposes of introduction to, or comment on, a work, or demonstration of a point'. At present, it is difficult to determine that the practices related to commercial AI development fall within the scope of the aforementioned fair use scenarios. However, many scholars have proposed that the scope of fair use could be expanded.

3.3 Remedies and Enforcement

To mitigate the risk of infringement, providers of AI systems may stipulate in user agreements that users are prohibited from uploading content that infringes upon the intellectual property rights of others. In cases where users upload infringing content, generate infringing outputs, or customize lightweight AI models that result in infringement, AI system providers typically invoke the 'safe harbour' defence. Courts may then assess the provider's level of fault (whether they known or should have known) by considering the existing technological capabilities of the AI system service at the time of the infringement. This assessment ultimately determines whether the AI system provider is liable for contributory infringement.

3.4 Summary

At the current stage of AI development in China, the use of AI systems is typically discussed in conjunction with training or output. There is a relative scarcity of research focusing solely on the issues related to the use of AI systems. Therefore, this chapter provides only a brief analysis as mentioned above.

4. AI-GENERATED OUTPUT

4.1 Protection of AI-Generated Content

In general, the issues concerning the copyright law in the output of AI models primarily focus on several aspects. First, whether the content produced by AI models is eligible for protection under copyright law. Chinese scholars have developed two main perspectives on this matter: affirmative and negative perspectives. Building upon the affirmation of its eligibility for copyright protection, scholars further explore the issue of rights attribution regarding AI model outputs. In this regard, scholars' opinions concentrate on two aspects: the protection of AI output content as a work and the protection thereof as neighbouring rights objects, thereby determining the issue of rights attribution.

Secondly, the infringement issues concerning the output of AI models. Scholars' exploration of this matter encompasses various aspects including, but not limited to, the types of infringed rights, the entities responsible for infringement liability, and the principles of liability attribution. The following sections will outline the main viewpoints of Chinese scholars on the issues above.

4.1.1 *Copyright Protection of AI Output*

4.1.1.1 *Justification of Authorization*

Regarding the viewpoint that AI model outputs constitute works in the sense of copyright law, scholars consider various factors, primarily based on the interpretation of 'works' in current copyright law and factors such as the subject and legislative purpose of copyright law.

First, concerning the interpretation of 'works' in copyright law, a representative perspective in the Chinese academic community is the 'objective standard of originality'. Represented by Professor Yi Jiming of Peking University, this perspective asserts that the determination of the copyrightability of AI model outputs should lean towards an objective judgment standard, focusing on whether they are consistent with existing works in form rather than being entangled in whether natural persons created them during the creative process.[23] If the expression of AI model outputs is indistinguishable in form, from human-created works, then they should be deemed to have originality. Scholars who share similar views advocate for considering 'originality' as the sole criterion for determining the 'work' nature of AI intellectual achievements, while 'originality' serves as the objective criterion for determining whether intellectual achievements qualify as works.[24] Building upon the 'objective standard of originality' some perspectives further suggest adopting 'minimal creativity' as an objective criterion to assess the originality of AI model outputs.[25] At the level of identifying works, there are also perspectives advocating for adopting reader-centred hermeneutics with the separation of subject and object, transferring the interpretation right of works from authors to readers, with readers' perceptions and understandings serving as the basis for judging the originality of works, and authorship is no longer being a constituent element for the protection of works.[26] This perspective, to some extent, acknowledges the 'objective standard of originality' proposed by the aforementioned scholars.

In addition to advocating for the application of the objective standard of originality, there are also perspectives suggesting that AI outputs should not only objectively resemble traditional works but also be authored by humans. For instance, Professor Li Yang of China University of Political Science and Law asserts that the focus of originality determination in copyright law lies not only in whether the objective result constitutes a work but also in whether the subjective source possesses the human category of intention. That is, the author's positioning of the work, the author intends for the work to be perceived by the anticipated audience and classified into a certain category, and the author intends to specify how the work should be

23. Yi Jiming, *Are AI Model Outputs Subject to Copyright Protection as Works?*, 5 Legal Science of Northwest University of Political Science and Law 139 (2017).
24. Li Weimin, *The Correctness of Artificial Intelligence Intellectual Achievements in Copyright Law – Discussion with Professor Wang Qian'*, 3 Dongfang Law Review 160 (2018).
25. Yang Lihua, *Exploration of Copyright Issues in AI Model Output Content*, 4 Modern Legal Science 105 (2021).
26. Xu Xiaoben, *On the Copyrightability and Ownership of Algorithmic Works*, 3 Eastern Jurisprudence 49 (2021).

treated. At the same time, Professor Li Yang also suggests that the determination of the originality of AI outputs can be maintained at the 'minimal creativity standard' traditionally used for identifying works, which will not directly lead to tragedies of anti-commons or a 'spurt' of rights, mainly because the exclusive rights scope of AI outputs is limited to the content finally generated, and individual prompt words belong to unprotected factual materials.[27]

Secondly, some scholars argue that AI model output content should be protected from the perspective of copyright subjects._This perspective asserts that Chinese copyright law does not explicitly limit the subject of copyright to natural persons. Therefore, on the basis of the absence of explicit contrary provisions in current Chinese copyright law, AI can also be inferred as a potential subject of copyright law, and the expression achievements created autonomously by AI in the field of literature and art should also be granted protection under copyright law.[28] Some perspectives also point out that with the development of society, it is conceivable for non-living entities to become legal subjects, with legal entities being the best example. Under this premise, AI can be deemed as the author, or the developers, managers, etc., of AI can be deemed as the authors of AI model outputs.[29] However, regarding the perspective that AI can also be a subject of copyright law, some scholars who support the protection of AI output content under copyright law have faced criticism. For instance, Professor Li Yang argues that AI lacks the independent consciousness and emotional abilities of humans, as well as the capacity to enjoy rights, fulfil obligations, and bear responsibilities, thus making it ineligible to be deemed as a legal subject. Forcing AI to be deemed as a legal subject disregards the requirements for legal subject qualifications and violates the principle that subjects and objects cannot be interchangeable, and it also contradicts the incentive theory of intellectual property law.[30]

Furthermore, there are also minority perspectives that argue from the legislative purpose, value, and theoretical perspectives of copyright law that AI output content should be considered as works. For instance, some perspectives assert that from the perspective of the legislative purpose of Chinese copyright law, copyright protection aims to provide certain incentives to creators to promote the prosperity of the cultural market and social development. Granting copyright protection to AI model outputs is of significant importance in the era of 'strong artificial intelligence'.[31] There are also perspectives that, from the perspectives of the labour theory of value and

27. Li Yang & Tu Teng, *On the Copyrightability Standards of AI-Generated Content*, 1 Intellectual Property Rights 75-83 (2024).
28. Zhu Mengyun, *A Feasibility Study on Copyright Protection for AI-Generated Content*, 3 Publishing Science 56 (2019).
29. Li Weimin, *Reconstruction of the System of Works Made in the Course of Employment and Path Selection for Copyright Ownership of AI Works*, 3 Legal Review 110 (2020).
30. Li Yang & Li Xiaoyu, *Discussion on the Copyright Issues of Artificial Intelligence Generated Works from the Perspective of Kant's Philosophy*, 9 Law Journal 47-49 (2018).
31. Mei Yizhe & Dong Xinyi, *Copyright Law Risks and Regulatory Frameworks for Strong Artificial Intelligence: A Case Study of ChatGPT*, Science and Management 4-5 (29 March 2024).

property theory, protecting content generated by AI is reasonable.[32] At the theoretical level of copyright law, Professor Li Yang proposed that the mainstream legitimacy interpretation of copyright law, namely, the incentive theory, is constructed on the imbalance between the cost of creating works and the cost of replication. To address the problem of insufficient supply of public goods caused by low-cost reproduction or free-riding phenomena, copyright law must establish scarcity above the expression of originality, enabling authors to charge prices higher than marginal costs through limited monopolies free from competition, thereby incentivizing authors to engage in continuous creative activities. However, this scarcity and incentive theory will not be completely eliminated or invalidated by the emergence of generative AI. Instead, they will be transferred to human intellectual activities behind the content generated by AI. The behaviour of humans continuously selecting, arranging, adapting, and modifying prompt words during the process of using AI to generate content possesses the scarcity characteristics of original creative expression. Therefore, copyright law is needed to incentivize this creative intellectual input.[33]

4.1.1.2 Attribution of Rights

Regarding the issue of rights attribution for AI model outputs, Chinese scholars have proposed various perspectives, including attribution to the designer, investor, user, according to contractual agreements, considering AI as the author, or discussing it on a case-by-case basis.

Scholars advocating for attribution to *the designer or creator* argue that works created by AI models should enjoy copyright protection, but they cannot exercise rights like natural person authors or legal entity authors. In this case, the provisions of copyright law regarding the service work could be referenced, where the rights should be enjoyed and exercised by the 'person' who created the machine rather than the machine itself.[34] Some scholars argue that AI-generated results can be considered as creative actions representing the will of the designer or trainer, and thus, they can adopt the institutional arrangement of legal entity works, with the rationale that the copyright should be attributed to the owner of the AI, representing the owner's intention.[35]

Scholars advocating for attribution to *the investor* argue that when AI model output content qualifies as the work of a legal entity, a service work, or a commissioned work, attributing rights to investors is more economically and practically feasible. This is because granting copyright ownership of AI-generated works to

32. Feng Gang, *Preliminary Exploration of Legal Protection Paths for Artificial Intelligence Generated Content*, 1 China Publishing 6 (2019).
33. Li Yang & Tu Teng, *On the Copyrightability Standards of AI-Generated Content*, 1 Intellectual Property Rights 71 (2024).
34. Wu Handong, *Institutional Arrangements and Legal Regulations in the Era of Artificial Intelligence*, 5 Legal Science (Journal of Northwest University of Political Science and Law) 131–132 (2017).
35. Xiong Qi, *Copyright Determination of Artificial Intelligence Generated Content*, 3 Intellectual Property Rights 8 (2017).

investors maximizes benefits.[36] Additionally, it is suggested that the attribution of rights for AI model outputs could combine with the provisions of the special service work in China, establishing an attribution system primarily based on investors and supplemented by contractual agreements.[37]

Scholars advocating for attribution to *the user* argue that users are the direct cause of each specific work's production and should be incentivized as the entity responsible for promoting cultural prosperity and encouraging creativity. Therefore, rights can be granted to users. At the same time, granting rights to users encourages them to review, modify, and adjust works, bringing excellent works to the public's attention.[38] Additionally, some perspectives, starting from the viewpoints of the 'artificial intelligence creation tool' advocate that the rights to AI outputs should, in principle, belong to the user, with exceptions attributed to the employer or the commissioner. Specifically, whoever creates the generated content (i.e., works) using AI is considered the author of that work and enjoys copyright unless otherwise specified by copyright law. Such special provisions refer to the provisions in Articles 16 and 17 of Chinese Copyright Law, which respectively regulate the attribution of service works and commissioned works.[39] There are also perspectives advocating for establishing the user as the primary principle of rights attribution for AI model outputs while considering a rights attribution system that balances investor interests. Specifically, AI model outputs that meet the characteristics of works should, in principle, belong to the user of AI. However, if the creation of AI-generated works is the result of significant investment by an investor, copyright law should also flexibly apply special provisions such as legal entity works, commissioned works, and service works, actively protecting the interests of relevant investors.[40] Moreover, some perspectives suggest respecting the autonomy of the parties involved, determining the attribution of rights based on contractual agreements, and if there are no agreements, the rights should, in principle, belong to the user.[41]

Scholars advocating for *establishing ownership based on contractual agreements* argue that the controversy over the subject of AI model output copyrights in the field of copyright law has yet to be settled. At this stage, directly establishing copyright in a stable position through contracts can be a concise and flexible way to allocate rights.[42]

36. Li Xiaoyu, *Discussion on the Copyrightability and Rights Allocation of AI Model Output Content*, 6 Electronic Intellectual Property 42 (2018).
37. Li Aizhen, *Exploration and Enlightenment of Copyright Protection for AI Model Outputs in the United States*, 11 Journal of Electronic Intellectual Property 91 (2020).
38. Zhang Linghan, Zhang Jiyu, Guo He, et al., *A Symposium on Copyright Protection for Content Generated by Artificial Intelligence (AIGC)*, 1 Digital Governance 22 (2024).
39. Li Yang & Li Xiaoyu, *Discussion on the Copyright Issues of Artificial Intelligence Generated Works from the Perspective of Kant's Philosophy*, 9 Law Journal 52–53 (2018).
40. Yang Lihua, *Exploration of Copyright Issues in AI Model Output Content*, 4 Modern Legal Science 111 (2021).
41. Mei Yizhe & Dong Xinyi, *Copyright Law Risks and Regulatory Frameworks for Strong Artificial Intelligence: A Case Study of ChatGPT*, Science and Management 7 (29 March 2024).
42. Ye Zhaochi, *Tort Liability and Resolution Pathways of AI Model Output Content*, Journal of South-Central Minzu University (Humanities and Social Sciences) 6 (11 January 2024).

Scholars proposing *AI as the author* argue that regarding AI as the inventor or author is essentially a division of authorship qualification and exercise of authorship rights into two stages. Regarding resource allocation, they advocate for strict adherence to contribution, arguing that AI makes the greatest contribution to the completion of the invention or creation. Regarding the exercise of rights, scholars propose that it should be carried out by the owner or user on behalf of AI. Based on this, scholars believe it is necessary to make appropriate institutional arrangements for intellectual property ownership, such as defaulting to the owner or user of AI as the rights holder. Designers or users can be seen as 'employers' while AI programs can be seen as 'employees', thereby applying the system of inventions made in the course of employment, with the 'employer' enjoying the rights.[43]

Scholars advocating for discussing the attribution of rights *on a case-by-case basis* argue that the determination of rights attribution for AI model outputs should be discussed based on different stages of AI development. At the stage of 'quasi-intelligence', the user should be the rights holder. At the stage of algorithmic intelligence, the provider of materials or the user should be the copyright holder. However, since the user's use of AI cannot be separated from the pre-set algorithm, the programmer should rightfully enjoy some copyrights (such as the right of authorship). At the stage of full brain simulation, even if AI is recognized as the author, the initial programmer should still be considered a co-author, mainly because AI cannot bear legal responsibilities.[44]

4.1.2 Neighbouring Rights Protection of AI Output

4.1.2.1 Justification of Authorization

In advocating for the protection of AI model outputs as objects of neighbouring rights, most scholars believe that categorizing them as works would contradict traditional theories of copyright law. However, it is still necessary to provide a certain degree of protection under copyright law for the results of AI generation. At this point, protection can be provided through the neighbouring rights system, allowing the generated results to be treated as objects of neighbouring rights in a broad sense.[45] This perspective differs from the criteria for judging works and the objective standard of originality. It suggests that recognizing AI model outputs as having 'originality' would deviate from the purpose of copyright law, as it does not meet the requirement

43. Liu Qiang, *Research on Legal Issues of Artificial Intelligence Intellectual Property* 49 (Law Press 1st ed. 2020).
44. Wang Xiaoxia & Fu Qiang, *Sighs on the Copyright Issues of AI Model Output Content*, 3 China Publishing 36 (2017).
45. Tao Qian, *On the Protection of Copyright Law for Artificial Intelligence Generated Results – Evidence of the Right of Data Handlers as Neighboring Rights*, 4 Law (2018); Yu Kaijie, *A Study on the Legal Issues of Copyright of AI Generated Content (From the Perspective of Humanism)* (Intellectual Property Publishing House, 1st ed. 2024).

of personality attributes stipulated by copyright law,[46] thus rendering them ineligible for copyright protection.

4.1.2.2 *Attribution of Rights*

Before addressing the issue of rights attribution for AI model outputs, most Chinese scholars advocate for the establishment of new neighbouring rights under the current neighbouring rights system to clarify matters such as rights holders, objects, content, and protection periods. Currently, the new neighbouring rights proposed by academics include, but are not limited to, the establishment of *'data processor rights', 'data regenerating rights', 'investor rights in AI creative works' and 'rights of AI model output content creators'.*

Regarding *'data processor rights'*, this refers to the rights enjoyed by the user of the program or device that generates data over the results of such data. On the basis of establishing this right, scholars propose that the identification of the rights holder should first adhere to contractual agreements, with the right belonging to the user of the AI program in the absence of clear contract provisions. Additionally, scholars point out that restrictions should be imposed on the exercise of this neighbouring right. In terms of the scope of rights, the entitlements associated with 'data processor rights' should be more limited than those granted under copyright, and they could be modelled after the rights of sound recording and video recording producers over their products. Regarding the terms of production, scholars suggest that the protection period for data results should be shorter than that of copyright property rights and general neighbouring rights. In terms of the exercise of rights, other entities should not be restricted from using technology to extract and utilize the results generated by AI.[47]

Regarding *'data regeneration rights'*, this represents a new form of neighbouring rights established for content created through AI technology. Regarding the subject of rights, scholars propose that contractual agreements should be followed, and in the absence of such agreements, the rights should belong to the user of the AI. At the object level, scholars advocate for the inclusion of independently generated works by AI. In terms of the content of rights, scholars suggest that they include distribution rights, reproduction rights, and the right of communication to the public on information networks. Regarding the term of protection, scholars propose a period of five to ten years as reasonable.[48]

Regarding *'investor rights in AI creative works'*, this refers to the protection of AI-generated content under the neighbouring rights system, which aligns well with the function of the neighbouring rights system. Therefore, it is deemed necessary to establish such rights. Regarding the subject of rights, scholars propose that contractual

46. Yu Kaijie, *A Study on the Legal Issues of Copyright of AI Generated Content (From the Perspective of Humanism)* 215 (Intellectual Property Publishing House, 1st ed. 2024).
47. Tao Qian, *On the Protection of Copyright Law for Artificial Intelligence Generated Results – Evidence of the Right of Data Handlers as Neighboring Rights*, 4 Law 15 (2018).
48. Qin Tao and Zhang Xudong, *On the Logic and Path of Copyright Protection for AI Model Output Content*, 6 Journal of East China University of Science and Technology (Social Sciences Edition) 85–86 (2018).

agreements should be followed, and in the absence of agreements, the rights should belong to the investor in AI creative works. In terms of the content of rights, scholars suggest that moral rights should include authorship rights and publication rights, while property rights may include reproduction rights, distribution rights, and the right of communication to the public on information networks. Regarding the term of protection, reference can be made to the database protection period in the EU, with a protection period of fifteen years from the date of publication.[49]

Regarding *'rights of AI model output content creators'*, the establishment of this right aims to protect the interests of stakeholders related to AI model outputs, and the protection scope can extend downstream to the dissemination of AI model outputs. Regarding the identification of the subject of this right, scholars propose an adherence to contractual agreements, with the right belonging to the creator of the AI model outputs in the absence of such agreements, namely the user or owner of the AI. At the object level, AI model outputs are the subject of these rights. In terms of the content of rights, moral rights may include authorship rights, while property rights may include reproduction rights and the right of communication to the public on information networks. Regarding the term of protection, scholars suggest a period of three to ten years from the date of publication of AI model outputs.[50]

4.1.3 Negative Perspective

Scholars opposing the protection of AI model outputs under copyright law primarily argue from two main perspectives: abstract theories of copyright law and specific institutional theories of copyright law.

First, at the abstract theoretical level of copyright law, scholars discuss from the standpoint of the legislative purpose and objectives of copyright. Regarding the legislative purpose of copyright, scholars advocating the negative view, represented by Professor Wang Qian from East China University of Political Science and Law, contend that copyright law is intended to encourage creativity. They argue that only humans can understand and utilize the incentive mechanism of copyright law; therefore, only creative works by humans are eligible for protection under copyright law. Professor Wang Qian criticizes the 'objective standard of originality' proposed by proponents, arguing that it contradicts the legislative purpose of copyright law and lacks legal basis.[51] He asserts that to achieve the legislative purpose of encouraging creativity in copyright law, it is crucial that the subjects of encouragement established by legislation can understand and utilize this incentive mechanism. Since AI cannot comprehend this incentive mechanism, its outputs cannot be incentivized under

49. Xu Mingyue & Tan Ling, *On the Protection of Neighboring Rights for AI Model Output Content: Theoretical Proof and Institutional Arrangement*, 6 Comparative Law Research 51–52 (2018).
50. Liu Qiang, *Research on Legal Issues of Artificial Intelligence Intellectual Property* 178–182 (Law Press 1st ed. 2020).
51. Wang Qian, *Revisiting the Qualification of AI-Generated Content in Copyright Law*, 4 Forum on Politics and Law 19 (2023).

copyright law.[52] Scholars holding similar views also propose that the purpose of copyright law should be to encourage humans to create 'robots capable of creating works' rather than encouraging robots to create works.[53] Furthermore, Professor Wang Qian criticizes other scholars who hold affirmative views in his article, including the 'simulated authorship theory' 'creative tool theory' 'investment incentive theory' and 'unity of rights and obligations theory'.

Regarding the 'simulated authorship theory',[54] Professor Wang Qian argues that AI does not possess the legal capacity of subjects, such as civil rights, actions, and responsibilities, and therefore cannot be designated as legal subjects. The perspective that investors, developers, and managers of AI should be designated as authors of content generated by AI in a legal sense also reverses the logical relationship in law. The premise for the application of Article 11(3) of the Chinese Copyright Law, which provides for 'deemed as the author', is the existence of works protected by copyright law rather than first establishing an 'author' through legal designation and then recognizing its content as 'works'.

Regarding the 'creative tool theory',[55] Professor Wang Qian argues that this perspective disregards the requirements of 'creation' under copyright law and cannot stand. In the context of Chinese copyright law, 'creation' implies an act based on free will directly determining expressive elements. This means that the author's free will plays a decisive role in the final expression of the work. Since developers or users of AI only have a circumstantial influence on the content generated by AI, they cannot be deemed as the 'authors' of content generated by AI.

Regarding the 'investment incentive theory',[56] Professor Wang Qian argues that it overlooks the different commercial ecosystems between investing in AI and creating works. Using the film industry as an example, he argues that films are recognized as works under the law and provided with copyright protection because

52. Wang Qian, *Revisiting the Qualification of AI-Generated Content in Copyright Law*, 4 Forum on Politics and Law 20 (2023).
53. Chen Hu, *On the Non-Copyrightability of AI-Generated Content: Centered on Expression Forms*, Journal of Chongqing University (Social Science Edition) 11 (5 July 2021).
54. This perspective suggests establishing a virtual legal personality for the intellectual property protection of AI-generated content, following the historical logic of legal personhood being deemed as the author. It proposes either attributing authorship to the artificial intelligence itself or designating the investors, developers, and managers of the artificial intelligence as legal authors of the AI-generated works. This approach aims to protect, in legal terms, the achievements of 'humans', thereby formally circumventing the legal obstacles of copyright law's inability to recognize and protect outcomes originating from non-human sources. See: Wang Qian, *Revisiting the Qualification of AI-Generated Content in Copyright Law*, 4 Forum on Politics and Law (2023).
55. This viewpoint argues that artificial intelligence is a tool created by humans, and thus, the relevant content should be recognized as created by humans using artificial intelligence as a means. Therefore, humans are considered the authors of such content. See: Wang Qian, *Revisiting the Qualification of AI-Generated Content in Copyright Law*, 4 Forum on Politics and Law (2023).
56. From the perspective of incentivizing investment in artificial intelligence technology and promoting industrial development, this perspective suggests that AI-generated content should be protected under copyright law. See: Wang Qian, *Revisiting the Qualification of AI-Generated Content in Copyright Law*, 4 Forum on Politics and Law (2023).

films that require significant investment are vulnerable to unauthorized reproduction, distribution, and various means of dissemination. However, the mode of economic benefit for developers of AI differs from that of the film industry. They do not achieve economic profits by regulating the reproduction, distribution, and various dissemination behaviours of the generated content itself. Moreover, the ways in which they realize technological profitability are diverse. Therefore, not recognizing content generated by AI as works and providing copyright protection will not affect investment in AI technology.

Regarding the 'unity of rights and obligations'[57] theory, Professor Wang Qian argues that 'rights' here are not limited to copyright or other statutory rights but refer broadly to interests. In other words, while obtaining corresponding benefits, it is usually necessary to assume corresponding obligations, thereby achieving the mutual unity of 'rights' and 'obligations'.

Regarding the legislative objectives of copyright law, some perspectives argue that the basic objective of copyright law is to promote social and cultural development, and granting authors copyright is a systemic tool, provided that the encouraged works contribute to the basic objectives of copyright law. Although it may be difficult to superficially distinguish between works created by AI and those created by natural persons, the essence of works created by AI may be an imitation of works by natural persons, with no necessarily incremental contributions in terms of knowledge, thoughts, emotions, and lacking guarantees in terms of moral or value systems, thus failing to provide the copyright value of promoting social and cultural development.[58]

Secondly, at the specific institutional theoretical level of copyright law, scholars further discuss the perspectives of the subject theory, object theory, and the inapplicability of neighbouring rights systems. Regarding the subject theory of copyright, some scholars propose that authors under copyright law are limited to human beings, so only when the author is a natural person can they possess the minimum level of thought and engage in original expression.[59] Regarding the object theory of copyright law, scholars propose that besides the form of expression, the originality determination of works under Chinese copyright law also needs to consider the intention of creation, which AI model outputs may not possess.[60] Some scholars also analyse the characteristics of works, arguing that besides being created by human authors, works also need to have diversity, value, and scarcity, which AI model

57. This viewpoint argues that holding only the developers of artificial intelligence responsible for infringement of AI-generated content without granting them the copyright to such content violates the principle of unity of rights and obligations. See: Wang Qian, *Revisiting the Qualification of AI-Generated Content in Copyright Law*, 4 Forum on Politics and Law (2023).

58. Liu Yinliang, *On the Copyright Status of Artificial Intelligence Works*, 3 Politics and Law 12 (2020).

59. Liu Yinliang, *On the Copyright Status of Artificial Intelligence Works*, 3 Politics and Law 5 (2020); Lan Chunjie, *From Generated Content to Basic Data: A New Direction for Legal Protection of Artificial Intelligence*, 3 Science and Law 25 (2020).

60. Chen Hu, *On the Non-Copyrightability of AI-Generated Content: Centered on Expression Forms*, Journal of Chongqing University 9 (Social Science Edition) 11 (5 July 2021); Yuan Bo, *On the Falsification of Copyright in the Field of Literature by Artificial Intelligence*, 6 Electronic Intellectual Property 26 (2018).

outputs may lack.[61] Regarding the applicability of neighbouring rights systems, some scholars point out from the perspectives of the establishment reasons for neighbouring rights and the reasons for advocating neighbouring rights protection that it is not appropriate to protect AI model outputs with this system. This perspective suggests that the establishment of neighbouring rights is due to significant capital investment in certain results and difficulty in identifying the authors, which do not apply to AI model outputs. Furthermore, neighbouring rights protection is closed, and current provisions cannot provide protection for AI model outputs.[62]

Although scholars holding the negative view believe that AI model outputs cannot be protected under copyright law, some suggest regulating behaviours in the field of AI through other means. Some scholars' perspectives suggest that it may be considered to regulate behaviour in the field of AI by establishing specialized management mechanisms, such as through classification, registration, time limits, and automatic licensing systems, to implement weak protection of property rights for AI model output content.[63] Others suggest shifting the focus from content generated by AI to the legal protection of the basic data used by AI, classifying and protecting various data according to their nature.[64] Some scholars propose adopting a competition law model to construct a protection path for AI model outputs, which has obvious advantages compared to the rights-based model, as it can regulate unfair competition behaviours that harm the interests of operators of AI model outputs based on the existing Anti-Unfair Competition Law.[65]

4.2 AI-Generated Output Infringes Existing Copyright

Regarding the first question, Chinese scholars assert that the content generated by AI may infringe upon the original author's rights, such as reproduction rights, adaptation rights, and the right of communication to the public on information networks. Some scholars propose that in the process of AI output, AI may extensively learn from the works of a particular author over a period, resulting in outputs with a style highly similar to that author's, potentially infringing upon the original author's reproduction rights.[66] Moreover, because the process of AI decomposing, learning, and recombining original works may produce adapted or compiled works, this may infringe upon the original author's adaptation and compilation rights.[67] Some scholars also point out

61. Liu Yinliang, *On the Copyright Status of Artificial Intelligence Works*, 3 Politics and Law 6-8 (2020).
62. Lan Chunjie, *From Generated Content to Basic Data: A New Direction for Legal Protection of Artificial Intelligence*, 3 Science and Law 26 (2020).
63. Liu Yinliang, *On the Copyright Status of Artificial Intelligence Works*, 3 Politics and Law 13 (2020).
64. Lan Chunjie, *From Generated Content to Basic Data: A New Direction for Legal Protection of Artificial Intelligence*, 3 Science and Law 26-29 (2020).
65. Rao Xiancheng, *Dilemmas and Ways Out: Choosing and Constructing the Protection Path of Artificial Intelligence Creations*, 11 Publishing Research 86 (2020).
66. Ye Zhaochi, *Tort Liability and Resolution Pathways of AI Model Output Content*, Journal of South-Central Minzu University (Humanities and Social Sciences) 6 (11 January 2024).
67. Ye Zhaochi, *Tort Liability and Resolution Pathways of AI Model Output Content*, Journal of South-Central Minzu University (Humanities and Social Sciences) 6 (11 January 2024);

that AI model outputs may infringe upon the author's right of communication to the public on information networks and broadcasting rights.[68] For instance, if the results of machine learning data analysis are publicly disclosed online in real time, it may constitute a violation of broadcasting rights; if the disclosure is delayed, it may infringe upon the right of communication to the public on information networks.

Additionally, some scholars argue that AI model outputs may also infringe upon personality rights, such as the right of portrait and privacy. Some argue that when AI outputs information, it may illegally use others' personal information to respond to users' queries, leading to the leakage of personal information and privacy. Furthermore, as generative AI can automatically generate images and videos, with the development of generative AI, it becomes increasingly difficult to distinguish from deepfakes, potentially infringing upon individuals' portrait rights.[69]

4.3 Remedies and Enforcement

Regarding the identification of the infringer and the remedies available, there are currently two main perspectives in academia. One perspective argues that the party bearing the liability for infringement should be the service provider of AI, while the other that different scenarios should be distinguished to clarify the legal liability of different entities. Scholars who advocate for the service provider to bear the liability for infringement believe that the service provider controls the pre-training data, optimization data, and algorithm design of generative AI products, thereby having significant control and decision-making power over the generated content, justifying their designation as the liable party.[70] Scholars who advocate for distinguishing different scenarios to determine liability argue that legal liability can be differentiated between AI users and service providers. If the service provider of generative AI develops products that generate false information or content with infringing properties, they should be held liable for infringement. Similarly, if users intentionally induce generative AI to produce false information and then disseminate it, this may also constitute infringement.[71]

Regarding the question of how to determine the principle of liability for infringement, the main perspective of Chinese scholars is that the principle of fault liability should be applied. For instance, some scholars propose that the civil liability of generative AI product providers can be determined based on the principle of fault liability, considering illegal acts, causality, and facts of damage.[72] Some scholars

---

Jiao Heping, *Copyright Risks and Resolutions in Data Acquisition and Utilization within AI Creation*, 4 Contemporary Law Science 132 (2022).

68. Jiao Heping, *Copyright Risks and Resolutions in Data Acquisition and Utilization within AI Creation*, 4 Contemporary Law Science 133 (2022).
69. Wang Liming, *Legal Responses to Infringements by Generative Artificial Intelligence*, 5 Chinese Journal of Applied Jurisprudence 29 (2023).
70. Sun Qi, *Research on the Legal Issues of Regulating Providers of Generative Artificial Intelligence Products*, 7 Politics and Law 167–169 (2023).
71. Wang Liming, *Legal Responses to Infringements by Generative Artificial Intelligence*, 5 Chinese Journal of Applied Jurisprudence 43 (2023).
72. Sun Qi, *Research on the Legal Issues of Regulating Providers of Generative Artificial Intelligence Products*, 7 Politics and Law 173 (2023).

advocate for differentiating scenarios for applying the principle of attribution, suggesting that the principle of presumption of fault should apply when service providers collect personal information on a large scale, while in other situations, the principle of fault liability should generally apply.[73] Some scholars suggest applying the principle of presumption of fault because the complexity and technical characteristics of generative AI make it difficult for plaintiffs to prove fault on the part of the provider.[74] Although there is no consensus on whether to apply the principle of fault liability or presumption of fault, scholars generally agree that the principle of strict liability should not be applied independently.

4.4 Summary

Regarding the issue of how to determine the principle of liability for infringement in the context of copyright issues related to generative AI output, the academic community has focused on in-depth discussions concerning the protection of AI-generated content, infringement issues, and remedies and liability determination.

In terms of the legal protection of generative AI output, the academic community has formed two major camps: the affirmative view and the negative view. Scholars advocating the affirmative view argue that AI-generated content should be included within the scope of copyright law protection and further explore the issue of rights attribution, including the feasibility of protecting the output as a work or subject of neighbouring rights under copyright law. Some scholars have argued for the copyrightability of generative AI output from perspectives such as the objective standard of originality, the subject theory of copyright law, and the legislative purpose, and have proposed various rights attribution schemes, such as attributing rights to the designer, investor, user, or based on contractual agreements. However, scholars holding the negative view criticize the copyrightability of generative AI output from the perspectives of the legislative purpose of copyright law, subject theory, and characteristics of the subject matter, arguing that it does not conform to the purpose and requirements of copyright law.

Regarding the determination of infringement in generative AI output, scholars generally believe that AI-generated content may infringe upon the copyright holder's rights, such as the right of reproduction, adaptation, compilation, and communication to the public on information networks, and may also involve infringement of personality rights, such as the right to portrait and privacy. In terms of remedies and liability allocation, the main viewpoints in the academic community include identifying the AI service provider as the liable party for infringement or distinguishing liability based on different scenarios. Concerning the principle of liability for infringement, scholars generally tend to apply the principle of fault liability or the presumption of fault, excluding the sole application of strict liability.

73. Wang Liming, *Legal Responses to Infringements by Generative Artificial Intelligence*, 5 Chinese Journal of Applied Jurisprudence 43 (2023).
74. Zhou Xuefeng, *Analysis of Liability for Infringement by Generative Artificial Intelligence*, 4 Comparative Law Research 125 (2023).

5. CONCLUSIONS

Artificial intelligence technology has developed rapidly in the past two years, and AI-generated content has achieved incredible expressive presentations. However, it must be said that groundbreaking AI-generated content is still in its infancy. It is premature to make final legal determinations about it at this stage. Currently, various viewpoints and discussions about AI-generated content in the fields of legislation, judiciary, academia, and industry are of positive significance in China and around the world. Essentially, they will play a role in safeguarding, promoting, regulating, and reflecting on the development of the AI industry. Law is not the primary driver of social development; in addressing the issues of AI development, considerations of safety, fairness, and efficiency are needed. We should start from the principle of maximizing human rights and prioritize the values of economics, sociology, anthropology, and technology ethics over jurisprudence.

China has clearly stated in the 'Interim Measures for the Management of Generative Artificial Intelligence Services' that the country adheres to the principle of giving equal importance to development and security, combining the promotion of innovation with governance according to law, and adopting effective measures to encourage the innovative development of generative AI services, implementing inclusive, cautious, and graded supervision.

In the legal regulation of AI training and outputting processes, a principle of balanced severity should be adopted. For example, by imposing strict intellectual property compliance obligations on AI developers during activities such as pre-training and optimization training of AI models, it may not be appropriate to require developers to bear strict liability for infringement during the AI content generation process. Conversely, if the reasonableness of using intellectual property data during AI model training is explained based on theories such as fair use, then clear allocation of potential liabilities for infringement and administrative responsibilities should be made during the AI content generation process, otherwise, it may lead to regulatory failure.

From the current development trend of AI, in the foreseeable future, AI will coexist and symbiotically evolve as a tool to assist human creativity, as a collaborator with humans, and as an independent generator. We tend to believe that if AI users can consciously use, instruct, select, and intervene in the final expression of AI-generated content, thereby representing human creative will and embodying human wisdom contributions, then the AI-generated content work should be protected by copyright law. Anthropologist Yuval Noah Harari once said, 'Human beings have been on earth for 2 million years, and all existing countries and religions/cultures are products of the past 5,000 years. All our "ancient traditions" are actually very new'.

AI-generated content should serve humanity, be determined by humanity, and belong to humanity.

Chapter 5

Finland

Elisa Huusko

1. INTRODUCTION

The copyright questions relating to training and use of artificial intelligence (AI) and AI-related works is a relatively novel matter in the Finnish legal system. The Finnish Copyright Act[1] does not contain any express terminology for AI and there is no case law from the Finnish courts either. The practitioners must rely on interpretation and use legal sources on a lower hierarchical level to support the interpretation. While legal certainty may be yet to be established, there are plenty of important legal rules and principles that will be considered by courts when they eventually take decisions in AI-related matters.

The most recent proposal for amendment of the copyright law refers to the EU publication, *Study on Copyright and New Technologies*,[2] but the written law is silent on any special treatment of AI-related works. Thus, it has been a conscious decision, that in the absence of further guidance from EU court of Justice,[3] the subject matter

1. Tekijänoikeuslaki 404/1961, unofficial translation https://finlex.fi/api/media/statute-foreign-language-translation/443836/mainPdf/main.pdf?timestamp=1961-07-08T00%3A00%3A00.000Z.
2. *Study on Copyright and New Technologies: Copyright Data Management and Artificial Intelligence*, Crowell & Moring, Directorate-General for Communications Networks, Content and Technology (European Commission), IMC University of Applied Sciences: Krems, Philippe Rixhon Associates, Technopolis Group, UC Louvain; EU publications 2022 (7 May 2024 https://op.europa.eu/en/publication-detail/-/publication/cc293085-a4da-11ec-83e1-01aa75ed71a1/language-en)
3. Since EU has legislated directives in the field of copyright, the national courts must ensure that the national law is interpreted in the light of the EU case law. *Flaminio Costa v. ENEL*, Case 6/64 (1964).

of copyright and AI is similarly assessed as copyright and any other written or artistic creation.[4] The section 1 of the Copyright Act holds that:

> '*A person*' who has created a literary or artistic work shall have copyright therein, whether it be a fictional or descriptive representation in writing or speech, a musical or dramatic work, a cinematographic work, a photographic work or other work of fine art, a product of architecture, artistic handicraft, industrial art, or expressed in some other manner.
>
> Maps and other descriptive drawings or graphically or three-dimensionally executed works and computer programs shall also be considered literary works.

Section 1 of the Finnish Copyright Act is understood to cover all kinds of works including software. The EU Court of Justice has a line of case law concerning the interpretation of concept of *work* and the same definition and criteria must be applied in and followed by the Finnish courts.[5]

The hierarchy of legal sources holds that courts cannot decide a case contrary to the express wording of the written law. The constitution can override regular law, and national decrees are of lower value than laws, but the conflict between written law and other legal sources must be decided in favour of the written law. Therefore, also in AI cases, the written law will be the point of departure in all interpretations. Written law (such as EU regulations and the national Copyright Act) is a so-called *compulsory legal source* and supersedes the case law and preparatory works that are used in the interpretation of the written laws. Case law and preparatory works are on the second level of the hierarchy and take the precedence over the third group of *other available legal sources*.

There exists a hierarchy within these three types of sources and especially in the second category, the value of case law depending on the court. A lower instance must comply with the decisions of higher instances and the market court, District Courts and Court of Appeal are expected to comply with the decisions of the EU Court of Justice and the Supreme Court of Justice and the Supreme Administrative Court of Justice – if the particulars of the case are similar. The value of case law and preparatory work may also depend on the language. If the casuistic nature of a decision is stressed by highlighting the exceptional circumstances, then the source is of lesser value than another decision that is formulated in a more general manner.

While legislating through court decisions is considered acceptable and some flexibility has often been intentionally left for the courts to take various circumstances and factors into account, legislating through preparatory works/*travaux préparatoires* is received with more cautiousness. If there is no case law, preparatory works will be followed, but it is to some extent expected that the case law will gain more significance over time while the preparatory works lose their importance as the time passes and society and surroundings change.

4. The Finnish Copyright Act (404/1961) Section 1 was renamed by Act (607/2015), paragraph 1 was amended by Act 446/1995 and paragraph 2 by Act (34/1991).
5. '*Work*' has become an *autonomous concept* in EU law and in addition to the effective parts of the EU Court of Justice's judgements the national courts observe the underlying reasonings.

The compulsory legal sources are then supplemented with available legal sources that contain research, peer reviewed articles, literature, international legal comparisons, and legal principles. The courts may find conclusions in literature convincing and can take them as a basis for decisions but in some difficult matters may need to be decided on the basis of the balancing of principles. The effects of the judgement (teleological interpretation) are of great importance especially if the decision is formulated to present a general rule and thereby given the value of a precedent. Balancing of fundamental rights and economic considerations will all play a role in the assessment of difficult cases.

One of the principles relating to copyright law is technological neutrality. The Copyright Act has been amended several times and the EU Court of Justice has introduced clarification of concepts and sometimes overruled prior national case law, but there are wordings and underlying principles in the law that date back to the time before 1960s. Harmonization of written law does not necessarily harmonize the principles, especially in cases where the written law lacks coherence. Technological neutrality has been an essential part of the Finnish system throughout its existence, and its role has been ensuring coherence and legal certainty. The concept of reproduction is at the core of copyright, and it has been of great importance that any kind of copying falls under the concept regardless of the level of automation and regardless of the methods or tools used or whether the reproduction is digital or analogue. Prohibition of the circumvention of technical measures was a notable exception to the principle of neutrality but increasing EU case law and Directives that address the use of technical measures have raised questions as to whether the principle remains alive or not. At least the principle should be noted and understood

Written law

(constitution,
EU regulations, Acts,
directives, degrees)

Case law, preparatory works

(higher instance supercedes lower, new
supersede old, general supersede casuistic)

Available sources

for example literature (preferably peer reviewed), committee
considerations, legal comparison, established practices, legal
principles, practical, ethical, moral, economic arguments

before one can assess whether it should have any effect on an individual matter. Exceptions and limitations to copyright may entail exceptions and limitations to underlying principles but extending an exception to a principle through interpretation may be found more undesirable than technologically neutral options that are fully in line with the principles.

Since *work* is an autonomous concept in the EU, relevance is given to the AI-related debate in the EU while the legal instruments and cases in other jurisdictions may be given informative value in legal comparison. The legal literature discussing EU case law is an acceptable source of legal information in Finnish courts, but as the number of research articles on the EU level makes comprehensive assessment impossible, and as there are many interest groups whose roles, incentives and intentions may not always be apparent to the judges, and further, as there exist related theories together with a wide range of opinions and underlying national law, the research articles and national literature, that have already been adapted to national surroundings may be more convincing and play a greater role in national courts.

AI matters currently rely on available sources of legal information.

The EU has approached AI through risk analysis and enacted an AI Act that is a regulation by its nature. While it is compulsory legislation and confirms that EU Directives on copyright must be respected, its preamble states that the AI Act does not affect the enforcement of copyright. It contains rules about transparency that the providers of foundation models must observe and expect, providing sufficient information to copyright owners to monitor and defend their rights. The providers of foundation models should have a specific policy in place about respecting copyright.

2. TRAINING AI MODELS

2.1 Training AI with Copyright Protected Works

Machine learning requires a great amount of material and most often it includes works that are copyright protected. While it is technically possible to use only material that is in the public domain and works that are excluded from copyright (such as laws, decisions, and official documents), the creation of generative AI that is of interest for non-lawyers requires much broader use of literary and artistic training material, which are most works in the meaning of copyright law. The use of open source or open licence documents (Creative Commons licences, open source software) is unlikely to solve the problem as the terms and conditions did not foresee the possibility of reproduction and storing for the purpose of creating commercial algorithms. Any contractual restrictions are legally binding irrespective of whether they protect economic or moral rights or intend to exclude liabilities.[6] Furthermore, the creation of large language models, or foundation models, require great amounts of training material to ensure sufficiency of generalization especially when the purpose

6. The attribution and notice requirements are legally binding on the user of open source material whether it has monetary value or not.

is training the AI to use natural language, and, in such case, it would be impractical or even impossible to collect the entire corpus from open source data.[7]

Using works in the training of AI systems requires taking several steps and some of them involve copying and/or reproduction of works. Section 2 of the Finnish Copyright Act holds that:

> Within the limitations imposed hereinafter, copyright shall provide the exclusive right to control a work by reproducing it and by making it available to the public, in the original form or in an altered form, in translation or in adaptation, in another literary or artistic form, or by any other technique.
>
> The reproduction of a work shall comprise making copies of the work in whole or in part, directly or indirectly, temporarily, or permanently and by any means or in any form whatsoever. The reproduction of a work shall also comprise the transfer of the work on to another device, by which it can be reproduced or communicated.

As the written law has been formulated very broadly, consent from the copyright holder is needed to train the AI unless one or more of the exceptions and limitations of copyright apply. Since creation of AI has been seen as desirable new technology and collecting consent would be practically impossible, the discussion on overcoming legal obstacles is ongoing and possibilities for broad interpretation of existing copyright exceptions are being debated.

The training of general-purpose AI aims at providing a language model that can then be used as a foundation in developing AI powered tools for more specific uses. The foundation loses its creative capabilities in the specialization process but gains in accuracy. The foundation model is a tool that creates text, pictures, and sounds, and with highly capable prompting it can produce content that is credible and could be taken for a human made. The foundation model can be unreliable and provide disinformation but is highly unlikely to replicate important parts of individual works because of the great amount of training material. It can be a powerful tool for creating new work-like content. When the general foundation model is further trained for a specific purpose, the training material is much more limited and has a stronger effect on the output. Specialized AI is a relevant competitor for human created content. It can imitate use styles and recognizable elements, and it can be instructed to produce new ones. AI powered tools are highly efficient and already in commercial use.

EU copyright does not differentiate between general-purpose AI and specialized AI. The act of training is similar with the exception that in the development of special-purpose AI, the training material is curated. A chat bot, for example, can be developed by training the model with questions and answers and by using product information and service descriptions, which are often lawfully available for the entity

---

7. Juha Vesala, *Developing Artificial Intelligence-Based Content Creation: Are EU Copyright and Antitrust Law Fit for Purpose?*, 54 ICC International Review of Intellectual Property and Competition Law 352 (2023), and Inger B. Ørstavik, *Access to Data for Training Algorithms in Machine Learning: Copyright Law and 'Right-Stacking'*, in Artificial Intelligence and the Media: Reconsidering Rights and Responsibilities 276–277 (Pihlajarinne & Alèn-Savikko eds 2022).

that trains the bot. In general, the training of general language models is perceived as desirable as it opens the market for developers of more specific AI. On the other hand, the training of specialized AI with copyrighted material made by a certain author or by a small group of known authors, is perceived as unfair and not desirable as it may affect the livelihood of impacted authors when it aims to overtake the market of specific kinds of works. Views are divided – allowing the training of a machine that can copy certain authors' personal style to produce work-like expressions that cause a likelihood of confusion with the author's recognizable style is perceived as unfair but the same applies to preventing or burdening of technological development that could increase productivity.

The EU AI Act puts the transparency obligations on providers of 'general-purpose' AI [sic] to allow copyright owners in creative industries to monitor whether their works have been used. Similar obligation would have been even more desirable in connection with more specific AI, at least for the time being, but eventually the general-purpose AI is likely to be developed to respond to needs that currently require more specialized programs, while commercial programs with limited use are likely to be trained in new tasks.

AI was not considered at the time the most recent digital single market package was discussed and when the Copyright Directive was enacted. None of the current exceptions seems to sufficiently cover all necessary steps of training AI and as all exceptions should always be interpreted narrowly, it seems that there is a need for a new legal instrument. A new exception could be a possibility, but since harmonization and enacting new laws is a slow process, there has been pressure to seek solutions through interpretation.[8] Even if broad application of an existing exception is adopted, it may relieve the pressure but fails to address the matter for the future.

2.2 Exceptions and Limitations Allowing Training of AI

AI is already widely used, and it has a material role in various kinds of business strategies. The change has been fast and new AI powered services and AI produced content is being made available at an increasing pace. Some organizations consider how to use AI in performing current tasks and others consider how to disrupt the market by creating services and performing tasks where AI is native, and some consider both. The world is currently adapting to the changing surroundings, and several interest groups already have expectations relating to limitations and the limitation of the limitations. Ideally the legal rules are focused on addressing the protectable and justified interest without affecting others and without creating obstacles for trade.

2.2.1 Temporary Reproduction

An existing exception concerning technically necessary temporary reproduction has been identified as one of the exceptions that could be available for authorizing AI

8. Juha Vesala, *Developing Artificial Intelligence-Based Content Creation: Are EU Copyright and Antitrust Law Fit for Purpose?*, 54 ICC International Review of Intellectual Property and Competition Law, 354–355 (2023).

training. Section 11a of the Finnish Copyright Act states that the reproduction right does not apply to temporary reproduction which is a) transient or incidental; b) integral and essential part of a technological process; c) the sole purpose of which is (to enable a transmission of a work in a network between third parties by an intermediary or) a lawful use of a work; and d) which has no independent economic significance.[9] While it is understandable that pressure to find justification for the exception is strong, this section cannot be applied without difficulties. It simply does not cover reproduction of material from a source of the developer's choice when the use has independent economic significance and when the reproduction is needed to create new tools and commercial products. Some academics and researchers consider that the economic significance is not with the use of any individual work, but with the use of great number of works, which is which is a convincing argument, but the exception continues to be challenge because copying is not incidental. At least in the training of curated foundation models, the sources are carefully selected. Transiency is arguable with respect to certain phases of AI training,[10] but no matter how the training is organized, the desirable space for allowing AI training remains incomplete. There exists a need for allowing collection and saving of entire corpuses of source material and the said process involves copying in one or the other phase. The copies are reproductions whether centralized or de-centralized, and there is a requirement of *lawful use*, that cannot be ensured when the training corpus is not curated, and further, as conditions of temporary reproduction exception were not drafted to allow AI training and as all exceptions are generally interpreted narrowly, there are important problems with this approach.[11] Therefore, as some kind of exception is needed for training of AI and a temporary copying exception seems insufficient for the purpose, researchers have turned to another exception concerning text and data mining.[12]

2.2.2 Text and Data Mining

Since data mining is defined as 'any automated analytical technique aimed at analysing text and data in digital form in order to generate information which includes but is not limited to patterns, trends and correlations' in the DSM Directive, it does seem to cover the kind of systematic repeated learning that takes place in the teaching of

9. The text is similar to Art. 5(1) of Directive 2001/29/EC of the European Parliament and of the Council on the harmonisation of certain aspects of copyright and related rights in the information society (InfoSoc Directive).
10. Giorgio Franceschelli & Mirco Musolesi, *Copyright in generative deep learning* el-17-6, el 17-8 (Cambridge University Press, Data & Policy 4, 2002). Authors note that if the data is stored in random access memory and then erased, the reproduction is transient, but since the creation and storage of the model is not transient by its nature, the condition remains problematic.
11. Juha Vesala, *Developing Artificial Intelligence-Based Content Creation: Are EU Copyright and Antitrust Law Fit for Purpose?*, 54 ICC International Review of Intellectual Property and Competition Law 360–365 (2023).
12. Jan Bernd Nordemann & Jonathan Pukas, *Copyright exceptions for AI training data – will there be an international level playing field?*, 17:12 Journal of Intellectual Property Law & Practice 973–974 (December 2022).

AI.[13] Data mining exceptions apply to use of lawfully accessible works by research organizations' data mining as well as commercial data mining if the copyright or database right owner has not expressly and appropriately reserved the right. The Finnish Copyright Act 13 b § holds that:

> One who has lawful access to the work may make copies of it for use for text and data mining and keep copies exclusively for that purpose, unless the author has expressly and appropriately reserved this right.
>
> Research organizations and cultural heritage institutions that have lawful access to the work may make copies of it for text and data mining in scientific research and keep them for scientific research, including for later verification of research results, provided that copies of the work are only available to those entitled to do so. What is stipulated in this paragraph above cannot be deviated from by agreement, nor can it be prevented by technical means.

The problem with this exception is that the works are available *for use in data mining only* and while the data mining and training of AI have technical overlaps, they are used for different objectives. If we overlook the fact that the interpretation is not in line with the express wording of law, there are also other problems with the scope of the exception. It has the criterion of lawful access, which is prima facie balanced, but very difficult to observe. Sometimes the distinction between lawful and unlawful appears relatively easy to make. Using an electronic library containing public domain works is free from copyright concerns, and using an online library containing books, music, audiovisual material, or news articles behind a payment wall, constitutes unlawful use if no payment is made. All material acquired by circumvention of technical measures is by definition unlawful in the EU.[14] For anything in between public domain and material with technical restrictions, 'lawful access' may be a challenging condition to meet. Consent makes the use lawful, but the consent may have been granted or denied for a specific kind of reproduction and making available to the public. The interpretation of such consent is narrow, and it may not cover the act of data mining or machine learning merely because the possibility was not considered at the time of publication. It should also be borne in mind that 'lawful access' has also been found to mean use of material that falls outside the exclusive right of the copyright owner, for example extracts that are so small that they could not be considered works as they fail to meet the requirement of originality.[15]

The EU AI Act (2024/1689)[16] Recital 105 suggests that text and data mining could be a suitable exception to authorize the training of AI. The Recital holds that

13. Inger B. Ørstavik, *Access to Data for Training Algorithms in Machine Learning: Copyright Law and 'Right-Stacking'*, in Artificial Intelligence and the Media: Reconsidering Rights and Responsibilities 286 (Pihlajarinne & Alèn-Savikko eds 2022).
14. Juha Vesala, *Developing Artificial Intelligence-Based Content Creation: Are EU Copyright and Antitrust Law Fit for Purpose?*, 54 ICC International Review of Intellectual Property and Competition Law 357–359 (2023).
15. Inger B. Ørstavik, *Access to Data for Training Algorithms in Machine Learning: Copyright Law and 'Right-Stacking'*, in Artificial Intelligence and the Media: Reconsidering Rights and Responsibilities 290 (Pihlajarinne & Alèn-Savikko eds 2022).
16. Regulation (EU) 2024/1689 of the European Parliament and of the Council of 13 June 2024 laying down harmonised rules on artificial intelligence and amending Regulations (EC)

that text and data mining techniques may be used in the training of a language model and then continues that if these techniques are used, then the opt out (reservation) in the text and data mining exception must be observed. Article 53 of the AI Act discusses general-purpose AI providers' transparency obligations. The providers of general-purpose AI must publish technical documentation and documentation about their compliance with EU laws. According to Article 53(1)(c), general-purpose AI providers must have a copyright policy in place. This policy should observe the reservations that copyright holders can make against commercial text and data mining.

It is likely that despite the different purpose, text and data mining is considered at least one of the exceptions that apply to the training of AI. It is also likely that 'lawful access' and conditions for effective reservation will be further specified by the CJEU. It would be very difficult to argue that the acts that have been previously held unlawful, would be lawful for AI training and data mining purposes without accepting special treatment of AI technology.[17] Furthermore, uncontrolled AI training uses all websites including those that contain obviously unlawful material, such as the contents of pirate sites, and it remains to be seen how the courts react to using them in language model training. Training AI for commercial purposes may be difficult to fit within the data mining exception without liberal interpretation of 'lawful'. The conditions for the text and data mining exception for research purposes is easier to fulfil because the potential reservations prohibiting data mining can be ignored and there is at least some room for allowing storage of material for research purposes, the requirement of 'lawful access' applies to research as well.[18]

The database right has also been identified as a potential challenge for machine learning and can be an obstacle for use of databases as source material. The right applies only to databases where obtaining, verification or presentation of data has required substantial investment and it could potentially protect source material used for the training, although many databases are collected in a manner that falls outside the definition of a protected database.[19] If the database right was to be applied to data collection used in the teaching of AI, then a licence for use of a third party owned database is needed unless a specific restriction applies. The exception applies to the

No. 300/2008, (EU) No. 167/2013, (EU) No. 168/2013, (EU) 2018/858, (EU) 2018/1139 and (EU) 2019/2144 and Directives 2014/90/EU, (EU) 2016/797 and (EU) 2020/1828 (Artificial Intelligence Act) (AI Act).

17. The law strives to be technology-neutral and the threshold for accepting different treatment of AI technology through interpretation is likely to be high.
18. Juha Vesala, *Developing Artificial Intelligence-Based Content Creation: Are EU Copyright and Antitrust Law Fit for Purpose?*, 54 IIC International Review of Intellectual Property and Competition Law 359 (2023).
19. Court of Justice of the European Union Case C-444/02 Fixtures Marketing Ltd v. Organismos prognostikon agonon podosfairou AE (OPAP), 9 November 2004, ECLI:EU:C:2004:697 'databases refers to any collection of works, data or other materials, separable from one another without the value of their contents being affected, including a method or system of some sort for the retrieval of each of its constituent materials, The expression 'investment in ... the obtaining ... of the contents' of a database in Article 7(1) of Directive 96/9 must be understood to refer to the resources used to seek out existing independent materials and collect them in the database. It does not cover the resources used for the creation of materials which make up the contents of a database'.

normal exploitation of a database and extracting and use of insubstantial parts of a database which are authorized for any user who has lawfully acquired the database.[20] Like copyright exceptions, the database exception contains several problems and as the data mining exception covers both copyright and database right and as it could therefore solve the problems relating to both forms of protection, many researchers consider it a more lucrative choice for authorizing AI training.

Despite the problems, many researchers are of the opinion that the data mining and temporary reproduction exceptions could be interpreted broadly and applied to the training of AI, because the interpretation is an internal matter in the EU and while it may not be the most elegant way of endorsing the system coherence and reading the law, at least the broad interpretation is unlikely to conflict with international agreements. AI has created a need for creative interpretation of existing copyright exceptions and the three-step test of the Berne Convention[21] for legislating and applying copyright exceptions could be satisfied. The test requires that the exempted use is for a special need, does not conflict with the normal exploitation of the work and safeguards the legitimate interests of the author. If the copyright holder has not made any reservations concerning data mining, its interests are likely to remain unharmed even in the case that the datamining exception would be used to authorize AI training.[22]

A German court, Landgericht Hamburg, rejected temporary copying in the case *Robert Kneschke v. LAION e.V.*, (Case No. 310 O 227/23) and instead applied the text and data mining exception to allow training of AI.[23] The German court observed the indirect reference to the exception in Article 53 of the AI Act when considering applicability of the exception and conducted the three-step test. The decisions of German courts are not binding on Finnish courts, but the decision falls into the category of allowed legal sources that may be observed in decision making. Although Germany has implemented the DSM Directive using different wording than the Finnish legislator, the case contains interpretations of the same concepts. The court decided that copying of pictures on a freely available web page falls under the text and data mining exception and took a view that the reservation made on the web page is

20. Inger B. Ørstavik, *Access to Data for Training Algorithms in Machine Learning: Copyright Law and 'Right-Stacking'*, in Artificial Intelligence and the Media: Reconsidering Rights and Responsibilities 282–284 (Pihlajarinne & Alèn-Savikko eds 2022).
21. The three-step test: 1) special case; 2) no conflicts with normal exploitation of the work; and 3) no unreasonable prejudice to the legitimate interests of the rightholder. Art. 9(2): 'It shall be a matter for legislation in the countries of the Union to permit the reproduction of such works in certain special cases, provided that such reproduction does not conflict with a normal exploitation of the work and does not unreasonably prejudice the legitimate interests of the author.'
22. Discussion on the difficulties in verifying such reservation, for example Juha Vesala, *Developing Artificial Intelligence-Based Content Creation: Are EU Copyright and Antitrust Law Fit for Purpose?*, 54 ICC International Review of Intellectual Property and Competition Law 351–380 (2023); and Inger B. Ørstavik, *Access to Data for Training Algorithms in Machine Learning: Copyright Law and 'Right-Stacking'*, in Artificial Intelligence and the Media: Reconsidering Rights and Responsibilities (Pihlajarinne & Alèn-Savikko eds 2022).
23. It rejected the temporary copying exception as the copying was not incidental nor part of an independent technical process and deleting of the corpus afterwards was not done automatically.

valid as it is express and sufficiently specific.[24] Reservation in machine readable and standard form would be more desirable when automated processes are used, but at least for the time being, human understandable, express and specific disclaimer is sufficient. The court applied text and data mining exception for scientific use because the copying was done by a scientific association. It did not make the distinction that the AI had thereafter been used commercially.[25] The case speaks in favour of accepting text and data mining as one of the available exceptions and limitations.

As previously mentioned, no AI-related cases have been tried in the courts in Finland and the possibility of some kind of creative justification in case law cannot be entirely excluded. Such creative authorization may be found from interpretation of existing copyright exceptions, but other alternatives are also possible. For example, before linking rules were specified by the EU Court of Justice, the Finnish law tolerated the existence of a *silent consent (implied licence)*[26] for hyperlinking, where normal users of the internet were assumed to understand the possibility of using hyperlinks to provide access to a publicly available work.[27] An implied licence is and instrument that has not been examined in the AI-related literature, but there would be at least some institutional support for applying it in Finland. For the time being and although the matter is being debated, in the absence of further instructions from courts, the legal status remains unclear.[28]

2.3 Remedies and Enforcement

According to the Finnish Copyright Act section 56g, if a person infringes copyright, the Court of Justice may prohibit him or her from proceeding with or repeating the act.

24. Hamburg Regional Court, Germany [2024]: *Robert Kneschke v. LAION e.V.*, Case No. 310 O 227/23 paragraph 9 cites the disclaimer on the web page 13.01.2021 https://www...com/de/usage.html on 13.1.2021: 'You may not use automated programs, applets, bots or the like to access the [XXX].com website or any content thereon for any purpose, including, by way of example only, downloading content, indexing, scraping or caching any content on the website'.
25. Regional Court of Hamburg, judgment of 27.09.2024, case no. 310 O 227/23 (REWIS RS 2024, 7778)
26. An implied licence is an instrument that has not been examined in the literature, but there would be at least some institutional support for applying it in Finland. Juha Vesala approaches the implied licence when assessing the interpretation of the data mining exception when he asks if a lack of express denying can be an authorization and when questioning whether a payment wall is any restriction that would protect the material from data mining at all. The purpose of the contract is to ensure income from the availability of works for consuming and not for the purpose of preventing machines from learning.
27. TN 2015:3. The Copyright Council of Finland has issued an opinion where silent consent to linking was deemed to exist. The basis for this opinion relied on Finnish legal literature: Taina Pihlajarinne, *Lupa linkittää – toisen aineiston hyödyntämisen tekijänoikeudelliset rajat* 222–223 (2012), and Katariina Sorvari, *Vastuu tekijänoikeuden loukkauksesta erityisesti tietoverkkoympäristössä* 258–259 (2005), where the silent consent was seen as a possibility, if the acts of the parties can be objectively assessed to be in line with the existence of such consent and nothing refers to the contrary.
28. Kristiina Harenko, Martti Kivistö, Valtteri Niiranen & Pekka Tarkela, *Tekijänoikeus* 179–180 (2024).

Whenever an author makes a demand on the basis of copyright infringement, he or she can demand that the court prohibits reproducing the work and making it available to the public, in the original form or in an altered form, in translation or in adaptation, in another literary or artistic form, or by any other technique. In such a case, the provider of AI must remove the infringing work from the corpus of the AI. Furthermore, the corpus should not contain any portions of the infringing work if these portions meet the threshold of originality, and it should not contain any adapted and altered versions of the work.

It is unlikely that the court would find further AI infringement after the deletion of infringing copies of works. If a work has been used at some part of the process and removed thereafter, there is naturally no evidence of further infringement either.

Should there be unauthorized copying, the court has the power to confirm that the act constitutes an infringement, and it can decide to deny further infringements. The court can place a permanent or temporary interruption order against continuing the infringement. If the infringer is unknown, prevention of the infringement may be available under certain conditions.

Section 57 holds that the infringer must pay reasonable compensation to the author. The amount of reasonable compensation is normally close to typical licence fee for authorized use of the work for similar purposes. In addition, if the copyright infringement is intentional, then the infringer must pay damages for actual losses. There are no punitive damages available and therefore the infringed party is able to recoup only those losses that can be shown. In reality the infringement may cause loss of opportunities and loss of potentially available commercial contracts, but these losses are not compensated. The same loss of licence fee cannot be demanded twice. The remedies are small for an author whose individual work has been used to train un-curated general AI.

Regular infringement is a civil law matter but there are also criminal sanctions available, and fines can be imposed on infringers whose infringement is intentional or considered gross negligence. These sanctions are available against infringements including importing or exporting of works that are produced in circumstances that would have been punishable in Finland.[29] While AI may have been produced in circumstances where copyright infringement takes place, the condition of importing or exporting a *work* must be fulfilled. If the matter is indeed punishable, the order that the infringing copy is confiscated or destroyed is under the Finnish Copyright Act section 58.[30]

3. USE OF AI SYSTEMS

The previous chapter discusses the training of AI and the role of the training material. Training AI is about reproducing material whereas commercial use of AI is making available an algorithm with or without the training material. Whenever the collection of training material, corpus, contains works, the temporary and permanent reproduction and making the corpus available to the public fall within the scope of copyright holder's exclusive right. Permission from copyright holders is required

29. Finnish Copyright Act, Art. 56a.
30. Finnish Copyright Act, Art. 58.2.

for the commercial use of the corpus. However, if an algorithm is used without the corpus and the use of AI does not involve making available the works or parts of works modified or unmodified, then making available of the algorithm only does not fall within the exclusive right of the authors.

Commercial AI applications and open-source AI applications are distributed with terms and conditions that specify the rights and obligations of the parties, including the scope of the licence grant and related restrictions. The terms and conditions are also likely to address the rights relating to prompts. AI can be instructed by prompts (or commands) which are unlikely to be works in the meaning of the Copyright Act. The Copyright Council of Finland has a relatively long list of interpretations of copyright on short expressions. Normal sentences and names of works are most often considered to lack copyright protection. The Council considers whether anyone could create and use the same short expression in describing the same kind of outcome. If so, the expression is not a work as it does not meet the threshold for originality.[31] For example, the normal conjugation of verbs is normal use of everyday language while notable variations from normal grammar rules and spelling can express free and creative choices to the extent that a sentence is original in the sense of copyright. While it is possible to use works such as poems as prompts, normal prompts are unlikely to be anything but use of common language because of their nature as clear and precise instructions. Cautiousness is however advisable when AI applications summarize or translate documents as the documents can be used as training data.[32]

Training of AI through users' prompting with works is a matter that a provider of AI must consider when mitigating risks. Drafting licence restrictions, indemnification clauses and termination clauses may provide some security against unintentional infringements, and the prompt data can be curated to exclude unauthorized copies of works from the corpus. The use of algorithm that has been trained without collecting corpus does not involve acts that fall within the scope of copyright and in such case, the temporary copy of the prompt work is done by the user.

If the user is a private person, taking a single copy of a work for private use is subject to an express limitation of copyright and it does not constitute a copyright infringement. The private use exception does not cover copying of works from databases, copying of computer programs, musical works and cinematographic works and the user cannot use the work for any other purpose.[33] Therefore, if movie rating

31. TN 2010:11, a sentence published in a book ('kuningas kutsui narrin luokseen' / 'the king called the jester to him') was not a work as it was descriptive expression that could have been written by anyone who wishes to express the same interaction with the persons. TN 2011:2, a name of publication series ('rockin korkeat korot' / 'high heels of rock') was a typical and short name that anyone could have come up with when connecting rock and roll and women artists. TN 2010:2, an extract of lyrics that contain two untypical expressions with rhythmic appearance was a work ('kaikki on vinksin vonksin tai ainakin heikun keikun') even if the two untypical expressions ('vinksin vonksin' and 'heikun keikun') did not, as such, meet the originality threshold.
32. It can be difficult to verify the effectiveness of any potential contractual restriction as the likelihood of becoming aware of its breach is very small. The problem of uneven information is not however unique to AI licences and there are mechanisms to ensure negative incentives against harmful conduct.
33. Finnish Copyright Act, Art. 12.

AI or series digest AI or music mashup AI become commonplace, the providers of databases, software, movies and music may need to consider how their own terms and conditions address the matter, but they do not need to worry about losing control over the works, because the private copies cannot be used for any purpose other than private use.

Making reproductions of works and making works available for commercial use falls within the scope of copyright protection. Most small and medium-sized companies lack the resources for building large foundation models. Instead, they design, develop and provide AI applications by using commercially available products that use the algorithms of pre-trained foundation models. Many of the commercially available foundation models have been optimized for a certain particular purpose and are provided for further adaptation. The potential infringing nature of training foundation models is solved in a jurisdiction that creates and controls the foundation model while the small users of them can develop their applications in a more secure environment. The adaptation and use of the foundation model through application provider interface does not reproduce or make available the works that were used in the training of the foundation model (large corpus of works) and many foundation models contain encoded restrictions that prohibit the reproducing of more than certain small amount from a single source material. The local AI application providers can therefore avoid the greatest risks in training and use of AI and focus on controlling their own use, adaptation and making available of the AI application of their choice. They build and control their own corpus, and the training and use of the AI product does not conflict with the rights of any copyright owners if the adaptation (final training) is done by using own material or material that is created or licensed for this particular purpose. Also, open source material and open data can be used if the licence does not contain restrictions with respect to economic or moral rights.

AI applications can be computer programs that are subject to copyright protection whenever and to the extent they are programmed by persons who make independent, free and creative choices in the programming work.[34] The rights to such AI applications are originally with the programmers, but the copyright law automatically transfers the copyright to the employer of the programmer.[35] Therefore, the company who provides the AI application is likely to own the exclusive right to the program, its preparatory works and related vector databases unless otherwise agreed with the employees or with the provider of the foundation model. However, although human creativity and effort may be essential in the programming and initial preparations for the training of the algorithm, the AI may develop over time and eventually the algorithm may have changed to something that has not been made

34. Taina Pihlajarinne, Alexander Thesleff, Leo Leppänen & Sini Valmari, *The European Copyright System as a Suitable Incentive for AI-Based Journalism* 221 (https://www.elgaronline.com/ at 4 March 2024).
35. According to the Finnish Copyright Act 40 b § 1, if a computer program and a work directly associated with it have been created in the scope of duties in private employment, the copyright in the computer program and the work shall pass to the employer. The same shall correspondingly apply to a computer program and a work directly associated therewith, created within the scope of a civil service post.

by the developers and something that was not even predictable by the developers.[36] If the causal link between author's free and creative choices and the work is lost, the copyright protection is no longer applicable in the light of the current EU law. The EU law does not provide copyright on the basis of causing of the work to come into existence, but on the free and creative choices that cause the work to be made.[37]

The Finnish Copyright Council (which operates under the Ministry of Culture and Education) provides recommendations for the interpretation of originality requirement and although it has not clarified its view on AI-created computer programs, it has previously discussed computer programs. The author's free and creative choices will be stressed in originality considerations and the author's personality must be somehow reflected in the AI application for it to become copyright protected. Therefore, AI created computer programs and algorithms are unlikely to meet the threshold of being a work in the meaning of Finnish copyright law. The recommendations highlight the importance of independent choices and authors creativity in connection to copyright in computer programs and the Council has held that technically obvious or required outcomes do not meet the required level of originality already prior to EU Court of Justice's decisions on the matter. There are no signs that the line of interpretation will change without any new legislative measures.[38]

It should also be borne in mind that copyright and trade secrets have always been complementary when protecting software. Trade secrets can also be useful with AI and according to Kallioniemi, secrecy may be a better form of protection for AI than copyright as it can cover the information on how to compile and organize the optimal training material, set targets, and create connections and prioritization. This information may even be the most valuable part of the training process as it affects the way AI adjusts over time even though the system may thereafter learn new connections and prioritization while performing as expected. In addition, there is no requirement that a secret should be made by a person.[39]

36. Taina Pihlajarinne, Alexander Thesleff, Leo Leppänen & Sini Valmari, *The European Copyright System as a Suitable Incentive for AI-Based Journalism* 222–223 (https://www.elgaronline.com/ at 4 March 2024).
37. Rognstad Ole Andreas, *Creations caused by humans (or robots)? Artificial intelligence and causation requirements for copyright protection in EU law*, in Artificial Intelligence and the Media: Reconsidering Rights and Responsibilities 181–182 (Pihlajarinne & Alèn-Savikko eds 2022).
38. Anette Alén-Savikko, Rosa Ballardini & Taina Pihlajarinne, *Tekoälyn tuotokset ja omaperäisyysvaatimus – kohti koneorientoitunutta tekijänoikeutta?*, 7–8 Lakimies 985, 989–990 (2018)
39. Ismo Kallioniemi *Tekoälyoikeus* 19, 55, 59–61 (Alma Talent 2022). Kallioniemi discusses the identification of a trade secret as part of a definition of trade secret and as a condition for protecting secret information. Machines can create secrets, but problems arise if a person is an owner of a secret, that she does not know herself. Also, questions relating to secrecy of information that concern use of publicly available information are being discussed, but maintaining secrecy of this type of information may be very challenging in any event.

4. OUTPUT OF AI AND COPYRIGHT ISSUES

4.1 Copyright Protection of AI-Generated Content

Following the hierarchy of legal sources there are solid grounds to assume that the output of AI is not a work in the meaning of copyright, as only a natural person (human being) can be an author. The written law states that 'a person' shall have copyright. The same can be concluded from the CJEU case law concerning the definition of work and originality threshold. The Court has repeatedly required human characteristics such as reflecting of author's personal touch, reflecting of author's personality and expression of author's creative abilities when assessing whether the author has made sufficiently free and creative choices. A similar conclusion on requirement of human authorship dominates legal discussions and peer reviewed articles, although some considerations about the potential of *sui generis* laws for robot and AI created works does exist.[40]

AI can make inventions and produce output that is unique. The more autonomous the AI, the stronger the need to find someone or something that is accountable for its acts, including IPR infringements, but instead of allowing AI and robots to hold rights and obligations or legal personhood, other instruments such as insurance could be investigated to address the problem. If AI robots develop the ability to independently assess morals and ethical consequences and the ability to make independent and unique creative works and provided that the AI copyleft is found inefficient to incentivize desirable technological development, there may be room to challenge the criterion of originality requirement and to consider some *sui generis* rights for the protection of the output, but there is a consensus that such changes would require new legislative measures.[41]

While a machine cannot be an author, the user of AI can be an author of an AI assisted work. In such case, the user has a creative input in the expression and AI has the role of a tool. Copyright law has already previously been found to have some tolerance for works where the exact expression is dictated partially by a factor other than the author. The author must in such cases use free and creative choices in the setup and conditions where the work is created.[42] While the protection of AI assisted works is widely accepted, there also exists a demand for recognizing some rights to AI created works or alternatively AI as the author. Such futuristic arguments are reasoned with arguments such as ensuring investment incentives, political

40. Rosa Maria Ballardini, Kan He & Teemu Roos, *AI-Generated Content: Authorship and Inventorship in the Age of Artificial Intelligence*, 6–9, 11–13 (2018).
41. Rosa Maria Ballardini & Robert van den Hoven van Genderen, *Artificial intelligence and intellectual property rights: the quest or plea for artificial intelligence as a legal subject*, 209–214 (https://www.elgaronline.com/ at 4 March 2024).
42. Ole-Andreas Rognstad, *Creations caused by humans (or robots)? Artificial intelligence and causation requirements for copyright protection in EU law*, in Artificial Intelligence and the Media: Reconsidering Rights and Responsibilities 185–189 (Pihlajarinne & Alèn-Savikko eds 2022).

considerations, use of other alternative and more restrictive means of protection, and practical difficulties of identifying the human input, for example.[43]

The output of AI is unlikely to be a reproduction of any pre-existing work, but the possibility of such event cannot be entirely excluded. While independently created expressions do not infringe the copyright of others, AI created output is unlikely to be found independent. The output can infringe the copyright of authors of the works that have been used in the training material. However, the risks relating to infringement may be substantially reduced by preventing the AI from reproducing long extracts from a single source and by using large amounts of training data.

The legislator has already taken steps to ensure that the greatest risks related to AI will be mitigated in the EU and in Finland as a member state of the EU. The AI Act will be imperative law, and requires that companies are open about their use of AI. It should, therefore, be clear whether the output has been generated by AI or by a person. This information should be informative of whether anyone can claim exclusive rights to the output, but it remains to be seen if there exists a need to legislate about false attribution. Using training material from a single artist could make partial reproductions more likely and reproduce a certain artist's style in a manner that confusion may arise as to whether a work is authentic in the sense that it has been made by the artist in question. Personal handwriting and handwritten signatures for example may also be vulnerable to misuse in future.

4.2 Protection of AI-Generated Content Through Neighbouring Rights

Copyright law has evolved throughout its history and there are documents that recognize the need to protect authors' rights against unauthorized commercial use of their works from the past 1,500 years. It is obvious that the rules develop over time, old rules become outdated, and new ones need to be enacted. One way to fix and patch the system has been laws relating to neighbouring rights. Neighbouring rights are almost like copyright as they are related to copying or recording. They protect the results of effort and investment rather than the personal relation between the author and the work, and therefore there are no obstacles to conclude that a producers' rights to a recording could cover AI created content.

The producer is the person who has first recorded the sound or audiovisual content. According to current praxis, one who is technically or mechanically involved in the process is not the producer, but it is the one who carries economic responsibility for making the recording. There are no requirements with respect to the recorded sound. It does not need to be a work in the meaning of copyright law, and it does not need to be a result of a person's activity. Any kind of sound is sufficient. Sounds in nature whether created by flora or fauna and events such as a storm can be recorded by a producer and protected with producer's rights.[44]

A producer who carries economic and operational responsibility for recording AI-generated sounds could enjoy producer's rights to the recording, and similarly

43. Mikko Antikainen, *Surviving Technological Change: Towards More Coherent Regulation of Digital Creativity Through EU Copyright and Design Law*, 61–63 (2021).
44. Kristiina Harenko, Martti Kivistö, Valtteri Niiranen & Pekka Tarkela, *Tekijänoikeus* 499 (2024).

the producer of video content could have video producer's rights to the recording of audiovisual or visual content. The scope of protection is almost the same in sound and movie recordings, but sound recordings are protected against performing the same publicly to an audience present at the performance. Double protection is however not possible as the sound recording right only applies if movie recording does not.[45]

A phonograph record or any other device on which sound has been recorded shall not, without the consent of the producer:

1) be transferred on to a device by means of which it can be reproduced;
2) be performed publicly to an audience present at the performance;
3) be communicated to the public by wired or by wireless means, including communication of the recorded material to the public in a manner which enables members of the public to access the work from a place and at a time individually chosen by them;
4) be distributed to the public

until fifty years have elapsed from the year during which the recording took place

The protection subsists until seventy years have elapsed from the year during which the recording was published or made available to the public for the first time. The law contains mechanisms for terminating the protection or transfer agreement if the recording remains unused and unpublished for fifty years.

The producer's right is not entirely free from problems as it was not intended to protect AI-generated content. Copyright protection has always been held to be better and have a form of protection with greater cover, and whenever this broader right is available then the neighbouring right does not apply. The Finnish Copyright Council has decided that computer games are not movies or audiovisual content where producer's rights could apply and the same has been outlined in the *travaux préparatoires* of the Finnish Copyright Act section 46a.[46] Traditionally computer games and videogames have not been deemed to be 'movies' as they are intended for playing and they are controlled by the user. In case AI created movies are to be protected by producer's rights there may be a reason to reconsider the definition of a movie and whether it should be extended at least partially to games or alternative story telling. The Beijing Treaty on Audiovisual Performances of 24 June 2012, would not prevent broader interpretation. According to Article 2 '"audiovisual fixation" means the embodiment of moving images, whether or not accompanied by sounds or by the representations thereof, from which they can be perceived, reproduced, or communicated through a device'.[47]

Furthermore, Finnish Copyright Act section 47 holds that a sound recording that has been published for commercial purposes and copies of which have been distributed or which has been communicated to the public, may be used: 1) directly or indirectly in a public performance; 2) in an original communication to the public in a manner other than one enabling members of the public to access the recorded performance or material at a place and time chosen by them; 3) for simultaneous and unaltered retransmission of a radio or television broadcast for reception by the

45. Finnish Copyright Act Art. 46.4.
46. HE 287/1994, s. 80 and TN1992:3 (*Nintendo*).
47. World Intellectual Property Organization (WIPO) TRT/BEIJING/001.

public. In other words, there is a compulsory licence that allows the use of recordings that are published and commercially available. The radio broadcasters and event organizers, restaurants and other public performances can play the commercially available music recording if fees are paid to a collecting society. Performers should not be compensated but the publisher's right falls within the scope of section 47. This section applies only to public performance that takes place in Finland and applies to recordings that are made in Finland and are commercially available.

4.3 Remedies and Enforcement

Remedies concerning infringement of publishers' rights are in principle the same as for copyright infringements but since the scope of neighbouring rights is much narrower, they are assessed in a different manner. Civil law remedies cover all acts that are contrary to copyright law whereas criminal law sanctions are written to protect copyrighted works and authors' economic and moral rights. Moral rights cannot be infringed or remedied when there is no moral right, and whenever there is a compulsory licence that applies to the use of neighbouring right, only outstanding licence fees can be demanded as compensation.

Like in infringement of copyright also in infringements of neighbouring rights, the court can order discontinuing of the infringing acts and that the infringer to pay compensation for the use of neighbouring right. Furthermore, damages for wilful infringements are available.

5. CONCLUSIONS

While only a human can be an author, a human can use tools in his or her free and creative process of making works. Therefore, a person can create a work or a compilation work that contains or comprises AI-generated parts. The AI-generated parts are, however, excluded from the scope of copyright protection and the exclusive right covers only the creative parts or the overall appearance of the compilation. Neighbouring rights are more liberal when it comes to the creative process and use of intellectual and personal expressions. Producers' rights could be a possibility to gain protection to a recording that contains AI created sounds, movies, or audiovisual content.

Training AI can be done by teaching the algorithm with a corpus that is curated, or with a corpus that contains everything from the internet or from other available sources. The reproduction of works for the purpose of AI training appears to require consent from the copyright holders, but it is yet to be decided whether temporary reproduction or data mining could authorize the AI training. There is a possibility for alternative interpretations such as implied licence or the problem could be solved by enacting new legislation. Technological development puts increasing pressure on existing legal uncertainty while there are other interest groups who are worried about imitation of distinctive personal styles.

The use of AI is the use of algorithms and trade secrets and is most often based on licence agreements. The AI of others should not be copied without permission as it may include trade secrets and copyrighted code, trademarks and commercial signs, design rights (design patents), look and feel and other protected or protectable subject matter even if the algorithm would develop itself over time. Instructive prompts are very seldom works and can be used by the AI developer, provided, however, that the user is informed and agrees to the use of its data.[48]

According to the AI Act the output should contain information as to whether it is AI created. If the output is AI created, no copyright restricts the use of it. If it is AI assisted, then copyright may limit the use of such material. Texts for various purposes, pictures, music, and audiovisual content may be freely available for consumption, but calculations and models used by the industry or research are likely to be kept secret or published for the benefit of all, if we manage to keep the data uncorrupted and secure from malicious actors.

Research discusses the difficulties from AI provider's perspectives and the desirability of investment in AI technology is widely accepted, but it is nevertheless worth noting that current legal uncertainty concerns both AI providers and users. The rights and obligations should be balanced, and both parties should have efficient measures to defend their rights. In EU member states such as Finland, where the use of class action is limited, the enforceability of copyright against AI providers can be very problematic.[49]

48. The use must be compliant with the Regulation (EU) 2016/679 of the European Parliament and of the Council on the protection of natural persons with regard to the processing of personal data and on the free movement of such data, and repealing Directive 95/46/EC (General Data Protection Regulation) and Regulation (EU) 2023/2854 of the European Parliament and of the Council on harmonised rules on fair access to and use of data and amending Regulation (EU) 2017/2394 and Directive (EU) 2020/1828 (Data Act).
49. Only the Consumer Ombudsman can file a class action in a court of law in Finland and only in cases where consumers have similar demands against the same legal entity, and, as copyright matters fall outside of its scope, the unauthorized use of works in creating a successful foundation model is likely to bring more gains than actualization of risks causes losses. The authors of works or other copyright or *sui generis* rights holders must show the infringement by identifying the work and unauthorized use, corrective measures are available for many only in theory. If authors file a case against an AI supplier in Finland and succeed in showing infringement, the AI supplier can remove or disable the parts that are infringing. The obligation to cover legal expenses of the winning parties is likely to be the greatest loss if the AI supplier loses, as the compensation for the use of works is value based and actual damages that were caused by the infringement are likely to be small.

Chapter 6

France

Stefan Naumann

1. INTRODUCTION

French and EU copyright law provide a robust framework and arguably adequate guidance for businesses and practitioners to make informed decisions when dealing with and/or using generative artificial intelligence (AI) in connection with copyright protected works and copyright protection (or not) of AI-generated content.

This country chapter for France includes a presentation of relevant fundamental copyright rules in effect in France and an overview of how the French courts would ordinarily apply them in the event of litigation related to the training and use of AI to generate content.

At the outset, it must be kept in mind that in France a creative work may be protected by copyright without any registration requirement so that no Intellectual Property Office gets to determine or take a position on whether or not a creative work is copyrightable or registrable.[1]

1.1 EU Regulation of Artificial intelligence – the AI Act

EU Regulation 2024/1689 of 13 June 2024, laying down harmonized rules on artificial intelligence and amending Regulations (EC) No. 300/2008, (EU) No. 167/2013, (EU) No. 168/2013, (EU) 2018/858, (EU) 2018/1139 and (EU) 2019/2144 and Directives 2014/90/EU, (EU) 2016/797 and (EU) 2020/1828 (the 'AI Act') was adopted by the European parliament by an overwhelming majority and unanimously by the 27 EU Member States and entered into force on 2 August 2024.

1. Article L111-1 of the French intellectual Property Code provides that 'The author of a work of the mind shall enjoy in that work, by the mere fact of its creation, an exclusive incorporeal property right which shall be enforceable against all persons.'

The AI Act is principally concerned with the protection of society, citizens and consumers from the potentially very harmful effects of AI, notably in terms of surveillance, manipulation and automated decision making without human oversight. The AI Act is therefore focused on compliance, data protection, non-discrimination, biometric identification, classification of persons and transparency, and provides limited but relevant guidance regarding AI and copyright.[2]

The AI Act contains a legal definition of AI that is relevant to the analysis of AI and copyright.

> *Article 3 Definitions*
>
> For the purposes of this Regulation, the following definitions apply:
>
> (1) 'AI system' means a machine-based system that is designed to operate with varying levels of autonomy and that may exhibit adaptiveness after deployment, and that, for explicit or implicit objectives, infers, from the input it receives, how to generate outputs such as predictions, content, recommendations, or decisions that can influence physical or virtual environments;
>
> ...
>
> (29) 'training data' means data used for training an AI system through fitting its learnable parameters;
>
> (30) 'validation data' means data used for providing an evaluation of the trained AI system and for tuning its non-learnable parameters and its learning process in order, inter alia, to prevent underfitting or overfitting;
>
> (31) 'validation data set' means a separate data set or part of the training data set, either as a fixed or variable split;
>
> (32) 'testing data' means data used for providing an independent evaluation of the AI system in order to confirm the expected performance of that system before its placing on the market or putting into service;

---

2. In the words of the AI Act itself: 'Article 1 Subject matter ... 2. The purpose of this Regulation is to improve the functioning of the internal market and promote the uptake of human-centric and trustworthy artificial intelligence (AI), while ensuring a high level of protection of health, safety, fundamental rights enshrined in the Charter, including democracy, the rule of law and environmental protection, against the harmful effects of AI systems in the Union and supporting innovation. This Regulation lays down: (a) harmonised rules for the placing on the market, the putting into service, and the use of AI systems in the Union; (b) prohibitions of certain AI practices; (c) specific requirements for high-risk AI systems and obligations for operators of such systems; (d) harmonised transparency rules for certain AI systems; (e) harmonised rules for the placing on the market of general-purpose AI models; (f) rules on market monitoring, market surveillance, governance and enforcement ...;" see also 'Article 5 Prohibited AI Practices 1. The following AI practices shall be prohibited: (a) the placing on the market, the putting into service or the use of an AI system that deploys subliminal techniques beyond a person's consciousness or purposefully manipulative or deceptive techniques, with the objective, or the effect of materially distorting the behaviour of a person or a group of persons by appreciably impairing their ability to make an informed decision, thereby causing them to take a decision that they would not have otherwise taken in a manner that causes or is reasonably likely to cause that person, another person or group of persons significant harm; ...' and following paragraphs.

(33) 'input data' means data provided to or directly acquired by an AI system on the basis of which the system produces an output;

...

(63) 'general-purpose AI model' means an AI model, including where such an AI model is trained with a large amount of data using self-supervision at scale, that displays significant generality and is capable of competently performing a wide range of distinct tasks ...'

The Preamble of the AI Act contains a number of references to general-purpose AI models, in particular generative AI models capable of generating text, images and other content, and to copyright. These references address but do not regulate copyright and AI issues. The Preamble nevertheless provides meaningful and clear guidance on the issues surrounding generative AI and copyright:

(105) General-purpose AI models, in particular large generative AI models, capable of generating text, images, and other content, present unique innovation opportunities but also challenges to artists, authors, and other creators and the way their creative content is created, distributed, used and consumed. *The development and training of such models require access to vast amounts of text, images, videos, and other data. Text and data mining techniques may be used extensively in this context for the retrieval and analysis of such content, which may be protected by copyright and related rights. Any use of copyright protected content requires the authorisation of the rightsholder concerned unless relevant copyright exceptions and limitations apply. Directive (EU) 2019/790 introduced exceptions and limitations allowing reproductions and extractions of works or other subject matter, for the purpose of text and data mining, under certain conditions. Under these rules, rightsholders may choose to reserve their rights over their works or other subject matter to prevent text and data mining, unless this is done for the purposes of scientific research.* Where the rights to opt out has been expressly reserved in an appropriate manner, providers of general-purpose AI models need to obtain an authorisation from rightsholders if they want to carry out text and data mining over such works.[3]

(106) Providers that place general-purpose AI models on the Union market should ensure compliance with the relevant obligations in this Regulation. To that end, *providers of general-purpose AI models should put in place a policy to comply with Union law on copyright and related rights, in particular to identify and comply with the reservation of rights expressed by rightsholders pursuant to Article 4(3) of Directive (EU) 2019/790. Any provider placing a general-purpose AI model on the Union market should comply with this obligation, regardless of the jurisdiction in which the copyright-relevant acts underpinning the training of those general-purpose AI models take place.* This is necessary to ensure a level playing field among providers of general-purpose AI models where no provider should be able to gain a competitive advantage in the Union market by applying lower copyright standards than those provided in the Union.

(107) *In order to increase transparency on the data that is used in the pre-training and training of general-purpose AI models, including text and data protected*

3. Preamble paragraph 104 contains a similar provision for AI under free and open-source licences.

> *by copyright law, it is adequate that providers of such models draw up and make publicly available a sufficiently detailed summary of the content used for training the general-purpose AI model. While taking into due account the need to protect trade secrets and confidential business information, this summary should be generally comprehensive in its scope instead of technically detailed to facilitate parties with legitimate interests, including copyright holders, to exercise and enforce their rights under Union law, for example by listing the main data collections or sets that went into training the model,* such as large private or public databases or data archives, and by providing a narrative explanation about other data sources used. It is appropriate for the AI Office to provide a template for the summary, which should be simple, effective, and allow the provider to provide the required summary in narrative form.
>
> (108) With regard to the obligations imposed on providers of general-purpose AI models to put in place a policy to comply with Union copyright law and make publicly available a summary of the content used for the training, the AI Office should monitor whether the provider has fulfilled those obligations without verifying or proceeding to a work-by work assessment of the training data in terms of copyright compliance. *This Regulation does not affect the enforcement of copyright rules as provided for under Union law.*
>
> (109) Compliance with the obligations applicable to the providers of general-purpose AI models should be commensurate and proportionate to the type of model provider, excluding the need for compliance for persons who develop or use models for non-professional or scientific research purposes, who should nevertheless be encouraged to voluntarily comply with these requirements. *Without prejudice to Union copyright law,* compliance with those obligations should take due account of the size of the provider and allow simplified ways of compliance for SMEs, including start-ups, that should not represent an excessive cost and not discourage the use of such models. …' [emphasis added].

The AI Act thus explicitly leaves the enforcement of copyright to copyright law, notably as regards copyright holders' reservation of rights with respect to the limitation of text and data mining.

On this last point, Article 53 of the AI Act provides the only specific obligation with respect to copyright:

> *Article 53 Obligations for providers of general-purpose AI models*
>
> Providers of general-purpose AI models shall:
>
> …
>
> (c) put in place a policy to comply with Union law on copyright and related rights, and in particular to identify and comply with, including through state-of-the-art technologies, a reservation of rights expressed pursuant to Article 4(3) of Directive (EU) 2019/790;
>
> (d) draw up and make publicly available a sufficiently detailed summary about the content used for training of the general-purpose AI model, according to a template provided by the AI Office.'[4]

4. Article 56(9) of the AI Act mandates that the European AI Office prepare codes of practice by 2 May 2025. The AI Office published the second draft of the General-Purpose AI Code of Practice on 14 November 2024.

1.2 Text and Data Mining

EU Directive 2019/790 on copyright and related rights in the digital single market ('DSM Directive') provides for two text and data mining exceptions:

> *Article 3 – Text and data mining for the purposes of scientific research*
>
> Member States shall provide for an exception to the rights provided for in Article 5(a) and Article 7(1) of Directive 96/9/EC, Article 2 of Directive 2001/29/EC, and Article 15(1) of this Directive for reproductions and extractions *made by research organisations and cultural heritage institutions* in order to carry out, *for the purposes of scientific research*, text and data mining of works or other subject matter to which they have lawful access [emphasis added].
>
> *Article 4 – Exception or limitation for text and data mining*
>
> 1. Member States shall provide for an exception or limitation to the rights provided for in Article 5(a) and Article 7(1) of Directive 96/9/EC, Article 2 of Directive 2001/29/EC, Article 4(1)(a) and (b) of Directive 2009/24/EC and Article 15(1) of this Directive for reproductions and extractions of lawfully accessible works and other subject matter for the purposes of text and data mining.
>
> 2. Reproductions and extractions made pursuant to paragraph 1 may be retained for as long as is necessary for the purposes of text and data mining.
>
> 3. The exception or limitation provided for in paragraph 1 shall apply on condition that the use of works and other subject matter referred to in that paragraph has not been expressly reserved by their rightsholders in an appropriate manner, such as machine-readable means in the case of content made publicly available online.
>
> 4. This Article shall not affect the application of Article 3 of this Directive.

The text and data mining exception for the purpose of scientific research pursuant to Article 3 of the EU Directive restricts the benefit of the exception to certain types of organizations but does not provide for an opt-out of rights holders, unlike the text and data mining exception of Article 4 of the EU Directive.

France transposed both exceptions, now in Article L.122-5-3 of the French Intellectual Property Code, and set up a regulatory framework for these two exceptions in Articles R.122-23 to R.122-28 of the French Intellectual Property Code.

1.3 AI and Copyright Law

As has frequently been the case when new modes of creation or exploitation of copyright protected works have been developed, one must look within copyright law itself for answers and guidance to assess the legal effects of generative AI on the use and output of creative works.

Under EU and French copyright laws, the substantive issues connected to the use of generative AI can be parsed as follows:

- training AI models with copyright protected works;
- use of copyright protected works in running AI systems;
- copyright protection of AI-generated output.

2. TRAINING AI MODELS

2.1 Training AI with Copyright Protected Works

The use of copyrighted works to train generative AI may require the reproduction or copying of these works.

The French Intellectual Property Code provides, in relevant part, the following:

> Article L122-3 Reproduction shall consist in the physical fixation of a work by any process permitting it to be communicated to the public in an indirect way. It may be carried out, in particular, by printing, drawing, engraving, photography, casting and all processes of the graphical and plastic arts, mechanical, cinematographic or magnetic recording.

While Article L.122-3 of the French Intellectual Property Code requires that the reproduction allow a work to be communicated to the public in an indirect way, it must be interpreted in conformity with Article 2 of Directive 2001/29/CE, which does not contain an express requirement that the reproduction must permit communication to the public. In fact, Article 2 of Directive 2001/29/CE provides that the right of reproduction encompasses "the direct or indirect, temporary or permanent reproduction by any means and in any form, in whole or in part" of works and other protected subject-matter.[5]

When an AI model memorizes or ingests training data extracted from a copyright protected work that allows the AI model to reproduce in whole or in part the copyright protected work described by the training data, the AI model permits the work to be communicated to the public in an indirect way.

The process by which the copyrighted work is fixated does not influence the conclusion that the right of reproduction is implemented.[6]

2.2 Exceptions/Limitations Allowing Training of AI

Training of generative AI with copyright protected works may however fall under one or more exceptions or limitations to the exclusive rights of the copyright holder, in

5. This is consistent with Article 9(1) of the Berne Convention, which mandates the protection of reproduction "in any manner or form" and WIPO Copyright Treaty, Agreed Statements concerning Article 1(4) and WIPO Performances and Phonograms Treaty, Agreed statement concerning Articles 7, 11 and 16 that clarify that the right of reproduction "fully appl[ies] in the digital environment."
6. In France as elsewhere, some authors have questioned whether training data reproduces a copyrighted work since the training data merely contains information about the copyrighted work extracted from said work. However, the process of fixation appears irrelevant under Article 2 of Directive 2001/29/CE ("direct or indirect, temporary or permanent reproduction by any means and in any form, in whole or in part") so long as it allows the communication to the public in an indirect way. *See* Austro-Mechana, C-433/20, EU:C:2022:217, paras 16–18; *see also* by way of analogy Opinion of Advocate General Szpunar in Mircom, C-597/19, EU:C:2020:1063, paras 48–49; for a detailed discussion, *see* Eleonora Rosati, Infringing AI: Liability for AI-Generated Outputs under International, EU, and UK Copyright Law, European Journal of Risk Regulation (2024), 1–25, doi:10.1017/err.2024.72.

particular the text and data mining exception and possibly the temporary reproduction exception.

France transposed the text and data mining exception of Article 3 of EU Directive 2019/790, but did so with some substantive modifications regarding who may benefit from the exception.

Article L.122-5-3 II of the French Intellectual Property Code thus provides as follows:

> II. – Digital copies or reproductions of lawfully accessed works may be made without the authorization of the authors for the purpose of text and data mining carried out solely for scientific research by research organizations, publicly accessible libraries, museums, archives or institutions holding cinematographic, audiovisual or sound heritage, or on their behalf and at their request by other persons, including in the context of a non-profit partnership with private actors.
>
> The provisions of the preceding paragraph do not apply when a company, shareholder or associate of the organization or institution conducting the mining, has privileged access to their results. ...
>
> An agreement concluded between the organizations representing copyright holders and the bodies and institutions mentioned in the first paragraph of this section II. may define best practices relating to the implementation of its provisions.

French law allows research organizations to benefit from the scientific research exception notably where they enter into non-profit partnerships with private actors. This arguably implies that, in keeping with French practice, only non-profit research organizations can benefit from the exception, and not private actors such as businesses.

This view is reinforced by the provisions of Decree 2022-928 of 23 June 2022 (codified in Articles R.122-23 to R.122-26 of the French Intellectual Property Code) that only refer to "institutions", thus arguably excluding private actors such as businesses from directly benefitting from the exception.

France also transposed the text and data mining exception of Article 4 of the EU Directive 2019/790 in Article L.122-5-3 of the French Intellectual Property Code as follows:

> 'I – Text and data mining, within the meaning of 10° of Article L. 122-5, means the implementation of a technique for the automated analysis of texts and data in digital form to extract information, in particular patterns, trends and correlations.
>
> ...
>
> III – Without prejudice to the provisions of II, *digital copies or reproductions of works that have been lawfully accessed may be made* for the purpose of text and data searches carried out by any person, *whatever the purpose of the search, unless the author has objected in an appropriate manner*, in particular by machine-readable processes for content made available to the public online' [emphasis added].

Absent an opt-out by the copyright holder, access to and use of copyright protected works is in principle lawful whatever the purpose of the data search. The purpose thus can include access and use for the purpose of training AI.

Once the provider or user of the AI has lawfully copied a copyrighted work under the text and data mining exception to the rights holder's exclusive rights, the reproduction or representation of the work during the use by the AI, such as training, testing, validation, would not require the rights holder's authorization.

But if a rights holder has opted out of the data mining exception, making digital copies or reproductions would require the rights holder's authorization unless the text and data mining is carried out (i) for scientific research (ii) by a research organization.

The temporary reproduction exception could potentially also be relevant:

> Article L122-5 Once the work has been disclosed, the author may not prohibit: … 6° The temporary reproduction having a transitory or accessory nature, when it is an integral and essential part of a technical process and its sole purpose is to enable lawful use of the work or its transmission between third parties via a network using an intermediary; however, this provisional reproduction, which may only concern works other than software and databases, must have no economic value of its own.

Article L122-5-6° of the French Intellectual Property Code transposed into French law Article 5(1) of Directive (EU) 2001/29, which provides:

> 1. Temporary acts of reproduction referred to in Article 2, which are transient or incidental [and] an integral and essential part of a technological process and whose sole purpose is to enable: (a) a transmission in a network between third parties by an intermediary, or (b) a lawful use of a work or other subject-matter to be made, and which have no independent economic significance, shall be exempted from the reproduction right provided for in Article 2. 2.

The application of this temporary reproduction exception to the use of protected works as training, validation, testing and/or use data for generative AI has not been assessed by French courts.

In the seminal *Infopaq* case, the CJEU found that the exemption for temporary reproductions only applies if (i) all the conditions of Article 5(1) are fulfilled,[7] (ii) the use does not conflict with a normal exploitation of the work and does not unreasonably prejudice the legitimate interests of the rights holder,[8] and (iii) the storage and deletion of the reproduction is not dependent on discretionary human intervention.[9]

The CJEU concluded that:

> 64. In the light of the foregoing, the Court finds that an act can be held to be 'transient' within the meaning of the second condition laid down in Article 5(1) of Directive 2001/29 only if its duration is limited to what is necessary for the proper completion of the technological process in question, it being understood that that process must be automated so that it deletes that act automatically,

7. CJEU Case C-5/08, *Infopaq International A/S v. Danske Dagblades Forening*, 16 June 2009, ECLI:EU:C:2009:465, paragraphs 54 and 55.
8. CJEU Case C-5/08, *supra*, paragraph 58.
9. CJEU Case C-5/08, *supra*, paragraph 62.

> without human intervention, once its function of enabling the completion of such a process has come to an end.

Both AI providers and users should either verify and monitor that their use of copyrighted works as training, validation and/or testing data fully meets the strict conditions for this exception or obtain appropriate authorizations from rights holders.

In this context, it may in particular be difficult to demonstrate in the event of litigation that a temporary act of reproduction of a copyrighted work for the purpose of training an AI model or creating a data set to train an AI model has no independent economic significance.

All of the foregoing exceptions are subject to the requirement that they do not interfere with the normal exploitation of the copyright protected work nor cause an unjustified damage to the author's legitimate interests (Article L.122-5 of the French Intellectual Property Code).

2.3 Remedies and Enforcement

Use of copyrighted works as training, validation and/or testing data that does not fall within the exceptions to copyright protection could constitute copyright infringement and could subject the user to the ordinary civil sanctions applicable to copyright infringement including injunctions, removal of infringing content, damages, publication of the judgement, reimbursement of the rights holder's legal costs and court costs pursuant to Articles L.331-1, L.331-1-3, L.331-1-4 of the French Intellectual Property Code and Articles 699 and 700 of the French Code of Civil Procedure.

Rights holders could have copyright infringement seizures carried out by a bailiff before and during litigation to gather evidence of the alleged infringement and request that the court order the defendant to provide information regarding the scope of infringement during litigation (Articles L.332-1 and L.331-1-3 of the French Intellectual Property Code).

Copyright infringement may also constitute a criminal offence pursuant to Articles L.335-2 and L.332-3 of the French Intellectual Property Code. The latter notably provides that "[i]t is also a criminal offense of infringement to reproduce, represent or distribute, by any means whatsoever, a work of the mind in violation of the author's rights, as defined and regulated by law."

3. USE OF AI SYSTEMS

3.1 Permission to Reproduce and Make Available to the Public

The use of copyrighted works by AI may also require the reproduction or copying of these works.

The French Intellectual Property Code provides that:

> Article L122-1 The right of exploitation belonging to the author shall comprise the right of performance and the right of reproduction.

> Article L122-4 Any complete or partial performance or reproduction made without the consent of the author or of his successors in title or assigns shall

> be unlawful. The same shall apply to translation, adaptation or transformation, arrangement or reproduction by any technique or process whatsoever.

In principle, the use of copyright protected works thus requires the authorization of the rights holder unless the use falls within an exception to copyright protection.[10]

3.2 Exceptions/Limitations Allowing Use of AI Systems

The text and data mining exceptions and the temporary reproduction exception are discussed in section 2.2 above.

End users of AI systems may benefit from the private use exception that could apply to the reproduction of copyright protected works so long as the reproductions are not destined for collective use (Article L.122-5-2° of the French Intellectual Property Code).

As with all exceptions to copyright protection under French law, the private use exception is subject to the requirement that it not interfere with the normal exploitation of the copyright protected work nor cause an unjustified damage to the author's legitimate interests (Article L.122-5 of the French Intellectual Property Code).

3.3 Remedies and Enforcement

The remedies and sanctions discussed in section 2.3 above would apply if the use of copyrighted works by or in the AI system infringes rights holders' copyrights.

4. AI-GENERATED OUTPUT

More complex copyright issues revolve around AI-generated output, in particular whether the output can itself be protected by copyright and, if so, who the author is, whether it infringes copyright protected works and the enforcement of copyright protected works that include AI-generated elements.

Fortunately, these issues are not entirely new in copyright law. Photography, colourization of black and white audiovisual works, user interfaces and computer-generated graphics have over time raised the same and/or similar existential copyright questions.[11]

---

10. The right of representation or communication to the public of a protected work set out in Article L122-2 of the French Intellectual Property Code may generally not be immediately relevant for training, validation and/or testing data for generative AI. If it does come into play however, it would not fall within the strict requirements of the exception of Article L122-5(6) or (10) of the French Intellectual Property Code and would require the authorization of the rights holder.
11. By way of example Cour de cassation, *Huston v. Turner*, 28 May 1991, RIDA July 1991, pp. 197 and 161; Versailles Court of Appeal, *Huston v. Turner*, 19 December 1994, RIDA April 1995, p. 389.

4.1 Protection of AI-Generated Output

Generative AI uses training, validation and/or testing data, data accumulated from previous user interactions and user prompts to generate output such as music, pictures, graphic art, audiovisual works and text that could qualify as a creative work.

Unlike computer programs, an instruction or prompt does not result in the same output each time it is used, since the training, validation and/or testing data and prior interactions will vary over time and since the algorithm and structure of AI by design allow multiple responses to a single instruction or prompt.

Two aspects are particularly relevant to determine whether the AI-generated output may be protected by copyright.

For one, the variation of output using the same prompt is not the result of creative choices by the generative AI.

Secondly, the user's prompt is the only element directed to the specific output or work.

Neither the selection of the training, validation and/or testing data, nor the construction of the algorithm(s) of generative AI could support a claim that the generated content reflects the personality of the individuals who programmed and trained the generative AI since their efforts are directed to developing and running the generative AI, and not to any specific output it generates.

4.1.1 Copyright Protection of AI Output

EU and French law and case law require a work to be original and reflect the personality of the author.[12] The courts use various expressions to describe this foundational rule of French and EU copyright law, such as the author's creative choices and the degree of freedom available to the author. In determining whether a work is copyrightable, courts do not assess the merits of the work, nor take into account the amount of effort.[13]

When AI is used to generate creative content drawn from the training, validation and/or testing data it received and from prior interactions, the AI-generated output can only reflect the personality of the person who issues the prompts to arrive at the specific content.

French courts would thus ordinarily consider that the user of generative AI is the author of a specific work provided that his or her prompts show that the work is original and reflects his or her personality. The prompts are in essence a memento of his or her creative choices in arriving at the particular work for which copyright protection is claimed.

Where the prompts are too general, generic or superficial, the AI-generated output would reflect the AI's training, validation and/or testing data, and data

12. By way of example, Paris Court of Appeal, *Lalique v. Habitat*, 15 February 2023, RG 21/14049; Paris Court of Appeal, *Baan v. Cherie Sheriff*, 21 June 2023, RG 21/08929; CJEU, Case C-145/10, *Eva Maria Painer v. Axel Springer AG*, 1 December 2011, ECLI:EU:C:2011:798.
13. Article L112-1 of the French Intellectual Property Code provides that 'The provisions of this Code shall protect the rights of authors in all works of the mind, whatever their kind, form of expression, merit or purpose.'

accumulated from previous user interactions, not the user's creative choices or personality. The resulting output would not be a work protected by copyright under current French and EU law and case law.

As a practical matter, it is advisable to collect and store prompts when creating works with generative AI to be able to establish the user input in the creative process and his or her authorship of the work created with the assistance of AI.

4.1.2 Potential Additional Authors of Works Created with Generative AI

The French Intellectual Property Code provides in relevant part the following:

> Article L113-2 'Work of collaboration' shall mean a work in the creation of which more than one natural person has participated. 'Composite work' shall mean a new work in which a preexisting work is incorporated without the collaboration of the author of the latter work. 'Collective work' shall mean a work created at the initiative of a natural or legal person who edits it, publishes it and discloses it under his direction and name and in which the personal contributions of the various authors who participated in its production are merged in the overall work for which they were conceived, without it being possible to attribute to each author a separate right in the work as created.

A work created with the assistance of generative AI would not be a work of collaboration unless the various authors worked together to create the specific work. The programmer(s) and trainer(s) of the AI ordinarily did not collaborate with the user to create a specific work, so that the resulting work could not be considered a work of collaboration for which they could potentially claim to be co-authors.

Could an AI-generated output be considered a composite work? If the AI-generated output incorporates preexisting works, it would still need to reflect the personality of an author (and be original) to benefit from copyright protection. Here too, the programmer(s) and trainer(s) of the AI could not be considered authors of the specific output for which protection is claimed. Nor are they authors of the training, validation and/or testing data composed of pre-existing works created by third parties.

Could an AI-generated output be considered a collective work?

French courts may be reluctant to reach this conclusion with respect to the programmer(s) and trainer(s) of the AI since any personal contributions of the programmer(s) and trainer(s) of the AI are not merged into an overall work for which they were conceived, but are indiscriminate with respect to the specific outputs generated by the AI once it is operational.

However, software and its documentation can be protected by copyright under French and EU copyright law.

The French Intellectual Property Code provides in relevant part the following:

> Article L113-9 Unless otherwise provided by statutory provision or stipulation, the economic rights in the software and its documentation created by one or more employees in the execution of their duties or following the instructions given by their employer shall be the property of the employer and he exclusively shall be entitled to exercise them.

The individuals who developed the generative AI and selected the training, validation and/or testing data could potentially be authors of the software and/or of the documentation if one considers the training, validation and/or testing data to constitute part of the software's documentation.

4.1.3 Neighbouring Rights Protection of AI Output

Several neighbouring rights may attach to copyrighted works and could be violated by AI-generated output.

Article L.211-1 of the French Intellectual Property Code provides that:

> Neighbouring rights do not affect the rights of authors. Accordingly, no provision of this Title shall be construed so as to limit the exercise of copyright by its owners.

French law provides for neighbouring rights for performers, producers of sound recordings and videos, audiovisual communication businesses and press publishers, respectively in their performance, sound recording, video, broadcast and press publication.[14] The scope of their respective rights differs slightly but all have in common the right to authorize (and hence to prohibit) the reproduction of their respective rights.

Performers may in addition prohibit the separate use of the sound and images of their performance. Producers and audiovisual communication businesses may prohibit the communication to the public. Press publishers may prohibit the digital communication to the public by online communication providers.[15]

4.2 AI-Generated Output Infringes Existing Copyright

Article L.122-4 of the Intellectual Property Code provides that:

> Any representation or reproduction in whole or in part made without the consent of the author or his successors in title or assigns shall be unlawful. The same shall apply to translation, adaptation or transformation, arrangement or reproduction by any art or process whatsoever.

14. Articles L.212-3, L.213-1, L.215-1, L.216-1 and L.218-2 of the French Intellectual Property Code.
15. Article L.211-3-1 of the French Intellectual Property Code provides a limitation to the press publishers' rights. The press publishers' rights and their limitation have given rise to significant litigation in France against Google: Competition Authority, 9 April 2020, No. 20-MC-01, D. 2020.1181, Dalloz IP/IT 2020.560; Paris Court of Appeal, Pole 5, Ch. 7, 8 October 2020, RG 20/08071, Prop. Intell. 2021, No.78, p. 63; Competition Authority, 21 June 2022, No. 22-D-13, Légipresse 2022.335.

Only an author's expression can be protected, not ideas.[16] Case law considers that infringement is assessed based on the similarities between the earlier and later work,[17] that a partial reproduction of the expression of the earlier work may be infringing and that a risk of confusion is irrelevant, provided that the element(s) reproduced are original and reflect the personality of the author of the earlier work.[18]

In principle, the use of an author's style could only be considered infringing if the later work partially reproduces elements of one or more specific earlier works, and if these elements are original and reflect the personality of the author of the earlier work(s).[19] Only later works that reproduce one or more earlier works in whole or in part may be infringing, provided that the element(s) reproduced is (are) original and reflects the personality of the author of the earlier work.

In case the use of a prior copyrighted work to train the AI system is covered by an exception, the AI-generated output would ordinarily not be infringing unless the exploitation of the output conflicts with a normal exploitation of the earlier work, or causes unjustified prejudice to the legitimate interests of the author of the earlier work (Article L.122-5 of the Intellectual Property Code).[20]

In case a prior copyrighted work has not been used to train the AI system, *outputs* generated by an AI system could nevertheless be qualified as infringements of that copyrighted work if the physical author of the AI-generated output knew about and/or had access to the earlier work.[21]

In case the use of a copyright protected earlier work to train the AI system has been authorized, the AI-generated output may nevertheless be infringing in cases where the exploitation of the output conflicts with the normal exploitation of the earlier work, or causes unjustified prejudice to the legitimate interests of the author of the earlier work, AI-generated works would no longer benefit from the exception (Article L.122-5 of the French Intellectual Property Code).

---

16. Cour de cassation, civil division, 17 June 2003, No. 01-17.650 '[w]hereas literary and artistic property does not protect ideas or concepts, but only the original form in which they are expressed'; Paris Judicial Court, 19 October 2005, RG 02/14370: a glass plate bearing irregular parallel lines is original, even if the scratch pattern on glass 'is not in itself susceptible of copyright protection'; *see also*, Paris Court of Appeal, 14 November 2003, Gaz. Pal. 6 January 2005, p.33.
17. Paris Court of Appeal, Pole 5, Ch.1, 17 December 2019, RG 17/09695: a sculpture reproducing the original characteristics of an earlier photograph was deemed to be infringing, even if 'the presence of the bouquet of flowers in the boy's hand has the effect of giving the statue a different meaning to that of the photograph'; in the case of software, Douai Court of Appeal, 8 February 2024, RG 22/03719.
18. Paris Court of Appeal, Pole 5, Ch.2, 7 January 2011, RG 09/16251; in the case of data, CJEU, Case C-5/08, *supra*, paragraphs 35 and 48; CJEU, Case C-604/10, *Football Dataco Ltd et al. v. Yahoo! UK Ltd et al.*, 1 March 2012, ECLI:EU:C:2012:115, point 38.
19. Paris Court of Appeal, Pole 5, Ch.2, 14 June 2024, RG 22/20621: bags that do not reproduce 'in an identical combination or at least a combination that reproduces in the same arrangement the characteristic elements' of previously created bags cannot constitute an act of counterfeiting.
20. CJEU, Case C-5/08, *supra*, paragraph 58; Versailles Court of Appeal, 7 September 2018, RG 16/08909.
21. Cour de cassation, civ., civil division, 5 October 2022, No. 20-23.629.

4.3 Remedies and Enforcement

France has not as of the date of writing this chapter had any copyright infringement litigation based on works created with generative AI. Yet here as elsewhere, creative industries and creators are embracing AI to create new works (movies, music, design, photography, fashion).

In litigation, the owner of a creative work has the burden of proof of showing that it is copyrightable, i.e. that it is the result of the author's creative choices.

A defendant may or will argue that AI-generated elements of a creative work (i) cannot be used to determine the overall copyrightable character of the work and/or (ii) must be excluded from the determination of infringement since they are not themselves copyrightable.

This may open a can of worms for the rights holder, notably:

- Is AI-generated content an identifiable part of the work?
- How much input from the human author is sufficient to make the work copyrightable?
- If the work is copyrightable, can an infringer avoid liability for copying parts of a work that are solely AI-generated (i.e. for which the rights holder cannot establish a human author's creative choices that reflect his or her personality)?

These questions confirm the importance of documenting the creative choices and input of the person using generative AI. Only the prompts of the human author can show that the work is the expression of the author's creative choices and reflect his or her personality.

The remedies and sanctions discussed in section 2.3 above would apply in the event a court finds the AI-generated output to be infringing.

Chapter 7

Germany

Alexandra Wachtel and Athina Theodoridis

1. INTRODUCTION

Artificial intelligence (AI) is not only a central topic in technological development but also has far-reaching effects on many societal and legal areas. AI is particularly relevant in copyright law, as it is used in various fields, from image generation to text production and music composition. With its growing presence, new legal questions arise that necessitate a thorough examination of the existing legislation.

One of the key issues in this context concerns the training of AI systems. AI systems are trained on vast amounts of data, often sourced from protected works. But who owns the rights to these training datasets? Is it permissible to use protected works to train an AI model without infringing copyright? The lack of clear regulations in Germany leaves many of these questions unanswered, creating uncertainty for developers, authors, and users.

Another fundamental issue is the legal classification of AI-generated outputs. If an AI system creates an artwork, writes a text, or composes music, who is the author? Is it the developer of the AI who trained the model, or should AI itself be recognized as the author?

These uncertainties are intensified by rapid technological development. AI is evolving at a pace that often surpasses the ability of lawmakers and legal experts to keep up. Given AI's significant impact on creative industries such as art, music, literature, and software development - industries heavily shaped by copyright law - there is an urgent need for legal clarity.

This chapter provides a detailed examination of the current legal framework in Germany concerning AI and copyright. It identifies key legal issues and discusses possible solutions. The discussion follows a three-step approach, distinguishing between three phases: the creation of datasets and their use for training the artificial neural networks (Stage 1a and 1b, see section 2), the application of AI models to generate new content (Stage 2, see section 3), and the ultimate AI-generated output (Stage 3, see section 4).

2. TRAINING AI MODELS

2.1 The Training of AI with Protected Works

In the legal discussion, a distinction is made between the input and output side of the use of AI. While the output side (Stage 3, see section 4) concerns the question of whether AI-generated content enjoys copyright protection and who is entitled to the rights to it,[1] the input side focuses on the collection and processing of training data and the training process itself (Stage 1a and 1b). This Section is dedicated to the input side.

Within the literature, there is agreement that the creation of data sets for training purposes constitutes a reproduction within the meaning of Section 16 of the German Copyright Act (hereinafter referred to as the 'Copyright Act')[2] and Article 2 of Directive 2001/29/EC. In this respect, the intermediate storage in the working memory through downloading and processing the work in an identical and transformed form are to be considered.[3] It is irrelevant whether the digital protected work is only temporarily stored. What is relevant is whether it is still perceptible to the human senses in its essential features.

There is also broad agreement that training an AI, i.e. analysing the training material, does not usually constitute an act of reproduction relevant to copyright law. No copies of the protected works are stored in the neural network of the AI model; only the information is extracted.[4] The training data is therefore not systematically transferred in compressed form to the parameters of the AI models, but can only be reconstructed in individual cases through skilful text input by the end user (see sections 3 and 4).[5] The finished AI model should not generate images of training data, but rather 'freely' create new content. This is achieved by applying a training approach with data sets hundreds of times, in which the AI model learns to form abstract relationships and generalize data.[6]

It follows from all this that the use of copyright-protected data (in the broadest sense) for the training of AI systems is in any case subject to the author's monopoly on the exploitation of his work (cf. Section 15 et seq. Copyright Act). It is therefore

1. *Baumann* NJW 2023, 3673, 3676 f.
2. https://www.gesetze-im-internet.de/englisch_urhg/englisch_urhg.html#p0018.
3. See *Hacker* ZGE 12 (2020), 239, 256; *Pesch/Böhme* GRUR 2023, 997, 1004; *de la Durantaye* ZUM 2023, 645, 647; *Hofmann* ZUM 2024, 166, 167 f.; *Schack*, NJW 2024, 113;.*Dregelies*, GRUR 2024, 1484.
4. *Pesch/Böhme* GRUR 2023, 997, 1001; *Pukas* GRUR 2023, 614, 618; *Maamar* ZUM 2023, 481, 482; *Raue* ZUM 2021, 793. Cf. on the relationship between training data and AI models: *Käde* ZUM 2024 174.
5. Cf. on the training of generative AI for image generation: *Pesch/Böhme*, GRUR 2023, 997, 1004.
6. *Pesch/Böhme*, GRUR 2023, 997, 999.

only permitted with the consent of the rights holder or if a copyright limitation provision applies.

In the case of basic AI models, which serve as the basis for various AI applications, the former case, i.e. the existence of the rights holders' consent to the reproduction of the work, will have to be negated. AI models are trained on large, diverse data sets that are obtained by means of automated collection and extraction from publicly accessible websites (so-called web scraping). The scraped data is often protected by copyright. A prominent example is the GPT model, which is trained with general language data. This raises the question of whether a limitation provision applies.

In contrast to this, the rights holders have generally given their consent to the training of so-called AI systems. These systems are further developed and optimized on the basis of AI models for special purposes. One example is ChatGPT, which was optimized for interaction with users through further training steps based on the GPT model. The fine-tuning of AI systems is achieved with the help of specialized data sets that are not obtained through web scraping. Instead, licence agreements are concluded for the data sets. The use of data to train AI systems is therefore often covered by consent. In this case, it is not important whether limitation provision applies.

2.2 The Intervention of Limitation Provisions

With regard to training AI models with scraped data, it was previously unclear whether and under what conditions the collection and creation of data sets is permissible.

In Germany, there is no general fair use limitation as in the USA, which allows a flexible balancing of user and rights holder interests. Instead, the enumeration principle applies, according to which the use of protected works is only permitted if one of the exhaustively regulated limitations is applicable. Since these limitations constitute exceptions to copyright protection, their conditions of application must be interpreted strictly.

German copyright law does not provide for any limitation that explicitly addresses the training and use of AI models. Therefore, the existing catalogue of exceptions must be used, whereby the applicability of the exceptions for so-called text and data mining (TDM, cf. Section 44b, 60d Copyright Act) is discussed in particular.[7] TDM is the automated analysis of digitized protected works to identify information such as patterns, trends and correlations (Section 44b para. 1 Copyright Act). It can serve scientific purposes (Section 60d Copyright Act) or commercial purposes (Section 44b Copyright Act). Section 44d and Section 60d Copyright Act transpose the DSM Directive (Article 3, 4 DSM Directive) into German law. While Section 60d Copyright Act was already introduced in 2018, Section 44b Copyright Act has been supplementing the Copyright Act with the commercial TDM limitation since 7 June 2021.

Section 60d Copyright Act authorizes the reproduction of protected works under the TDM for scientific purposes, provided that the reproduction is made by a

7. Critical: *Schack* NJW 2024, 113, 114 and GRUR 2021, 904, 907 see further; *Baumann*, NJW 2023, 3673, 3675; *Pukas* GRUR 2023, 614, 615.

research organization and not in collaboration with a private company (Section 60d para. 2 Copyright Act).

In contrast, Section 44b Copyright Act covers commercial TDM. According to Section 44b para. 2 Copyright Act, the reproduction of legally accessible works is permitted, provided that the rights holder has not reserved the right to use protected works accessible online in machine-readable form (cf. Article 4 (3) DSM Directive, Section 44b Para. 3 Copyright Act). The provision is a novelty in the landscape of copyright limitations. Contrary to the traditional idea of copyright law, according to which an act of use without the consent of the rights holder is generally prohibited, the legislator has introduced a solution of opposition with Section 44b Copyright Act:[8] the commercial exploitation of the work for the purpose of TDM is possible without permission if the rights holder has not actively 'provided for the legal situation'. The provision also contains a rule on the burden of proof, according to which the rights holder bears the secondary burden of substantiation with regard to the scope of the reserved rights of use. [9]

Occasionally, there are also discussions as to whether the intermediate storage of the data could be a temporary, fleeting reproduction in the sense of Section 44a Copyright Act. However, this is predominantly denied with the argument that the reproduction is carried out in a targeted manner for the later analysis of the data (set) and is therefore not coincidental.[10]

2.3 Hamburg Regional Court

In September 2024, the Hamburg Regional Court (judgment of 27 September 2024, case no. 310 O 227/23 – *Kneschke v. LAION*)[11] ruled on the permissibility of using protected works for AI training. The Court ruled that the creation of AI training data sets in accordance with Section 60d Copyright Act does not infringe the copyrights of third parties if it serves scientific research purposes. This is the first ruling by a German and European court to address the copyright implications of using training data for AI models and TDM for AI training purposes.

In the proceedings, a photographer ('the plaintiff') filed a lawsuit against a non-profit organization ('the defendant') that had provided open data sets to support AI research. The disputed data set comprised 5.85 billion image-text pairs with hyperlinks to publicly accessible images and textual image descriptions. Among the images was a photograph by the plaintiff that he had licensed to a stock photo agency. The terms of use of the stock photo website prohibited the photos from being used for 'automated programs'. The plaintiff considered the download of the photograph as part of the analysis process to be a copyright infringement. The Court dismissed the claim.

Although the decisive factor for the dismissal of the action was Section 60d Copyright Act, the Court analysed the requirements of Section 44b Copyright Act in detail. The reasoning is set out below:

8. *Wachtel* ZUM 2025, 77 f.; *Maamar*, ZUM 2023, 481, 483 f. see further under footnote 24.
9. Dreier/Schulze/*Dreier*, 8th ed. 2025, Copyright Act Section 44b para. 9 see further.
10. LG Hamburg ZUM 2025, 64, 67 with reference to ECJ, GRUR 2014, 654 para. 43.
11. LG Hamburg ZUM 2025, 64.

The Court found that the requirements of *Section 60d Copyright Act* were met and emphasized that the creation of the data sets formed the basis for the subsequent training of an AI system as part of scientific research and was aimed at subsequently gaining knowledge. In this respect, the fact that the data sets created by the defendant could also be used by commercial companies due to their public accessibility and that the training data sets may thus have indirectly contributed to the generation of profit does not preclude their classification as a non-commercial activity.[12] With this provision, the Court gives Section 60d Copyright Act a broader scope of application and promotes AI innovation research in Europe.[13]

Regarding the applicability of *Section 44b Copyright Act* to the creation of AI training data sets, the Court stated the following:

- The next focus of the judgement was on the requirement of 'reproduction for the *purpose of TDM*' and the question of whether the training of AI in its entirety is covered by the statutory permission of use or whether reproductions for the purpose of training generative AI are to be excluded from its scope of application.[14] The representatives of the latter view justify this by the fact that training the AI model creates a product that is in competition with the (digital) work. The Court countered the latter view by referring to the various stages of AI.[15] According to the Court, the focus during dataset creation (Stage 1a) is on the information hidden in the data; in contrast, a later creation of new content (Stage 3), possibly based on the specific content of the dataset, is only conditioned by the as yet unclear success of the training of the AI model (Stage 1b), which has yet to be carried out. The Court points out that the judgement thus only concerns the preparation of the subsequent act of using the AI, but not the training itself.
- The Court then addressed the reservation of use in Section 44b para. 3 sentence 1 Copyright Act. Any specific, individual wording with which the scope of the reservation can be determined beyond doubt is sufficient. It must only be possible to recognise which protected works and which acts of use the reservation of use extends to.[16] With this broad interpretation of the reservation of use, the Court takes into account the protection of the rights holder in the context of the opposition solution.[17]
- Finally, the Court argues in favour of a broad interpretation of the machine readability of the reservation of use in Section 44b para. 3 sentence 2 Copyright Act. In doing so, it provides clarity at a point of intersection that is relevant in practice: so far, there has been discussion as to whether 'machine readability' requires technically coded information,[18] or can also be assumed

12. LG Hamburg ZUM 2025, 64, 71.
13. *Wachtel* ZUM 2025, 77, 78.
14. Critical: *Schack* NJW 2024, 113, 114; *Pukas* GRUR 2023, 614, 615.
15. LG Hamburg ZUM 2025, 67ff.
16. LG Hamburg ZUM 2025, 67, 69.
17. *Wachtel* ZUM 2025, 77, 79.
18. *Gausling* CR 2021, 609, 611; *Maamar*, ZUM 2023, 481, 484; *Müllerter Jung/Rexin* CR 2022, 169, 174; *BeckOK/Bomhard*, 43rd ed. 2024, Copyright Act Section 44b para. 28.

in the case of declarations written in natural language.[19] Neither Article 4 para. 3 nor Recital 18 of the DSM Directive – as the primary text for the TDM – provide any indications in this regard. The Court has now ruled that a reservation of use drafted 'in natural language' is also machine-readable, whereby the assessment of the (technical) machine readability is based on the point in time of the use of the work, i.e. the act of reproduction.[20]

Overall, the judgment of the Hamburg Regional Court brings initial clarity and a modicum of legal certainty to what is still a young area. Even though the Court only considers Section 60d Copyright Act to be directly relevant to its decision, it does deal comprehensively with the technical peculiarities and legal implications of AI. In doing so, the Court interprets the concept of TDM broadly, but emphasizes that the interests of rights holders must be taken into account.

In this way, despite the absence of an AI-specific limitation in German and European copyright law, it is possible to promote technological progress while at the same time taking into account the protection of rights holders under Article 17 (2) of the EU Charter of Fundamental Rights. The Court locates the consideration in Section 44b para. 3 Copyright Act, which, with its opt-out solution, has an unusual system for traditional copyright law. With its differentiated approach, the Court is thus contributing to a copyright law that is open to technology. However, it should be noted that there is great innovation potential in the commercial sector in particular due to the high resource requirements for creating training data sets. It remains to be seen whether the guidelines developed by the Court and the strict separation between scientific and commercial TDM will enable sufficient exemption for AI use.

2.4 Other Current Developments in This Context

It should be noted that the judgment of the Hamburg Regional Court is not legally binding. In November 2025, with financial support from the 'Collecting Society Bild-Kunst' ('*Verwertungsgesellschaft Bild-Kunst*'), the plaintiff appealed against the judgment of the Hamburg Regional Court.[21]

In addition, further proceedings concerning the training of AI with copyright-protected data are pending in German courts.

GEMA (German Society for Musical Performing and Mechanical Reproduction Rights) filed a lawsuit against OpenAI in November 2024, alleging that ChatGPT reproduced protected song lyrics without acquiring licences or remunerating the authors.[22] ChatGPT was trained on a large number of protected texts, including protected works by around 95,000 GEMA members. The problem lies in the fact that OpenAI did not pay a license for the use of these protected works to train the AI or

19. Dreier/Schulze/*Dreier*, 7th ed. 2022, Copyright Act Section 44b para. 9; Wandtke/Bullinger/*Bullinger*, 6th ed. 2022, Copyright Act Section 44b para. 10.
20. LG Hamburg ZUM 2025, 67, 69 f.
21. https://www.bildkunst.de/news/news.12.text-und-data-mining-entscheid-des-landgerichts-hamburg/.
22. https://www.gema.de/de/w/gema-erhebt-klage-gegen-openai.

to reproduce them, which, under copyright law, requires a licence to make these protected works publicly available.[23]

A central point of the lawsuit concerns the question of whether the copyright exception for TDM (Section 44b Copyright Act) also applies to the training of AI. This exception allows the use of data from protected works for analysis purposes.[24] The judgment of the Hamburg District Court, which already ruled that the training of an AI is permissible, could serve as a precedent here. However, GEMA emphasizes that its works may only be used with the appropriate license to ensure that the authors receive a fair share of the revenue. The lawsuit is supported by numerous well-known musicians and their publishers, who have also not received any compensation for the use of their lyrics by ChatGPT.

In addition, GEMA filed another lawsuit in January 2025,[25] this time at the Munich I District Court against the US company Suno. The company is said to have used protected musical works without permission to create new pieces of music using an AI tool.[26] Well-known songs such as 'Atemlos', 'Mambo No. 5', and 'Cheri Cheri Lady' were used as templates without the creators of the original works being compensated. GEMA is demanding that artists receive a fair share of the revenue; it hopes that the lawsuit will spark a broader discussion about how AI is used in the creative industry.[27]

GEMA represents the rights of around 95,000 members in Germany and over two million rights holders worldwide. In its lawsuit, it criticizes the fact that AI providers such as Suno profit from the protected works of their members, while the authors 'go away empty-handed' financially. In this respect, it emphasizes that the results generated by AI systems often compete with the original protected works.

It remains to be seen how other courts will decide on the applicability of the TDM exceptions to the creation of training data sets and on the question of remuneration for authors.

3. USE OF AI SYSTEMS

The following section concerns the end user's use of the AI system. Overlaps with copyright law may arise if the user uploads copyrighted material to the AI system or incorporates it (even in part) into their own instruction (known as a prompt). The latter is done with the aim of obtaining a specific AI-generated result. The prompt can be in the form of text, code, images or other data.

Assuming that the material entered constitutes a protected work within the meaning of Section 2 Copyright Act and that the AI user is not the rights holder, the question arises as to whether the use requires consent within the meaning of Section 15 et seq. Copyright Act. Examples include uploading a photograph or text

23. https://www.gema.de/de/w/gema-erhebt-klage-gegen-openai.
24. https://www.lto.de/recht/nachrichten/n/gema-verklagt-openai-chatgpt-urheberrechtsverletzung-lg-muenchen-i-42o1413924.
25. https://www.gema.de/de/w/pm-klage-gegen-suno.
26. https://www.gema.de/de/w/pm-klage-gegen-suno.
27. https://www.gema.de/de/w/pm-klage-gegen-suno.

to ChatGPT and asking the AI system to modify, shorten or otherwise incorporate the photograph or text into a new product.

The assessment depends heavily on the technical details of the AI system and how it is used. Reproduction is any 'physical fixation that is capable of making the protected work perceptible to the human senses, either directly or indirectly'. It is sufficient that the protected work can only be made perceptible in further intermediate steps or through independent, technically necessary reproductions, provided that the core creative characteristics have been adopted.[28] It is sufficient that the work can only be made perceptible in further intermediate steps or through independent technically necessary reproductions, provided that the creative characteristics in their essence have been adopted.[29] For this reason, the storage of the work in a different format[30] or as a compressed version is to be regarded as a reproduction, as are rearrangements of the work that lack creative expression of their own.[31]

Uploading a protected work by an end user to an AI system can therefore be considered an infringing reproduction within the meaning of Section 16 Copyright Act, provided that the AI system stores the content for a legal second.[32] If, on the other hand, only information from the protected work is extracted in the neural network of the AI system, without its concrete fixation and thus its perceptibility being important, then there is no reproduction.[33]

The following can thus be noted as an assessment guideline: an infringing act of use according to Section 16 Copyright Act is thus only deemed not to have occurred if the AI system does not translate the protected work information or only translates it in a highly incomplete manner and if this specified information does not enable the AI system to permanently reconstruct the protected work while retaining the creative characteristics.[34] As a rule, an accumulation of these exclusion conditions will be denied, with the result that an act of use requiring consent exists.

The use of the protected work in the form of making it publicly available in accordance with Section 19a Copyright Act does not require approval. The prerequisite for this would be that a work is made available to an unspecified number of people through a deliberate act of reproduction.[35] This is lacking. A protected work is fed into an AI system with the sole aim of generating a result that can be accessed by the user, and not publicly. The protected work is therefore not made publicly available on a permanent basis. At the same time, there is no act of communication, because the AI-generated result is produced on the basis of the user's individual request, so the protected work is not directly communicated. The same applies to a constellation

28. BGH GRUR 2020, 738 – Internet-Radiorecorder; GRUR 2017, 793 – Mart-Stam-Stuhl; Pesch/Böhme, GRUR 2023, 997, 1002.
29. Wandtke/Bullinger/*Heerma*, 6th ed. 2022, Copyright Act Section 16 para. 6; Dreier/Schulze/*Raue*, 8th ed. 2025, Copyright Act Section 16 para. 37.
30. BGH GRUR 1966, 503 – Apfel-Madonna; BGH GRUR 1990, 669 – Bibelproduktion.
31. BGH GRUR 2010, 628 (629) – Vorschaubilder.
32. Temporary or transient storage also falls under the concept of reproduction, see Spindler/Schuster/*Wiebe*, 4th ed. 2019, Copyright Act Section 16 para. 3.
33. Cf. comments in connection with AI training: *Pukas* GRUR 2023, 614, 618; Maamar ZUM 2023, 481, 482; *Raue* ZUM 2021, 793; similarly: *Pesch/Böhme*, GRUR 2023, 997.
34. Also on the training of AI models: *Pesch/Böhme*, GRUR 2023, 997, 1005.
35. See ECJ, GS Media, C-160/15.

in which third parties come into contact with the protected work in the context of a later use of the AI system (for the classification as an act of reproduction, see section 4.2.1).

Limitation provisions, in particular Section 44a, 44b, 60d Copyright Act, are not applicable to the use of AI systems according to their regulatory purpose (see section 2.2). This is because the act of reproduction is carried out with the aim of generating an AI result – and not in order to obtain information about patterns, trends and correlations or similar. Moreover, at the mere usage level, the fixation of the work required for the application of Sections 51 and 51a of the German Copyright Act is lacking. A meaningful engagement with the specific work – as is essential for parody or quotation – does not occur in AI-assisted training or prompting. Instead, the user interaction primarily involves the unaltered reproduction of the third-party work, without critical engagement or transformative use.

Assuming that a copyright infringement has occurred, the question of liability arises. The user uploads the protected work to the AI system or enters it in some other way. In doing so, they take the adequate and causal action for the copyright infringement and are therefore the passive party in the lawsuit (see section 4.3 on liability, Section 97 et seq. Copyright Act).[36]

It should be noted that there are considerable legal uncertainties regarding the use of AI systems. Rights holders are therefore advised to regulate the use of their publicly accessible digital works at an early stage. Such usage restrictions can be based on Section 44b para. 3 Copyright Act, for example, and combined with technical protection measures against web scraping. The exclusion declaration can be exercised in the imprint, the general terms and conditions of a website or through collective rights management. [37]

Compliance with such reservations of use is relevant against the background of Article 53 para. 1 lit. c Regulation (EU) 2024/1689 (AI Act). This obliges the provider of generative AI models to ensure compliance with all reservations of rights holders, even when limitations are invoked (see Article 3 and 4 of the DSM Directive, see sections 2.2), by means of technical protection measures.

4. AI-GENERATED RESULTS

4.1 Protection of AI-Generated Content

4.1.1 Copyright Protection of AI-Generated Results

A central problem that keeps coming up in connection with AI-generated content is the question of authorship: Who is considered the author of a work if it was created by an AI system? Is it the AI itself, the developer of the AI, the user who employed the AI, or possibly no one at all? This question leads to fundamental legal considerations, since copyright law traditionally only recognizes natural persons as authors.

---

36. Dreier/Schulze/*Specht-Riemenschneider/Raue*, 8th ed. 2025, Copyright Act Section 97 para. 23.
37. Cf. recital 18 of the DSM Directive; *Pukas* GRUR 2023, 614 614 f.

According to Section 2 (2) Copyright Act, a protected work is a personal intellectual creation, and according to Section 7 Copyright Act, the author is the natural person who created the protected work. A work must exhibit a certain individuality and reach a minimum level of creativity in order to enjoy copyright protection.[38]

So far, an AI system cannot generate new content independently and without human intervention.[39] Human intervention or activation in the form of a prompt is necessary for an AI system to work. Should it be possible in the future for an AI to create works completely autonomously, the current legal situation is that such works would not enjoy copyright protection. This is because, under Section 2, 7 Copyright Act, AI cannot be considered the author.[40]

However, the more relevant question concerns the situation in which a human uses an AI system to create a work. In this case, there is currently a lack of clear legal regulation. In the relevant literature, there is widespread agreement that the human being must be recognized as the author if he or she has had a significant creative influence on the result.[41] The fundamental principle of German copyright law is also relevant in the context of using AI systems: the principle of authorship, as enshrined in Section 2 (2) Copyright Act ('only the authors own'), requires that humans should not be dominated by machines. AI must therefore serve merely as a tool.[42] However, the more an AI takes over artistic decision-making, the less clear the boundaries are. It is therefore necessary to examine each individual case to see whether the human contribution can be considered sufficiently creative to uphold the principle of authorship.[43]

In Germany – unlike in the USA[44] – the question of whether an AI can be considered the author of a work has not yet been decided in court. However, there has already been a significant decision by the Federal Court of Justice (BGH) on the subject of naming inventors in patent law.[45] In the so-called DABUS decision, the BGH clarified that only natural persons can be named as inventors in the patent register.[46] The BGH justified this with the fact that an AI is not a legal entity and therefore cannot fulfil the requirements of patent law.[47] This decision is based on the fundamental view that the inventor, like the author, must be a natural person who has contributed intellectual creativity. As copyright law, like patent law, is intended to honour the human creative process, this reasoning could also be transferable to

---

38. *Wandtke/Bullinger/Bullinger*, Copyright Act Section 2 para. 21 et seq.
39. BGH GRUR 2024, 1315 para. 40 – DABUS; *Dornis* GRUR Patent 2023, 14 para. 12 f.; *Gärtner* GRUR 2022, 207.
40. *Lauber-Rönsberg* GRUR 2019, 244; *Legner* ZUM 2019, 807; *Hetmank/Lauber-Rönsberg* GRUR 2018, 574, 579; *Dornis* GRUR 2019, 1252; *Gerecke* GRUR-Prax 2023, 381.
41. Federal Ministry of Justice, file://f0112475/Ordnerumleitung$/N1247500000008248/Downloads/240305_FAQ_KI_Urheberrecht%20(2).pdf; *Kraetzig* NJW 2024, 697.
42. *Kraetzig* NJW 2024, 697; *Dreier/Schulze/Schulze*, Urheberrechtsgesetz Section 7 para. 2; *Dornis* GRUR 2019, 1252; *Mamaar* ZUM 2023, 481.
43. *Theodoridis* NJW 2025, 689.
44. U.S. District Court for the District of Columbia, August 18, 2023 – 22-1564 GRUR 2024, 287; *Kaesling*, GRUR 2024, 260.
45. BGH GRUR 2024, 1315 – DABUS.
46. BGH GRUR 2024, 1315 – DABUS.
47. BGH GRUR 2024, 1315 – DABUS.

copyright law.[48] A product that is created exclusively by an AI could therefore not fulfil the protective purpose of copyright law, as there is no human creative power in it.[49]

Despite the differences[50] between copyright and patent law, the regulatory objective of both rights is comparable: they are intended to protect, promote and thus incentivize the creative or inventive contribution of humans.[51] However, AI-generated creations lack a human contribution, which precludes copyright protection for such products.

Whether a work generated by AI enjoys copyright protection therefore also depends on how the AI result was created. The decisive factor is the activity of a human being. However, the question arises as to what degree of creativity is sufficient in this context. To assess this, the personal contribution of the human being must be examined in each individual case. A list of the features that are intended to determine the objective design of the subsequent product is sufficient.[52] The more detailed the prompt, the easier it is to control the AI output – with the result that the AI system is used as a tool and is given little creative leeway. For industrial property rights, this means the following according to Section 2 Copyright Act: if a human being enters differentiated and detailed prompts, they may contribute to the individual design of the product. For example, an artist could give an AI instructions on colour selection, composition and style and then manually edit the generated result. Changes made to the product by a human being also suggest the creation of a protected work, provided that these changes significantly shape the unique core of the product.

In contrast to this, a prompt with the following content: 'Create an impressionistic landscape' is opposed to the protection of the work. Such a work of art comes about without any recognizable human influence because the prompt only contains a valuation ('impressionistic') but without specifying the work modalities in detail. In this respect, it should be noted that neither the artistic style nor an abstract idea[53] are protected by copyright in themselves.[54] Finally, copyright protection must be denied if the human being merely makes a selection between different AI outputs (so-called 'curating') – because here there is absolutely no creative achievement in the aforementioned sense.

48. *Theodoridis* NJW 2025, 689.
49. *Theodoridis* NJW 2025, 689.
50. In this respect, in particular see the provisions on moral rights in Section 11 et seq. Copyright Act, which in this do not exist in patent law. Copyright law protects the author 'in his intellectual and form personal relationship to the work [...].'
51. *Theodoridis* NJW 2025, 689.
52. In this respect, the following principle applies within the meaning of Section 2 Copyright Act: Only those forms of expression that are perceptible and 'identifiable with sufficient precision and objectivity' can be protected as a copyright work; see ECJ C-310/17, para. 40, 42 – Levola Hengelo; ECJ C-683/17, para. 32, 34 – Cofemel; BGH GRUR 2021, 1290 para. 58 – Architect's right of access; GRUR 2022, 899 para. 29 – Porsche 911.
53. On the protection of literary figures: BGH ZUM 2011, 151 para. 36 – Perlentaucher; BGH ZUM 2014, 234 para. 25 f. – Pippi-Langstrumpf-Kostüm; similarly: LG Köln ZUM-RD 2024, 410 with annotation Wachtel ZUM-RD-2024, 420.
54. Likewise with regard to the style limitation in AI results: Maamar ZUM 2023, 481 (489); Baumann, NJW 2023, 3673; Hoffmann, ZUM 2024, 166.

4.1.2 *Protection of AI-Generated Results by Other Rights*

If an AI product is not protected as a work under Section 2 Copyright Act, it is in the public domain.[55] However, other legal mechanisms and property rights may apply:

- *Database rights (Section 87a et seq. Copyright Act)*: if AI results are part of a structured database, that database as a whole could be protected if a substantial effort was made to create it. However, it should be noted that every digital product consists of individual data values with independent values. If the protection of AI-generated results under Section 87a et seq. Copyright Act is affirmed, the question therefore arises as to whether all digitized products should not be protected by the database maker's right.[56] It is then questionable whether this is compatible with the legislative intent.
- *Trade secrets*: results generated by AI that remain confidential (e.g. in a company) could be protected by the Trade Secrets Protection Act (GeschGehG).
- *Design protection*: AI-generated results that constitute a design could, under certain circumstances, be protected as a registered design if they are novel and distinctive.
- *Trademarks*: certain AI results (e.g. logos or advertising graphics) could be protected by trademark law if they can be registered as a trademark.

As an alternative approach to protecting AI products, supplementary protection should be considered.[57] The ancillary copyrights regulated in Section 70 et seq. Copyright Act, like the copyright under Section 2 Copyright Act, grant certain exclusive rights. However, they are not based on human performance, but on investments. The focus is not on protecting the relationship between the author and their protected work (see Section 11 Copyright Act for the moral rights component), but rather on the economic effort behind the product.[58] Similar to the enumeration principle of the limitations and exceptions catalog (see Section 44a et seq. Copyright Act, see section 2.2 below), German copyright law only grants supplementary protection to certain products.[59]

It is already possible to consider additional protection for an AI-generated product in the case of sound recordings (Section 85 et seq. Copyright Act), databases (Section 87a et seq. Copyright Act), press products (Section 87f et seq. Copyright Act) and in the case of light and motion pictures (Section 92, 95 Copyright Act). However, the respective requirements for protection are narrow, so that the question of an alternative protection concept arises: introducing a separate intellectual property right for AI results could be considered, in order to define the requirements for the (economic) effort and the exclusive rights granted.[60]

55. Lauber-Rönsberg GRUR 2019, 244; Dornis GRUR 2021, 784 (785 f.); v. Welser GRUR-Prax 2023, 57 (58 f.); Gerecke GRUR-Prax 2023, 381; Hofmann, ZUM 2024, 166.
56. *Baumann* NJW 2023, 3673, 3676, see further under footnote 39.
57. *Baumann* NJW 2023, 3673, 3676.
58. Dreier/Schulze/Dreier, 8th ed. 2025, Copyright Act before Section 70 para. 1 et seq.
59. Dreier/Schulze/Dreier, 8th ed. 2025, Copyright Act before Section 70 para. 14.
60. Baumann NJW 2023, 3673, 3676.

4.2 AI-Generated Results Infringes Existing Copyright

4.2.1 Infringement of Rights

From the above, it follows that AI-generated content that has been created without significant human creative input is generally not considered to be protected by copyright. Works originally generated by an AI system are therefore generally in the public domain. If there are no contractual restrictions, third parties can therefore freely exploit the AI-generated products without having to rely on copyright exceptions.

However, it is not uncommon for supposedly independent AI products to contain recognizable elements of protected works or even reproduce them in full. A copyright infringement occurs when the AI-generated result recognizably adopts parts of a protected work. In this case, there may be an infringement of the right of reproduction (Section 16 Copyright Act) or the right of adaptation (Section 23 Copyright Act). However, this only applies if the protected work in question was actually used to train the AI (see section 2.1 on training AI models and the objective of independent reconstruction). If, on the other hand, an AI randomly generates a work that resembles an existing protected work without having been trained with it, this is a double creation that does not pose any copyright problems.[61]

For outsiders, however, i.e. for the rights holders of the digital works that may have been infringed, as well as for AI users and the courts, it is often not possible to determine whether the act of reproduction is infringing or whether it is a permissible, reconstructive new creation of the pre-existing digital protected work. This is because how the output is generated and which data the neural network of the AI system accesses is rarely disclosed by the operators. This will lead to considerable evidentiary difficulties, since the existence of a copyright infringement under Section 16, 23 Copyright Act can only be conclusively determined if the technical processes are known. It is to be feared that the resulting legal uncertainties will have to be borne by the rights holders of the digital protected works. Against this background, attention is drawn once again to the necessity of reservations of use and the setting up of technical protection measures to protect the rights holders (see sections 2.3 and 3). GEMA has addressed this topic before the District Court Munich I. It is demanding that the operators of the AI models OpenAI and SUMA pay a flat-rate fee to the authors. However, it is linking this to the training of the AI models with protected works – and not to the infringing output. One reason for this early link is the legal uncertainties regarding the AI-generated result, as discussed above.

In practice, however, there will be more cases in which AI-generated content is so similar to existing protected works that it will be difficult to deny the adoption of creative characteristics. On the technical side, this will be due to an almost complete and permanent translation and storage of the work information in the neural network as part of the training of the AI models (sections 2.1 and 3).[62]

---

61. Similarly: Maamar ZUM 2023, 481, 489; Baumann, NJW 2023, 3573, 3677; Hofmann, ZUM 2024, 166, 172 in detail on 'double creations': Konnertz WRP 2023, 796 (803); F. Hofmann WRP 2024, 11 (17).
62. Likewise: Maamar ZUM 2023, 481, 489; Baumann, NJW 2023, 3573, 3677. On the relationship between the training data and the output: Käde, ZUM 2024 174, 182.

In such cases, a copyright infringement under Section 16, 23 Copyright Act may be considered, whereby the degree of similarity is crucial. The decisive factor is whether essential elements of the protected work, in which the individual artistic handwriting of the author is reflected, can be recognized in the AI output.[63] In this respect, an overall assessment must be carried out, whereby the following guideline can be used for the individual case assessment:[64] if the distinctive features of the pre-existing work remain recognizable in the AI-generated product, while the deviations are minor and limited to details, the overall picture will be one of infringing appropriation. However, the situation is different if, in addition to minor deviations, completely different design features also appear in the AI-generated product – because then recognizability is to be denied.

4.2.2 The Intervention of Limitation Provisions

Insofar as it is established that a protected work or a recognizable part thereof is used in an AI-generated result, the question arises as to whether the associated copyright infringement can be legitimized by a limitation.

There are two liability scenarios here: either third parties who use the AI-generated result or the operators of AI systems could be held liable. In the former case, the general copyright law provisions apply. It is necessary to check whether the respective conditions of the limitation regulation are met.

If an AI system processes protected works or recognizable parts thereof, the following limitations of the Copyright Act could apply:

- Temporary acts of reproduction according to Section 44a Copyright Act: the intermediate storage of AI outputs constitutes a reproduction according to Section 16 Copyright Act. However, third parties cannot invoke Section 44a Copyright Act because the storage is not purely technical, but serves to display the AI output.
- Quotations according to Section 51 Copyright Act: if an AI system outputs parts of protected works as a quotation, this could be justified by Section 51 Copyright Act depending on the situation. However, a quotation must meet high standards; in addition, a source must be cited (Section 63 Copyright Act). AI systems usually do without this.[65]
- Caricature, parody or pastiche according to Section 51a Copyright Act: even if an AI-generated output can be objectively classified as a caricature, parody or pastiche (Section 51a Copyright Act; Article 5 (3) (k) Directive 2001/29/EC),[66] the question arises as to whether an AI system can invoke artistic

63. On the criterion of recognisability: ECJ NJW 2019, 2913 para. 39 – Pelham (Metall auf Metall III); Dreier/Schulze/Schulze Copyright Act Section 23 para. 47 et seq.
64. See BGH GRUR 2022, 899 para. 56 f. – Porsche 911. For detailed information on the system of dependent creations and the relationship between Section 16, 23 UrG: *Wachtel*, Derivative Works in the Digital Age. An Examination of Internet-Memes.
65. *Hofmann*, ZUM 2024, 166, 173.
66. On the requirements: Dreier/Schulze/Dreier, 8th ed. 2025, Copyright Act Section 51a; on the current discussion surrounding the concept of pastiche and its applicability to remixes: *Wachtel*, ZUM-RD-2024, 420.

freedom (Article 13 EU Charter of Fundamental Rights) at all. However, both the operators of an AI system and the users who have the system generate content in a targeted manner can invoke the relevant fundamental rights.[67]

- Reproduction for private use under Section 53 Copyright Act: a copy for private use could be permissible, but this requires that the reproduction be carried out by a natural person. It is questionable whether a user who has an AI output generated 'technically accomplishes' this action or controls it sufficiently in normative terms. If this is not the case, Section 53 Copyright Act is not applicable.

4.3 Legal Remedies and Enforcement

If the AI-generated work reaches the level of copyright protection, the following enforcement options are available to the author:

The author can demand cessation under Section 97 para. 1 Copyright Act to prevent further infringements. Furthermore, he or she can claim damages for unauthorized use of the protected work under Section 97 para. 2 Copyright Act. The damages can be calculated in three ways: licence analogy (remuneration that would have been due for legal licensing), surrender of the profits made by the infringer, or compensation for the specific damage suffered by the copyright holder. The copyright holder can also demand destruction or recall under Section 98 Copyright Act and assert a claim for information and accounting under Section 101 Copyright Act.

A cease-and-desist letter is a cost-effective and fast way to enforce claims such as injunctive relief or damages. It is often the first step before a court dispute. In the case of urgent infringements, such as the unauthorized distribution of AI-generated content, the rights holder can apply for a preliminary injunction to stop the use immediately. In Germany, the civil courts are often responsible for copyright disputes. Depending on the amount in dispute and jurisdiction, the action is brought before the district court or local court. For industrial property rights such as trademarks or designs, the Federal Patent Court may also be responsible.

5. CONCLUSIONS

The legal issues surrounding AI and copyright are undoubtedly complex and require an urgent examination of existing legislation. In particular, the questions of authorship of content generated by AI and the use of protected works to train AI models remain unresolved and give rise to considerable uncertainty. It has been shown that the Hamburg Regional Court has already made a good start in its 'first AI judgement' by applying the existing limitations on TDM for the creation of training datasets and has taken the interests of all parties involved adequately into account (see section 2.3).

Nevertheless, it is clear that the existing legal framework is currently insufficient to adequately address the new challenges posed by the use of AI models and AI systems. An adaptation and expansion of the copyright law as well as the European legal framework is therefore essential in the long term. On the one hand, creative,

67. *Baumann* NJW 2023, 3673, 2677 f.; *Hofmann* ZUM 2024, 166, 173.

innovative and inventive human achievements must be protected, but on the other hand, technical progress and the further development of AI technologies must not be hindered. Otherwise, Germany and Europe risk falling behind the USA and Asia in the global technological competition.

To counteract this development, new regulations are needed that take into account both the traditional creative process and the use of AI systems as tools in the creative process - and possibly even as independent creative actors. In this context, the introduction of a neighbouring right along the lines of Section 70 et seq. Copyright Act ('Related Rights', see section 4.1.2). While traditional copyright law is based on individual creative achievement, related rights primarily protect economic exploitation interests, regardless of the requirement of personal intellectual creation (Section 11 et seq. Copyright Act), as required for the protection of works under Section 2 Copyright Act. The introduction of a new intellectual property right for AI-generated content could therefore provide a legal basis for adequately capturing the value of AI-generated content without fundamentally changing the existing copyright system.

The challenge for legislators, legal experts and society in the future will be to find a balanced solution that both protects the rights of authors and ensures the necessary freedom for the development and use of AI systems. This will require an ongoing dialog between technology, law and ethics to ensure that the legal framework can keep pace with developments in the field of AI.

Chapter 8

Hong Kong

Ian Liu

---

1. INTRODUCTION

Under Hong Kong law, the Copyright Ordinance (Cap. 528) (CO), as amended and came into force on 1 May 2023, is the main legislation governing copyright issues. While the Hong Kong Government has conducted a consultation and proposed a plan for legislations, there is currently no specific legislation which regulates artificial intelligence (AI) or generative AI or addresses its copyright issues under Hong Kong law. Existing legislation and judicial precedents are applicable.

2. TRAINING AI MODELS

2.1 Training AI with Copyright Protected Works

Currently, the training of AI requires the input of training data. Depending on the type of AI model, i.e. modality, such data for training an AI model may comprise texts, images, music, videos, codes, and/or other forms of works that are copyrighted works. As of the time of writing, in Hong Kong, as it has not been tested in court, the legality of using third-party copyrighted materials without a licence for AI training purposes remains unsettled, and it is also uncertain whether the fair dealing exceptions would apply in such cases.

Under Section 23(2) CO, copying means 'reproducing the work in any material form' and includes storing the work in any medium by electronic means. As provided by Section 22(3) CO, copying can be of the whole or a substantial part. In *Sony Computer Entertainment Inc & Another v. Lik Sang International Ltd & Others* [2003] HKEC 521, the Hong Kong Court of First Instance dealt with an application for summary judgment over the alleged infringement of copyright in a video game through mod chips and modified consoles. The Court relied on *The Modern Law of Copyright and Designs*, second edition, which states that 'the measure of whether a copy is a substantial part is relative more to quality than to quantity', and that 'substantiality is a matter of degree and quantity, not quality'. In that case, the Court accepted the plaintiff's test that 'when a counterfeit game disc is played for only a brief time, that is sufficient for a substantial amount of the material to be recorded in the RAM and from there to be reproduced only the screen'.

Arguably, when a copyright work is extracted and fed to an AI as training data, there would be copying and storage of the work as the work would be required to be downloaded or copied and stored in computer memory. It is, therefore, assumed that there may be copyright infringement when a person without authorization trains an AI model, subject to any fair dealing exceptions.

2.2 Exceptions/Limitations Allowing Training of AI

There is no general 'fair dealing' exception for the use of copyright works under Hong Kong law. Instead, the CO provides for several fair dealing exceptions only for specific use scenarios, including:

(a) research and private study;[1]
(b) criticism, review, quotation, and reporting and commenting on current events;[2]
(c) parody, satire, caricature and pastiche;[3]
(d) incidental inclusion of copyright material;[4]
(e) giving or receiving instruction for education;[5] and
(f) public administration.[6]

To rely on the fair dealing exceptions, it must be satisfied that the use in dispute is fair dealing and falls under the specified use scenarios. The CO provides for non-exhaustive factors under each scenario for the courts to consider whether there is fair dealing, which generally includes the purpose and nature of the dealing (such as whether it was for profit), the nature of the work, the amount and substantiality of the portion dealt with in relation to the work as a whole, and the effect of the dealing on the potential market for or value of the work. For the exception of criticism, review, quotation, and reporting and commenting on current events under Section 39 CO, a sufficient acknowledgement of the copyright work is specifically required.

In *Capcom Co. Ltd v. Pioneer Technologies Ltd*,[7] the Hong Kong District Court dealt with an application for summary judgment and the leave to appeal against a decision for dismissing the plaintiffs' application for summary judgment and granting unconditional leave to the first defendant to defend the action. The plaintiff alleged copyright infringement over its video game and 'charts and data of the game'. The defendant ran a business of publishing magazines. It did not dispute that it imported

1. CO s. 38.
2. CO s. 39.
3. CO s. 39A.
4. CO s. 40.
5. CO s. 41A.
6. CO s. 54A.
7. [2008] HKEC 682 and [2008] HKEC 392.

images identical or substantially similar to frames from the film, and claimed a defence of fair dealing 'for the purpose of criticism or review' within the meaning of Section 39(1) CO. There was no dispute that the magazine contained an acknowledgement of the plaintiff's copyright and the plaintiff did not claim that the acknowledgement was not sufficient. The Court quoted a passage by Robert Walker L.J. in *Pro Sieben A.G. v. Carlton Television Ltd* [1999] 1 W.L.R. 605:

> 'Criticism or review' and 'reporting current events' are expressions of wide and indefinite scope. Any attempt to plot their precise boundaries is doomed to failure. They are expressions which should be interpreted liberally ...

It can therefore be seen that whether a fair dealing exception would apply is highly fact-sensitive and must be determined on a case-by-case basis.

As of the time of writing, there is no specific exception under the existing fair dealing exceptions of the CO for the training of an AI model. It is noted that the fair dealing exceptions under the CO require that an otherwise infringing act is done 'for the purpose of' a specific use scenario, as specified in the CO. However, as seen in *Capcom Co. Ltd.* above, the court may adopt a liberal approach in interpreting the purposes and avoid giving a rigid definition.

While the fair dealing exceptions are limited by scenarios, it is yet to be seen whether a court would consider that training of an AI model would satisfy one or more of the purposes of 'researching', 'private studying', or 'reviewing' under the existing fair dealing purposes.

As of the time of writing, according to the Public Consultation on Copyright and Artificial Intelligence (2024) ('2024 Consultation Paper'), the Hong Kong Government proposes to introduce a specific Text and Data Mining Exception ('TDM Exception') into the CO for the purposes of computational analysis and processing of text, images, data and/or other types of information, which shall cover (a) conventional text and data mining; and (b) computational data analysis and processing for enhancing the performance of a computer program, such as the development, training and enhancement of AI models.

The TDM Exception aims to promote increased accessibility in copyright works for developing and training AI systems, and to provide legal certainty for copyright users. Users can save time and transaction costs expended on rights clearance, provided that all conditions for the exception are complied with. The conditions may include that the users should have lawful access to the works and other subject matter, the copy should be accompanied by a sufficient acknowledgement, and the copyright owners may 'opt out' and prevent their works from being used in AI training. Also, the exception should not apply in cases which unreasonably prejudice the interests of the owner.

2.3 Summary

Currently under Hong Kong law, prior to the introduction of the TDM Exception for using third-party training data for the purpose of training an AI model, licences from copyright owners of training data would likely be required.

3. USER OF AI SYSTEMS

3.1 Permission to Reproduce and Make Available to the Public

Under the CO, copying of a work and communicating a work to the public by any mode of electronic transmission are acts restricted by copyright unless an exception applies. However, it is yet to be decided by courts whether an AI model may infringe copyright works of others. Due to the design of AI models, neural networks do not store a full or exact copy of the training data in the classical sense; instead, they process information through tokenization and input data is tokenized. However, overfitting can cause AI to memorize specific details, potentially reproducing substantial parts of input data in outputs.

It is evidenced that AI models may however memorize a substantial part of a piece of training data and reproduce it in its outputs, and AI may be instructed or prompted to substantially reproduce whole or substantial part of the user input data. Courts have yet to decide if an AI model's memory or content constitutes a 'substantial reproduction' of a copyright work. This determination is likely fact-dependent. Similarly, the extent to which AI reproduction of user input data amounts to copying will require case-by-case analysis.

With regard to communicating the work to the public, such determination is again highly fact sensitive depending on the operation of the AI model and how the AI model is used. The CO provides that making a work available to the public is reference to making the work available, by wire or wireless means, in such a way that members of the public in Hong Kong or elsewhere may access the work from a place and at a time individually chosen by them (such as by making works available through the internet).[8] A person is to be regarded as having communicated a work to the public if the person has determined the content of the communication.[9] The CO further clarifies that acts which are not considered as 'determined the content of the communication', i.e. a person does not determine the content of a communication only because the person takes one or more steps for the purpose of (a) gaining access to what is made available by someone else in the communication, or (b) receiving the electronic transmission of which the communication consists.[10] For example, an internet user does not determine the content of a communication to him only because he clicks on a link to gain access to a webpage. The CO also clarifies that the mere provision of facilities by any person for enabling or facilitating the communication of a work to the public does not of itself constitute an act of communicating the work to the public.[11] Therefore, determining whether use of AI systems can constitute copying or communicating the work to the public under the CO will be highly fact-sensitive, focusing on who controls the generation of the content.

8. CO s. 28A(3).
9. CO s. 28A(4).
10. CO s. 28A(5).
11. CO s. 28A(6).

3.2 Exception/Limitations

The CO provides for several fair dealing exceptions for specific use scenarios. Depending on the factual scenario, one or more of the fair dealing exceptions may be applicable, including research and private study and criticism, review, quotation, and reporting and commenting on current events. In determining whether any dealing with a work is fair dealing, for instance, under research and private study and criticism and review, the court shall take into account all the circumstances of the case and, in particular (a) the purpose and nature of the dealing, including whether the dealing is for a non-profit-making purpose and whether the dealing is of a commercial nature; (b) the nature of the work; (c) the amount and substantiality of the portion dealt with in relation to the work as a whole; and (d) the effect of the dealing on the potential market for or value of the work. The court will also consider whether the dealing is accompanied by a sufficient acknowledgement, where appropriate.[12]

3.3 Summary

The determination of whether use of AI systems may constitute 'substantial reproduction' of copyrighted works under the CO remains uncertain, hinging on how AI models are created and used. While neural networks typically tokenize data rather than store exact copies, risks like overfitting or user prompting may reproduce protected content. Courts have yet to clarify if such outputs infringe copyright, as this depends on context-specific factors like memorisation extent and user contribution.

4. AI-GENERATED OUTPUT

4.1 Authorship of AI-Generated Literary, Dramatic, Musical or Artistic Work

Although the application of Section 11(3) is yet to be tested by the Hong Kong courts, the CO recognizes the authorship of computer-generated outputs of certain works. Section 11(3) CO provides that, in the case of a literary, dramatic, musical or artistic work ('LDMA Work') which is computer-generated, the author is taken to be the person by whom the arrangements necessary for the creation of the work are undertaken. In relation to AI-generated LDMA Work, the person deemed to have made the arrangements necessary for the creation of the work could include a) the developer/programmer/trainer of the AI model, b) the operator of the AI system who has configured or fine-tuned the AI model, and c) the user who inputs prompts to the AI system to create the AI-generated work, and moreover any or more of the aforementioned persons. The determination of the author and the first copyright owner of the work will be fact-specific and shall be determined on a case-by-case basis.

12. CO s. 38; CO s. 39.

4.2 Protection of AI-Generated Content

The CO recognizes the subsistence of copyright of computer-generated outputs of LDMA Works. Under Section 17(6) CO, a computer-generated work expires at the end of the period of fifty years from the end of the calendar year in which the work was made. 'Computer-generated' work is defined as work that is generated by a computer in circumstances and there is no human author of the work.

According to the 2024 Consultation Paper, the existing provisions governing LDMA works generated by a computer in the CO are capable of protecting AI-generated LDMA works on the basis that these works are computer-generated without a human author, and that they satisfy the originality requirement. On the other hand, the protection afforded to sound recordings, films, broadcasts, cable programs and the typographical arrangement of published editions ('non-LDMA Works') in the CO applies regardless of whether such works are created by human or computers, including AI-generated works. The current position of the 2024 Consultation Paper is that the existing CO contains the necessary provisions which are applicable to provide copyright protection to AI-generated works.

4.3 AI-Generated Output Infringing Existing Copyright

The CO is applicable to determine copyright infringement of existing copyright protectable works arising from the creation and use of AI-generated works. Under the CO, if the creation or use of an AI-generated work involves doing any acts restricted by the CO in relation to the whole or any substantial part of the work (such as copying or making an adaptation, or communicating the work to the public through any mode of electronic transmission), the person doing such acts would commit copyright infringement. This applies unless the person is authorized or has obtained a licence from the copyright owner or the act in question falls within any copyright exception under the CO.

4.4 Remedies and Enforcement

The CO is applicable to provide remedies to copyright infringement arising from the creation and use of AI-generated works. There are statutory exceptions to rights that can be conferred on computer-generated works. Section 91 CO makes clear that the moral right to be identified as author or director does not apply to any computer-generated works. Further, Section 93 CO provides that the right to object to derogatory treatment of work does not apply to computer-generated works.

4.5 Summary

The CO currently already recognizes computer-generated LDMA Works, and through the 2024 Consultation Paper, the Government put forward the proposal that computer-generated non-LDMA Works are also afforded protection under the CO.

5. CONCLUSIONS

5.1 Areas for Further Development

In 2024, the Hong Kong Government commenced the consultation process for the amendment of the CO to specifically address the copyright issues arising from AI-generated works. As mentioned, the 2024 Consultation Paper states that the existing provisions of the CO already provide copyright protection on AI-generated works. With regard to this, the Hong Kong Government invites the public to submit views on, among other things, (i) whether the existing CO offers adequate protection on AI-generated works; (ii) whether the existing legal framework is broad enough to address the liability issues on copyright infringement arising from AI-generated works based on the individual circumstances; and (iii) the possible introduction of a TDM Exception as mentioned in section 2.2 into the new legislation. Additionally, there may be a need for new legislation that takes into account the emerging technology of training AI systems with large datasets.

5.2 Recommendations for AI Users

In light of the current position of Hong Kong law, which provides a certain level of copyright protection on AI-generated work, we recommend AI users implement internal control measures to afford maximum protection to AI-generated work and avoid infringing third parties' rights. AI users should conduct due diligence on AI training methodology and datasets where possible for both using online and offline AI solutions. To reduce risk of infringement, checks should be conducted to ensure that the AI output is not substantially similar to any unlicensed copyright work of a third party.

As to use of online AI services, users should carefully review the terms and conditions or contractual terms as to whether the AI service providers had proper licences from the owner of the copyrights of the training data, and as to indemnity, representations, and warranties.

To formally demonstrate the originality of LDMA Works, it is advisable to maintain a comprehensive record of the creative process. This includes retaining documentation such as inspiration materials, concept notes, drafts, and correspondence related to the creation of the works. Additionally, contemporaneous records of discussions and decisions made during the development process should be preserved.

For works generated using AI, such as large language models or image generation tools, it is essential to track and document the evolution of prompts, inputs, and parameters utilized in their creation. This documentation will serve to evidence the exercise of skill, judgment, and labour expended in the production of the works, thereby supporting claims of originality.

Chapter 9

India

Neel Mason

1. INTRODUCTION

The Copyright Act, 1957 (the 'Copyright Act') governs copyright law in India. Under Section 16 of the Copyright Act, any right or defence in relation to copyright has to fall within the four corners of the legislation.

While reviewing the IPR regime in India, the 161st Parliamentary Report[1] recommended creating a separate category of rights for artificial intelligence (AI) and AI-related works. However, the Minister of Commerce and Industry in a differing opinion stated that the existing IPR regime is well-equipped to protect AI-generated works thus indicating no necessity to establish a separate category of rights and no intent to amend the provisions of the Copyright Act.

The Government of India further made a statement[2] that while they are reviewing laws in relation to data protection and information technology there is no proposal to consider amending the Copyright Act at present to meet the challenges of AI. The Government at present is of the view that the law should be sufficient to deal with challenges raised by AI. However, the Government has also specified that the Copyright Act obligates the user of the AI to obtain permission/licence from the copyright owner to use their works which are not covered under the fair dealing exceptions.[3]

1. Parliamentary Statutory Committee Report No. 161, para. 8.5, 23 July 2021.
2. Ministry of Commerce & Industry, Government of India, Advisory, *Existing IPR regime well-equipped to protect AI generated works, no need to create separate category of rights*, 9 February 2024.
3. Copyright Act, 1957, Section 52.

2. TRAINING AI MODELS

2.1 Training AI with Copyright Protected Works

At present we have no judicial pronouncements in relation to whether AI can be trained using copyright protected works. Recently ANI, a news agency, filed a suit[4] against OpenAI alleging infringement of copyright. While OpenAI has a system that facilitates entities to opt out, ANI claims, being primarily a news syndication agency, that the opt out mechanism is of no value as its syndicate partners/licensees cannot be compelled to opt out. The Indian Music Industry, the Federation of Indian Publishers and the Digital New Broadcasters have intervened[5] in the present matter and may be permitted to make arguments on a point of law. It appears that this matter may set down markers for the way the courts view the issue of training AI models with content that is subject matter of copyright.

Section 14 of the Copyright Act grants the owner of copyright exclusive rights which are set out below:

> *14. Meaning of copyright*
>
> For the purposes of this Act, 'copyright' means the exclusive right subject to the provisions of this Act, to do or authorise the doing of any of the following acts in respect of a work or any substantial part thereof, namely: -
>
> (a) in the case of a literary, dramatic or musical work, not being a computer programme, -
>
> (i) to reproduce the work in any material form including the storing of it in any medium by electronic means;
>
> (ii) to issue copies of the work to the public not being copies already in circulation;
>
> (iii) to perform the work in public, or communicate it to the public;
>
> (iv) to make any cinematograph film or sound recording in respect of the work;
>
> (v) to make any translation of the work;
>
> (vi) to make any adaptation of the work;
>
> (vii) to do, in relation to a translation or an adaptation of the work, any of the acts specified in relation to the work in sub-clauses (i) to (vi);
>
> (b) in the case of a computer programme, -
>
> (i) to do any of the acts specified in clause (a);
>
> (ii) to sell or give on commercial rental or offer for sale or for commercial rental any copy of the computer programme:
>
> Provided that such commercial rental does not apply in respect of computer programmes where the programme itself is not the essential object of the rental.
>
> (c) in the case of an artistic work, -

4. *ANI Media Pvt. Ltd. v. OpenAI Inc & Anr.*, CS(COMM) 1028/2024.
5. Aditi Agrawal, *DNPA, HT, Express, NDTV seek to join ANI lawsuit against OpenAI*, Hindustan Times (27 January 2025) https://www.hindustantimes.com/india-news/dnpa-ht-express-ndtv-seek-to-join-ani-lawsuit-against-openai-101737959742260.html.

(i) to reproduce the work in any material form including –
  (A) the storing of it in any medium by electronic or other means; or
  (B) depiction in three-dimensions of a two-dimensional work; or
  (C) depiction in two-dimensions of a three-dimensional work;
(ii) to communicate the work to the public;
(iii) to issue copies of the work to the public not being copies already in circulation;
(iv) to include the work in any cinematograph film;
(v) to make any adaptation of the work;
(vi) to do in relation to adaptation of the work any of the acts specified in relation to the work in sub-clauses (i) to (iv);

(d) in the case of a cinematograph film, –
(i) to make a copy of the film, including –
  (A) a photograph of any image forming part thereof; or
  (B) storing of it in any medium by electronic or other means;
(ii) to sell or give on commercial rental or offer for sale or for such rental, any copy of the film;
(iii) to communicate the film to the public;

(e) in the case of a sound recording, –
(i) to make any other sound recording embodying it including storing of it in any medium by electronic or other means;
(ii) to sell or give on commercial rental or offer for sale or for such rental, any copy of the sound recording;
(iii) to communicate the sound recording to the public.

An adjudication will need to be made as to what are the rights that are violated by a training module using content that is subject matter of copyright. As present it appears that the storage of data that is subject matter of copyright would amount to a violation of one of the exclusive rights to an owner granted under Section 14 of the Copyright Act. While there are defences for transient or incidental storage, in the view of the author this is unlikely to be a valid defence given that the storage is not incidental to the activity involved. The defence of fair use will be looked at later in this chapter as will the issue of scraping of content.

In the event that permission is required, the entity training the data would require a licence from the owner of copyright. The Copyright Act envisages the manner in which a licence can be granted by the owner to a user. A licence under the Copyright Act must adhere to the following principles:

(a) It needs to be in writing signed by the licensor or an authorized agent.
(b) The licence shall identify the work and specifically the rights that have been licensed including the duration and the territorial extent of the said licence.
(c) The licence should specify the amount of royalty and other consideration payable to the licensor.
(d) If the licence does not set out a time period, it will be deemed to be for a period of five years.
(e) If the territory is not specified, it shall be presumed to extend within India.
(f) Where a licence does not exercise rights within a period of one year, the licence in respect of the rights so granted will be deemed to have lapsed.

The above principles can be contracted to the contrary in both a licence as well as an assignment agreement. The above principles do become relevant in cases where the training modules may give an opt-out clause or expect copyright owners to take some positive steps to ensure that the content that is subject matter of copyright is not utilized in the training of the AI system. It is arguable that any such unilateral declaration or offer will be invalid under the Copyright Act if it fails to follow the principles set out above.

2.2 Exceptions/Limitations Allowing Training of AI

At present there is no legislative proposal to amend the Copyright Act. Certain trade bodies have proposed incorporating an exception for data mining in India.

Under the existing Copyright Act, it is possible however, for an entity to rely on the defence of 'fair dealing'. Fair dealing is an exception to copyright infringement, which has been enumerated under Section 52 of the Copyright Act:

> 52 (1) The following acts shall not constitute an infringement of copyright, namely:-
> (a) fair dealing with any work, not being a computer programme, for the purposes of -
> (i) Private or personal use, including research;
> (ii) Criticism or review, whether of that work or of any other work;
> (iii) The reporting of current events and current affairs including the reporting of an lecture delivered in public.
> Explanation: the storing of any work in any electronic medium for the purposes mentioned in this clause, including the incidental storage of any computer programme which is not itself an infringing copy for the said purposes, shall not constitute infringement of copyright.

From a plain reading of the Section, it is evident that storage for a purpose which falls under the three exceptions of fair dealing will be permitted. The question that really needs clarity is whether the activities for which the storage of works is being done is covered by the three exceptions. Not only will it have to be fair dealing with the works, but it would need to be pigeon holed into one of the exceptions that have been set out above.

Further, the courts in India have been fairly liberal in relation to interpreting the concept of fair dealing, with the Division Bench in *India TV Independent News Service (P) Ltd. v. Yashraj Films (P) Ltd.*[6] having adopted a four-factor test to determine fair dealing relying on the statute in the United States of America (even though the US statute refers to 'fair use' and, in my view, does not have similar limitations). These four factors as observed by the court are as follows: '(i) the purpose and the character of the use, including whether such use is of a commercial nature or is for non-profit educational purposes; (ii) the nature of the copyrighted work; (iii) the amount and substantiality of the portion used in relation to the copyrighted work as a whole; and (iv) the effect of the use upon the potential market for or value of the copyrighted

6. 2012 SCC OnLine Del 4298.

work'.[7] In my view, there will have to be a fact-based decision to understand how the training model uses the content that is the subject matter of copyright to enable the courts to decide the defence. If this defence is held not to be applicable then it is open to the owner of the AI training system to license content from the owner of copyright to avoid a claim of infringement of copyright.

3. USE OF AI SYSTEMS

3.1 Permission to Reproduce and Make Available to the Public

As set out earlier in section 2.1, under Section 14 of the Copyright Act, the owner of the copyright in each and every class of work is given a different set of rights.

For instance, the owner of copyright in a literary, dramatic or musical work that is not a computer program has a right to reproduce the work in any material form (including the storing of it in any medium by electronic means),[8] to make copies of the work, to perform the work in public or communicate it to public, to make a translation or adaptation, to make a cinematographic film or sound recording in respect of the said work. The rights given to the owner are wide in my view, and consequently, feeding such copyright material to train an AI would require a licence. A significant issue being argued in the *ANI* case is that of scraping of content on the internet. Courts will consider whether this will fall within the four corners of the Section 14 of the Copyright Act.

In relation to sound recordings and cinematographic films, storing such works in any medium by electronic or other means amounts to a violation of the exclusive rights of the copyright owner. Therefore, even in this case, it would be necessary to procure a licence for such use to train an AI.

3.2 Exception/Limitations Allowing AI Training

The exceptions that can be used as a defence against unauthorized use of copyright protected works has already been covered under section 2.2 above.

The rights of communication to the public are distinct from the reproducing of the work in any material form and it is therefore arguable that even if the work that is created is distinct from any work that has been used in training the AI system, while that may be a defence to communication to the public, it will not be a defence in relation to 'to reproduce the work in any material form including the storing of it on any medium by electronic means'.

7. 2012 SCC OnLine Del 4298, para 42.
8. Section 14(1)(a)(i) of the Copyright Act, 1957.

4. AI-GENERATED OUTPUT

4.1 Protection of AI-Generated Content

4.1.1 Copyright Protection of AI Output

4.1.1.1 What Would Constitute Works That Would Qualify Within the Copyright Act?

Section 13 of the Copyright Act recognizes original, literary, dramatic, musical and artistic works as well as cinematographic films and sound recordings as 'works'. In India, while the word 'original' is used for literary, dramatic, musical and artistic works, but the work being original is not required for cinematographic films and sound recordings. All works falling in these categories may not be considered the subject matter of copyright.

To be considered the subject matter of copyright, for several decades, the Indian position was based on the 'sweat of the brow test'. The Supreme Court of India, in the case *Eastern Book Company & Ors. v. D.B Modak*[9] ('*Eastern Book*') held that the test is a minimal degree of creativity. The Court held:

> 57. The Copyright Act is not concerned with the original idea but with the expression of thought. Copyright has nothing to do with originality or literary merit. Copyrighted material is that what is created by the author by his own skill, labour and investment of capital, maybe it is a derivative work which gives a flavour of creativity. The copyright work which comes into being should be original in the sense that by virtue of selection, coordination or arrangement of pre-existing data contained in the work, a work somewhat different in character is produced by the author ...
>
> ...
>
> 60 ... for establishing a copyright, the creativity standard applied is not that something must be novel or non-obvious, but some amount of creativity in the work to claim a copyright is required. It does require a minimal degree of creativity.

4.1.1.2 Authorship

In India at present, there has been no authoritative judgment on authorship in relation to AI-generated works. This becomes significant as under Section 17 of the Copyright Act, the first owner of a work shall be the author of the work subject to certain exceptions.

Further, Section 2(d) of the Copyright Act defines an author as:

(i) for a literary or dramatic work it is the author of the work;
(ii) in relation to a musical work it is the composer;

9. 2008 1 SCC 1.

(iii) in relation to an artistic work other than a photograph it is the artist;
(iv) in relation to a photograph, the person taking the photograph;
(v) in relation to a cinematographic film or sound recording it is the producer; and
(vi) in relation to any literary, dramatic, musical, artistic work which is computer generated it is the person who causes the work to be created.

4.1.1.3 Can AI be an Author?

The courts in India have adopted a conservative approach to interpreting the term 'person'. Notably, the High Court of Delhi in *Rupendra Kashyap v. Jiwan Publishing House Pvt. Ltd.*[10] examined the question of whether the Central Board of Secondary Education (CBSE) can claim copyright in a set of question papers. The Court stated that the CBSE, being an artificial person, cannot claim copyright unless it proves that it had engaged persons to prepare the question papers. Subsequently, in 2014, the High Court of Delhi in the case of *Tech Plus Media Private Ltd. v. Jyoti Janda*[11] held:

> 20 ... The plaintiff is a juristic person and is incapable of being the author of any work in which copyright may exist. However the plaintiff can be the owner of a copyright under an agreement with the author of the said work...

Further, the aforesaid position has also been upheld in the case of *Navigators Logistics Ltd. v. Kashif Qureshi & Ors*,[12] wherein it was observed that the authorship cannot lie in a juristic person, although it may be the copyright owner. Consequently, it is clear that the courts in India have adopted a conservative approach in interpreting the term 'person' being a 'natural person' under the Copyright Act. In view of this approach, the question remains: who is an author of an AI-generated work?

In 2020, the Copyright Office of India granted joint authorship to an AI painting app, Raghav. Raghav, which created *Suryast*, a painting autonomously combining Vincent van Gogh's painting *Starry Night* and a photograph taken by Mr Ankit Sahni. The Copyright Office received two applications for registration of *Suryast*. The first application claimed Raghav, the AI painting app, as the sole owner which the Copyright Office turned down. The second application claimed Raghav as the joint author along with Mr Ankit Sahni, who is the owner of the painting. The second application was accepted by the Copyright Office, thus awarding an AI joint authorship in such a work. However, subsequently, a withdrawal notice was sent, seeking clarification of the legal status of Raghav. Mr Ankit Sahni responded to this notice stating that the Copyright Act does not contain any express provision under which it has the power to review its own decision.

Therefore, at present we see potential conflict as to whether AI can claim authorship in relation to literary, dramatic, musical and artistic works. However, in relation to cinematographic films and sound recordings, the producer is deemed to be the author. A producer in relation to a cinematograph film or sound recording

10. 1996 (38) DRJ 81.
11. (2014) 60 PTC 121.
12. (2018) 254 DLT 307.

means a person who takes the initiative and responsibility for making the work.[13] As regards sound recordings and cinematographic films it does pose the question as to who the person is who takes the initiative and responsibility to make the work.

While there may be a bar for AI claiming authorship for original literary, dramatic, musical or artistic works, the case may be different for computer-generated literary, dramatic, musical or artistic works. In my view, in both the case of computer-generated works as well as sound recordings or cinematographic films, the Copyright Act may be wide enough to address the issue of AI-generated works being protected. However, one must bear in mind that there is a distinction between the AI-generated software and the work generated by an AI. In my view, the person who uses the generated software to generate uses/ create the work would be considered to be the author. Issues such as the level of involvement need to be clarified, detailing by the person giving the input have not been considered under the Copyright Act by a judicial pronouncement and one expects that one will get clarity on all these issues in the near future.

4.1.1.4 Infringement by AI-Generated Output

India, like all significant jurisdictions, follows the idea/expression dichotomy in relation to copyright.

The Supreme Court in the case *R.G. Anand v. Deluxe Films*[14] held:

> 2. Where the same idea is being developed in a different manner, it is manifest that the source being common, similarities are bound to occur. In such a case the Courts should determine whether or not the similarities are on fundamental or substantial aspects of the mode of expression adopted in the copyrighted work. If the defendant's work is nothing but a literal imitation of the copyrighted work with some variations here and there it would amount to violation of the copyright. In other words, in order to be actionable, the copy must be a substantial and material one which at once leads to the conclusion that the defendant is guilty of an act of piracy.
>
> 3. One of the surest and the safest tests to determine whether or not there has been a violation of copyright is to see if the reader, spectator or the viewer after having read or seen both the works is clearly of the opinion and gets an unmistakable impression that the subsequent work appears to be a copy of the original.

As mentioned earlier on in this chapter, Section 14 of the Copyright Act confers the right to reproduction and right to adaptation on the copyright owner to the exclusion of others.

Section 51(a)(i) states that a copyright is infringed when a person without a valid licence does anything which is the exclusive right of the copyright owner.

Further, under the Copyright Act the definition of an 'infringing copy', in respect of literary, dramatic, musical or artistic works, refers to a reproduction; while the

13. Section 2(uu), Copyright Act, 1957.
14. (1978) 4 SCC 118.

term 'reproduction' is not defined under the Copyright Act, colloquially it refers to the action/process of copying in most cases identically and even imitatively.

It is clear from the above that in case any AI-generated work/output is literally or substantially similar to any works protected by copyright, likely used to train the generative AI model, it would amount to an infringement. As to the question of who is responsible, the law at present does not specifically deal with the issue relying on existing law, it could potentially be the person who was responsible for using the AI to generate the content or the person who exploits the work. This is something we await clarity on.

4.1.2 Neighbouring Rights Protection of AI Output

As mentioned earlier, India recognises literary, dramatic, artistic and musical works that are original, and in relation to sound recordings and cinematographic films there is no requirement of it being original. The exclusive rights granted to the owner of a sound recording and cinematographic work under Section 14 of the Copyright Act is reproduced in section 2.1 above.

India also recognises performers' rights and broadcasters' special rights:

> *37. Broadcast reproduction right*
>
> (1) Every broadcasting organisation shall have a special right to be known as 'broadcast reproduction right' in respect of its broadcasts.
>
> (2) The broadcast reproduction right shall subsist until twenty-five years from the beginning of the calendar year next following the year in which the broadcast is made.
>
> (3) During the continuance of a broadcast reproduction right in relation to any broadcast, any person who, without the licence of the owner of the right does any of the following acts of the broadcast or any substantial part thereof, –
> (a) re-broadcast the broadcast; or
> (b) causes the broadcast to be heard or seen by the public on payment of any charges; or
> (c) makes any sound recording or visual recording of the broadcast; or
> (d) makes any reproduction of such sound recording or visual recording where such initial recording was done without licence or, where it was licensed, for any purpose not envisaged by such licence; or
> (e) sells or gives on commercial rental or offer for sale or for such rental, any such sound recording or visual recording referred to in clause (c) or clause (d)
>
> shall, subject to the provision of Section 39, be deemed to have infringed the broadcast reproduction right.
>
> *38. Performer's right*
>
> (1) Where any performer appears or engages in any performance, he shall have a special right to be known as the 'performer's right' in relation to such performance.
>
> (2) The performer's right shall subsist until [fifty years] from the beginning of the calendar year next following the year in which the performance is made.

38A. Exclusive right of performers

(1) Without prejudice to the rights conferred on authors, the performer's right which is an exclusive right subject to the provisions of this Act to do or authorise for doing any of the following acts in respect of the performance or any substantial part thereof, namely: -

(a) to make a sound recording or a visual recording of the performance, including -

(i) reproduction of it in any material form including the storing of it in any medium by electronic or any other means;

(ii) issuance of copies of it to the public not being copies already in circulation;

(iii) communication of it to the public;

(iv) selling or giving it on commercial rental or offer for sale or for commercial rental any copy of the recording;

(b) to broadcast or communicate the performance to the public except where the performance is already broadcast.

(2) Once a performer has, by written agreement, consented to the incorporation of his performance in a cinematograph film he shall not, in the absence of any contract to the contrary, object to the enjoyment by the producer of the film of the performer's right in the same film: Provided that, notwithstanding anything contained in this sub-section, the performer shall be entitled for royalties in case of making of the performances for commercial use.

In relation to performers' rights, an issue of attribution will need to be considered. It is possible that new works will be generated creating either the likeness of similar aspects of a performer, such as singing in the voice of a well-known singer. So, while the work that may be created may not originate from the performer, it does contain elements that are attributable to the performer. While we do not have a decision on the issue in relation to generative AI, certain actors have taken action in relation to their image rights against third parties who were using either images or a likeness or a voice to create content. This is an area which would require adjudication as this would fall under the wider issue of attribution. The courts' ex-parte injunction orders in the cases *Anil Kapoor v. Simply Life India*[15] and *Amitabh Bachchan v. Rajat Nagi & Ors*[16] against unauthorized commercial exploitation of a performer's attributes is indicative of the successful efforts of the actors. Further, the judgment of the Delhi High Court in *Digital Collectibles Pte Ltd. v. Galactus Funware Technology Pvt. Ltd.*,[17] recognizes the right of a celebrity to commercially exploit their attributes only to the extent of restraining false endorsements and advertisements and the right does not extend to facts or information relating to the celebrity that are neither personal nor private. Additionally, the judgement in *Krishna Kishore Singh v. Sarla A. Saraogi*[18] has also drawn a distinction between personality rights between celebrities who are alive and those who have passed on, posing a conflicting view to the cases

15. CS(COMM) 652/2023.
16. CS(COMM) 819/2022.
17. 2023 SCC OnLine Del 2306.
18. 2021 SCC OnLine Del 3818.

mentioned earlier, though strictly speaking that would come under privacy rights and not the Copyright Act.

5. REMEDIES AND ENFORCEMENT

The Copyright Act provides both civil and criminal remedies to the owner of copyright. Sections 55 (civil remedies) and 63 (criminal remedies) of the Copyright Act and other applicable Indian laws broadly cover these.

5.1 Civil Remedies

A. Interim remedies such as: (a) interlocutory injunction, which requires the satisfaction of the following (i) establishing a prima facie case; (ii) favourable balance of convenience; and (iii) result in irreparable injury; (b) Anton Pillar Order;[19] (c) a Mareva Injunction;[20] (d) John Doe (Ashok Kumar) Order;[21] and/or (e) a Norwich Pharmacal Order.[22]

B. Pecuniary remedies: (a) damages equivalent to the amount of unlawful profit; (b) compensatory damages; and/or (c) conversion damages attributable to the value of the work.

C. Specific remedies: (a) search and seizure of infringing material; and/or (b) delivery/handover of infringing material to the copyright owner.

5.2 Criminal Remedies

A. Criminal remedy against wilful infringement: (a) imprisonment up to three years but not less than six months; (b) monetary fine no less than INR 50,000, extendable up to INR 200,000.

B. Where infringement has not been made for gain in the course of trade or business: imprisonment for a term of less than six months or a fine of less than INR 50,000.

---

19. Derived from the case *Anton Pillar AG v. Manufacturing Processes* (1976) 1 All ER 779 – includes an injunction restraining the defendant from destroying infringing material, search and seizure and a direction to disclose names of suppliers/consumers.
20. Provided under Order XXXVIII, Rule 5 of the Civil Procedure Code, 1908 (originally derived from *Mareva Compania Naviera SA v. International Bulkcarriers SA* [1980] 1 All ER 213) – involves an instruction to place the defendant's property in whole or a part thereof under the court's disposal to satisfy the decree, in the event of delay/obstruction of decree execution.
21. Derived from the case *Taj Television v. Rajan Mandal* (2003) FSR 22 – involves an order that allows a person or entity to take legal action against an unknown party or parties.
22. Derived from the case *Souza Cruz v. N.K. Jain* (1995) 3 IPA 28 – involves an order to determine relevant information from third parties for gathering supporting evidence to establish infringing activities.

5.3 Jurisdiction

An issue arises as to the jurisdiction of the courts of India in both civil as well as criminal remedies. The Copyright Act extends to the territory of India. Therefore, a question arises as to what the remedies are when training of data which is subject matter of copyright takes place outside the territory of India. While India is a member of most significant conventions and Indian works will be protected in different jurisdictions, it is arguable that while Indian works may be protected, if the allegedly infringing activity is taking place outside the territory of India, then the owner may need to look at the territory where the activities are taking place. It is also possible that courts in India will look at whether the entity training the AI offers their services in India.

6. CONCLUSION

While there is no proposed change to the laws to deal with the challenges of AI, one expects that the decisions in the *ANI* case and other conflicts may lead to calls for legislation depending on the outcome of the said decisions. In my view, rather than to look at creating an exception under the Copyright Act, perhaps the legislature can consider statutory licensing for training AI. This would ensure revenue for the creative industry and certainty for the AI/tech industry. Currently, since statutory licensing does exist for cover versions,[23] FM radio and TV broadcasts[24] under the Copyright Act, it may be worth exploring if a version of statutory licensing can be considered for AI-related challenges.

23. Section 31C, Copyright Act, 1957.
24. Section 31D, Copyright Act, 1957.

Chapter 10

Paraguay

Aldo Fabrizio Modica

1. INTRODUCTION

The rapid development of artificial intelligence (AI) poses significant challenges to copyright law worldwide, including in Paraguay. Paraguay's primary legislation governing copyright is Law No. 1,328/98 on Copyright and Related Rights, which was enacted long before AI's widespread use in content creation. This law does not explicitly address issues related to AI-generated works or the implications of AI training on copyrighted material. In this context, the legal framework's lack of specific provisions for AI highlights the pressing need for modern legislative solutions. This article provides an in-depth examination of the current Paraguayan copyright framework and proposes adjustments to address the transformative impact of AI on intellectual property rights.

2. TRAINING AI MODELS

2.1 Training AI with Copyright-Protected Works

The training of AI models often involves processing extensive datasets that may include copyright-protected works. Paraguayan copyright law stipulates that any reproduction, adaptation, or public communication of a work requires prior authorization from the copyright holder. This means that AI training using copyrighted materials without explicit permission constitutes an infringement. To mitigate these challenges, the following measures are critical:

- contracts and licensing: clear licensing agreements should delineate the terms of use for copyrighted works in AI training datasets;
- public databases: leveraging publicly available databases containing works licensed for AI use could serve as a practical solution;

- responsibility assignment: entities commissioning or developing AI systems must bear the responsibility for ensuring compliance with copyright requirements.

2.2 Exceptions/Limitations Allowing Training of AI

Under Paraguayan copyright law, the existing exceptions and limitations, such as those related to private use or educational purposes, do not extend to the training of AI systems. Unlike jurisdictions that recognize specific exemptions for text and data mining, Paraguay's legislation lacks provisions that would facilitate AI training activities within lawful bounds. This gap restricts the potential for innovation and collaboration in AI development and underscores the need for:

- introducing specific exceptions that allow the use of copyrighted works for AI training under tightly controlled conditions;
- defining permissible purposes, such as non-commercial research or public interest initiatives, to strike a balance between innovation and rights protection.

2.3 Remedies and Enforcement

The enforcement of copyright law in Paraguay is governed by the provisions of Law No. 1,328/98, which offers remedies for infringement through civil and criminal channels. These include compensation for damages, cessation of infringing activities, and punitive measures against violators. Applying these principles to unauthorized AI training involves:

- civil remedies: allowing rights holders to claim damages and seek injunctions against entities training AI with copyrighted content without authorization;
- criminal enforcement: penalizing deliberate and large-scale violations to deter misuse;
- preventative frameworks: establishing monitoring mechanisms to ensure that datasets used for AI training adhere to copyright laws.

2.4 Summary

The absence of specific legal provisions for AI training in Paraguay highlights significant regulatory gaps. Establishing tailored exceptions, licensing frameworks, and robust enforcement mechanisms is essential to enable lawful and ethical AI development.

3. USE OF AI SYSTEMS

3.1 Permission to Reproduce and Make Available to the Public

The integration of AI systems, such as ChatGPT, in reproducing and distributing content raises critical copyright considerations. Under Paraguayan law, reproducing or publicly disseminating copyrighted works requires prior authorization. Key factors include:

- licensing agreements: securing permissions for using copyrighted materials in AI applications;
- liability frameworks: determining whether liability for potential infringements lies with the user, developer, or both.

3.2 Exceptions/Limitations Allowing AI Training

Paraguayan copyright law does not currently provide exceptions that could be directly applied to AI training. However, adapting existing provisions, such as those related to private study or research, could offer limited scope for non-commercial applications of AI systems. Legislative clarity in this area is crucial to foster both compliance and innovation.

3.3 Remedies and Enforcement

In cases where AI systems are used in a manner that infringes copyright, the remedies and enforcement mechanisms in Law No. 1,328/98 apply. These include:

- injunctions: halting the use of AI systems that violate copyright;
- compensation claims: allowing affected rights holders to recover losses incurred due to unauthorized use;
- proactive measures: encouraging AI developers to implement safeguards that minimize the risk of infringing outputs.

3.4 Summary

The use of AI systems for reproducing and distributing copyrighted content must be regulated through comprehensive permissions and tailored exceptions to ensure legal compliance.

4. AI-GENERATED OUTPUT

4.1 Protection of AI-Generated Content

4.1.1 Copyright Protection of AI Output

Paraguayan copyright law traditionally protects works that are original and human-made. This framework challenges the protection of AI-generated content, as AI lacks the legal status of authorship. Potential solutions include:

- assigning economic rights to the individual or entity controlling the AI system;
- recognizing outputs derived from specific human prompts as eligible for copyright protection when originality criteria are met.

4.1.2 Neighbouring Rights Protection of AI Output

Neighbouring rights could provide an alternative means of protection. Unlike copyright, neighbouring rights are not linked to originality or creativity, as they do not involve a creative act. Instead, they protect economic activities related to copyright.

Currently, Paraguayan law only recognizes neighbouring rights for performers, phonogram producers, and broadcasting organizations. However, recognizing such rights for the protection of AI output could potentially provide a suitable solution.

Defining the extent and scope of these rights remains essential to address the specific issues surrounding AI-generated content.

4.2 AI-Generated Output Infringing Existing Copyright

AI outputs that replicate existing copyrighted works raise serious concerns about infringement. When an AI-generated output is a "copy" or "very similar" to a copyrighted work, it may constitute infringement under Paraguayan law, which prohibits unauthorized reproduction or adaptation. The responsibility for such infringement generally lies with the entity operating or programming the AI, as well as the user commissioning the specific output.

However, the determination of infringement depends on:

- substantial similarity: evaluating whether the AI-generated work is sufficiently similar to the original to constitute a derivative work;
- intent and use: considering whether the output was created intentionally to replicate the original or as part of an allowable use under exceptions.

While copyright law offers remedies for such cases, it is essential to clarify that protection of artistic style is not explicitly covered by copyright but may be addressed under unfair competition laws. These laws aim to prevent unauthorized exploitation of a creator's distinctive methods or reputation, providing a complementary avenue for rights holders to seek redress.

4.3 Remedies and Enforcement

Addressing infringement by AI-generated outputs requires:

- establishing liability frameworks that define responsibilities for developers and users;
- implementing technical safeguards to prevent AI from generating infringing content.

4.4 Summary

A balanced approach is essential to protect the rights of original creators while enabling the ethical use of AI-generated content.

5. CONCLUSIONS

The challenges posed by AI technologies to Paraguayan copyright law are unprecedented but present opportunities for legal and technological innovation. To ensure a balanced and forward-looking framework, the following measures are essential:

Adapting legislative frameworks: Paraguay must introduce specific provisions to address the unique challenges posed by AI in copyright. This includes clear definitions of authorship, liability, and the scope of copyright protections for AI-generated works.

Balancing innovation and protection: by encouraging responsible innovation, Paraguay can foster a thriving AI ecosystem while ensuring the protection of intellectual property rights. Legislative amendments should promote technological development without compromising the rights of creators.

Strengthening exceptions and limitations: introducing narrowly tailored exceptions, such as for text and data mining, would enable AI development in non-commercial and public interest contexts. These provisions should ensure that rights holders are not unduly prejudiced while supporting research and innovation.

Clear enforcement mechanisms: robust enforcement measures are critical to deterring unauthorized uses of copyrighted works in AI training and outputs. This includes mechanisms for rights holders to claim damages, obtain injunctions, and resolve disputes efficiently.

International collaboration: AI and copyright are global issues. Paraguay should collaborate with international organizations and other countries to align its legal frameworks with best practices and emerging standards.

Educational initiatives: public awareness and education on AI's impact on copyright can empower stakeholders, including creators, developers, and policymakers, to navigate this evolving landscape effectively. Comprehensive guidelines and resources can support compliance and innovation.

Monitoring and adaptation: as AI technologies evolve, continuous monitoring of their impact on copyright is necessary. Regular updates to the legal framework will ensure that Paraguay remains adaptable to new challenges and opportunities in the AI era.

By embracing these measures, Paraguay can not only address the challenges posed by AI but also position itself as a regional leader in intellectual property regulation. This proactive approach will ensure that the country's legal framework supports both the protection of creators and the advancement of cutting-edge technologies.

Chapter 11

Poland

Martyna Czapska

1. INTRODUCTION

Artificial intelligence (AI) has not been defined under Polish law. For now, the only legal definitions relating to that subject matter that function in the Polish legal systems are those which are present in the EU Artificial Intelligence Act[1] (AI Act) that entered into force on 1 August 2024. The main definition is 'AI system' which started to apply on 2 February 2025. An AI system means: 'a machine-based system that is designed to operate with varying levels of autonomy and that may exhibit adaptiveness after deployment, and that, for explicit or implicit objectives, infers, from the input it receives, how to generate outputs such as predictions, content, recommendations, or decisions that can influence physical or virtual environments'.[2]

Ultimately, the AI Act does not define 'generative AI' as such, but it points out that generative AI models are a typical example of general-purpose AI models and that they allow for flexible generation of content, such as in the form of text, audio, images or video, that can readily accommodate a wide range of distinctive tasks.[3] In simple terms, it could be said that generative AI creates new data, such as text, images, music, or video.[4] Examples of generative AI are: ChatGPT,[5] GitHub Copilot,[6]

1. Regulation (EU) 2024/1689 of the European Parliament and of the Council of 13 June 2024 laying down harmonized rules on artificial intelligence and amending Regulations (EC) No. 300/2008, (EU) No. 167/2013, (EU) No. 168/2013, (EU) 2018/858, (EU) 2018/1139 and (EU) 2019/2144 and Directives 2014/90/EU, (EU) 2016/797 and (EU) 2020/1828 (Artificial Intelligence Act), Official Journal of the European Union L Series, 12.7.2024, hereinafter referred to as 'AI Act'.
2. Article 3(1) of AI Act.
3. AI Act, recital 99.
4. See: https://en.wikipedia.org/wiki/Generative_artificial_intelligence (10 Apr. 2025).
5. https://chat.openai.com/ (10 Apr. 2025).
6. https://github.com/features/copilot/plans (10 Apr. 2025).

Gemini,[7] and Dall-E2.[8] Due to the very nature of operations performed with the use of generative AI (usually outputs resemble, more or less, human works), this type of AI seems to be the one generating main challenges related to copyright.

In addition, there are no works on bills in Poland that relate to AI and copyright. The only regulation that is a part of Polish law is, as mentioned above, the AI Act. As of the time of finalizing this chapter, the Polish government is working on an Act incorporating the AI Act into the Polish law. As of now there is no case law regarding AI and copyright in Poland and no landmark cases that could serve as a benchmark for potential future cases.

The primary source of copyright law in Poland is the Act of 4 February 1994 on Copyright and Related Rights (Copyright Act).[9] Poland is a member, among others, of the Berne Convention and WIPO Copyright Treaty.

Under Article 1 of the Copyright Act:

> The subject matter of copyright is each individual creative work, embodied in any form, regardless of its value, designation, or medium of expression (work). In particular, the subject matter of copyright encompasses: 1) works expressed in words, mathematical symbols or graphics (literary, journalistic, scientific, cartographic and computer programs); 2) artistic works; 3) photographic works; 4) works of string instrument craftsmanship; 5) works of industrial design; 6) works of architecture, urban architecture, and urban planning; 7) musical works and textual and musical works; 8) dramatic works, dramatic works with music, choreographic works, and pantomimes; 9) audiovisual works (including motion pictures). Copyright protection only applies to the medium of expression, and it does not extend to discoveries, ideas, procedures, methods and principles of operation or mathematical concepts. A work is the subject matter of copyright from the moment it is fixed, even if it is unfinished. An author is entitled to protection regardless of his compliance with any formal requirements.

The Copyright Act does not state so explicitly, but it is the commonly accepted consensus in Polish legal doctrine is that the author of a copyrightable work can only be a human being.[10]

2. TRAINING AI MODELS

2.1 Training AI with Copyright Protected Works

A question of whether AI can be trained using copyrighted works should be considered in the context of the provisions of the Copyright Act.

7. https://gemini.google.com/ (10 Apr. 2025).
8. https://openai.com/dall-e-2 (10 Apr. 2025).
9. Full text (available in Polish only): https://isap.sejm.gov.pl/isap.nsf/download.xsp/WDU19940240083/U/D19940083Lj.pdf, unified text: Journal of Laws of 2022, item 2509 (6 Apr. 2025), hereinafter referred to as 'Copyright Act'.
10. See for example: *Ustawa o prawie autorskim i prawach pokrewnych. Komentarz* (E. Ferenc-Szydełko ed., Legalis 4th ed. 2021) (7 Apr. 2025); *Prawo autorskie. Komentarz* (A. Niewęgłowski ed., 2021), Art. 8, Lex (7 Apr. 2025); R. M. Sarbiński [in:], *Prawo autorskie i prawa pokrewne. Komentarz,* W. Machała ed., 2019, Art. 8, Lex (7 Apr. 2025).

The Polish copyright system is dualistic; therefore authors have both moral and economic copyright to the works they create.

Moral rights are regulated in Article 16 of the Copyright Act. Per this provision:

> Unless this Act states otherwise, the moral rights shall protect the link between the author and his/her work which is unlimited in time and independent of any waiver or transfer, and, in particular, the right:
> 1) to authorship of the work;
> 2) to sign the work with the author's name or pseudonym, or to make it available to the public anonymously;
> 3) to have the contents and form of the author's work inviolable and properly used;
> 4) to decide about making the work available to the public for the first time;
> 5) to control the manner of using the work.

Moral rights cannot be waived or transferred, so they will remain with the original author even if economic rights are sold or otherwise transferred. Moral rights to works constituting computer programs are limited to the right to authorship of the work and the right to sign the work with the author's name or pseudonym, or to make it available to the public anonymously.

Economic copyright is author's exclusive right to use the work and to dispose of its use throughout all the fields of exploitation and to receive remuneration for the use of the work (Article 17 of the Copyright Act). It can be transferred to other persons or entities.

Taking the above provisions into consideration, training AI with copyright protected works can be seen as violating the author's or rights holder's (as the case may be) exclusive rights to use and dispose the work. This concerns primarily the right to reproduce works (and other objects protected by copyright, in particular artistic performances, phonograms, and videograms), as well as the right to download data and/or reuse them in whole or in significant part.[11] As a consequence, this means that a work could be used to train AI if either a proper authorization is obtained or if one of the exceptions apply, as described in section 2.2 below.

Authorization can be granted by means of a relevantly scoped licence agreement where a rights holder grants a licence. Under the Copyright Act, a licence agreement must specify the scope, territory, time of use and so-called fields of exploitation, which in other words are areas of use of the work[12] and, as a rule, they must be explicitly indicated in the licence agreement. A non-exclusive licence agreement can take any form, including being a part of terms and conditions on a website, while an exclusive licence must be in writing under pain of nullity (thus, in accordance with Polish law, either with a wet ink signature or signed with a qualified electronic signature recognized under Polish law). Licensing could also take the form of an

11. R. Markiewicz, *ChatGPT i prawo autorskie Unii Europejskiej*, ZNUJ. PPWI 2023, no. 2, pp. 142–171, Lex (10 Apr. 2025)
12. Statutory fields of use are indicated in Article 50 of the Copyright Act.

author distributing their work under of the Creative Commons licences[13] (up to the point when they give their work up for public domain).

As indicated above, moral rights to works cannot be transferred or waived, so it is possible that a rights holder that acquired economic copyright grants a licence to use the work to train AI, while the actual author claims such training violates the author's moral rights to the work. In practice, economic copyright transfer agreements often include provisions where the author commits not to enforce their moral copyright and authorizes a purchaser of economic copyright to execute moral copyright to the work on their behalf. This construction may raise some doubts under the Copyright Act, however, it is a widely adopted market practice and as of now, it has not been challenged by court in a landmark case that would change it.

Lastly, using copyrighted works to train AI would generally be allowed in case of works that are in the public domain, meaning monetary copyright to the works has expired. Apart from author deliberately putting their work in the public domain[14] as mentioned above, the general rule is that monetary copyright expires seventy years after the author's (or the last author's) death.[15] It should be noted, however, that with respect to moral copyrights, in some cases they can be exercised after the author's death. Unless the author provided otherwise, upon the author's death, the lawsuit for the protection of moral rights of the deceased author may be brought by the spouse, and if such does not exist, by descendants, parents, siblings, and descendants of siblings, in that order and, unless the author provided otherwise, these persons are to be authorized in the same order to exercise the moral rights of the deceased author. In addition, unless the author provides otherwise, the lawsuit referred to above may also be brought by the relevant association of authors according to the type of creative activity, or the organization for collective administration of copyright and neighbouring rights which had been administering copyright of the deceased author. As a consequence, even in case of works to which economic copyrights have already expired, using such works to train AI may still be seen as violation of author's moral rights which can be exercised even after author's death by certain persons or entities. Thus, the possibility to use works in the public domain to train AI is not absolute.

2.2 Exceptions/Limitations Allowing Training of AI

The Copyright Act contains a number of cases of the so-called permissible use of the protected works. Permissible use applies to works that have already been disseminated, is free of charge and for purposes of personal use without the permission of the author. It does not, among other things, authorize to use electronic databases possessing the features of a work unless this applies to one's own scientific use not

13. For details see the Creative Commons website: https://creativecommons.org/ (7 Apr. 2025).
14. Legal effectiveness and consequences of such action under the Polish law can be discussed, but details are deliberately left out of this chapter.
15. Article 36 of the Copyright Act indicated the detailed rules applying to different types of works: co-authored works, works where the author is not known, works with respect to which the author's economic rights are, under statutory law, enjoyed by a person other than the author, audio-visual works and textual and music works.

connected with any profit-gaining purposes. Permissible use of copyrighted works is described in Chapter 3 of the Copyright Act and indicates a number of cases, including citation, parody and pastiche.

An exception that is primarily relevant to training AI is the text and data mining (TDM) exception indicated in Article 26(3) of the Copyright Act. TDM is defined as the analysis of text and data solely using automated techniques for analysing text and data in digital form in order to generate specific information, including in particular patterns, trends and correlations. According to this provision, it is permitted to reproduce distributed works for the purpose of TDM, unless the rights holder opts out. Opt-out should be made expressly and appropriately to the manner in which the work has been made available. In case of works made publicly available via the internet, the opt-out should be made in a machine-readable format together with metadata.[16] Works reproduced in accordance with the TDM exception may be stored solely for the purpose of TDM, for as long as necessary to achieve this purpose. That last requirement may be problematic to satisfy. First of all, determining a moment when works are no longer necessary to achieve the TDM permissible purposes may be disputable in particular cases. Secondly, if the works are not removed after that moment, a person or entity would start to be in violation of the rights holder's rights. In Poland there have not yet been any landmark disputes regarding TDM, however, the collective management organizations have opted out from using their data for TDM and are actively encouraging authors and rights holders to do the same by, among other things, sharing a robots.txt file to be used on individual websites.[17] TDM is allowed without the opt-out limitation for specifically indicated types of entities, including cultural heritage institutions, for the purposes of scientific research, if TDM is not performed for the purpose of achieving direct or indirect financial benefits (Article 26(2) of the Copyright Act).

2.3 Remedies and Enforcement

It is not yet established under Polish law whether the mere use of copyrighted work for training AI constitutes violation of monetary or moral copyrights. As indicated above, there is no case law that would help to indicate how Polish courts approach this. Regarding whether the use of copyrighted works for training AI could violate the author's moral rights, it is sometimes perceived as a possible violation of the right to authorship and the right to integrity (sometimes even when a work is used as input but cannot be identified in the AI output). In the opinion of others, such an assessment seems unjustified. The argument here is that mere fact of processing works in AI memory, without the user being able to familiarize themselves with the

16. Within the meaning of Art. 2 point 7 of the Act of 11 August 2021 on open data and the reuse of public sector information (Journal of Laws of 2023, item 1524), i.e.: machine-readable format means a file format structured so that computer programs can identify, recognize, and retrieve specific data and its internal structure.
17. An example of Society of Authors ZAiKS. For details see: https://zaiks.org.pl/en/ai (9 Apr. 2025)

results of such proceedings, cannot be the basis for violation of moral rights even with a broad approach to their protection.[18]

An author whose moral copyrights have been threatened by third party's actions may demand that this action be discontinued. In the event of an infringement, the author may also demand that the person who committed the infringement takes the actions necessary to remove its effects, in particular that they make a public statement of appropriate content and form. If the infringement was culpable, the court may award the author an appropriate sum of money as compensation for the harm suffered or – at the author's request – oblige the perpetrator to pay an appropriate sum of money for a social purpose indicated by the author.

Regarding economic copyrights, protected works to train AI without a relevant legal basis could be considered as violation of these rights, as an author (or a rights holder) has the exclusive right to use the work and to dispose of its use throughout all the fields of exploitation and to receive remuneration for the use of the work. The rights holder whose economic copyrights have been infringed may demand from the person who infringed these rights:

1. to cease the infringement;
2. to remove the effects of the infringement;
3. to compensate the damage caused:
   a. in general terms according to the Polish law provisions regarding damages and compensation[19] or
   b. by paying a sum of money in the amount of two times the appropriate remuneration that would be due at the time of its claim for the consent granted by the rights holder to use the work;
4. to hand over the obtained benefits.

Regardless of the claims specified above, the rights holder may demand a single or repeated publication in the press of a statement of appropriate content and form or disclosing to the public of part or the whole of the court decision issued in the case under consideration, in the manner and to the extent specified by the court.

Alternatively, to demand ceasing the infringement or removing its effects, the court may order the person who has infringed economic copyrights, to pay an appropriate sum of money to the rights holder, if ceasing the infringement or removing the effects of the infringement would be disproportionately burdensome for the infringing party. Depending on the exact nature of copyright infringement in a particular case, ceasing infringement or removing its effects might be hard to achieve. It seems possible that it could even lead to the point where a trained AI would have to be withdrawn from the market. While removing particular works from datasets used for training might be possible, "untraining" AI with respect to particular data will likely be a challenge. In such cases, using this provision appears to be a solution. However, it requires three conditions that might not always be met. First, a perpetrator's request; secondly, the consent of the rights holder, who may simply

18. For details and overview of these positions see: R. Markiewicz, *ChatGPT i prawo autorskie Unii Europejskiej*, ZNUJ. PPWI 2023, n. 2, pp. 142–171., Lex (29 Apr. 2024).
19. These are primarily described in the Polish Civil Code (Act of 23 April 1964, unified text: Journal of Laws of 2024, item 1061).

not want to give it; and thirdly, the infringement must be unintentional, which will call for proving, for example, whether the perpetrator was aware or should have been aware of the possibility that the copyrighted work was used to train AI.

When deciding on the infringement of the law, the court may rule, at the request of the rights holder, on the unlawfully produced items and the means and materials used to produce them, in particular it may rule on their withdrawal from the market, awarding the entitled party the compensation due, or their destruction. When ruling, the court shall consider the gravity of the infringement and the interests of third parties. The question arises as to whether an AI model or system could be recognized as: an unlawfully produced item (when trained on protected works without a relevant legal basis), or material used to produce an unlawful item (AI used to train another AI?). This seems possible, in theory at least.

The above remarks regarding practical difficulties that may occur with respect to ceasing the infringement and removing its effect apply also to infringement of the moral right, given that the author whose moral rights have been threatened by a third party's actions may demand that this action be discontinued. In the event of an infringement, the author may also demand that the person who committed the infringement takes the actions necessary to remove its effects.

When it comes to responsible parties, according to the Polish Civil Code, not only the person who directly caused the damage is liable, but also the person who persuaded another person to cause the damage or assisted such perpetrator, as well as the person who consciously benefited from the damage caused to another person. Depending on the particular case, various entities might be deemed liable for copyright infringement, for example: the provider of the AI, the deployer, the final user and other persons, depending on the circumstances. The liability of a direct perpetrator is independent of fault. The direct perpetrator is responsible for the mere fact of the infringement leading to the occurrence of damage. In case of an indirect infringement, if a person is at least aware that they may contribute to unlawful copyright infringement, it might be sufficient to deem such a person liable.

It is also worth noting that, according to Article 53(1)(c) and (d) of the AI Act, providers of general-purpose AI models are obliged to (i) put in place a policy to comply with EU law on copyright and related rights, and in particular to identify and comply with, including through state-of-the-art technologies, a reservation of rights expressed pursuant to Article 4(3) of Directive (EU) 2019/790,[20] which is implemented in Polish law though the TDM exception and (ii) draw up and make publicly available a sufficiently detailed summary of the content used for the training of the general-purpose AI model, according to a template provided by the AI Office. These two obligations became effective on 2 August 2025, when Chapter V (along with other provisions) of the AI Act start to apply.

20. Directive (EU) 2019/790 of the European Parliament and of the Council of 17 April 2019 on copyright and related rights in the Digital Single Market and amending Directives 96/9/EC and 2001/29/EC, Official Journal of the European Union L 130/92.

2.4 Summary

In the current state of Polish law, training AI with copyrighted works is possible only when there is a relevant legal basis. As of now, such basis would primarily be a licence or the TDM exception, provided however, that the rights holder has not opted out or that the entity who intends to use the works to train AI falls within the statutory catalogue.

The Polish copyright system is dualistic, which means authors have both moral and economic copyright to the works they create. In consequence, unauthorized use of protected works to train AI may violate both types of copyright. Moral rights are non-transferrable and cannot be waived, so there is a possibility that the original author could have claims towards the person violating author's moral rights, even if economic rights have been transferred. Remedies regarding both sets of rights include the right to demand ceasing violation and removing its effect, which may cause technical difficulties and even lead to demanding withdrawing particular AI from the market altogether.

As of now, there has been no landmark court case involving AI, so the practical application of these provisions to the AI-related issues is yet to be tested.

3. USE OF AI SYSTEMS

3.1 Permission to Reproduce and Make Available to the Public

Permissions to both reproduce and make available to the public are exclusive rights of an author or rights holder in case the economic copyrights have been transferred. Thus, the use of AI systems in a way that involves protected works without a proper authorization may infringe copyrights, both moral and economic. Remarks regarding AI training in section 2.1 apply to the use phase as well.

It is worth noting that under the AI Act's provider transparency obligations, the outputs generated by AI should generally be labelled in a clear and visible manner, with some exceptions provided for in the applicable provisions of the AI Act.[21]

3.2 Exception/Limitations Allowing AI Training

Remarks regarding AI training in section 2.1 apply to the use phase as well.

3.3 Remedies and Enforcement

Remarks regarding AI training in section 2.1 apply to the use phase as well.

3.4 Summary

Copyright infringement may occur at different stages of the AI life cycle, not just the training phase. Whether an infringement takes place or not will heavily depend

21. Chapter IV of AI Act, which will start to apply on 2 August 2026.

on, among other things, the technical details of how the particular AI-based tool works. For example, it may not use the whole works to train and the used fragments may not satisfy the statutory criteria of work (they may not be creative enough, plainly speaking). When it comes to the use phase (for output remarks see section 4 below), it is a question of whether the works are still present in the AI-based tool or whether they have been removed and are not directly used anymore. While the legal framework for copyright infringement remains the same, the circumstances of a particular case, including the characteristics and features of a specific AI, will likely play a crucial part.

4. AI-GENERATED OUTPUT

4.1 Protection of AI-Generated Content

As indicated above, there is a consensus in the Polish legal doctrine that an author must be a human being. By an analogy to the use of an 'ordinary' computer program (one not involving AI), works could sometimes be computer-generated images (graphics or computer animation) if they are the work of a human being and not just a computer.[22] A computer program is seen merely as a tool. It seems to be the consensus that the creator of, for example, graphics is not, as a rule, the creator of the graphics program (used to create it), unless the images generated on the computer screen would be the result of mechanical implementation of instructions for using the program (e.g., the user only duplicates the instructions in order to generate a specific drawing by the computer and then print it out).[23]

This view leads in turn to a conclusion that output generated solely by AI, without any human contribution, cannot be copyrighted at all.[24] If human contribution exists, then it should be assessed, on a case by case basis, whether the effect of it satisfies the statutory requirements for being deemed as a copyrightable work[25] (as a reminder: it should be an individual creative work, embodied in any form, regardless of its value, designation, or medium of expression). And even if so, another analysis must be made in each case: whether the effect of the human contribution that constitutes a copyrightable work is only a part of output or the whole of it, hence, whether the whole output could be copyrighted or not. In any case, under the above consensus, outputs that are fully computer-generated, without any human contribution, cannot be copyrighted.[26] Some scholars are of the opinion

22. *Prawo autorskie. System prawa prywatnego. Tom 13*, edited by J. Barta, 4th edition, 2017, Chapter II, §1(3), Legalis (10 Apr. 2025).
23. See for example: *Prawo autorskie. System prawa prywatnego. Tom 13*, edited by J. Barta, 4th edition, 2017, Chapter II, §1(3), Legalis (10 Apr. 2025).
24. See for example: *Prawo autorskie. System prawa prywatnego. Tom 13*, edited by J. Barta, 4th edition, 2017, Chapter III, §9(1), Legalis (10 Apr. 2025); D. Flisak [in:] M. Bukowski, Z. Okoń, P. Podrecki, J. Raglewski, S. Stanisławska-Kloc, T. Targosz, D. Flisak, *Prawo autorskie i prawa pokrewne. Komentarz*, 2015, Art. 8, Lex (10 Apr. 2025).
25. A. Bar, *Prawo autorskie w erze sztucznej inteligencji Uwagi na tle historii 'Portretu Edmonda de Belamy'*, PME 2022, n. 1, p. 17, Legalis (10 Apr. 2025).
26. See for example: R. Markiewicz, *ChatGPT i prawo autorskie Unii Europejskiej*, ZNUJ. PPWI 2023, n. 2, pp. 142–171, Lex (10 Apr. 2025); A. Bar, *Prawo autorskie w erze sztucznej*

that AI-generated outputs should in fact remain in the public domain because the investment outlays and intellectual effort are sufficiently rewarded by the fact that an AI system itself can be copyrighted and thus one can make money by licensing it to the users.[27]

Another conclusion presented in the Polish legal doctrine is that in the current state of law, AI outputs could have a similar status as ghostwritten works, meaning that a work will be distributed under the name of a person who ordered it (in this case: a user who initiated creative operation).[28]

Leaving the above conclusion to one side, it is worth noting that several options regarding who should be the owner of copyright to the output (assuming output could be copyrighted) are presented in the Polish legal doctrine. These are, among others:[29] developers of an AI system; trainers and/or data providers; feedback providers; the 'owner' of an AI system; the user of an AI system who initiates creative operation; the purchaser of an AI product; government entities; those using a work-for-hire model to generate an AI output. Sometimes it is considered that copyright should be assumed to AI itself, but this is a margin view and one that is not possible under the current legal system, where AI does not have any legal personality.[30] Unless that changes, AI cannot have any rights attributed to itself.[31]

Most of these options are based on a human contribution, achieved one way or another. The question is whose contribution is the most significant and creative in the sense of satisfying the requirements of the Copyright Act. Is it a developer who developed the AI system and possibly designed the way it works ('thinks')? Is it a user who initiates a creative operation? That would probably depend on whether such initiating is limited to 'pushing the button' or whether indeed a creative input is needed to use an AI tool. Similar logic applies to other options: one could argue that the creative nature of the output depends on the set of data used to train an AI or that a person who gives feedback (in order to improve an output and/or to choose the best one). Attributing copyright merely to a purchaser of an AI product does not

---

inteligencji Uwagi na tle historii 'Portretu Edmonda de Belamy', PME 2022, n. 1, p. 17, Legalis (10 Apr. 2025).

27. See for example A. Bar, *Prawo autorskie w erze sztucznej inteligencji Uwagi na tle historii 'Portretu Edmonda de Belamy'*, PME 2022, n. 1, p. 17, Legalis (10 Apr. 2025).
28. A. Nowak-Gruca, *Artystyczna twórczość cyborgów*, IUSNOVUM 2022, No. 2, p. 79, Legalis (10 Apr. 2025).
29. Review cited as made by A. Nowak-Gruca, *Artystyczna twórczość cyborgów*, IUSNOVUM 2022, n. 2, p. 79, Legalis (10 Apr. 2025).
30. There is, however, an alternate conception in the Polish legal doctrine, according to which authorship of output would be attributed to an AI itself, but not within the meaning of attributing monetary or personal copyrights to an AI but leaving potential rights of such an 'author' unprotected. Authors propose other solutions outside of the copyright regime, such as a special tax imposed on using AI or granting rights to an output to a national or international foundation created for purpose of handling them. See: P. Księżak, S. Wojtczak, *Prawo autorskie wobec sztucznej inteligencji (próba alternatywnego spojrzenia)*, PiP 2021, n. 2, pp. 18–33., Lex (10 Apr. 2025).
31. As a side note, it is not really determined what should be considered as an AI in this context. As indicated above, the AI Act defines the terms 'AI system', which in my view is clearly a tool. Granting AI with legal personality would first require identifying what an AI as such is and defining it properly, which is unlikely to happen in foreseeable future.

seem to be convincing, as there is no contribution-related component and mere fact of purchasing a product is not even in a remote way related to creating its output. Regarding using a work-for-hire model (if at all possible, under the continental law regime, it would be somewhat limited compared to the common law system[32]) and the government as an owner of copyright, we will not get into details here. It is worth noting that another solution that is being proposed is creating a *sui generis* right,[33] similar to those protecting the investments in databases. This last option is an interesting direction that shifts the focus from copyright protection to protecting investing in an AI system instead. This seems like a direction worth exploring. A similar proposition, when it comes to the purpose of protecting investment, is creating a new related (neighbouring) right.[34]

4.2 AI-Generated Output Infringes Existing Copyright

If an AI-generated output is similar to the copyrighted work, to the point that it could be considered a derivative work, the above considerations apply. Under the Copyright Act, a work deriving from another person's work, such as in particular a translation, transformation, or adaptation of an original work, is the subject matter of copyright, notwithstanding the right in the original work. The Copyright Act uses the notion of work, meaning that a derivative work still must satisfy the statutory criteria for being deemed as a copyrightable work.[35] Thus, the above considerations regarding whether AI-generated output can be copyrighted apply.

At the same time, an input that is too similar to an existing protected work may violate the author's or rights holder's copyrights. For example, it could be so-called plagiarism. "Plagiarism" is not a term defined in the Copyright Act and may in fact be used to describe different violations. Often it will mean self-attribution with respect to somebody else's work or, which in case of AI outputs seems to be more relevant, an unlawfully acquired fragment of another person's work, for which the perpetrator of the infringement claims authorship. Polish legal doctrine distinguishes numerous types of plagiarism, depending, among other things, on how exactly perpetration acquired somebody else's work into their own. Determining a specific form of violation depends on the circumstances of a particular case, but the general conclusion is that AI-generated output can infringe existing copyright. Violation can also take place with respect to moral copyrights, as in the case of training AI.

As a side note, in case an author or a rights holder believes that the output violates their rights, they could also seek legal basis for claims in legal provisions

---

32. See the details and literature cited in P. Juściński, *Prawo autorskie w obliczu rozwoju sztucznej inteligencji*, ZNUJ. PPWI 2019, n. 1, pp. 5–44, Lex (10 Apr. 2025).
33. A. Bar, *Prawo autorskie w erze sztucznej inteligencji Uwagi na tle historii 'Portretu Edmonda de Belamy'*, PME 2022, n. 1, p. 17, Legalis (10 Apr. 2025).
34. See for example: A. Bar, *Prawo autorskie w erze sztucznej inteligencji Uwagi na tle historii 'Portretu Edmonda de Belamy'*, PME 2022, n. 1, p. 17, Legalis (10 Apr. 2025); P. P. Juściński, *Prawo autorskie w obliczu rozwoju sztucznej inteligencji*, ZNUJ. PPWI 2019, n. 1, pp. 5–44, Lex (10 Apr. 2025).
35. See also: A. Auleytner, *Prawnoautorska ochrona rezultatów działalności intelektualnej człowieka obejmujących wytwory sztucznej inteligencji*, supplement to MOP 2020, n. 20, p. 125, Legalis (9 Apr. 2025).

other than the Copyright Act. For example if an output is parasitic on other people's work (for example an output that imitates a particular work or a style of a particular author,[36] and such style will not necessarily satisfy the premises to be deemed a copyrightable work), claims could potentially be based on an Act of 16 April 1993 on Combating Unfair Competition[37] as such parasitic use could be deemed as an act of unfair competition. In the lack of a landmark court case in Poland, and in general no case law that would be broadly described whatsoever, this concept has not yet been tested and for now remains a theoretical (although in my opinion a fairly good) legal possibility. Another potential legal possibility is to claim infringement based on the provision regarding the so-called personal rights, one of which is the right of creativity.[38]

4.3 Remedies and Enforcement

Remarks regarding AI training in section 2.1 apply to using the output as well.

4.4 Summary

Polish law does not contain copyright provisions that would explicitly refer to AI-generated outputs. Thus, the general rules of copyright law apply. There is a widely adopted consensus in the Polish legal doctrine that an author must be a human being. It seems unlikely that this view will be questioned in the foreseeable future. This leads to the conclusion that outputs generated by AI, without any significant human involvement which would be creative within the meaning of applicable laws, cannot be copyrighted. The required extent and type of human involvement and the means to prove it pose questions that have not yet been answered or challenged within the Polish legal landscape.

Outputs may infringe a person's copyright (or other rights). Considering the dualistic copyright in Poland, such infringement may concern either moral or economic copyright or both at the same time. The type of violation will depend on the circumstances of a particular case. It is yet to be seen how the remedies for copyright infringement will be applied in practice when it comes to AI-generated output.

36. As an example of AI which learned from one person's works and created an output that is clearly based on a particular's author works and style, see project *The Next Rembrandt*, as a result of which a 'new' Rembrandt's painting was created. Of course, Rembrandt himself is long dead and this project was more of a scientific nature. The purpose of referring to it is to illustrate the potential mechanism discussed for the purposes of this paragraph. For more details see: https://www.vml.com/work/next-rembrandt (9 Apr. 2025).
37. Consolidated text: Journal of Laws of 2022, Item 1233. The Act implements Directive 97/55/EC of European Parliament and of the Council of 6 October 1997 amending Directive 84/450/EEC concerning misleading advertising so as to include comparative advertising.
38. Article 23 of the Polish Civil Code.

5. CONCLUSIONS

AI is a great legal challenge, even more so within the copyright area. Starting from training AI, which requires massive amounts of data, the question is whether protected works can be used for that purpose. In the United States, rights holders are opposing it which is resulting in numerous lawsuits. In Poland some collective management organizations opted out of the TDM exception and are encouraging authors to do the same. For now, the safest, from the legal point of view, option to train AI on protected works without the risk of a lawsuit would be to obtain a relevantly scoped licence from the rights holders. Under Polish law, however, authors' non-transferrable, non-waivable moral right must also be taken into consideration. The Copyright Act provides several remedies for authors (and rights holders) whose rights are violated, including ceasing the violation and removing the effect of it. This raises the question of how to achieve such effect when it comes to AI trained on someone's work where it may be technically difficult or even impossible to, for instance, remove the works from AI already trained. This has not yet been tested in court practice in Poland.

When it comes to using the AI-generated output, the possibility that it may violate intellectual property rights is one risk factor. Another one is that rights to such output are not clearly regulated, and it is doubtful whether it can be copyrighted. Under Polish law, only humans are eligible for being recognized as authors, so this would depend on the extent of human involvement in creating the final form of such output. Output generated solely by AI will not be eligible for copyright protection under Polish law. This means that, on the grounds of copyright law at least, exclusive rights to such output could not be claimed. That in turn creates a risk for example for anyone who would like to use such output for commercial purposes. In practice it seems that persons wanting to use AI-generated output and use the protection available under the Copyright Act might simply claim authorship of such outputs, even if against the provisions of the AI Act. The question is whether there will be tools allowing to verify it.

Given the growing numbers of AI use and how easily AI can generate outputs that closely resemble human works, to the extent they even can be presented as originals, legal developments in this area are to be expected. It remains to be seen which direction they will take, whether they will focus on, for example, creating a new *sui generis* law to protect investment efforts undertaken to create AI-generated output (or AI capable of generating them) or maybe changing the definition of works under the copyright laws to somehow include the outputs, or maybe expanding neighbouring rights to achieve the same. Time will tell. It seems probable that these kinds of developments may happen on the European Union level in order to harmonize the approach and regulations across the member countries.

Chapter 12

Sweden

Malin Ekstrand and Sofia Sars

1. INTRODUCTION

The Swedish Act on Copyright in Literary and Artistic Works (1960:729) (SCA) grants authors exclusive rights to their original literary or artistic works without any registration required. The exclusivity of authors entails the exclusive right to reproduce and make available their works to the public, Section 2, first paragraph SCA. These rights aim to ensure that rights holders maintain control over how their works are exploited, reproduced and distributed, principles that are facing new challenges by the rapid development and use of artificial intelligence (AI).

The SCA also provides certain exclusive rights to performing artists and producers, so called 'neighbouring rights'. In the following, the author (the creator of a work) and/or the person or entity that has subsequently acquired rights to the protected work, and/or the person or entity holding a neighbouring right (as a producer, performing artist or assignee), will be referred to as the 'rights holder'. Further, references to 'protected works' will entail materials eligible for protection by copyright or neighbouring rights.

At the European level, the European Union (EU) has played a significant role in shaping the regulatory landscape for both AI and copyright. One of the key EU legislative acts in this area is the so-called Infosoc Directive (2001/29)[1] which harmonizes copyright legislation across EU Member States. The Infosoc Directive has been central in adapting copyright protections also in a digital context, ensuring that authors and creators continue to have control over their protected works in digital environments.

1. Directive (EC) 2001/29 on the harmonisation of certain aspects of copyright and related rights in the information society ('Infosoc Directive').

In addition, the so-called digital single market directive (2019/790)[2] ('DSM Directive') introduced specific provisions related to text and data mining (TDM). TDM is a crucial activity for the training of AI models, which involves the analysis of large datasets to extract information and patterns. The DSM Directive introduced exceptions that may allow the use of copyrighted works in connection with TDM, with the purpose of making it easier for AI developers to access the data they need without facing legal barriers.

More recently, the EU has established a regulatory framework for AI technologies with a focus on ensuring safety, transparency and accountability by adopting the Artificial Intelligence Act (2024/1689)[3] ('AI Act'). While the AI Act is primarily concerned with risk management in AI development, it has implications for intellectual property law. It introduces a transparency requirement for AI companies, obliging them to implement a policy on how they comply with EU copyright law, including respecting opt-outs, and to provide a sufficiently detailed summary of the training data used for their AI models.

As a Member State, Sweden's legal landscape in the fields of copyright and AI is closely tied to developments at the EU level. This means that Sweden's approach is not only a matter of national legal practice, but also a reflection of a broader European approach. This chapter provides an overview of how Sweden navigates the intersection of AI and copyright.

2. TRAINING AI MODELS

2.1 Training AI with Copyright Protected Works

In order to program a general-purpose AI model, especially a generative AI model, the AI model must be trained on great quantities of already existing information and materials, which may include text, images, videos and sound recordings. Such materials are often protected works. In general, during the training phase of a generative AI model, such existing protected works are reproduced, and such reproductions are then analysed. Information and data about the protected works are extracted from the reproductions of protected works, and such information is used to train the AI model.[4]

Provided that a reproduction of a protected work is made when a generative AI model is trained, this is an act that falls within the exclusive rights of the rights holder. The act of reproducing a protected work, as a rule, requires the rights holder's authorization, unless an exception or limitation to the exclusivity of the rights holder applies.

---

2. Directive (EU) 2019/790 on copyright and related rights in the Digital Single Market and amending Directives 96/9/EC and 2001/29/EC.
3. Regulation (EU) 2024/1689 laying down harmonized rules on artificial intelligence and amending regulations (EC) No. 300/2008, (EU) No. 167/2013, (EU) No. 168/2013, (EU) 2018/858, (EU) 2018/1139 and (EU) 2019/2144 and Directives 2014/90/EU, (EU) 2016/797 and (EU) 2020/1828 (Artificial Intelligence Act).
4. See the AI Act, recital no. 105.

When applying certain exceptions or limitations to the exclusivity of the rights holder under EU copyright law, the so-called three-step rule as introduced in the Berne Convention[5] must be adhered to.[6] The three-step rule entails, in short, the following: i) an exception or limitation may only be applied in certain specific cases, meaning the exception or limitation must be clearly defined and delimited for certain purposes; ii) an exception or limitation may not be applied in a way that conflicts with normal exploitation of the protected work; and iii) an exception or limitation may not be applied in a way that unreasonably prejudices the legitimate interests of the rights holder.[7] The three-step rule must be applied by the legislator, when introducing new exceptions or limitations to the exclusivity of the rights holder, and also by courts when applying such exceptions and limitations.[8]

2.2 Exceptions/Limitations Allowing Training of AI

2.2.1 Temporary Reproductions

As described above, Swedish copyright law is the result of implementation of EU legislation. The Infosoc Directive introduced and codified a number of exceptions and limitations to the exclusivity of rights holders in copyright law. One such exception is the exception for so-called temporary reproductions of protected works under Article 5.1 of the Infosoc Directive.

A temporary reproduction of a work, which is transient or incidental, and is an integral and essential part of a technological process, whose sole purpose is to enable either a) a transmission in a network between third parties by an intermediary, or b) a lawful use, is exempted from the rights holder's exclusive right to reproduction, provided such reproduction does not have any independent economic significance. According to Article 5.5 of the Infosoc Directive, the three-step rule must be adhered to when applying the exception or limitation for temporary reproductions as provided in Article 5.1.

The exception for temporary reproductions has been implemented into Swedish law in Section 11a SCA. Although the reproductions of protected works created during the training of an AI model likely fulfil the requirements of being transient or incidental and are an integral and essential part of a technological process, it is not certain that the purposes necessary for permissibility of the reproductions, as outlined in Section 11a SCA, are present. The purpose of enabling a transmission in a network between third parties by an intermediary primarily aims at temporary copies created on servers or in the cache memory of computers when someone is lawfully accessing a protected work online.[9] As this is not applicable to the reproduction of protected works for the purpose of training an AI model, the remaining purpose outlined in Section 11a for the temporary copies is to enable a lawful use. This

5. The Berne Convention for the Protection of Literary and Artistic Works, adopted in 1886.
6. See Art. 5.5 in the Infosoc Directive.
7. See for example Swedish preparatory works, SOU 2024:4, p. 121.
8. See case law from the Court of Justice of the European Union, case C-435/12, and case law from the Swedish Supreme Court in case NJA 2016 p. 212 'Wikimedia'.
9. See the Swedish preparatory works, prop. 2004/05:110 p. 381.

means, the exception from the copyright exclusivity under Section 11a SCA cannot be independently applied on the reproduction of protected works for the training of AI models, and the exception is therefore not ideal to rely on for such acts.

2.2.2 Text and Data Mining

Through the DSM Directive, the EU legislator introduced new exceptions or limitations to the rights holder's exclusive rights under copyright law for the purposes of TDM. According to Article 2.2 of the DSM Directive, TDM is an automated analytical technique aimed at analysing text and data in digital form in order to generate information which includes, but is not limited to, patterns, trends and correlations.

The new general exception or limitation for TDM is established in Article 4 of the DSM Directive and allows for anyone to reproduce or extract protected works for the purpose of TDM, provided that such works have been lawfully accessed. Reproductions and extractions of such protected works may be retained for as long as is necessary for the purposes of TDM. However, rights holders to protected works have the option of expressly reserving the right of reproducing or extracting the protected works for the purpose of TDM, a so-called 'opt-out' (see Article 4.3, DSM Directive). Such reservation must be made in an appropriate manner, which regarding content made publicly available online entails that the reservation is expressly made by machine-readable means.

For research organizations and cultural heritage institutions that perform TDM on protected works for the purpose of scientific research, a special exception or limitation is established in Article 3 of the DSM Directive. Under this exception, research organizations and cultural heritage institutions may retain reproductions or extractions of protected works created through TDM for as long as is necessary for such scientific research. Rights holders to protected works cannot prevent such TDM as is described in Article 3 of the DSM Directive, by expressly reserving such use, as opposed to the general exception for TDM under Article 4 of the DSM Directive. As is the case for certain other exceptions and limitations to the rights holder's exclusivity under EU copyright law, the three-step rule also applies to the TDM exceptions.[10]

Articles 3 and 4 of the DSM Directive have been implemented into Swedish law in Sections 15a (general TDM exception) and 15b (TDM exception for scientific purposes) of the SCA. In Section 15a SCA, the Swedish legislator has clarified that the exception applies only for the purpose of TDM, and any reproductions or extractions of protected works may not be used for any other purposes. Regarding the requirement of lawful access to the relevant protected works, the Swedish legislator has clarified in preparatory works that this means access with authorization from the rights holder or otherwise with a legal basis, and that reproductions may only be made from a lawful copy of the protected work.[11]

So far, there is no case law in Sweden regarding the application of the TDM exceptions under Sections 15a-15b SCA, but the general understanding is that these exceptions are applicable to the reproduction of protected works that take place when training AI models. It is still relatively unclear exactly how a rights holder should

10. See Art. 7.2 of the DSM Directive.
11. Swedish preparatory work, prop. 2021/22:278 p. 220.

appropriately reserve its right to perform TDM on its protected works, in order for such reservation to be respected.

The EU legislator has however clarified that the providers of general-purpose AI models are required to adopt a policy on how it complies with copyright law and specifically the rights holders' possible reservation of the use of their protected works for TDM in accordance with Article 4 of the DSM Directive, through inter alia state-of-the-art technologies, see Article 53.1(c), AI Act. If a rights holder has made such a reservation, then the providers of general-purpose AI models must obtain an authorization from the relevant rights holder, in order to perform TDM on the relevant protected work.[12] Additionally, providers of general-purpose AI models are obligated to make available a sufficiently detailed summary about the content used for training its AI model, see Article 53.1 (d) AI Act.

2.3 Remedies and Enforcement

Under Swedish law, there are both civil and criminal sanctions against copyright infringements. Such sanctions may apply when a provider of a general-purpose AI model trains the AI model on protected works, despite the relevant rights holder having reserved the right to perform TDM acts on the relevant works.

Where such training on protected works, despite the rights holder's reservation, is carried out intently or grossly negligently, a provider of an AI model may be liable for criminal copyright infringement, Section 53 SCA. However, only natural persons can be liable for crimes under Swedish law, i.e. not a company or legal person. If the unlawful training of an AI model, which amounts to criminal copyright infringement, has resulted in any profits, such profits may be confiscated and forfeited subject to the Swedish Criminal Code (1962:700).[13]

Someone who unlawfully trains an AI model on protected works, despite the rights holder's reservation thereto, is liable to pay reasonable compensation to the rights holder, Section 54, first paragraph SCA. This applies regardless of the infringer's intent or negligence in relation to the unlawful training. If the unlawful training is performed with intent or negligence (i.e. not gross negligence), the infringer is also liable to pay damages to the rights holder, Section 54, second paragraph SCA. The damages shall compensate any additional damage caused by the infringement or violation, whereby particular consideration shall be given to lost profits, profits made by the party that committed the infringement or violation, non-pecuniary damage and the interest of the rights holder in avoiding infringements.

The infringing reproductions of the protected works, as created through unlawful training of an AI model, can be subject to injunction under Section 53b SCA. Such an injunction means the infringer is prohibited to continue to commit, aid or abet an act that constitutes infringement, such as using an infringing reproduction of protected works to train an AI model, by penalty of fines.

According to Section 55 SCA, a court may order that the infringing reproductions of protected works are recalled from the market, altered, destroyed or that another measure is taken against the reproductions.

12. See also Regulation (EU) 2024/1689, Recital 105.
13. See especially chapter 36, Sections 3–6.

Furthermore, a court may issue an information injunction by penalty of fines, according to Section 53c SCA, which entails an obligation for the recipient to provide information about infringing goods or services. The recipient of the injunction does not have to be the purported infringer, but can be anyone that has exploited the infringing goods and/or used services that the infringement concerns on a commercial scale, has provided an electronic communication service or other service used in connection with the infringement on a commercial scale, or has been identified by someone in the foregoing categories as involved in the production or distribution of goods or the making available of a service that the infringement or the violation concerns.

Lastly, a court may order an infringer to pay the costs for appropriate measures to be taken in order to distribute information about a judgment concerning copyright infringement or violation of the SCA, according to Section 53h SCA.

However, any of the above sanctions, such as injunction, recalling from the market or destruction, cannot be taken against the AI model itself, once training of the AI model is completed, where after training is completed, the reproductions of protected works are automatically deleted and are thus not retained in the AI model. This means, there are no longer any infringing reproductions to apply the sanctions against. The prerequisite of taking any such sanctions against the AI model itself, is that so-called memorization of the protected works can be proven, i.e. where fragments of such works are in fact retained in the AI model.[14] Additionally, it is not certain that a court will consider it proportionate to apply an injunction or destruction against an entire AI model, due to unlawful reproductions of just one or a few protected works.

2.4 Summary

To summarize, under Swedish copyright law there are exceptions from the exclusivity of the rights holders to their protected works that allow reproductions of such works for training AI models. The primary applicable exception is for TDM under Sections 15a and 15b SCA, provided that the rights holders have not reserved their right to perform TDM on their protected works.

If a provider of an AI model trains the AI model in a way that is not compliant with the above explained exceptions or without authorization from the rights holder in case of their reservation against TDM, this would likely constitute copyright infringement. The unlawful reproductions of protected works can be targeted with various sanctions, and the provider of the AI model could be liable for criminal copyright infringement and to pay reasonable compensation and damages to the rights holders.

14. See Emanuilov and Margoni, *Memorisation in generative models and EU copyright law: an interdisciplinary view*, Kluwer Copyright Blog, 26 March 2024, https://copyrightblog.kluweriplaw.com/2024/03/26/memorisation-in-generative-models-and-eu-copyright-law-an-interdisciplinary-view/ (accessed on 15 April 2025), and Carlini et al., *Extracting Training Data from Large Language Models*, Usenix Association, 2021.

3. USE OF AI SYSTEMS

3.1 Permission to Reproduce and Make Available to the Public

The making of a copy that constitutes a reproduction of the whole or part of an existing protected work, or the communication to the public of the whole or part of a copy of a protected work, are exclusive rights reserved for the rights holder. When the user provides instructions to the AI system, it could occur that, for instance, literary works are inserted as part of the prompt or as information the user would like the AI system to analyse. If such act is deemed to constitute a reproduction or making available to the public, or whether an exception or limitation to the exclusive rights would apply, depends on what technically happens with a protected work inserted by a user into an AI system. Sometimes AI systems use input provided by users as training data to continue the development of the AI model. If the AI system analyses the text but does not continuously store a copy of it in the AI system (other than a temporary copy the use of which may be covered by the exception set forth in Article 5.1 of the Infosoc Directive), it could be argued that this is not a use which requires authorization from the rights holder. On the other hand, if protected works are in fact stored in the AI model, this could constitute a copyright infringement. If stored in the AI system, making available to the public could possibly also occur, for instance, if protected works or parts thereof are included in output generated from the AI system.

Due to the nature of AI systems generally being based on learning from rather than storing materials, there is currently no clear answer as to whether an AI system provider could be considered to produce a reproduction or make available to the public in the sense of copyright law in the phase of generating output. Some AI training models may however be prone to include memorisation which could result in storing fragments of copyrighted training data in the AI system,[15] in respect of which no exception from the main rule in Article 2 Infosoc Directive applies.

3.2 Exception/Limitations Allowing AI Training

Articles 3 and 4 of the DSM Directive include exceptions for reproduction of protected works during the training phase and development of the AI model, however in relation to the subsequent use of an AI system this exception does not apply. If any reproductions of protected works were stored in the AI system this should require the authorization of the rights holders, and any making available to the public of the relevant copies would generally not fall within any exception or limitation.

3.3 Remedies and Enforcement

The usual civil and criminal sanctions for copyright infringement, such as criminal copyright infringement liability, confiscation of profits, injunction, destruction, recalling from the market, liability for damages and information injunction may

15. See *ibid* article and paper.

be available in the event that infringing acts occur in relation to the use of an AI system, although due to the nature of AI systems certain sanctions may be difficult to impose, as further described under Section 2.3 above. Further, a difficulty that arises in connection with use of AI systems is to determine for instance whether or not reproductions of protected works are stored in the system once the training of the AI model is completed. This would require access to the underlying model and training data etc., and in this regard the information injunction described above could be helpful, as well as transparency requirements under the AI Act.

3.4 Summary

Exceptions for reproduction of protected works during the training phase and development of the AI model are not necessarily available in relation to the subsequent use of an AI system. Whether any acts occurring during the use of the AI system would constitute copyright infringement would need to be assessed based on the general rules for reproduction and making available to the public (including whether any exception other than the TDM exception for training of AI models applies). Whether an infringement may occur during the use of the AI system depends on the functionality of the AI model itself, including, for instance, whether so-called memorization occurs in the AI model. Who should be liable for any possible reproductions or making protected works available to the public, is however not easily determined and must be ultimately decided based on the circumstances of each individual case.

4. AI-GENERATED OUTPUT

4.1 Protection of AI-Generated Content

4.1.1 Copyright Protection of AI Output

Under the SCA, the one who creates a literary or artistic work has copyright to the work, Section 1, first paragraph. According to Swedish preparatory works to this Section, the one who created the work is the author, composer or artist that have accomplished the work.[16] This means, the creator of the work must be a human being. Furthermore, the object of copyright, i.e. what can be protected, is also closely connected to human creation. As the SCA has now been harmonized with EU copyright law, the term 'work' under Swedish copyright law is defined in accordance with the Infosoc Directive and applicable EU case law. The Court of Justice of the European Union (CJEU) have clarified that in order for a work to be protected by copyright, it must be 'original in the sense that it is its author's own intellectual creation'.[17] Moreover, only such works that are the result of the author's own intellectual creation, through his or her free and creative choices, can be granted protection.[18]

16. See Swedish preparatory works, SOU 1956:25, p. 83.
17. See CJEU case C-5/08 *Infopaq I*, p. 37 and p. 45.
18. See CJEU case C-145/10 *Painer*, p. 89.

This means, in order for a work to be regarded as a 'work' in the sense of the SCA and thus deemed protected by copyright under Swedish (and EU) law, the work in question needs to be created by a human. Since the requirement of human creation is strict, all things created by non-humans are therefore not covered by copyright, including for example content independently generated by AI models. AI technology today has reached a level of sophistication, which means generative AI models may autonomously decide how to interpret a user's prompt in accordance with their understanding of possible content to generate, gained through training, and independently decides the final expression of the output generated. This means that the output generated by a generative AI model may be deemed created primarily by the AI model itself and therefore not eligible for copyright protection under Swedish and EU law.

However, distinctions should be made regarding what role the AI system has played in the creation of the work in question. If a human uses an AI system as a means for their own creation, meaning that the human user has substantial impact over the final expression, has made all the decisions and has control over the ultimate result, the AI system could instead be seen as nothing but a tool, meaning that a user could be deemed to create a protected work.

Currently, there exists no case law at EU level or in Sweden concerning AI-generated content and clear guidance is missing, but in general the level of the user's free and creative choices in relation to the level of autonomy of the AI model at hand should be relevant factors to address in an assessment of whether content generated by means of using an AI model could be deemed eligible for copyright protection.

4.1.2 Neighbouring Rights Protection of AI Output

Neighbouring rights do not have a requirement of human creation in order for the protection to be granted. For instance, sound recordings and audio-visual recordings are protected as such, regardless of whether the content of the recording is eligible for copyright protection. In the preparatory works to Section SCA 46, it is stated that the producer, which could be the company that arranged the recording, is the one that will be granted the exclusive rights.[19] The rights of the producer of the sound or audio-visual recording are essentially the same as for a rights holder of a copyright protected work; the producer has an exclusive right to make reproductions of the recording and to make the recording available to the public. Since protection for sound recordings, for example, is granted regardless of the content of the recording being copyrightable, a sound recording generated by an AI model could possibly be considered protected under Section 46 SCA. However, there exists no relevant case law or other clear guidance in respect to whether generative AI output could be deemed a protectable recording under the SCA.

If, for instance, AI-generated sound recordings would be protectable under Section 46 SCA, the question of who should be granted the exclusive rights naturally arises. Only a physical or legal person can be the producer of a sound or audio-visual recording under Section 46 SCA. Thus, the AI model, being neither a physical nor legal person, cannot hold any such rights. It would need to be determined whether

19. See Swedish preparatory works, prop. 1960:17, p. 245.

it would be the user of the AI model, or the provider of the AI model, who would enjoy a neighbouring rights protection (if any), which could possibly differ depending on the nature of the AI model at hand.

4.2 AI-Generated Output Infringes Existing Copyright

When it comes to infringing content generated by an AI model, there is no different assessment than what is usually made when deciding whether content infringes copyright. If an AI-generated work, objectively looking to the relevant circumstances in the case at hand, oversteps the exclusive rights of the rights holder to a protected work, it should be deemed a copyright infringement. Regarding neighbouring rights, there needs to be an actual reproduction of the original work (i.e. a copy), even if very short-lived, in order for the output to infringe the original, for example sound recording.[20] According to the CJEU, in cases of infringement of sound recordings, if a sound recording is modified to the extent that the original recording is undetectable to the human ear in the proposed infringing recording, there is no infringement.[21]

It may however be complicated to determine who should be liable for the infringing reproduction of a protected work that occurs when the AI model initially generates the infringing output. If the AI model is considered as having a low degree of autonomy, it is possible that the human user instructing the AI model to create infringing content, i.e. using the AI model as a tool, would be liable for the initial creation (reproduction) of the infringing content. If the AI model, however, has a higher degree of autonomy, in the sense that the AI model is considered as having autonomously generated the final expression of the infringing output, neither the provider of the AI model nor the user can be clearly determined to have initially generated the infringing output. In this situation, the question of who is liable for such infringement is more complex. Only natural or legal persons can be liable for copyright infringement under Swedish copyright law and for damages under Swedish tort law, meaning the AI model itself cannot under current law be held liable for the initial infringing reproduction. In certain cases a provider of an AI model, with a high degree of autonomy, could possibly be held liable for any infringing output that the AI model creates, if the purpose of providing the AI model is in itself improper, such as a purpose to create infringing content. In absence of case law regarding such liability, it is however not possible to give a definitive answer to who is liable for the creation of AI-generated output which infringes existing copyright.

Any subsequent use of infringing output, for instance where a person or entity makes the infringing content available to the public, for instance in channels outside the AI system, would not necessarily attribute any responsibility to the provider of the AI model, unless the provider itself is involved in the subsequent use.

20. CJEU case C-476/17, *Pelham*, see especially p. 29.
21. *Ibid* case, p. 31.

4.3 Remedies and Enforcement

There are no specific remedies or sanctions regarding AI-generated output that infringes protected works. The usual civil and criminal sanctions for copyright infringement, such as criminal copyright infringement liability, confiscation of profits, injunction, destruction, recalling from the market, liability for damages and information injunction as described under section 2.3 above, apply also to such content. The main difficulty that arises in connection with AI-generated output that infringes protected works, is who should be held liable for the initial creation of the infringing output (see section 4.2 above).

4.4 Summary

Under Swedish copyright law, copyright protection is granted only to original works that are the result of human creation. It could be argued that AI-generated output can be protected by copyright provided that the work is deemed created by a human in terms of creative control and that AI has only been used as a tool in the creative process. However, if an AI model is the stand-alone or main creator of a work and no human has had any (or limited) control over the final result, such work would not be eligible for copyright protection. Further, there is currently no definite answer as to whether AI-generated output is eligible for neighbouring rights protection under the SCA.

Regarding infringements where the content is AI generated, the usual considerations for determining whether a copyright infringement has occurred should be made. Consequently, the same remedies and sanctions as are applicable for other copyright infringements or violations of the SCA can be applied to infringing AI-generated output. Who should be liable for the initial creation of infringing output when the AI model has a high degree of autonomy is however not easily determined and must be ultimately decided based on the circumstances of each individual case.

5. CONCLUSIONS

Under Swedish law, training of AI models on reproductions of protected works is excepted from the exclusivity of the rights holders of protected works, when made in accordance with the TDM exceptions under Sections 15a – 15b SCA. This is clear especially in light of what is stated in the AI Act about the application of Articles 3 and 4 of the DSM Directive on the reproduction of protected works that take place when training general-purpose AI models.[22]

Following the rapid development of AI models, for the purpose of generating sound recording and audiovisual recordings, it has however been debated whether the intention of the EU legislator really was that Articles 3 and 4 of the DSM Directive would make lawful training of general-purpose AI models on vast quantities of protected works that have the potential of producing content that can directly compete with the rights holders of the protected works used in the training phase.

22. See the AI Act, Recital 105 and Art. 53.

It has further been debated whether it is suitable to apply the TDM exceptions on reproductions of protected works during the training of general-purpose AI models. It can be questioned whether the application of the TDM exceptions should be applicable to the training of such AI models on protected works, due to the second and third steps of the three-step rule, i.e. that the training and further provision of the AI model conflicts with normal exploitation of protected works, or that such training unreasonably prejudices the legitimate interests of the rights holder.

Furthermore, it can be questioned whether it is suitable to introduce an exception or limitation to the exclusivity of rights holders, which the rights holders can control the application of, by reserving their rights to perform TDM on their protected works. It is possible that all or the vast majority of rights holders make such a reservation, which would render the (general) TDM exception somewhat useless for providers of AI models. Further, it may impose difficulties for developers of AI models to identify which rights holders may have opted out and in relation to which protected works.

Regarding sanctions, it can be deemed unsatisfying that a provider of an AI model, which was trained unlawfully on protected works, may continue to provide and use the AI model commercially, since there may be difficulties in applying the existing sanctions of injunction, recalling from the market or destruction that can be applied to the AI model itself. If there would be a technical solution that allows the AI model to delete or 'forget' information it has been trained with, and the subsequent knowledge the AI model has developed therefrom, an injunction to perform such a deletion process or destruction of such information and/or knowledge within the AI model regarding the infringed protected works would be a preferable solution. However, such deletion process or destruction of specific information or knowledge may not be possible with current AI technology. Other sanctions such as damages or fines would be more appropriate, especially if only a few of all protected works an AI model has trained on was unlawfully reproduced. If reproductions of protected works are continuously stored (by memorization or otherwise) unlawfully in the AI system, the remedies available should however be applicable in relation to those copies.

The current regulation of the training phase of general-purpose AI models raises many questions regarding its application and consequences. Further clarification from the EU legislator, or the CJEU, on the abovementioned issues is necessary in order to achieve a higher degree of predictability for training AI models on protected works.

Regarding the issue of potential copyright protection for AI-generated content, it is a fundamental principle within copyright law, both in Sweden historically but also currently in the EU, that authorship is granted only to humans, and this principle must remain irrefutable. As current general-purpose generative AI technology currently works (as further discussed under section 4.1 above), the relevant 'creator' of content created by a generative AI model is the AI model itself, rather than the human user or the human provider or the AI model. Certainly, there are different types of generative AI technology, with different degrees of autonomy. In cases where the AI model has a low degree of autonomy, it is more likely that the AI model is used as a tool by the human user. In such cases, copyright protection can be granted for content generated with the AI model as a tool, however only to the extent that the relevant content fulfils the general requirements of the CJEU for copyright protection, i.e. that the content is the result of the author's own intellectual creation, through his or her free and creative choices. As far as Swedish copyright law is concerned, any future decisions and policies of the EU legislator and CJEU are ultimately decisive.

Chapter 13

Switzerland

Raphael Zingg

1. INTRODUCTION

Swiss courts have not yet been faced with legal disputes pertaining to the interaction of generative artificial intelligence (AI) and copyright. Nonetheless, the Swiss Copyright Act (CopA) as well as its interpretation established by case law set out a fairly clear framework for the development, training and testing of AI systems. While many open questions have been debated in depth by scholarship, it remains to be seen whether courts will follow suit.

This chapter addresses three key practical and doctrinal aspects of AI and copyright. Section 2 examines whether the use of copyrighted works for training AI systems is copyright-infringing. Section 3 focuses on the end-user use of copyrighted material within AI systems. Finally, section 4 investigates the copyrightability of AI outputs and the circumstances under which such outputs constitute infringing copies.

As in many other countries, the primary policy priority in this space is to establish regulation for the training of AI systems while introducing legal certainty for both technology firms investing in the technology and rights holders producing creative assets.

2. TRAINING AI MODELS

AI systems are trained on datasets oftentimes containing copyrighted material (text, images, video, music, etc.). Famously, Stable Diffusion was initially trained on a set of 2.3 billion images scraped on the internet, without authorization by or compensation for the rights holders. To avoid certain copyright issues, firms have started to train their models on Creative Commons-licensed works. As such, Google trained its tokenizer and autoregressive models of its text-to-music model MusicLM on the Free Music Archive dataset, which contains five million audio clips.

2.1 Training AI with Copyright Protected Works

The typical development and training of AI systems starts with, in the first stage (1), the *collection and assembling of a corpus of training data*. Large datasets of copyrighted works are web scraped, extracted, copied, and the data transformed for use in algorithms. The training data is typically stored in a file or database. In the second stage (2), training an AI model involves systematically presenting it with *training data*, which includes inputs and corresponding correct outputs, referred to as ground truth. The model uses this data to adjust its internal parameters – weights, through a process guided by a loss function, which quantifies the disparity between the model's predictions and the ground truth. This iterative optimization process aims to minimize the loss function, improving the model's accuracy.

Swiss law grants the copyright holder the exclusive rights to control the duplication or copying of their works (Article 10 CopA). The reproduction right is broad and encompasses temporary and permanent reproductions of the work.[1] Swiss courts would most likely rule in favour of a violation of the reproduction right, at the very least when works are permanently stored (stage (1) or certain algorithms in stage (2)).[2] When models are only trained in stage (2) – for instance on works stored on an external cloud server – the doctrine is divided as to whether this process constitutes a reproduction under copyright law.[3] The jurisprudence on this point will determine the fate of technology firms and the need for a legislative rewrite of the copyright exceptions.

2.2 Exceptions/Limitations Allowing Training of AI

Accordingly, AI firms presumptively will need to rely on copyright exceptions to shield themselves from copyright infringement liability.

A first potential exception to copyright is the use of works for the purpose of *scientific research* (Article 24d CopA). This norm was introduced as recently as 2020 with text and data mining in mind. For both commercial and non-commercial research, it is permissible to reproduce a work if the copying is due to the use of a technical process. According to the Swiss Federal Council, this exception requires that scientific research is the *main* purpose pursued.[4] The norm appears to encompass at best only certain use cases, for instance in the development of a new AI system. For instance, in the German litigation against LAION, the court recognized the research purpose of the process, as the organization was making its datasets freely available

1. Pfortmüller, *SHK-Urheberrechtsgesetz*, Art. 10 Rz 5 (2012).
2. Marmy-Brändli/Oehri, *Das Training künstlicher Intelligenz*, sic! 658 (2023); Thouvenin/Picht, *AI & IP: Empfehlungen für Rechtsetzung, Rechtsanwendung und Forschung zu den Herausforderungen an den Schnittstellen von Artificial Intelligence (AI) und Intellectual Property (IP)*, sic!, 517 (2023).
3. On the view that pattern extraction constitutes a reproduction under copyright law, Cherpillod, *Intelligence artificielle et droit d'auteur*, sic! 446 (2023); contrary view Städeli/Mary, *Künstliche Intelligenz und Urheberrecht*, SJZ 120, 248 (2024).
4. Message of the Federal Council on revision of copyright law, BBl 17.069, 628.

and accessible to all, including researchers in the field of neuronal networks.[5] On the other hand, after commercial deployment, the retraining of AI systems over new data can hardly be qualified as pursuing a main research objective.

Secondly, Swiss law grants an exception for *temporary copies* (Article 24a CopA). This norm is written narrowly and addresses browsing and caching. The copies must in particular have no independent economic significance - which is typically not the case for training data - and the use of the work must be lawful. This would only be the case if one of the exceptions to copyright would apply.[6] Other authors argue that the temporary reproduction in view of the generation of an output is lawful, so that the key question is whether the data has independent economic significance or not.[7] Further, temporary copies must represent an integral part of a technological process; downloading data for software analysis is not incidental to a technical software analysis but rather a prerequisite step for data analysis. Importantly, permanent copies are excluded *per se*, so that the AI training process as a whole will not be shielded.

A last route may be via the *private use* exception. Swiss copyright law gives companies the right to copy works for internal information and documentation (Article 19 CopA). However, the company must not seek to achieve revenues through the use of the works[8] and owns the author remuneration. This remuneration can only be asserted by authorized collective rights management remunerations (Article 20 CopA). With the exception of isolated authors,[9] the majority doctrine holds this exception as non-applicable, in particular because the copies do not aim at internal information but at developing external, often commercial software services.[10]

2.3 Remedies and Enforcement

As illustrated by the first court cases in the United States and in Germany, the typical defendants in these lawsuits will be the organization collecting, downloading, extracting and making available datasets for AI training (see above stage (1), e.g. LAION) as well as the technology companies training their AI models on such data (see above stage (2), e.g. Stability Diffusion was trained on LAION datasets). See section 4.3. for more detail on remedies.

2.4 Summary

The question of whether the use of copyrighted work for training AI systems constitutes copying within the meaning of copyright law has not yet been decided by Swiss courts. Under the current interpretation of the Swiss Copyright Act, various

5. Landgericht Hamburg, 310 O 227/23.
6. Gilliéron, *Intelligence artificielle: la titularité des données*, RSDA 440 (2021).
7. Salvadé, *Comment licencier l'utilisation d'œuvres préexistantes pour entraîner l'intelligence artificielle?*, sic! 89 (2024).
8. Swiss Federal Supreme Court, BGE 143 II 617.
9. Schönberger, *Deep Copyright: Up – and Downstream Questions Related to Artificial Intelligence (AI) and Machine Learning (ML)*, in: De Werra, Droit d'auteur 4.0 / Copyright 4.0, 145 ff. (2018).
10. Marmy-Brändli/Oehri, *Das Training künstlicher Intelligenz*, sic! 660 (2023).

steps in the training of AI systems infringe the reproduction right and there is no one-size-fits-all exception to copyright allowing for such copy.

3. USE OF AI SYSTEMS

The use of third-party material in AI systems by end-users remains an under-studied area, with unanswered questions regarding the legality and consequence of such use. A typical example would be a user uploading Harry Potter books into an AI system such as ChatGPT and requesting an analysis or summary thereto.

3.1 Permission to Reproduce and Make Available to the Public

Under Swiss copyright law, uploading copyrighted work into an AI system or more generally, prompting using copyrighted works, constitutes a reproduction and may infringe the right to make the work available to the public (Article 10 CopA). This means that, in principle, any such action would require explicit permission from the copyright holder. Consequently, the terms of use of major players including OpenAI require users to warrant that they possess all necessary rights, licences and permissions to provide said copyrighted input to their services.

3.2 Exception/Limitations Allowing AI Training

The exceptions to copyright outlined in section 2.2, in particular regarding private use and scientific research, may potentially be invoked by end-users. Under Swiss law, uploaded works must be restricted to a close circle of relatives or friends to quality as private use. Since AI companies may typically store and utilize input data for training and feedback purposes, this exception is unlikely to apply. There are scenarios in which private use could be applicable, for instance when a user runs a local version of an AI system – this would typically require a massive amount of computational power and storage capacity. There are, however, a number of chatbots like Nvidia's ChatRTX that can be installed locally and would be private.

3.3 Remedies and Enforcement

The responsibility of end-users may be engaged in case of copyright infringement, although the risk of detection is very low. See section 4.3. for more details on remedies.

3.4 Summary

Feeding copyrighted works into AI systems requires permission from the copyright holder and exceptions for private use and scientific research do not provide protection for users in this context.

4. AI-GENERATED OUTPUTS

AI systems generate literary and artistic outputs, such as text, music, video and the like. As an example, MusicML generates high-quality music from text descriptions. The prompt 'A rock'n'roll melody with two guitar riffs' will generate minutes-long audio which, for the unaware listener, might not be of inherently different quality than (or even undistinguishable from) an instrumental song released by a rock band. In this vein, AI-generated outputs have won photography, digital art and animated music video competitions, competing and winning against human creativity.

4.1 Protection of AI-Generated Content

Swiss law is clear about the copyrightability of autonomously generated content: an output solely generated by AI does not qualify as copyrighted work.

4.1.1 Copyright Protection of AI Output

Under Swiss copyright law, *works are literary and artistic intellectual creations with individual character* (Article 2 CopA). The Swiss Federal Supreme Court recognizes that as an 'intellectual creation', the work must be based on human will – it must be an expression of human thought.[11] Material autonomously generated by an AI system – that is, the user is only prompting – would thus not be deemed copyrightable works.[12] As such, from the standpoint of copyright law, AI-generated outputs may be used freely by third parties.

Swiss law even explicitly defines the *author* of the copyright as the '*natural* person who has created the work' (Article 6 CopA) and grants him/her moral rights such as the recognition of authorship (Article 9 CopA) and the right to integrity of the work (Article 11 CopA). The author's death determines the term of protection (Article 29 para. 2 CopA). For a recognition of AI systems as authors and AI-generated materials as copyrighted works, the entire structure of Swiss copyright law would need to be rewritten.

As a consequence, the use of AI technology should be limited to content of secondary value. Taking the example of video games, the generation of landscapes, buildings, non-playable characters, simple dialogues and soundtracks can be entirely automated, but not the creation of the main characters of a new game. Alternatively, rights holders will need to rely on unfair competition or contract law to protect these non-copyrighted assets. In the particular case of gaming, where licensing is the norm, a prohibition on copying game assets for AI purposes may well become a standard clause. Such obligations are limited in scope in that they can only be enforced against those accepting the licence terms, not all third parties.

On the other hand, as long as there is sufficient human input or intervention, material generated with the assistance of AI systems are copyrightable. In the context of photography, courts have long recognized that the selection of the depicted object,

11. Swiss Federal Supreme Court, BGE 130 III 168.
12. AIPPI Study Group, *Copyright in artificially generated works*, sic! 573 (2019).

the timing of the image capture, the adjustment of the focus or the processing of the negatives may be sufficient to fulfil the human criterion.[13] Accordingly, the arrangement and selection of AI-generated material or the modification of said material by a human should meet the standard for copyright protection.[14] For instance, an artist exhibiting a series of large-format printed posters with both prompts and the visual outputs they generate to showcase the divide between human and machine intelligence will be deemed the author of a copyrighted work.

The line between human intervention and autonomous generation will be a fine one in practice. Fashion designer Bach Mai used Midjourney to generate prints for fabrics. The creative process was described as follows: 'It's not like you can just go in, and all of a sudden you're a genius print designer. It's like a paintbrush that the print designers have. They can use it to enhance their work and their output. They're inputting their know-how, their technique'.[15] While these considerations are very much true, under the current understanding, merely prompting – no matter how much knowledge and creativity the prompt is the result of – and the choice and refinement of the output via further prompts – no matter how much know-how this required – will not be deemed to be sufficient for a material to be an expression of human thought.

In the instances where AI-generated outputs are eligible for copyright protection, the user of the AI systems – not the developer team – would be the author and initial copyright owner, similar to a designer using CAD software or a videographer using a camera. There might be rare individual cases where the software developer, rather than the program's user, is the one responsible for the creative work and copyright protection might thus be awarded to the developer personally.[16]

4.1.2 Neighbouring Rights Protection of AI Output

While copyright protects the creators of works, neighbouring rights safeguard the interests of those who perform existing works or produce copies of such works (rights of performers, phonogram producers and broadcasters).

If copyright protection is denied to AI-generated outputs, the artists executing such performances (musicians, singers, conductors) will typically not benefit of exclusive performers rights. Swiss law defines a performer as the person performing a 'work' or an 'expression of folklore' (Article 33 CopA) and AI-generated outputs will typically not meet this threshold.[17]

On the other hand, the rights of phonogram producers exist irrespective of whether the output was created by humans or by AI systems. Phonograms and

13. Swiss Federal Supreme Court, BGE 130 III 168.
14. Similarly, US Copyright Office Guidance issued 16 March 2023.
15. Fashionista, *AI-Generated Prints on the Runway Pose Existential Questions about Design's Future* (2024).
16. *Rearden LLC v. Walt Disney Co.*, No. 17-cv-04006-JST (N.D. Cal. 21 February 2018) in which the developers of a motion capture software contended that its software did the 'lion's share' of the work in translating animator's input into the digital, copyrighted output.
17. See Brem/Brem, *Künstliche Intelligenz und künstlerische Darbietung*, sic! 413 and 416 (2024).

audio-visual fixations encompass works, but also any other sound or image, such as bird songs or filmed depictions of sports events. The same is true for broadcasting organizations, which acquire rights independently of the qualification of the broadcasted content under copyright law.[18]

4.2 AI-Generated Output Infringes Existing Copyright

AI models memorize and regenerate individual copyrighted training data, illustratively recovering a *verbatim* sequence or producing a near-identical reconstruction from the training set. The likelihood of regeneration is being disputed by leading AI firms, with OpenAI arguing that infringement is 'an unlikely accidental outcome',[19] whereas a study estimates that Stable Diffusion samples have a 'significant amount of copying' in 1.88% of all random generations.[20]

Memorization and regeneration are problematic from a copyright standpoint, as such near-copies generated by AI systems are typically deemed infringing the right to reproduction, to modification or to derivative work as well as the right to the recognition of authorship.

AI-generated near-copies need not constitute a full, identical copy of the work to fall within its scope of protection. Rather, a *modified work*, for instance via deletion, reformation, excerpts, cropping or change in colour tones is copyright-infringing (see Article 11 CopA for the right to modification).[21] The scope of protection further extends to *transformations* in form (translation, dramatization, motion picture version) or in content (collage painting, recreation of a photograph, montage including film and music) (Article 10 CopA for the right to derivative works). Such works can be derivative works if the transformations incorporated by the second author have individual character (Article 3 para. a CopA). For AI-generated content, this will typically not be the case, as discussed in the next section.

Additionally, if, from the perspective of the generated output, a previous work is only recognizable as a source of inspiration and the borrowed elements fade into the background, there is *free use* ('*Neugestaltung*').[22] The style of an author, in the sense of abstract characteristics common to his or her works, is not protected by copyright.[23]

In 2020, Swiss law introduced protection for *photographic depictions* without individual character (Article 2 para. 3bis CopA), illustratively news photographs, product images, snapshots or family portraits. The scope of protection of such photographs is narrow, as they are only protected against copies, not transformations.[24]

18. Egloff, *Das neue Urheberrecht*, Art. 36 Rz 8 (2020).
19. OpenAI, *Comment Regarding Request for Comments on Intellectual Property Protection for Artificial Intelligence Innovation* (2019).
20. Somepalli/Singla/Goldblum/Geiping/Goldstein, *Diffusion Art or Digital Forgery? Investigating Data Replication in Diffusion Models* (2022).
21. Rehbinder/Haas/Uhlig, *OFK- Urheberrechtsgesetz*, Art. 3 Rz 2 (2022).
22. Swiss Federal Supreme Court, BGE 125 III 328.
23. Cherpillod, *Intelligence artificielle et droit d'auteur*, sic! 448 (2023) with reference to a prompt 'in the style of Warhol' which would generate a freely usable output.
24. Egloff, *Das neue Urheberrecht*, Art. 11 Rz 13 (2020) although this is controversial.

Developing AI systems on photographic training data (without individual character) might avoid specific copyright, as only generating virtually identical copies will be copyright-infringing. In practice, distinguishing between individual and non-individual photographs in large datasets appears to be a daunting and non-implementable task.

The author has the right to *recognition of his authorship, including the right to be named* (Article 9 CopA). When a near-copy is generated as the output of an AI system – whether in the form of an identical reproduction or a modified or a transformed version thereof – the author has the right to be recognized and named as author on the output.[25] This is not the current practice with AI systems, as exemplified by the 2022 class action versus Github, Microsoft, OpenAI and so on, which contends that all author information is removed by Copilot and DALL-E-2 from the images used to create derivative works. Even when relying on open-source data, the licences generally require *attribution of the author* (name of the creator, copyright notice, disclaimer notice). The lack thereof constitutes a violation of copyright and a breach of contract.

4.3 Remedies and Enforcement

In terms of liability, it remains to be seen who will be held responsible for copyright infringement. Most likely, the first set of lawsuits will be filed against large technology firms (AI model developers or providers), not against individual users.

AI system developers should be held primarily liable if they wilfully or negligently train their model on copyright-infringing material. Meanwhile, *AI systems providers*, could face secondary liability if they contribute or aid infringement of a copyright in a sufficiently causal manner. As to the *user*, establishing fault, which is needed for damages or criminal liability, will be difficult, since in most instances the user will not intentionally be generating a near-copy.

This can be exemplified as follows: in the video games industry, companies such as Scenario offer custom-trained AI models for generating game visuals via API in-game. In its terms of services, Scenario seeks to shift liability from the provider to users: generated outputs may be similar or identical to third party materials, but the user is solely responsible for its use. The terms expressly forbid users to create and exploit assets violating intellectual property rights. Under Swiss law, the provider should still be liable in case the machine learning models were trained on copyrighted materials, independently of such a clause. As to users, intent or negligence – which are required for a claim for damages – should be considered given when the assets are clearly similar or identical to copyrighted works (by resembling well-known characters such as Lara Croft, Link or Mario) or when users themselves train the models by uploading copyrighted characters, concept art or backgrounds.

The consequences of a negatory action are not clear: while the provider should be forced to delete the copyright-infringing image from the training dataset, it is not certain what the court would order with regard to the trained model, as the latter retains patterns from the original dataset.[26]

25. See Rehbinder/Haas/Uhlig, *OFK-Urheberrechtsgesetz*, Art. 3 Rz 13 and Art. 9 Rz 5 (2022).
26. See also Mühlemann/Ritter, *Copyright and AI: Responsibility of Providers and Users* (2024).

4.4 Summary

Near-copies generated by AI systems typically infringe the right to reproduction, to modification or to derivative work as well as the right to the recognition of authorship. In view of these developments, industry practices are already shifting. Steam, the largest distribution platform for PC games, has in 2024 introduced a disclosure obligation for AI-generated material. Developers must ensure that AI-generated content does not include infringing material and, for content generated in-game, have guardrails in place that make sure that AI systems do not create copyright-infringing material.

5. CONCLUSIONS

Despite its relative clarity, the Swiss copyright regime surrounding AI appears *too rights holder friendly* when it comes to the training of AI – most if not all technically necessary acts are deemed copyright-infringing reproductions of works – and, at the same time, *not rights holder friendly enough* when it comes to the production of AI-generated works – which are not deemed copyrightable despite the immense investment and know-how put into their generation.

As such, large rights holders such as Disney, Warner Bros, Nintendo, Sony Music and the like have a lot of control over the use of their existing copyrighted works by AI providers (assuming lawsuits will be filed and decided according to the current interpretation of Swiss law), at the expense of having third-parties being able to freely reproduce the non-copyrighted assets and materials they will be generating with AI tools. This precarious line does not seem to balance the interests of the authors in the control of their works and society's competing interest in the free flow of such works in a consistent manner. In our view, this gap should be remedied by the legislator.

In order to ensure that all stages and aspects of the training of AI systems do not infringe copyrights, there have been proposals for *courts* to interpret the reproduction right very narrowly. Under this viewpoint, the permanent and temporary copies of works in AI training processes would be deemed technically necessary and not relevant under copyright law. Alternatively and supported more broadly, proposals argue that the *legislator* should introduce a new copyright exception for AI development, testing and training, so that copyrighted works may be used lawfully in such processes. Finally, the role of *collective rights management organizations* is at a tipping point. If these organizations manage to offer large volumes of training data under easily accessible and cost-efficient conditions, they might well both solve the collective bargaining problem and grant compensation to the rights holders.

The Swiss Cooperative Society for Music Authors and Publishers only permits the use of the musical works of its members with a licence and explicitly opted-out of the European text and data mining exception. According to its policy, AI providers must obtain a licence to use these works for training purposes.

In Switzerland, the collective rights management organization could make use of the new instrument of extended collective licences and assert the exclusive rights of rights holders who are not represented by it (Article 43a CopA). Extended collective licences are subject to legal and practical uncertainties and complications due to the possibility of rights holders to opt-out. Nevertheless, they appear to be the only instrument currently available to both remunerate rights holders and grant fast data access to AI firms. Ideally, this regime should be international or subject to extensive international cooperation amongst the collective rights management organizations.

Chapter 14

United Arab Emirates

Divyendu Verma and Sarmad Hasan Manto

1. INTRODUCTION

The core tenets of copyright law – creativity and originality – are at the centre of legal debates surrounding artificial intelligence (AI)-generated content. These debates are highly relevant in the United Arab Emirates (UAE), where the legal framework is still adapting to the challenges posed by AI technologies. Central to these discussions are questions about whether AI-generated works can be considered 'original' and whether they meet the legal criteria for copyright protection under UAE law.

In the UAE the application of moral and economic rights to traditional works is relatively straightforward, as the author is typically a human creator with a clear connection to the work. However, AI-generated works present a challenge to this framework. Since AI systems do not have the legal capacity to hold rights, the question arises as to who if anyone should hold the moral and economic rights to AI-generated content. Current UAE law does not explicitly address this issue, leading to debates about whether the developer, the user, or another party should be considered the author of AI-generated works. This lack of clarity underscores the need for legal reform to address the unique challenges posed by generative AI. Accordingly, the UAE legal framework may benefit by introducing new categories of rights or clarifying how existing rights apply to AI-generated content.

2. TRAINING AI MODELS

AI is revolutionizing content creation, but its reliance on large datasets – including copyrighted works – raises complex legal questions. In the UAE, copyright law primarily protects the rights of authors, musicians, artists, and software developers under Federal Decree-Law No. 38 of 2021 on Copyright and Neighbouring Rights (UAE Copyright Law). However, this law does not explicitly address AI training, leaving developers and organizations to interpret existing legal provisions cautiously.

While some jurisdictions provide specific exceptions for AI model training, the UAE currently lacks such clear guidelines. This makes it crucial for AI developers and businesses to obtain proper permissions or rely on publicly available datasets to ensure compliance with copyright regulations.

2.1 Training AI with Copyright-Protected Works

AI models require vast amounts of data to learn and improve their capabilities. In many cases, such data includes copyrighted books, articles, images, music, and other creative works. However, using such materials without explicit authorization could lead to legal repercussions. The UAE Copyright Law does not currently provide a dedicated exemption for AI training, meaning that any unauthorized use of copyrighted works could be considered infringement. To avoid legal risks, organizations must rely on proper licensing agreements, direct permissions from rights holders, or publicly available content when training AI systems.

A possible way of dealing with these legal complications is by licensing and contractual agreements. AI developers can enter into agreements with copyright owners, which allow the use of certain works for training. Another method is using Creative Commons licences, where there are different levels of usage of the content subject to conditions provided. Alternatively, developers can use public domain and open-source data, which are free and do not involve any licensing. Several governments and institutions, even some in the UAE, are actively assembling such datasets to enable innovation while staying within the legal framework.

Responsibility for adhering to copyright laws in AI training is shared among multiple stakeholders. Developers and AI companies have to be proactive and ensure that their datasets are sourced legally. Companies employing AI have to be meticulous in doing background checks to prevent accidentally infringing upon copyright protections. At the same time, regulatory agencies in the UAE, such as the Ministry of Economy, could potentially play a very important role in formulating more definitive AI-related copyright policies in the future.

2.2 Exceptions/Limitations Allowing Training of AI

While UAE copyright law does not explicitly address AI training, there are certain exceptions that could, in limited circumstances, allow AI developers to use copyrighted materials. Some jurisdictions, such as the European Union, have introduced text and data mining (TDM) exemptions, which permit AI training on copyrighted works under specific conditions. However, no such provisions currently exist in UAE law.

The UAE Copyright Law does, however, include exceptions for research, education, and personal use. Under Article 22, copyrighted works may be used for non-commercial research or academic purposes. Article 23 allows limited reproduction of copyrighted content for personal use. These provisions suggest that AI training conducted in academic, or research settings might be permissible, provided that the use does not extend to commercial applications.

Globally, fair use doctrines are often cited as a justification for AI training, but the UAE does not have a formalized fair use provision similar to that of the United States. Instead, Article 22 of the UAE Copyright Law provides a comprehensive set of exceptions and limitations that cater to various public interest uses while safeguarding the rights of copyright holders. These exceptions are critical for enabling educational, cultural, and technological advancements, and therefore, these exceptions allow for the free flow of information and support the administration of justice. By permitting certain uses without requiring explicit permission, the law ensures that copyright protection does not become an impediment to creativity, education, or innovation, particularly in contexts such as AI development, research, and public discourse.

2.3 Remedies and Enforcement

The enforcement of copyright in the UAE is governed by a combination of civil, criminal, and administrative mechanisms. The UAE has established a comprehensive legal framework to protect the rights of copyright holders, which is supported by various enforcement agencies.

As AI-generated content becomes more common, the UAE is starting to encounter cases that challenge the current copyright laws. Although no major cases have been reported so far, the UAE's mechanisms for copyright enforcement and dispute resolution are strong and continue to adapt to the new challenges posed by AI-generated content. The existing legal framework offers a solid base for copyright protection, but the growing use of AI in creative processes is likely to drive further legal and enforcement developments.

2.4 Summary

The training of AI models using copyrighted content presents legal challenges in the UAE, particularly due to the absence of clear AI-specific provisions in the current UAE Copyright Law. AI developers must obtain proper licensing or rely on publicly available datasets to ensure they are not infringing on copyright-protected works. While research and education-related exceptions under Articles 22, 23 and 24 may provide limited allowances, commercial AI applications still require explicit authorization from rights holders.

Unauthorized AI training could result in civil liability, financial penalties, and enforcement actions by regulatory authorities. Given the growing adoption of AI across industries, there is a need for legislative clarity to balance copyright protection with technological innovation. Future amendments to the UAE Copyright Law may introduce specific data mining exemptions, AI-specific copyright protections, or clearer licensing frameworks for AI developers.

For now, businesses and AI firms operating in the UAE must exercise due diligence, implement strict compliance measures, and engage with legal experts to navigate the evolving regulatory landscape surrounding AI and copyright.

3. USE OF AI SYSTEMS

With the growth of AI, its use in content creation, copying, and dissemination is increasingly becoming the norm. AI machines can now create text, images, music, and other creative material that closely mirrors human created content. But this has several legal and ethical issues, especially under the UAE Copyright Law. While the UAE Copyright Law does not explicitly state that the person inputting data into AI is responsible, existing copyright and liability principles suggest that users who control AI input and distribution may be held accountable in cases of infringement or harmful content.

3.1 Permission to Reproduce and Make Available to the Public

The reproduction and distribution of AI-generated content in the UAE fall under the broader copyright framework governed by the UAE Copyright Law. The present law does not explicitly define AI-generated works as separate from human-created content. Instead, the legal status of AI-generated outputs is assessed based on traditional copyright principles.

Under the UAE Copyright Law, only human authorship is recognized, meaning AI-generated content does not automatically receive copyright protection unless there is significant human intervention in its creation. If an AI system reproduces an existing copyrighted work – such as generating an image that closely resembles a famous painting or producing text similar to a published article – such reproduction could constitute copyright infringement if done without authorization from the rights holder.

To legally distribute AI-generated works, individuals and companies must ensure proper licensing and permissions. This may involve licensing agreements between AI developers and copyright holders, particularly if the AI has been trained on copyrighted datasets. Many organizations rely on public domain content or open-source datasets to avoid legal disputes. Additionally, some jurisdictions are developing AI-specific licensing models, allowing creators to specify whether their works can be used for AI training and reproduction. The UAE has yet to introduce such provisions, meaning businesses must navigate licensing within the framework of existing copyright laws.

In terms of responsibility and liability, the legal question remains: who is accountable for AI-generated content that infringes copyrights? Since the UAE does not attribute authorship to AI, responsibility may fall on the developer, user, or platform distributing the AI-generated content. Courts may consider the level of human involvement in guiding the AI's creation to determine liability in copyright disputes. If AI-generated material is made available to the public without proper authorization, the party facilitating its distribution may be held legally accountable.

3.2 Exception/Limitations Allowing AI Training

Although UAE copyright law generally requires permission for reproducing copyrighted content, certain exceptions and limitations may apply, particularly in research and private study contexts. Articles 22 and 23 of the UAE Copyright Law provide exceptions that could allow for AI training under limited conditions.

For example, Article 22 permits the use of copyrighted materials for research or educational purposes, provided that such use does not affect the commercial exploitation of the original work. This suggests that non-commercial AI research conducted by universities or academic institutions might be protected under UAE copyright law, though commercial AI training on copyrighted materials would require explicit licensing. Similarly, Article 23 allows for the reproduction of works for scientific and educational purposes, which may be applicable in AI training scenarios.

When comparing UAE copyright law with international AI copyright exceptions, some countries – such as those in the European Union – have introduced TDM exemptions, allowing AI models to process copyrighted content for machine learning purposes under specific conditions. The UAE has yet to adopt such a framework, meaning AI developers must proceed cautiously when training models on copyrighted data.

Beyond legal considerations, the ethical implications of AI-generated reproduction must also be addressed. If AI systems create outputs that closely resemble copyrighted works, questions arise about the fairness of such reproductions and the impact on human creators. Some argue that AI should be transparent in citing its data sources, while others believe that copyright laws should evolve to address AI's growing role in content production. As AI capabilities expand, UAE policymakers may consider new guidelines on AI-generated works, fair use, and licensing models to balance innovation and copyright protection.

3.3 Remedies and Enforcement

If AI-generated content is distributed without authorization, it may constitute copyright infringement, leading to legal consequences under UAE law. Copyright owners whose works are reproduced by AI without permission may take civil, administrative, or criminal actions to enforce their rights.

Under Articles 41–46 of the UAE Copyright Law, unauthorized reproduction or distribution of copyrighted content may result in legal claims for damages and injunctions preventing further use. Rights holders can file lawsuits against individuals or organizations distributing AI-generated content that infringes their works. Courts will assess factors such as the extent of similarity between the AI output and the original work, whether there was intentional copying, and whether the AI's use of the work qualifies as transformative or derivative.

Enforcement mechanisms in the UAE include:

i. Civil lawsuits, where copyright owners can seek compensation for financial losses.
ii. Criminal penalties, which may involve fines or imprisonment in cases of wilful copyright infringement.
iii. Administrative enforcement, where authorities such as the Ministry of Economy or UAE regulatory bodies can take action against platforms distributing infringing content.

The UAE has taken strict measures against copyright violations, particularly in digital and online spaces. In recent years, cases involving digital content piracy and unauthorized reproductions have led to website takedowns, platform bans, and legal actions. If AI-generated content becomes a major source of infringement, future enforcement efforts may target AI systems and platforms facilitating unauthorized reproduction.

A notable case study in AI copyright infringement involves global legal debates on AI-generated images and text-based reproductions. While the UAE has yet to see high-profile AI copyright disputes, courts are likely to consider international precedents when interpreting AI-related infringement cases. As AI adoption grows, UAE regulators may introduce stricter policies governing AI-generated content to prevent misuse while fostering AI-driven creativity.

3.4 Summary

The use of AI systems in content reproduction and distribution presents legal and ethical challenges under UAE copyright law. While AI-generated works are not explicitly recognized under existing legal frameworks, their reproduction and availability to the public must comply with traditional copyright rules. Licensing and permission agreements remain essential for ensuring AI-generated outputs do not infringe existing works, and liability for AI-generated content may fall on developers, users, or distributors.

Although certain exceptions exist for research and private study, UAE law does not currently provide a broad AI training exemption, meaning commercial AI models must obtain explicit copyright permissions. Compared to international jurisdictions, the UAE has yet to introduce AI-specific copyright policies, but future legislative developments may address AI training, reproduction rights, and fair use provisions.

Unauthorized AI-generated content distribution could lead to legal consequences, including civil, criminal, and administrative penalties. UAE enforcement authorities have actively taken measures against digital copyright violations, and future AI-related cases may shape the country's evolving legal stance on AI and copyright enforcement.

As AI technology advances, businesses, developers, and content creators must navigate copyright laws carefully, ensuring compliance with existing legal standards while advocating for clearer AI copyright frameworks in the UAE.

4. AI-GENERATED OUTPUT

AI has transformed the way content is created, with AI systems now capable of generating text, music, images, videos, and even entire books with little to no human intervention. While this presents opportunities for innovation, it also raises important legal questions about ownership, copyright protection, and liability for infringement. The UAE, like many other jurisdictions, does not yet have specific legal provisions governing AI-generated works, which leaves room for interpretation within existing copyright laws and related intellectual property frameworks.

4.1 Protection of AI-Generated Content

As AI becomes more sophisticated, it can now generate content that is indistinguishable from human-created works. This raises the question: who owns AI-generated works, and are they eligible for copyright protection? The UAE's copyright laws currently do not explicitly recognize AI-generated content as an independent category, meaning its protection under existing intellectual property laws is subject to interpretation.

4.1.1 *Copyright Protection of AI Output*

Under the UAE Copyright Law, copyright protection is granted to human-created works that demonstrate originality and creativity. The law does not currently recognize AI-generated works as copyrightable unless there is significant human involvement in their creation.

In the absence of AI-specific copyright provisions, courts may rely on traditional copyright principles to determine ownership and authorship in cases where AI is used to generate content. For now, this means that:

i. AI cannot be recognized as an author since authorship under UAE law is tied to human intellectual effort.
ii. The individual or entity that programmed, operated, or provided input to the AI may be considered the owner or author if they contributed significantly to the creative process.
iii. If an AI-generated work is purely autonomous, its copyright status remains unclear, and it may fall into the public domain by default.

4.1.2 *Can AI-Generated Content Be Protected Under UAE Copyright Law?*

The UAE copyright framework requires human creativity as a fundamental requirement for protection. If AI is used as a tool where a human provides the core creative input, the human (user) may be recognized as the author. However, if an AI system fully generates a piece of content without human intervention, it is unlikely to qualify for copyright protection under current UAE law.

This issue is increasingly debated worldwide. Some jurisdictions, such as the UK, have laws that allow AI-generated works to receive copyright protection if a human makes the necessary arrangements for creation. The UAE has yet to adopt such provisions, but future amendments to copyright law may address this gap.

4.1.3 *Defining 'Authorship' in the Context of AI: Human versus Machine Authorship*

The question of authorship is at the core of the AI copyright debate. In the UAE, as in most jurisdictions, authorship is granted to a natural or legal person - not to machines or AI systems. The key question that UAE courts may need to address in the future is:

i. Does inputting a prompt into an AI system qualify as 'authorship'?
ii. If AI modifies an existing work, who owns the final version?
iii. If a company uses AI to generate an advertisement, does the company own the rights, or does the AI provider?

These questions remain unanswered in UAE, but legal developments in AI governance could introduce clearer rules regarding authorship and ownership.

4.1.4 Neighbouring Rights Protection of AI Output

Neighbouring rights typically apply to performers, producers, and broadcasting organizations rather than authors. In the context of AI-generated content, the role of a producer becomes complex:

i. If an AI system generates music, who is the 'producer' – the AI company, the user, or the business that deployed it?
ii. If AI-generated content is broadcast, does it qualify for neighbouring rights protection?

Since neighbouring rights laws were designed for human contributions, their application to AI-generated works is unclear under the UAE Copyright Law.

4.1.5 Legal Challenges in Recognizing AI Outputs as Eligible for Protection

AI-generated works face three main legal challenges in terms of protection:

i. Lack of human authorship: since UAE law requires human authorship, AI-generated works may be denied copyright protection.
ii. Difficulty in assigning ownership: if multiple people contribute to an AI's output, who owns the final product?
iii. Public domain concerns: many experts argue that fully AI-generated content should automatically fall into the public domain, limiting its commercial value.

4.1.6 International Approaches to Neighbouring Rights for AI Content

Countries worldwide are debating AI and neighbouring rights. Some, like the European Union, are considering extending neighbouring rights to AI-generated works in cases where there is significant human oversight. The UAE has yet to introduce such laws, but future amendments may address this emerging legal challenge.

4.2 AI-Generated Output Infringing Existing Copyright

One of the biggest concerns with AI-generated content is its potential to infringe on existing copyrights. If an AI system produces an image, text, or song that closely resembles an existing copyrighted work, it could be deemed an infringement, even if the resemblance was unintentional.

4.2.1 AI-Generated Works and the Risk of Infringing Artistic Styles

Many AI models are trained on datasets containing copyrighted content. If AI generates a painting in the style of a famous artist, does this infringe the artist's copyright? While UAE law does not explicitly protect artistic styles, courts could consider whether the AI output is 'substantially similar' to a protected work.

4.2.2 *Identifying 'Substantial Similarity' in AI Outputs*

The key legal test in copyright cases is whether the AI-generated work is 'substantially similar' to an existing copyrighted work. UAE courts may look at factors such as:

i. Is the AI-generated content a direct copy or a unique transformation?
ii. Does the output contain identifiable copyrighted elements?
iii. Did the AI use copyrighted materials in its training process?

If a work closely resembles a copyrighted work, courts may rule in favour of the original creator.

4.2.3 *Liability for Copyright Infringement: AI Developers versus Users*

Who is responsible if AI-generated content infringes on copyright? Possible liable parties include:

i. The AI developer (company that built the model).
ii. The AI user (person who inputs the prompt).
iii. The platform distributing the AI-generated content.

UAE law does not yet specify who is liable, but courts will likely analyse the degree of human involvement in AI outputs when determining responsibility.

4.3 Remedies and Enforcement

As already discussed above in section 3.3, the UAE Copyright Law already provides enforcement mechanisms that could be applied to AI-generated copyright disputes. This includes:

i. Cease-and-desist orders for unauthorized content.
ii. Monetary damages awarded to copyright owners.
iii. Fines and penalties for wilful infringement.

While AI-related copyright cases have yet to reach UAE courts, enforcement may involve:

i. Civil litigation initiated by copyright holders.
ii. Regulatory actions against AI platforms violating copyright laws.
iii. Website takedowns for AI-generated infringing content.

4.4 Summary

AI-generated content presents new legal challenges under UAE copyright law. Since UAE law does not currently grant AI-generated works copyright protection, ownership and liability issues remain open to legal interpretation. Courts will likely consider human involvement when assessing authorship, infringement, and liability. As AI continues to evolve, future regulations may introduce clearer legal frameworks for AI-generated content protection and enforcement.

5. CONCLUSIONS

The rise of AI in creative industries introduces significant legal and ethical challenges, particularly concerning copyright law. In the UAE, these challenges intersect with established principles of creativity, originality, and the protection of human creators.

AI's ability to create content – be it art, music, literature, or even software – raises profound ethical questions about authorship, ownership, and the value and degree of human creativity. Therefore, the ethical considerations are twofold: the impact on society and the implications for creators.

Consider an AI that composes music. The AI's outputs are often indistinguishable from human-composed music. If this music is released commercially, should the developer of the AI be credited as the composer, or should the AI itself be recognized as the author? This dilemma is further complicated if the AI's output is modified by a human before publication – does this make the human a co-author, or does the human merely act as a facilitator of the AI's creativity?

Further, an AI system trained on thousands of images creates a painting that wins an art competition. While the AI's creators celebrate the achievement, human artists express concern that their ability to make a living is being eroded by machines that can produce similar or even superior work. The ethical question arises: Is it fair for AI-generated works to compete directly with human-created works in contexts traditionally dominated by human creativity?

In addition, AI-generated content in the form of news articles, poetry, or visual art might start reflecting the biases inherent in the data it was trained on. For instance, an AI trained predominantly on Western media might produce content that marginalizes or misrepresents Arab culture. This could lead to a dilution of cultural identity and heritage, particularly if AI-generated content begins to dominate media and cultural spaces.

In October 2023, a cultural institution in the UAE, Tashkeel, showcased a collection of AI-generated art. The exhibition sparked a public debate about the role of AI in the art world, with some critics arguing that the inclusion of AI-generated works in prestigious cultural spaces could diminish the value of human artistic endeavours. While the exhibition was legally permissible under current copyright law, it highlighted the need for clearer guidelines on the ethical use of AI in cultural contexts.

The ethical implications of AI-generated content are complex and multifaceted, touching on issues of authorship, the valuation of human creativity, and the cultural impact of AI. In the UAE, these ethical considerations are becoming increasingly relevant as AI technologies are more widely adopted. The existing legal framework, while robust in many respects, may require further refinement to address the unique challenges posed by AI. As the country continues to innovate and lead in technology adoption, ongoing dialogue and legal development will be essential to ensure that the benefits of AI are realized while respecting the rights and contributions of human creators.

Imagine an AI system trained on millions of human-composed songs. The AI then produces a new song that is a unique combination of the patterns it has learned. While the song is technically new, the AI did not 'create' it in the traditional sense – it merely processed data according to its programming. Is this song truly 'original' in the way copyright law traditionally understands the term? Article 7 of the UAE Copyright Law emphasizes the originality of a work as a criterion for protection. The Article stipulates that copyright is granted to works that are the result of the author's personal intellectual creation. This raises challenges for AI-generated content, which, while potentially unique, does not result from human intellect in the traditional sense. The UAE legal system may need to address whether such content can be considered original and, if so, how it fits within the existing framework.

Creativity, as traditionally understood, involves human expression, intention, and choice. AI can mimic creativity, but its processes are fundamentally different, and it is based on algorithms, data processing, and pattern recognition. This raises questions about whether AI outputs meet the legal standards of creativity required for copyright protection. Further, If AI can produce high-quality content at scale, there is a risk that human creators may be marginalized. This could devalue human creativity and disrupt industries that rely on the production and distribution of original content. Legal frameworks must therefore consider how to balance the benefits of AI with the need to protect human creators. In the publishing industry, AI-generated texts could flood the market, making it difficult for human authors to compete. If these AI-generated works are considered original and copyrightable, they could potentially dominate the market, reducing opportunities for human authors and lowering the overall quality of creative works.

Article 23 of the UAE Copyright Law, which addresses the economic rights of authors, could be strained by the influx of AI-generated content. The law is designed to protect the financial interests of human creators, but if AI-generated works are granted the same protections, this could lead to a shift in market dynamics, potentially disadvantaging human authors.

Currently, the UAE Copyright Law does not explicitly address the status of AI-generated works. However, Article 7 could be interpreted to apply to AI, especially in contexts where the AI is seen as a tool used by a human author. Legal debates continue about whether AI should be considered a co-author or whether its outputs should be considered public domain.

AI's ability to generate content quickly and efficiently could lead to economic displacement of human creators. Article 20 of the UAE Copyright Law ensures that creators retain moral rights to their works, but the rise of AI could devalue these works in the marketplace, making it difficult for human creators to compete. As AI takes over more creative tasks, there is a risk that certain professions may diminish in importance or disappear altogether. For instance, AI-generated music or art might reduce the demand for human musicians or artists, leading to job losses and a shift in the professional landscape.

The introduction of AI into creative processes could transform industries such as publishing, entertainment, and advertising. While this transformation may lead to new opportunities and efficiencies, it could also result in the marginalization of human creators who cannot compete with AI's productivity and cost-effectiveness. The legal uncertainty surrounding AI-generated works, including issues of copyright ownership and liability, could lead to complex legal disputes. Industries relying heavily on AI may face challenges in ensuring that their AI-generated content complies with copyright laws, especially if the legal framework remains ambiguous.

The legal and ethical considerations surrounding AI-generated content within the UAE Copyright Law framework are complex and evolving. As AI technology advances, the law must balance the protection of human creators' rights with the potential benefits of AI in creative industries. Ethical implications, legal debates on originality and creativity, and the potential impact on human creators are all crucial areas that will shape the future of copyright law in the UAE.

In conclusion, the UAE Copyright Law offers a comprehensive framework for protecting the rights of authors and creators in an increasingly digital world. As AI technology advances, it challenges traditional concepts of creativity, authorship, and originality - principles fundamental to copyright law.

The rise of AI in creative industries raises significant ethical and legal questions, particularly regarding authorship attribution, the potential devaluation of human creativity, and the cultural impact of AI-generated works. While Articles 7 and 20 of the UAE Copyright Law provide a solid foundation for addressing these issues, there is a clear need for more precise guidelines to navigate the complexities introduced by AI.

Traditional copyright law in the UAE, emphasizing human intellectual effort as the basis for originality and creativity, must evolve to address the challenges posed by AI. Articles 2 and 7 highlight the importance of human authorship, but the ability of AI to generate content independently complicates this framework. The law must adapt to ensure that AI-generated works are appropriately classified and protected - or excluded - under copyright protection.

Moreover, the UAE's enforcement mechanisms, supported by civil, criminal, and administrative avenues, offer robust protection for copyright holders. However, the increasing use of AI in creative processes necessitates further development of these mechanisms, especially in judicial interpretation and the role of specialized committees, as outlined in Article 38.

In comparison to other jurisdictions, such as the EU and the US, the UAE's copyright law aligns well with international norms, particularly in its emphasis on human authorship. However, there is an opportunity for the UAE to lead by introducing specific provisions for AI-generated content. Drawing lessons from the EU's consultative approach and the US's clear stance on human authorship could guide future developments in UAE law.

The future of copyright law in the UAE depends on its ability to adapt to new realities while preserving the core principles of intellectual property protection. By proactively addressing the challenges posed by AI through thoughtful legislation, the UAE can maintain its position as a global hub for innovation, creativity, and cultural exchange.

In summary, the UAE Copyright Law stands at a critical juncture where careful consideration and timely updates are essential to address the growing influence of AI in creative industries. By adopting best practices, learning from other jurisdictions, and fostering ongoing dialogue with stakeholders, the UAE can ensure that its copyright law continues to support both innovation and the protection of creative works in an increasingly AI-driven world.

Chapter 15

United Kingdom

Ellen Keenan O'Malley

1. INTRODUCTION

1.1 Creative Works Dilemma

The creation and use of artificial intelligence (AI) within creative works is not a novel concept. British born, abstract painter Harold Cohen was one of the first artists to explore the use of AI in his creative work. Circa 1974, Cohen transitioned from traditional oil-on-canvas works to inventing and using the first AI software in the artworld entitled 'AARON' to produce fine-art in works such as *KCAT*. To create AARON's output, Cohen built his own plotters and painting machines, which interpret commands from a computer to make line drawings on paper with automated pens and add colour with brushes, but the output itself relied heavily on the creative input of the programmer, Cohen. Fast forward to today, we have tools such as DALL-E, Midjourney and Stable Diffusion which use text-prompt software that arguably requires less (if any) human creative input, which is where the traditional way of thinking about copyright law and software has been turned on its head, causing lawyers, academics and even policy makers in the UK to rethink the interaction between computers and the creative process.

This revolution is underpinned by the availability of increasingly powerful computing hardware and increasing volumes of data, and the development of machine learning software, a subset of AI that enables computers to learn how to perform tasks without being explicitly programmed how to do so by a human. Broadly speaking, machine learning software includes (1) a model, such as a neural network, which is arranged to generate an output in dependence on a given input and a set of adjustable parameters, and (2) a training algorithm which controls how the parameters are adjusted in dependence on so-called training data. Once trained, the model can generate outputs in dependence on new inputs, such as 'prompts' in the case of certain generative AI applications like ChatGPT. Models with larger numbers of parameters may be able to capture more complex and nuanced patterns in their training data and therefore have the potential to be more capable than models with fewer parameters but can require vast amounts of training data to achieve this.

From a copyright perspective, such capabilities could have huge implications. The computer program is arguably no longer just a tool (like a camera) because it now has the capabilities to make its own 'decisions' as part of the creative process without human intervention, giving rise to questions around authorship and ownership. It also raises the question as to whether such works should even attract copyright, and/or whether the creation of such works results in the infringement of third party owned copyrights. The question about legal liability of AI developers under English law can be divided into the following three stages:

(1) *pre-training stage* where copies are made of original works for use in training the model (i.e. the collection of data to be used to train the model);
(2) *training stage* where parameters of the model are updated to capture information within the original works (i.e. the creation of prompts); and
(3) *output stage* where AI-generated works may (or may not) attract their own copyright and may (or may not) infringe the original copyright works used to train the model.

When exploring these three stages under English law, it is important to remember what the objective of copyright law is – to reward authors for their skill and labour in the creation of original works by granting them (or their assignees) exclusive rights to control how their works are made available to the public to use and enjoy. There are exceptions to such exclusive rights (which are explored in more detail below), but as recognized in the TRIPS Agreement, the exceptions need to be restricted to 'certain special cases which do not conflict with a normal exploitation of the work and do not unreasonably prejudice the legitimate interests of the rights holder'.[1] However, as the current law was written in an era when the AI technologies that we know today did not exist, there are more question marks than answers right now regarding what qualifies as a permitted act in relation to AI. Consequently, we have seen a slew of cases being brought globally trying to seek clarity on these issues specifically, including in the UK.[2]

This chapter breaks down the potential legal liability relating to the three stages of AI development under existing legislation. It should be noted that at the time of writing this chapter the UK Government is considering amendments to copyright law, including in relation to AI and computer-generated works, but this chapter will focus on the existing UK laws and guidance currently in place.

1.2 Copyright Designs and Patents Act 1988

The Copyright Designs and Patents Act 1988 as amended (the 'CDPA') is the primary piece of legislation in the UK governing copyright in relation to AI at present and

1. Article 13 of the TRIPS Agreement.
2. *Getty Images (US) Inc & Ors v. Stability AI Ltd* [2023] EWHC 3090 (Ch) Case No: IL-2023-000007.

below we discuss the relevant sections which apply to AI models, their training and their output.

1.2.1 *Categories of Work and Authorship*

The CDPA protects the following categories of works:

- original literary, dramatic, and musical works;[3]
- databases;[4]
- artistic works;[5]
- sound recordings, films, broadcasts and cable programmes;[6] and
- typographical arrangements of published editions.[7]

Section 3(1) of the CDPA defines a literary work as including 'a computer program, the preparatory design material for a computer program' (which it is understood to include the source code for a computer program) and 'a database'. An AI model and its code would be considered to fall into these categories and so be treated under the CDPA as a 'literary work'.

That said, a work normally requires an author, who is defined as the person who creates it.[8] Yet, the CDPA acknowledges that a literary work which is computer-generated may not have a human author.[9] At the time of drafting the CDPA this was not a very common concept, but in light of the recent rise in 'big data', enhanced statistical and pattern recognition techniques, and greater computer processing powers, computer-generated works with no human author have become a commercial reality. In those scenarios, the author is taken to be the person by whom the 'arrangements necessary for the creation of the work' are undertaken.[10] Yet, who this person is, is still unclear under English law. Is it the entity which owns the code in the AI model and/or trained it or is it the user who prompts the model to produce works? In many cases, the terms and conditions of use of an AI model attempts to reduce this uncertainty by, for example, providing that the owner of any copyright in an AI-generated work is the user who prompts the model but whether this type of provision is effective in law remains to be seen. In the author's view it is likely that such a provision would be regarded as an equitable assignment of the copyright to the prompter if the prompter is not, under the CDPA, the first owner of the work.

The copyright protection for a computer generated work is fifty years, and no moral rights apply to this type of work.[11]

3. Section 3 of the CDPA.
4. Section 3A of the CDPA.
5. Section 4 of the CDPA.
6. Sections 5A–6 of the CDPA.
7. Section 8 of the CDPA.
8. Section 9(1) of the CDPA.
9. Section 178 of the CDPA.
10. Section 9(3) of the CDPA.
11. Section 12(7) of the CDPA.

1.2.2 *Originality*

To attract copyright protection, Section 1(1) of the CDPA requires that a literary work must be 'original'. English case law has defined this to mean that the author of the work must have applied more than a 'trivial amount of skill and labour' in the creation of the work.[12] However, EU case law (which still applies notwithstanding Brexit) has adopted a different test – it requires that the work is the expression of the author's 'intellectual creation'.[13] Further, it should be the result of an expression of 'free and creative choices'. Both tests are hard to reconcile with the concept of a work not created by a human author. (See section 4 below, which explores this further in the context of AI-generated outputs.)

1.2.3 *Ownership*

Section 11 of the CDPA provides that the first owner of the copyright in a work is the author of the work, which in the context of AI is 'the person by whom the arrangements necessary for the creation of the work are undertaken'.[14] (See section 1.2.1 above.)

2. TRAINING AI MODELS

2.1 Training AI with Copyright Protected Works

A highly debated topic is whether use of copyright-protected materials to train AI models infringes copyright. Copyright protects an author's creative work from being reproduced (without permission) in whole or in part in 'material form' which is stated to include 'storing the work in any medium by electronic means'.[15] Whether such a reproduction has occurred is determined in English law by asking whether the user has copied a 'substantial part' of the work. 'Substantial part' refers to the qualitative features of the work copied (i.e., the quality, importance, or significance of the extract); it is not just the volume of the work copied. Therefore, unauthorized copying of a relatively small but important extract of a work may be sufficient to infringe. In the context of AI training and modelling, under Section 17(6) of the CDPA copying includes 'the making of copies which are transient or are incidental to some other use of the work'.

In the context of generative AI, models may be trained on data obtained primarily through web scraping, which often includes the scraping of original copyright works. This process would appear to involve the copying of such works even if carried out in a manner which is transient (it does not appear to be possible to suggest it is incidental). The use of such material would, on the face of it, result in the infringement of copyright in the work unless the copying fell into one of the acts

12. *Infopaq International A/S v. Danske Dagblades Forening*, Case C5/08.
13. *Cofomel – Sociedade de Vestuário SA v. G-Star Raw CV*, Case C683/17.
14. Section 178 of the CDPA.
15. Section 17(2) of the CDPA.

of copying permitted under the CDPA, or the AI developer had a licence to use the data in this way. In addition, it might be a breach of the website terms and conditions of use which frequently prohibit scraping.[16] If the works taken are subject to the *sui generis* database right[17] the scraping may also be an infringement of the database right. Additionally, if bots are used, which impersonate real persons to mine data, it could also be said that this is deemed 'dishonestly making a false representation in order to make a gain for himself or another' in breach of Section 2 of the Fraud Act 2006, potentially a criminal offence. Lastly, such mining of material on the internet may also fall under the provisions of the Computer Misuse Act 1990, which states at Section 1 that a 'person is guilty of an offence if – (a) he causes a computer to perform any function with intent to secure access to any program or data held in any computer, (b) the access he intends to secure is unauthorized, and (c) he knows at the time when he causes the computer to perform the function that that is the case.'

Notwithstanding the above, as the original material used to train such AI models may not be visible, it could make it difficult for the owners of the creative material to obtain evidence of such use, incentivizing unethical companies to take the risk and use the copyright works for training purposes without a licence. There are, however, an increasing number of tools available to help content creators to search popular AI training databases to find out if their content has been included in such training databases, which could make the risk greater for AI companies.

In light of the growing debate around rights in input data used to train AI models and infringement of intellectual property rights in the UK (and worldwide), the UK Government is considering making amendments to the CDPA to address such use. On 17 December 2024 the UK Government launched a consultation on copyright and AI[18] ('Consultation'), which proposes a controversial change to copyright law. One of the key proposals is an exception to copyright for text and data mining (Section 29A), allowing AI developers to use copyrighted works to train AI models for commercial purposes without the need for a licence to use them, unless rights holders explicitly object (opt-out). This would bring Section 29A more in line with the EU opt-out model under Article 3 of the Digital Single Market Directive.[19] Nonetheless, this proposal has been met with strong opposition from the UK's creative industries[20] casting much doubt over whether it will be approved or if so, in what form. The Consultation closed on 25 February 2025, and it is expected that the outcome of the Consultation shall be published sometime in Spring 2025. Until then, the law remains unchanged.

2.2 Location of the Training and/or Development of a Model

When analysing whether there has been copyright infringement by the training and/or development of a model, it is important to consider the location. Under English

16. *Ryanair Ltd v. PR Aviation BV*, Case C-30/14.
17. Section 7 of the Copyright and Rights in Databases Regulations 1997.
18. https://www.gov.uk/government/consultations/copyright-and-artificial-intelligence/copyright-and-artificial-intelligence.
19. Digital Single Market Directive (Directive (EU) 2019/790).
20. UK's creative industries are estimated to contribute over £126 billion a year to the UK economy (DCMS, 2023).

law, copyright is a territorial right which confers protection on its holder only within the territory of the UK.[21] Therefore, if this process did not take place in the UK, it would not amount to copyright infringement of the UK rights.

2.3 Exceptions/Limitations Allowing Training of AI

There are certain exceptions that may authorize the use of copyright-protected data to train AI systems without the copyright holder's consent. These are set out in Chapter III of the CDPA. The most relevant exceptions in relation to training AI models are as follows:

2.3.1 Section 28A – Making Temporary Copies

Section 28A allows for the making of temporary copies during technological processes, such as browser caching. The temporary copies must be (i) transient or incidental, (ii) an integral and essential part of a technological process that has the sole purpose of enabling a transmission of the work in a network between third parties by an intermediary or a lawful use of the work, and (iii) have no independent economic significance. In the context of AI training (e.g., data collection and storage) there is much debate about whether this exception would apply. Some argue that the AI models' retention of copies of copyrighted works for prolonged periods could fall under the 'temporary copies' exception, as it is part of the technological process of training the model. However, the counter argument to this is that the copies created for training AI models are not truly 'temporary' if the model needs to remember and use the data for subsequent operations, especially if it is then used to generate new outputs. Further, the copies are also likely to have independent economic significance if they are used to create outputs for commercial purposes. Therefore, it may be quite difficult for AI companies to rely upon this exception.

2.3.2 Section 29 – Research and Private Study

Section 29 provides for the fair dealing of any copyright work for the purposes of research. However, it only applies to non-commercial research and must be accompanied by a sufficient acknowledgement of the source of the work. Therefore, it is possible that web scraping for non-commercial research purposes may be permitted.

2.3.3 Section 29A – Text and Data Mining Exception

Section 29A permits a 'copy of a work by a person who has lawful access to the work [and] does not infringe copyright in the work provided that – (a) the copy is made in order that a person who has lawful access to the work may carry out a computational analysis of anything recorded in the work for the sole purpose of research for a non-commercial purpose; and (b) the copy is accompanied by a sufficient

21. Paragraphs 43 to 78 of *Getty Images (US) Inc & Ors v. Stability AI Ltd* [2023] EWHC 3090 (Ch) Case No: IL-2023-000007.

acknowledgement (unless this would be impossible for reasons of practicality or otherwise).' If, however, that copyright work is transferred to another person without the copyright owner's consent or it is used for a purpose other than the purpose of research for a non-commercial purpose, this exception would not apply.[22]

As most AI models use the underlying input data to educate the model ultimately to produce an output for commercial purposes, it appears at first sight that this exception would not apply to such AI companies. An example of this is currently the subject of the *Getty Images* case. The dataset used to train the AI system Stable Diffusion, according to Stability AI, was initially built by LAION, a German AI non-profit entity for the purpose of non-commercial analysis and research. However, as Stable Diffusion is using the dataset for commercial purposes, it seems unlikely that the exception would apply.

2.3.4 *Section 30 – Criticism, Review, Quotation and News Reporting*

Section 30 applies where the 'fair dealing' of any copyright work falls within the four corners of one of the exceptions – criticism, review, quotation or news reporting – and it must be accompanied by a sufficient acknowledgement (unless this would be impossible for reasons of practicality or otherwise).[23] In the context of criticism or review, the use must be 'fair', relate to a work accessible to the public, and be used fairly. Ultimately, the review must not replace the original work protected by copyright. In the context of training AI, it seems unlikely that such an exception could apply.

In the context of output data from an AI model, the dealing with the work may not be considered 'fair' if its use is commercially competing with the interests of the copyright holder to exploit their own original work, for example, if the AI created work could be used as a substitute to using the original work. It would also not be fair to use a work that has not yet been published or made available publicly (i.e. was shared confidentially or to a small academic group for feedback). Further, it may not be 'fair' if a large amount of data has been reproduced unnecessarily. Therefore, reliance on this exception for general commercial training of AI models seems extremely rare.

2.3.5 *Section 30A – Caricature, Parody and Pastiche*

The Copyright and Rights in Performances (Quotation and Parody) Regulations 2014 amended, *inter alia*, Section 30 of the CDPA to add section 30A. This amendment allows fair dealing with a copyright work for the purposes of caricature, parody or pastiche. As Section 30A only came into effect on 1 October 2014 there is limited case law regarding it, in particular in relation to a pastiche defence.

In the case of *Shazam v. Only Fools The Dining Experience Ltd*[24] the Intellectual Property Enterprise Court (IPEC) had to consider whether the parody or pastiche defences under Section 30A could apply where the defendants had developed an

22. Section 29A(2) of the CDPA.
23. Sections 30(1), (1ZA) and (1A) of the CDPA.
24. *Shazam Productions Ltd v. Only Fools The Dining Experience Ltd* [2022] EWHC 1379 (IPEC).

interactive dining show, '*Only Fools The (cushty) Dining Experience*', using characters, mannerisms, voices and catchphrases from the well-known British television comedy *Only Fools and Horses*, in an action brought by the family of the script writer. Regarding what constituted pastiche, the judge concluded that each case should be assessed on its own merits and stressed the importance of not applying pastiche too widely, to cover any imitation or reproduction of subject matter, otherwise it ceased to be a 'special case' of protected expression. The judge claimed that if pastiche was applied too broadly it would encompass virtually any form of borrowing, imitation or reproduction, which was plainly not the intention of the European or UK legislature which created the exception for three limited specific types of use. Therefore, in the context of AI, it seems quite unlikely that an AI company could make a strong enough argument to rely on the Section 30A pastiche exception given that the output in general is not a one-off example, and it might be that the prompted output is precisely to imitate the style of another work because it has been trained to do so for that specific purpose. As such, it would seem that, in the event this exception does apply to an AI output, it would be very fact specific.

2.4 Remedies and Enforcement

The lack of transparency regarding the training data used in AI models might make it difficult to assess the extent of copyright infringement and therefore to identify what remedies might be available. This lack of transparency can also create uncertainties about liability, especially for those who use the AI model's output (see section 3.3 below). That said, if the copyright holder can prove that AI developers have used their data to train their AI models without proper consent (as in the case of *Getty Images*[25]) and such use does not fall within one of the exceptions under the CDPA, the copyright owner may be entitled to damages from the AI developer to compensate them for the loss they have suffered arising from such use – e.g. in the *Getty Images* case the lost revenue which Getty might have earned had the copyright protected works been reproduced with its consent. Additionally, they could also get an injunction to stop the AI model operating or to remove code or copy derived from copyright protected works, which would have an impact on the company's revenue and also no doubt result in reputational damage.

2.5 Summary

Under current English law and at the date of writing this chapter, the use of copyright works to train AI models is not permitted for commercial purposes unless the AI developer has a licence to do so, or it falls within one of the exceptions. This could, however, change following legislative amendments or judicial guidance from the *Getty Images* case once judgment is delivered.[26] Therefore, if an AI developer wants

25. In *Getty Images* the claimants were assisted by the retention on images generated by the Stability AI model of watermarks identifying the images as having copyright in them owned by the claimants, but this is not standard.
26. By an order of 22 April 2024, a trial on liability is set to be heard between 9 June 2025 to 31 July 2025.

to use copyright works to train its AI model in the UK, it requires consent from the copyright holder.

3. USE OF AI SYSTEMS

3.1 General Use of AI Systems

If an AI-generated work from an AI system infringes the copyright of another work, who is liable – is it the provider of the AI system or the user that prompts the system to produce the output? This is an area of some uncertainty. As a result, some AI platforms have terms and conditions which require users to bear liability for any infringing outputs they create whilst using the AI system, while other companies such as Microsoft and Adobe (albeit subject to acceptance on various conditions) have made assurances that users will not be liable for copyright infringements arising from the use of their AI systems (although the extent and efficacy of some of these can be questioned). Currently, liability of AI companies is done on a company-by-company basis, but the general approach taken by Microsoft and Adobe to offer indemnities to users may become market standard.

3.2 Exception/Limitations on the Use of AI-Generated Works

As set out above in section 2.3, there are certain exceptions under the CDPA that permit the copying of copyright works without consent. In particular, Section 29 of the CDPA provides for the fair dealing of any copyright work for the purposes of research for non-commercial purposes and such purpose must be to assist the user's research. Use of this exception is quite limited, and unlikely to be relevant where the user and rights holder are in commercial competition, which one may argue an AI developer and copyright holder are. If, however, the user of an AI system is using it for non-commercial research purposes then this exception could be relevant.

3.3 Remedies and Enforcement

Proving the use of copyright works in the training of the AI model may be difficult but it could be even harder to identify the use of the copyright works in the AI-generated content from an AI system, especially as the models become more advanced. Further, it may not be straightforward to ascertain who to enforce your rights against – the user of the AI system who innocently created infringing content and/or the supplier of the AI system. If, however, this hurdle can be overcome, then the copyright holder could be entitled to damages. In addition, the copyright holder could seek an injunction to stop the person from using the infringing content.

3.4 Summary

Given the uncertainty around liability for AI systems and use of AI-generated content both for companies operating AI systems and users of AI systems, it is recommended that a close review of the liability and indemnity provisions of the terms and conditions for use of particular AI systems are carried out prior to use. Further, it is strongly recommended that, if a company is training the AI model as well as creating and distributing the AI-generated content, it enters into a licence with the copyright holders to permit use their copyright protected works to mitigate the risks of copyright claims down the line.

4. AI-GENERATED OUTPUT

4.1 Protection of AI-Generated Content

As noted above in section 1.2.1, a work normally requires an author, which in the context of a computer-generated work, this is the person *'by whom the arrangements necessary for the creation of the work are undertaken'*. Initially one may consider it straightforward to determine who the author is, but in the context of an AI output, who undertook the necessary arrangements for the creation of an AI-generated artistic work could be a number of different persons. For example, it could be the person(s) who: (i) organized and/or funded the project; (ii) arranged the coding to be done before the AI was taught; (iii) arranged for the teaching of the AI; or (iv) chose and/or selected any input(s) and/or settings ('prompts') for the creation of the work. With the increasingly blurred boundary between human-authored and computer-generated works, authorship disputes become increasingly likely, especially as AI-generated works often arise in the course of collaborations between those providing AI software, those providing the data to train the AI and those using the AI to do a particular task.

The originality of the work needs to be assessed in order to see if the work can attract copyright protection. The CDPA implicitly recognizes that the requisite skill, labour and judgment under the English case law test can be provided by such a person who could be a company (acting via an employee) or a human being. However, it is not clear from the CDPA or any other existing legislation how the requirement of originality could be applied in a computer-generated work if the work must be the product of at least some element of skill and labour which does not involve a human being. For example, it is uncertain whether arrangements such as prompt-based generative AI would be sufficiently original to exhibit 'free and creative choices' to meet the originality threshold or whether there is a lower standard of originality for computer-generated work. The position is even less certain under UK law once the overlay of EU law is considered – in particular, how might an AI-generated work be considered to be 'the expression of the intellectual creation of the author'. Notwithstanding Brexit, EU case law has generally been preserved in English (and UK) law and so the requirement that for a work to attract copyright it must be the expression of the author's intellectual creation still stands (at least until a UK court or Parliament decides otherwise).

As such, it seems highly likely that for an AI-generated work to attract copyright protection, it will need to demonstrate a significant element of human involvement in its creation. Whether this can be supplied, for example, by a human making the arrangements necessary for the creation of the work undertaken is a matter that will need to be tested before the courts unless the UK Parliament brings forward laws to address this question (which is an issue included in the Consultation referred to above). We already know from a decision of the UK Supreme Court that a computer cannot be an inventor under UK patents law,[27] but this decision will not be determinative in relation to the question as to whether an AI-generated work can attract copyright since the question will turn on different legislation.

4.2 AI-Generated Output Infringes Existing Copyright

At the output stage of AI development, if copyright does not subsist in a work generated by an AI model, then there would be no copyright prohibition on people or machines copying and otherwise exploiting such works (although such use might be a breach of the terms and conditions which apply to the use of the AI model in question). If copyright does not subsist in the underlying input data used to train the AI model to produce the new work or the training and storage processes do not amount to infringement, then there should not be an issue of copyright infringement since the work would not have been generated by a process that infringes the original works. However, such scenarios seem relatively remote given the number of copyright cases being brought internationally in relation to copyright infringement by AI models. As such, the following sections explore the relevant laws that AI companies and users of such AI tools should be aware of in relation to their output.

4.2.1 Permission to Reproduce and Make Available to the Public

In relation to AI-generated content available to the public, where the AI model is used to generate a work that reproduces the whole or a substantial part of one or more of the copyright works, this may be contrary to the copying and communication to the public provisions of Section 16 of the CDPA. Section 16(2) states that copyright in a work is 'infringed by a person who without the licence of the copyright owner does, or authorises another to do, any of the acts restricted by the copyright.' For example, if an AI developer copies texts from Stephanie Meyer's *Twilight* novels to train its AI model to write vampire romance short stories, which are then published on their AI platform, this could amount to infringement of copyright by copying (Section 17) and infringement by issue of copies to the public (Section 18).

Any replication of the underlying copyright (irrespective of whether there was knowledge that the work is protected by copyright) in the new creative work could be deemed as infringement. Therefore, if the output of the AI model contains a material reproduction of the underlying original copyright work used to train the model (irrespective of whether they had knowledge of this) and the new creation is put on the market, this could amount to infringement. However, as mentioned earlier, proving this evidentially may be easier said than done. The claimant would need to prove subsistence of copyright in the work (including originality), authorship, ownership, copying and substantiality (i.e., that the scale of copying is sufficient to be justiciable), which can be more difficult the more advanced the AI models become.

To avoid such risk of the claimant proving infringement has occurred, and incurring legal costs and potential reputational harm, AI companies may choose

27. *Thaler v. Comptroller-General of Patents, Designs and Trademarks* UKSC/2021/0201.

to make a commercial deal with the copyright owner by way of a licence or a partnership, as demonstrated by Axel Springer and Open AI in 2023.[28] In that case, the parties entered into a licence enabling Open AI to continue using content from Axel Springer media brands to train its large language models. This is also an approach that is being considered in the Consultation, along with the use of collecting bodies.

4.2.2 Importing Copyright-Protected 'Articles' into the UK

Sections 22 and 23 of the CDPA make it an offence to import into the UK, sell or use in business copyright protected 'articles'. It is currently unresolved in English case law whether an 'article' as referred to in the CDPA includes something that is intangible by nature and therefore, such conduct could amount to secondary infringement. If it is, this could have huge repercussions for AI companies distributing content into the UK as their risk exposure could increase significantly.

Secondary infringement arises if a person imports into the UK an article which is, and which they know or has reason to believe is, an infringing copy of the copyright work.[29] Alternatively, if they (a) possess in the course of a business; (b) sell or let for hire, or offer or expose for sale or hire; (c) in the course of business exhibits in public or distributes; or (d) distributes otherwise than in the course of business to such an extent as to affect prejudicially the owner of the copyright, an article which is, and which they know or have reason to believe is, an infringing copy of the work, they could also be liable for secondary infringement.[30]

Therefore, the interpretation of the word 'article' in Sections 22 and 23 is critical for AI companies and is at the heart of the *Getty Images* secondary infringement claim. Getty Images argues that there are good policy reasons why 'article' should be read as meaning both tangible and intangible articles, including that, if Stability AI's construction were to be applied, 'there would be an infringing copy and secondary infringement if it had brought a copy of Stable Diffusion into the UK on a memory stick but because of developments in technology which mean this can now be achieved via a cloud-based service, there would be no infringement'. Mrs Justice Joanna Smith agreed with this and held that the correct statutory interpretation of the word 'article' shall be determined at trial but at present it remains unclear whether it could also cover intangible articles also.

4.2.3 Knowledge

In the context of secondary infringement (Sections 22 and 23 of the CDPA), knowledge is key to determining liability. A person is liable if they knew or had reason to believe they were dealing with an infringing copy. In the context of AI-generated outputs, this could be a grey area at present under English law, and therefore it would be prudent to ask questions about the source of the AI training data and, at the very least, check the liability provisions before commencing in using it.

28. https://openai.com/index/axel-springer-partnership/.
29. Section 22 of the CDPA.
30. Section 23 of the CDPA.

4.3 Remedies and Enforcement

As set out above, if copying can be evidenced then the copyright holder may be able to recover damages. However, it may be more difficult to enforce rights against a secondary infringer (at present at least), not just because it would be necessary to prove knowledge (or a reason to believe), but also because of the current ambiguity around whether or not 'article' under the CDPA includes intangible as well as tangible articles.

4.4 Summary

Under the current laws, it is unclear whether an AI-generated output would be able to obtain copyright protection. This is primarily because of the underlying requirement for human authorship including for computer-generated works. This may be addressed through legislative changes, especially as the UK wants to encourage more tech companies to develop and train their AI in the UK and the current Consultation process suggests that the law might be clarified to grant rights in the AI-generated outputs.

5. CONCLUSIONS

As evidenced throughout this chapter, the existing laws around AI and copyright are subject to a great deal of debate. Rights holders in the UK (and globally) are finding it difficult to control the use of their works in training AI models and seek to be remunerated for its use. Similarly, AI developers are finding it difficult to navigate copyright law in the UK and therefore, might feel deterred from developing AI tools in the UK through fear of infringing copyright. The UK Government claims that this legal uncertainty is undermining investment in and adoption of AI technology and as a consequence, has published the Consultation to change the way in which this is managed. Equally, the outcome of the *Getty Images* case, the first AI-related case to be heard in the UK, will no doubt shape how copyright law and the development of AI will co-exist.

Chapter 16

United States of America

Linda Lecomte and Hailey Bureau

---

1. INTRODUCTION

The intersection of artificial intelligence (AI) and copyright law is largely undeveloped in the United States. While the US Copyright Office does not recognize AI as an author for copyright purposes, there are additional considerations regarding training of AI systems on copyrighted materials and whether such constitutes copyright infringement.

Specifically, there is what is termed the Artificial Intelligence Disruption – that is, how does one protect the input, intermediates, and output of an AI system, and how does one determine originality and authorship? There are US precedents dealing with attempts to circumvent the human author requirement for copyright protection, stating that a human directed the AI system in a certain way with certain control. However, given the rapid nature of the advancements in AI, questions remain on the efficacy of this position.

The US Library of Congress oversees the registration of Copyrights in the US. The procedure for registering a copyright of a work is fairly simple, except when having to state who the actual author is of a work generated from an AI system.

US copyright protection is based on the Copyright Act of 1976, encapsulated in Title 17 of the United States Code, and is further shaped by significant federal and Supreme Court rulings. These statutory and judicial elements together form the bedrock of copyright protection in the US. Notably, the Copyright Act does not explicitly address the use of data in training AI systems. To address this gap and assist the public, the US Copyright Office published guidance regarding *US Copyrights and AI: Part 1: Artificial Intelligence Report of July 31, 2024*, and *Part 2: Artificial Intelligence Report of January 29, 2025*. The US Library of Congress announced that a Part 3 will be published at some point in the future to address, in part, the legal implications of training AI models on copyrighted works.

Training an AI system involves incredibly large amounts of data, which may or may not be within the public domain. Any data that is within the public domain is ineligible for copyright protection under US law. When copyrighted material is ingested for training, this may implicate the exclusive right to reproduce the copyrighted material, and may implicate the exclusive right to prepare derivative works, under 17 U.S.C. § 106. Thus, training an AI system with such data requires permission from the copyright holder unless an exception applies.

While US statutory law does not directly address the intersection of AI and copyright law and American courts have not yet issued binding rulings on the subject, there are various exceptions under copyright law that may apply to situations where copyrighted material is used to train AI. The 'fair use exception' is most likely to apply, and has been raised as defences in many of the pending litigations. Fair use is an exception under which certain uses of copyrighted materials without the copyright owner's permission are allowed for public policy reasons. The evaluation of the applicability of the fair use doctrine requires consideration of four statutory factors:

(1) the purpose and character of the use, including whether such use is of a commercial nature or is for nonprofit educational purposes;
(2) the nature of the copyrighted work;
(3) the amount *and* substantiality of the portion used in relation to the copyrighted work as a whole; and
(4) the effect of the use upon the potential market for *or* value of the copyrighted work.[1]

When a proposed use of copyright material does not fall within the scope of an exception, then a licence agreement from the copyright owner is required to engage in use of the copyrighted work.

At the time of this chapter, a recent ruling in the case of *Thomson Reuters v. Ross Intelligence* on 11 February 2025 by a US district court determined that fair use does not apply to non-generative AI trained on data obtained through third parties. See *Thomson Reuters v. Ross Intelligence*, No. 1:20-cv-613 (D. Del., Feb. 11, 2025).

2. TRAINING AI MODELS

2.1 Training AI with Copyright Protected Works

The training of AI systems on copyrighted works is a complex issue, with many concerned whether a licence or ownership is required, or if such training can be considered fair use of the copyrighted work. If such training cannot be considered fair use, and if copyright holders[2] do not agree to a licence or use, how will AI systems learn and progress in order to help the public good? Are AI system providers liable

1. See *Authors Guild v. Google, Inc.*, 804 F.3d 202 (2d Cir. 2015) (holding Google's digitization of books to make them searchable online was transformative and constituted fair use, as it provided significant public benefits without replacing the books); *see also Andy Warhol Foundation for the Visual Arts, Inc. v. Goldsmith*, 598 U.S. 508 (2023).
2. Throughout this chapter, 'holder' and 'owner' are used sometimes interchangeably to identify the person or entity having the right to enforce the copyrighted work.

for infringement, direct or indirect, by providing a system that pulls and uses others' copyright works? Are copyright holders being unfairly damaged by a devaluation of their work and rights? These are the questions with which the US courts are grappling, and the general public is asking US legislators to create specific laws and rules regarding new technologies.

Currently, there are no codified US laws specifically regulating the use of copyrighted data to train AI systems. Several cases have been pending in the US courts applying current statutory law. With this US statutory foundation regarding which works are protectable by copyright, the questions being asked include whether the use of or the way the use is occurring of copyrighted materials by an AI system infringes the copyright? Where is the benefit to the public good being afforded by the US copyright system if the public cannot benefit by an AI system training on third party copyrighted materials?

One can theorize the different ways in which an AI system may infringe a third party copyrighted work. For example, if the AI system generates an internal representation of the copyrighted work, is this considered an unauthorized copy or unlawful derivative work? Does it matter is the internal representation of the copyrighted work is in machine language code or a simple data set? If the AI system is copied from another copyrighted AI model, is this an infringement?

These questions are not all answered by the US judicial system, and certainly not by the US legislative system. Like with any situation, the facts of each case – such as the actual AI system being employed – as well as a consideration of the public good, appear to be key. How and to what extent the fair use exception is employable is currently being addressed by the US courts.

Several lawsuits have been filed alleging copyright infringement by AI systems training on copyrighted works. The US District Court for the District of Delaware issued an opinion on 11 February 2025, in *Thomson Reuters Enterprise Centre GmbH & West Publishing Corp. v. Ross Intelligence Inc.*, No. 1:20-cv-00613-SB (D. Del. Feb. 11, 2025), modifying its earlier opinion in *Thomson Reuters Enter. Ctr. GmbH & West Publishing Corp. v. Ross Intelligence Inc.*, 694 F. Supp. 3d 467 (D. Del. 2023). Specifically, the court '(1) grant[s] most of Thomson Reuters's motion for partial summary judgment on direct copyright infringement and related defenses, D.I. 674; (2) grant[s] Thomson Reuters's motion for partial summary judgment on fair use, D.I. 672; (3) den[ies] Ross's motion for summary judgment on fair use, D.I. 676; and (4) den[ies] Ross's motion for summary judgment on Thomson Reuters's copyright claims, D.I. 683.'[3] At present, the court has delayed its upcoming trial to determine, *inter alia*, whether certain Thomson Reuter's copyrights at issue are expired and if Ross intelligence copied Westlaw's Key Number System. This postponement allowed Ross Intelligence Inc.[4] to file an interlocutory appeal regarding the 11 February 2025

3. *Thomson Reuters Enterprise Centre GmbH & West Publishing Corp. v. Ross Intelligence Inc.*, No. 1:20-cv-00613-SB (D. Del. Feb. 11, 2025), modifying its earlier opinion in *Thomson Reuters Enter. Ctr. GmbH & West Publishing Corp. v. Ross Intelligence Inc.*, 694 F. Supp. 3d 467 (D. Del. 2023).
4. On 11 December 2020, Ross Intelligence Inc. announced that it would 'shut down operations at ROSS Intelligence' as of 31 January 2021, https://blog.rossintelligence.com/post/

opinion. On 4 April 2025, Judge Bibas issued an order, granting Ross's motion for interlocutory appeal and stay pending appeal, stating:

> Though I remain confident in my February 2025 summary judgment opinion, I recognize that there are substantial grounds for difference of opinion on controlling legal issues in this case. These issues have the potential to change the shape of the trial. I thus certify the following two questions to the Third Circuit: (i) whether the West headnote and West Key Number System are original; and (2) whether Ross's use of the headnotes was fair use.[5]

As no further opinion has been rendered yet in this case, we look to the 11 February 2025 opinion for its impact on the AI training of copyrighted material landscape.

In Judge Bibas's 11 February 2025 opinion,[6] the court explains that Thomson Reuters[7] provides a Westlaw platform allowing users to pay for access to 'case law, state and federal statutes, state and federal regulations, law journals, and treatises.'[8] Specifically, 'Westlaw also contains editorial content and annotations' like 'headnotes' which 'summarize key points of law and case holdings' and 'organizes its content using the Key Number System, a numerical taxonomy.'[9] In the same opinion, Ross is identified as a 'new competitor to Westlaw' who made a 'legal-research search engine that uses artificial intelligence' and '[t]o train its AI search tool, Ross needed a database of legal questions and answers.'[10] The opinion states that Ross asked to license Westlaw's content, but Thomson Reuters refused. Ross entered into business with LegalEase to obtain training data in the form of 'Bulk Memos' which were 'lawyers' compilations of legal questions with good and bad answers.' According to the opinion, 'LegalEase gave those lawyers a guide explaining how to create those questions using Westlaw headnotes, which clarifying that the lawyers should not just copy and past headnotes directly into the questions.'[11] LegalEase sold about 25,000 Bulk Memos to Ross, which 'Ross used to train its AI search tool.'[12] As the court states, 'Ross built its competing product using Bulk Memos, which in turn were built from Westlaw headnotes.'[13] Thomson Reuters subsequently sued for copyright infringement.

Accordingly, the court looked to 'whether the LegalEase Bulk Memo questions copied Thomson Reuters's headnotes or were instead taken from uncopyrightable

announcement. Further, Ross Intelligence states 'Although we are out of funds for our operations, ROSS has insurance for our litigation costs.' *Id.*

5. Order by Judge Bibas, U.S. District Court for the District of Delaware, April 4, 2025.
6. *Thomson Reuters Enterprise Centre GmbH & West Publishing Corp. v. Ross Intelligence Inc.*, No. 1:20-cv-00613-SB (D. Del. Feb. 11, 2025).
7. Thomson Reuters 'owns copyrights in Westlaw's copyrightable material.' *Id.* citing *Thomson Reuters Enter. Ctr. GmbH v. Ross Intel. Inc.*, 694 F. Supp. 3d 467 (D. Del. 2023).
8. *Id.*
9. *Id.*
10. *Id.*
11. *Id.*
12. *Id.*
13. *Id.*

judicial opinions.' In doing so, the court determined it more useful to create a side-by-side comparison of the Bulk Memo questions, headnotes and judicial opinions.[14]

With this in mind, the court proceeded to step through the issues. First, did Ross infringe Thomson Reuters's copyrights? The court states that to show direct infringement, 'Thomson Reuters must show both that (1) it owned a valid copyright and (2) Ross copied protectable elements of the copyrighted work. Feist, 499 U.S. at 361. The second element requires showing both that (2a) Ross actually copied the work and that (2b) its copy was substantially similar to the work. *Dam Things from Den. v. Russ Berrie & Co.*, 290 F.3d 548, 561–62 (3d Cir. 2002).'[15] However, to determine the validity of the Thomson Reuters's copyrights, the court admitted that an underlying factual dispute may render this determination unsuitable for summary judgment.[16] The court stated that Thomson Reuters provided the copyright registrations for the copyrightable content, with docketed registrations from 1981 to 2019, showing valid compilation copyright.[17] So, while copyright registrations are 'prima facie evidence of the validity of the copyright' if 'made before or within five years after the first publication of the work,' as per 17 U.S.C. §410(c), there is an issue:

> [...] if Thomson Reuters chooses to try this case based on a theory of infringement of individual headnotes as individual works rather than infringement of the compilation as a whole, there is still a factual dispute about which individual head-notes are both within the period covered by Thomson Reuters's registrations and not in the public domain. See D.I. 755, 757, 761, 763. So, if Thomson Reuters advances a theory of damages that depends on the infringement of specific headnotes, this evidentiary matter must be taken up at trial.[18]

That is, Thomson Reuters has a compilation copyright, and for a damages analysis, Thomson Reuters may look to a damages analysis regarding specific parts of the compilation copyright – but, those specific parts, separately, may not be 'original enough.'[19] However, the court stated that 'the originality threshold is "extremely low," requiring only "some minimal degree of creativity... some creative spark."' [20] That being said, the court stated that the 'key question [...] is whether a work is original, not how much effort went into developing it' and found that the headnotes

14. *Thomson Reuters Enterprise Centre GmbH & West Publishing Corp. v. Ross Intelligence Inc.*, No. 1:20-cv-00613-SB (D. Del. Feb. 11, 2025).
15. *Id.*
16. 'Copyright validity is a question of law, not fact, making it suitable for summary judgment. *See Silvertop Assocs. Inc. v. Kangaroo Mfg. Inc.*, 931 F.3d 215, 219 (3d Cir. 2019). But an underlying factual dispute remains here. So the jury may need to decide this issue, but for reasons different from the ones I gave in my prior summary judgment opinion.' *Id.*
17. *Id.*
18. *Id.*
19. 'Originality is central to copyright. The Constitution limits copyright protection to original works.' *Id.* citing *Feist*, 499 U.S. at 346. 'So even if Thomson Reuters gets a presumption of validity because of the copyright registrations, Ross could rebut the presumption by showing that the works are not original.' *Id.*
20. *Id.*, citing *Feist*, 499 U.S. at 348.

and Key Number System at least reach Feist's minimum threshold for originality.[21] The court found:

> The headnotes are original. A headnote is a short, key point of law chiseled out of a lengthy judicial opinion. The text of judicial opinions is not copyrightable. *Banks v. Manchester*, 128 U.S. 244, 253–54 (1888). And even if it were, Thomson Reuters would not get that copyright because it did not write the opinions. But a headnote can introduce creativity by distilling, synthesizing, or explaining part of an opinion, and thus be copyrightable. That is why I have changed my mind.
>
> First, the headnotes are a compilation. 'Factual compilations' are original if the compiler makes 'choices as to selection and arrangement' using 'a minimal degree of creativity.' *Feist*, 499 U.S. at 348. Thomson Reuters's selection and arrangement of its headnotes easily clears that low bar. More than that, each headnote is an individual, copyrightable work. [...] So too, even a headnote taken verbatim from an opinion is a carefully chosen fraction of the whole. Identifying which words matter and chiseling away the surrounding mass expresses the editor's idea about what the important point of law from the opinion is. That editorial expression has enough 'creative spark' to be original. Feist, 499 U.S. at 345. So all headnotes, even any that quote judicial opinions verbatim, have original value as individual works.[22]

The court further held that the Key Number System is also original, stating that:

> [e]ven if 'most of the organization decisions are made by a rote computer program and the high-level topics largely track common doctrinal topics taught as law school courses,' it still has the minimum 'spark' of originality. The question is whether the system is original, not how hard Thomas Reuters worked to create it. [...] To be original, a compilation need not be 'novel,' just 'independently created by' Thomson Reuters. Thus, I grant summary judgment for Thomson Reuters on whether the headnotes and the Key Number System are original enough to prevent Ross from rebutting any presumption of validity.[23]

Accordingly, next, in order to prove direct infringement, Thomson Reuters had the burden to prove both (a) actual copying and (b) substantial similarity. The court defined its process for determining actual copying as the following.

> Actual copying means that 'the defendant did, in fact, use the copyrighted work in creating his own.' *Tanksley v. Daniels*, 902 F.3d 165, 173 (3d Cir. 2018). One can prove this directly, with evidence that the defendant copied the work, or indirectly, by showing that the defendant had access to it and produced something similar ('probative similarity'). *Id.*[24]

In this case, the court commented that it may also consider expert opinions to evaluate copying.[25] The court found that the expert report submitted by Ross stated that 'the Bulk Memo questions for this batch [of headnotes at issue] closely resemble

21. *Id.*
22. *Id.*
23. *Id.*
24. *Id.* citing *Tanksley v. Daniels*, 902 F.3d 165, 173 (3d Cir. 2018).
25. *Id.* citing *Kay Berry, Inc. v. Taylor Gifts, Inc.*, 421 F.3d 199, 208 (3d Cir. 2005).

the headnotes' text and that the headnotes differ significantly from the text of the judicial opinions' and that '[h]er finding suggests that these questions were created by copyright Westlaw headnotes, not by summarizing the underlying opinions.'[26] The court determined that this showed 'Ross's expert conceding that the 2,830 [headnotes] were actually copied.'[27] In addition, the court 'compared how similar each of the 2,830 Bulk Memo questions, headnotes, and judicial opinions are, one by one' keeping in mind that LegalEase not only had access to Westlaw but also used it specifically to make the Bulk Memos.[28] The court concluded:

> But a Bulk Memo question that looks more like a headnote than it does like the underlying judicial opinion is strong circumstantial evidence of actual copying. My comparison of the questions, headnotes, and opinions can decide whether probative similarity is present, so long as I think no reasonable jury could reach a different conclusion. Access plus probative similarity adds up to evidence of actual copying. [...] Ross' counsel [...] twice confirmed that Ross had used 80% for initial training and 20% for later validation. D.I. 769 at 30 (10:48:35), 162 (14:36:24). So taking counsel at his word, Ross used practically 100% to train its AI. Having slogged through all 2,830 headnotes, I grant summary judgment to Thomson Reuters on actual copying, finding actual copying of 2,243. I grant summary judgment only on the headnotes for which actual copying is so obvious that no reasonable jury could find otherwise.[29]

Next, the court looked to determining whether there was substantial similarity proven by Thomson Reuters. The court explained the process for determining substantial similarity as follows.

> Substantial similarity requires evaluating whether 'the later work materially appropriates the copyrighted work.' *Tanksley*, 902 F.3d at 173. That means deciding which parts of the actually copied work are original expression and so protected by copyright. [...] The question is whether an ordinary user of a product would find it substantially similar to the copyrighted work. *Dam Things*, 290 F.3d at 562. As a lawyer and judge, I am myself an ordinary user of Westlaw headnotes. So I am well positioned to determine substantial similarity here.
>
> [...]
>
> Though I do not apply the Ninth Circuit's test explicitly, I do apply the concept underlying all these terms: The less protectable expression a work contains, the more similar the allegedly infringing work must be to it. Applying this standard, I grant summary judgment on substantial similarity for Thomson Reuters on the 2,243 headnotes listed in Appendix A, finding that the Bulk Memo questions were substantially similar to them. Again, I grant summary judgment only on the headnotes for which substantial similarity is so obvious that no reasonable jury could find otherwise. In practice, this means that I am granting summary judgment only on the headnotes whose language very closely tracks the language

26. *Id.*
27. *Id.* Notably, at least an additional 5,367 headnotes were left for determination of copyright infringement by a jury at trial.
28. *Id.*
29. *Id.*

> of the Bulk Memo question but not the language of the case opinion. The rest of the headnotes must go to trial.[30]

The court reviewed each of Ross' argued defences, including fair use, and found each of the defences to fail. These defences will be discussed later in this chapter. This case is ongoing, with the appeal to the Third Circuit, as well the additional headnotes, et al., left for trial.

In the case of generative AI tools and their outputs, the analysis becomes complex and for copyright owners there can be unique challenges in meeting the substantial similarity threshold. During the past few years, several cases have been filed and are pending alleging copyright infringement, among other claims, regarding the unauthorized training on copyrighted materials by generative AI and AI tools.[31] In one case, in its filed Complaint, Getty Images, Inc. filed suit against Stability AI, Inc. for 'brazen infringement of Getty Images' intellectual property on a staggering scale' claiming that 'Stability AI has copied more than 12 million photographs from Getty Images' collection, along with the associated captions and metadata, without permission from or compensation to Getty Images, as part of its efforts to build a competing business.'[32] According to the court dockets for several of these cases, trial is expected in 2025, which will hopefully bring some additional clarity.

2.2 Exceptions/Limitations Allowing Training of AI

There are various legal defences and exceptions that may allow for the training of AI systems. The most popular defence being put forth is the well-established fair use doctrine. Several articles, white papers, discussions have centred around the issue of whether AI system training on third party copyrightable data is allowable because it constitutes fair use. Generally, the fair use doctrine has been applied to allow for the limited use of copyrighted materials in situations of parody, criticism, education, transformative work, et al. So, the question is, does the AI system training fit in these

30. *Id.* '[S]ubstantial similarity is always a spectrum, whether the copyright is "thin" or "thick" and "[m]ore similarity is required when less protectable matter is at issue."' 4 Nimmer on Copyright.
31. See, *e.g.*, *Andersen v. Stability AI Ltd.*, No. 3:23-cv-00201 (N.D. Cal. Second amended complaint filed Oct. 31, 2024); *Tremblay et al. v. OpenAI, Inc., et al.*, No. 3:23-cv-03223-AMO (N.D. Cal., filed June 28, 2023) (Complaint alleges that ChatGPT infringed their copyrights by training on their copyrighted works, making summaries of and reproducing their works); *The N.Y. Times Co. v. Microsoft Corp.*, No, 1:23-cv-11195, (S.D.N.Y., filed Dec. 27, 2023) (Complaint alleges that OpenAI and Microsoft's large language models were trained without authorization on their copyrighted material); *In re Google Generative AI Copyright Litigation*, No. 5:23-cv-03440 (N.D. Cal. filed July 11, 2023); *Authors Guild v. OpenAI, Inc.*, No. 1:23-cv-08292 (S.D.N.Y. filed Sept. 19, 2023); *Kadrey v. Meta Platforms, Inc.*, No. 23-cv-03417-VC (N.D. Cal. Nov. 20, 2023); *Huckabee v. Bloomberg L.P.*, No. 1:23-cv-09152 (S.D.N.Y. filed Oct 17, 2023); *Concord Music Grp., Inc. v. Anthropic PBC*, No. 3:23-cv-01092 (M.D. Tenn. filed Oct. 18, 2023); *Nazemian et al. v. Nvidia Corp.*, No. 24-01454 (N.D. Cal. filed Mar. 8, 2024).
32. Complaint, *Getty Images (US), Inc. v. Stability AI, Inc.*, 1:23-cv-00135-UNA (D.Del. Complaint filed Feb. 3, 2023).

situations? Or, perhaps, AI system training should it be included in future legislation as another allowable situation?

The fair use doctrine, as applied to AI training on copyrightable works, is proving to be quite fact specific in the AI systems landscape. The four fair use factors to be reviewed include the purpose and character of use, the nature of the copyrighted work, the amount and substantiality of the portion taken, and the effect of the use upon the potential market.[33]

US statutory law does not directly address this question and the US Supreme Court has not yet issued binding rulings directly on the subject in the AI training system landscape. AI training typically involves large-scale ingestion and reproduction of copyrighted material, which would implicate the exclusive right to reproduce the copyrighted works in copies, and may arguably implicate the exclusive right to prepare derivative works, under 17 U.S.C. § 106. Thus, training an AI system with such data requires permission from the copyright holder unless an exception applies.

There is a general exception that authorizes the use of copyrighted data if it is determined that the use of such copyrighted data falls under a fair use exception. As noted earlier, this is a context dependent inquiry, and requires the evaluation of four factors:

(1) the purpose and character of the use, including whether such use is of a commercial nature or is for nonprofit educational purposes;
(2) the nature of the copyrighted work;
(3) the amount *and* substantiality of the portion used in relation to the copyrighted work as a whole; and
(4) the effect of the use upon the potential market for *or* value of the copyrighted work.

For example, in *Authors Guild v. Google, Inc.*,[34] the Second Circuit held that Google's digitization of books to make them searchable online was transformative and constituted fair use. The court further commented that such work provided significant public benefits without replacing the books.[35]

There are a handful of other exceptions that could apply in specific circumstances, but these generally involve libraries, archives, and educational and research uses and are unlikely to apply to commercial AI systems. Although not technically an exception, it is notable that AI systems also ingest large amounts of material that is within the public domain, meaning that it is ineligible for copyright protection under US law or its copyright protection expired remains another potential defence.

In the above-discussed *Thomson Reuters v. Ross*, the court looked to whether Ross met its burden of proof for the fair use affirmative defence.[36] Specifically, the court considered the four fair use factors required by 17 U.S.C. § 107(1)–(4): '(1) the use's purpose and character, including whether it is commercial or nonprofit; (2) the copyrighted work's nature; (3) how much of the work was used and how

33. *Andy Warhol Foundation for the Visual Arts, Inc. v. Goldsmith et al.*, 598 U.S. 508 (2023).
34. 804 F.3d 202 (2d Cir. 2015).
35. *Id.*
36. *Video Pipeline, Inc. v. Buena Vista Home Entertainment, Inc. et al.*, 342 F.3d 191, 197 (3d Cir. 2003).

substantial a part it was relative to the copyrighted work's whole; and (4) how Ross's use affected the copyrighted work's value or potential market.' The first and fourth factors weigh most heavily in the analysis.[37]

Specifically, with the first factor, the court looked to the purpose and character of Ross's use, determining whether it was commercial and/or transformative.[38] The court found that Ross's use of the headnotes is for commercial purpose which is similar to Thomson Reuters, and 'stands to profit from exploitation of the copyrighted material without paying the customary price.'[39] The court next looked to whether Ross's use of the headnotes is transformative, i.e., '[i]f an original work and a secondary use share the same or highly similar purposes, and the second use is of a commercial nature, the first factor is likely to weigh against fair use, absent some other justification for copying.'[40] The court determined that Ross's use is not transformative because it does not have a 'further purpose or different character' from the owner of the copyrighted works.[41] That is, the court determined that Ross used 'Thomson Reuters's headnotes as AI data to create a legal research tool to compete with Westlaw.' The court noted that 'Ross's AI is not generative AI,' that is, its AI does not generate new content. Instead, it was determined that 'when a user enters a legal question, Ross spits back relevant judicial opinions that have already been written.'[42] Further, the court noted that '[t]hat process resembles how Westlaw uses headnotes and key numbers to return a list of cases with fitting headnotes' and that 'Thomson Reuters uses its headnotes and Key Number System primarily to help legal researchers navigate Westlaw and (possibly, as the parties dispute this) to improve Westlaw's internal search tool.'[43] In response, Ross argued that Thomson Reuters's headnotes are not a part of the product it provides to its customers. Accordingly, the court recognized that the 'copying occurred at an intermediate step: Ross turned the headnotes into numerical data about the relationships among legal words to feed into its AI.'[44] While the court acknowledged that intermediate copying has been permitted under this fair use factor (1) in computer program cases,[45] the court differentiated those cases as essentially non-analogous, recognizing a difference between copying computer program code which has a functional purpose and copying 'written words.'[46] The court found that 'computer-programming cases about intermediate copying rely on

37. *Authors Guild v. Google, Inc.*, 804 F.3d 202, 220 (2d Cir.2015).
38. 17 U.S.C. § 107(1). See *Andy Warhol Found. for the Visual Arts, Inc. v. Goldsmith*, 598 U.S. 508, 529–31 (2023).
39. *Ross v. Thomson Reuters*, quoting *Harper & Row*, 471 U.S. at 562.
40. *Ross v. Thomson Reuters*, quoting *Warhol*, 598 U.S. at 532–33.
41. *Ross v. Thomson Reuters.*
42. *Id.*
43. *Id.*
44. *Id.*
45. *Id.* The court further cited *Google*, 593 U.S. at 30–32; *Sony Comput. Ent., Inc. v. Connectix Corp.*, 203 F.3d 596, 599, 606–07 (9th Cir. 2000) (copying source code to create its product was held to be transformative); *Sega Enters. Ltd. v. Accolade, Inc.*, 977 F.2d 1510, 1514–1515, 1522–23 (9th Cir. 1992) (copying source code to create games that are compatible with an existing gaming system is transformative).
46. *Id.* quoting *Google*, 593 U.S. at 21.

a factor absent here: [t]he copying was necessary for competitors to innovate.'[47] In the various cases reviewed, the court noted that that copying in computer programs was 'necessary for different programs to speak to each other.'[48]

Further, in other cases reviewed, the court found that intermediate copying was 'necessary to reverse engineer access to unprotected functional elements within a program.'[49] With the facts of the present case, the court found that there was 'no computer code whose underlying ideas can be reached only by copyright their expression. The "copying is [not] reasonably necessary to achieve the user's new purpose."'[50] Accordingly, the court found that neither case was true – this case is not about intermediate copying of computer program code and does not require copying in order to reach underlying information. Instead, the court decided that for this specific fact situation, the framework laid out in the *Warhol* case is applicable. The court stated that it did not need to go to looking whether bad faith had any impact since it had already found that Ross's use was commercial and not transformative,

The second fair use factor concerns the nature of the original work.[51] That is, what level of creativity is involved in the original work. While the court in *Ross v. Thomson Reuters* found that Westlaw's material had 'more than the minimal spark of originality required for copyright validity,' the original material was not that creative.[52] The court went so far as to compare Westlaw's headnotes as having editorial creativity and judgment, but lacking the higher creativity level of a novelist or artist 'drafting a work from scratch.'[53] The court determined that the Key Number System is a factual compilation and so also did not reach the higher creativity level.

The third fair use factor concerns 'how much of the work was used and how substantial a part it was relative to the whole.'[54] In this situation, the court looked to how much of the original material of the Westlaw headnotes was used – considering whether Ross took the 'heart of the work.'[55] The court found that Ross's output to an end user did not include a Westlaw headnote. The court stated '[w]hat matters is not the amount and substantiality of the portion used in making a copy, but rather the amount and substantiality of what is thereby made accessible to a public for which it may serve as a competing substitute.'[56] The court differentiated the various arguments made by the parties, clarifying that Ross wins on this factor because it did not make the Westlaw headnotes available to the public, not because (as Ross argued) the number of Westlaw headnotes used for the AI training amounted to a small percentage of the total number of Westlaw headnotes.

47. *Id.*
48. *Id.* quoting *Google*, 593 U.S. at 31.
49. *Id.* quoting *Google*, 593 U.S. at 22.
50. *Id.* quoting *Warhol*, 598 U.S. at 532.
51. 17 U.S.C. § 107(2). The court in *Ross v. Thomson Reuters* looked to 'the degree of creativity inherent to the work.' *Id.* quoting 4 Nimmer on Copyright § 13F.06.
52. *Id.*
53. *Id.*
54. *Id. See,* 17 U.S.C. § 107(3).
55. *Id.* (internal quotation marks omitted).
56. *Id.* quoting *Authors Guild*, 804 F.3d at 222 (internal quotation marks omitted).

The fourth fair use factor is considered 'the single most important element of fair use.'[57] For this factor, the court must determine the 'likely effect [of Ross's copying] on the market for the original.'[58] The court looked to both current markets and possible future markets for the product. Also, the court looked to any 'public benefits the copying will likely produce.'[59] The court determined that the current market for the Westlaw headnotes and for Ross's outputted product is the same - legal research platforms - and at least one potential market would be for data to train AI models. The court found that Ross's outputted product could be a market substitute for the Westlaw headnotes. The court also looked to whether Thomson Reuters would use or sell its Westlaw headnotes as data to train AI tools.[60] The court further looked to 'whether the public's interest is better served by protecting a creator or a copier.'[61] The court found that the factor was satisfied because of Ross's intention to provide a market substitute in direct competition to Westlaw, and not so much whether Thomson Reuters has used its data to train AI tools or a possible benefit to the public since legal opinions are publicly available. The court stated '[t]here is nothing that Thomson Reuters created that Ross could not have created for itself or hired LegalEase to create for it without infringing Thomson Reuters's copyrights.'[62] Accordingly, in *Ross v. Thomson Reuters*, the court rejected Ross' fair use defence, weighing factor (4) more heavily that the other factors, and weighing factor (2) less than the other factors.

Thus, the court in *Ross v. Thomson Reuters* found direct copyright infringement for the use of some Westlaw headnotes as underlying training data.[63] As with many cases cited herein, this case has not reached a final conclusion in the US courts and will hopefully provide additional guidance for copyright holders and AI tool owners.

Other exceptions or defences can be utilized by AI training tool owners, including innocent infringement, copyright misuse, merger, and scenes à faire.[64] Innocent infringement is just as it sounds - a claim by a party that it innocently infringed copyrighted material. However, this defence only applies when an infringed work does not have a copyright notice.[65] This defence does not limit liability for copyright infringement, but it does limit damages.[66] Copyright misuse is a viable defence when a copyright holder effectively weaponizes the copyright against the public interest, such as for 'anti-competitive behavior.'[67] The merger defence is when an idea and

57. *Id.* quoting *Harper & Row*, 471 U.S. at 566.
58. *Id.* quoting *Campbell*, 510 U.S. at 590.
59. *Id.* quoting *Google*, 593 U.S. at 35.
60. *Id.*
61. *Id.*
62. *Id.*
63. *Id.* Note, this opinion concerned specific questions and did not overrule or address the decision of the case underlying this case, concerning contributory liability, vicarious liability and tortious interference with contract.
64. These exceptions were also considered by the court in *Ross v. Thomson Reuters*, but were rejected.
65. 17 U.S.C. § 401(d).
66. 17 U.S.C. § 504(c)(2).
67. *Video Pipeline, Inc. v. Buena Vista Home Ent., Inc.*, 342 F.3d 191, 203–06 (3d Cir. 2003).

an expression are effectively inseparable.[68] An example of an inseparable idea and expression may be a visual traffic sign stating 'no turn on red' with a red circle surrounding and line through that text. The scenes à faire defence protects use of stock elements or tropes that follow from the nature of the work.[69] An example of such includes the commonplace 'damsel in distress' element in a historical romance genre. This is by no means an exhaustive list of possible defences that might be used by AI system or AI tool owners when accused of copyright infringement.

In the US, public benefit is a real consideration, and there is much debate regarding the potentially immense benefits from AI tools' use of and ability to learn from available material (not just public domain material) and generate new, creative content, without the restriction of requiring permission of use of the third-party owned material. However, the US courts are currently attempting to balance the public benefit with the effect that these AI tools may have in devaluing the underlying copyrighted material being used in the training of the AI tools, and the consequent erosion of the market for the underlying copyrighted material. The legal landscape surrounding the rights of AI tools to train on third party data continues to evolve, and will hopefully provide further clarification soon from the US judiciary and the US legislature.

2.3 Remedies and Enforcement

For the copyright owner, generally, US Copyright Law provides for remedies for infringement including injunctions,[70] impounding and disposition of infringing material,[71] damages and profits,[72] court costs and attorney's fees,[73] as well as criminal penalties.[74] For the copyright holder and user, compulsory licensing is available in limited circumstances for certain types of uses or copyrighted material for a statutory fee, or other compensation. Examples of possible compulsory licences in the US include music,[75] broadcasting,[76] and certain uses of sound recordings.[77] At this time, there does not appear to be any specific US legislation explicitly allowing for a compulsory licences of other copyrighted material such as text and images which is often used in AI tool training. Further, the available compulsory licences do not appear to read broadly enough to extend to covering AI training purposes. However, this is a consideration moving forward whether a compulsory licence should be established so that copyrightable data can be used for AI training purposes. Until then, AI tool owners have the option to license copyrighted material for training purposes from each copyright owner so as to avoid infringement.

68. 17 U.S.C. §102(b). See, *Educ.Testing Servs. v. Katzman*, 793 F.2d 533, 539 (3d Cir. 1986).
69. *Atari, Inc. v. N. Am. Philips Consumer Elecs. Corp.*, 672 F.2d 607, 616 (7th Cir.1982).
70. 17 U.S.C. § 502.
71. 17 U.S.C. § 503.
72. 17 U.S.C. § 504.
73. 17 U.S.C. § 505.
74. 17 U.S.C. § 506.
75. 17 U.S.C. § 115.
76. 17 U.S.C. § 111.
77. 17 U.S.C. § 114.

3. USE OF AI SYSTEMS

3.1 Permission to Use and Make Available to the Public

At present, in the US, the use of AI tools and systems on copyrighted works requires permission, unless a defence or exception applies. At the same time, there is a question as to possible derivative works generated by such AI tools and systems, which could be found to damage the integrity of the underlying copyright work or author. For example, in the class action suit filed against Stability AI, Midjourney and DeviantArt,[78] the plaintiffs alleged that the AI image generators generated reconstructed copies of the plaintiff's works which are arguably unauthorized derivatives. In looking at the original and the AI image generated images, one might argue that the generated image is not only infringing the copyright, but also damages the integrity of the author.[79]

Interestingly, UAB Planner 5D filed a copyright infringement and trade secret misappropriations case against Meta et al., and in its defences, Meta argued that Planner 5D's virtually created interior design scenes are not valid as copyrighted works since they lack a human author.[80]

3.2 Exceptions/limitations allowing AI training

US Copyright Law does not currently allow exceptions for AI training on copyright works. However, US Copyright Law, 17 U.S.C. §108, does provide for limited exceptions with respect to copyrighted works for acts by libraries or archives, among others, provided, *inter alia*, that 'the reproduction or distribution is made without any purpose of direct or indirect commercial advantage' and the collections of the library or archives are 'open to the public' or 'available not only to researchers affiliated with the library or archives or with the institution of which it is a part, but also to other persons doing research in a specialized field' and 'the reproduction or distribution of the work includes a notice of copyright that appears on the copy or phonorecord that is reproduced under the provisions of this section, or includes a legend stating that the work may be protected by copyright if no such notice can be found on the copy or phonorecord that is reproduced under the provisions of this section.'[81] The pending copyright infringement focused cases do not appear to meet these requirements (and, also, do not claim to); however, it is of interest whether a library or archive might utilize an AI tool which met the requirements of Section 108.

78. *Andersen v. Stability AI Ltd.*, No. 3:23-cv-00201 (N.D. Cal. Second amended complaint filed Oct. 31, 2024).
79. *Id.* See also, Complaint, *Getty Images (US), Inc. v. Stability AI, Inc.*, 1:23-cv-00135-UNA (D.Del. Complaint filed Feb. 3, 2023).
80. *UAB 'Planner5D' v. Meta Platforms, Inc.*, 3:19-cv-03132, (N.D. California, Complaint filed June 2019) (originally filed as *UAB 'Planner5D' dba Planner 5D v. Facebook, Inc.*, 3:19-cv-03132-WHO, Northern District of California, June 2019, and 3:20-cv-02198-WHO, Northern District of California, March 2020).
81. 17 U.S.C. § 108.

As discussed herein, in *Authors Guild v. Google, Inc.*,[82] the court looked to whether Google's digitization of allegedly more than 20 million books and other third-party copyrighted works without permission or payment of licence fees amounted to copyright infringement. The plaintiffs also claimed that Google maintained multiple copies of each book, including on its servers, backup tapes, et al. The Second Circuit found that Google's digitization of books to make them searchable online was transformative and constituted fair use, as it provided significant public benefits without replacing the books. Regarding Google 'snippets' gleaned from the digitized copies, the Second Circuit agreed that 'Google's making of a digital copy to provide a search function... augments public knowledge by making available information about [p]laintiffs' books without providing the public with a substantial substitute for matter protected by the [p]laintiffs' copyright interests in the original works or derivatives of them.'[83] Further, the Second Circuit found that Google's provision of the digital copies to libraries was non-infringing as well.

From this case and others, it is conceivable that libraries and archives, and possible other research institutions, will eventually benefit (if not already benefitting) from AI tools and systems, provided they are used in approved manner. At the same time, there appear to be persuasive arguments being made in current cases in order to extend such use in order to benefit the public. It would be beneficial if such large improvements in technology were expressly identified and address in US Copyright Law.

3.3 Remedies and Enforcement

As for all areas of copyright infringement – whether by an AI tool's unauthorized use of copyrighted material or output of an unauthorized derivative -- the same remedies and enforcement available are available. Notably, it is useful to mention that US courts have also recognized vicarious infringement, where a party profits from direct infringement while declining to exercise a right to stop or limit it.[84] Accordingly, while an AI tool or system provider may license their system to another, and especially if the use of such AI tool or large language model (LLM) system is geared only towards actions that would amount to copyright infringement, there is precedent for holding a provider – albeit not necessarily an AI tool or LLM system owner -- liable.

4. AI-GENERATED OUTPUT

4.1 Protection of AI-Generated Content

In the US, there have been consistent discussions concerning the protection of AI-generated content, referred to as 'output'. Like in US patent cases, the US courts and US Copyright Office have consistently held that the 'author' of a copyrightable work must be human.

82. *Authors Guild v. Google, Inc.*, 804 F.3d 202 (2d Cir. 2015).
83. *Id.*
84. *Metro-Goldwyn Mayer Studios, Inc. v. Grokster Ltd.*, 545 U.S. 913, 914 (2005).

Several US courts have explained in detail that 'author' must be a human. The courts ground their decisions in the US Constitution, Article 1, Section 8, Clause 8, which states that Congress has the power '[to] promote the Progress of Science and useful Arts, by securing for limited Times to Authors and Inventors the exclusive Right to their respective Writings and Discoveries.' In looking to the intent of the authors of the Constitution, as well as other reasonings, the US courts have been generally consistent in finding that 'author' means a human author, not a machine, monkey, or other non-human.[85] For example, the US Supreme Court in 1884, in *Burrow-Giles Lithographic Co. v. Sarony*, which questioned whether a photograph outputted by a camera (machine) was in fact a copyrightable work, held that the copyright laws permitted a photograph to be copyrightable 'so far as they are representatives of original intellectual conceptions of the author.' The Court defined 'author' as 'he to whom anything owes its origin; originator; maker; one who completes a work of science or literature' and repeatedly made references that 'authors' are humans or persons. 111 U.S. 53, 56 *et seq*. Further, in its published opinion, the Court referenced an English decision describing an author as the 'person' who was 'the cause of the picture which is produced.' 111 U.S. 53, 58.

Recent US district courts continue to consistently follow *Burrow-Giles* and later precedents, holding that an author must be a human. In March 2025, the US Court of Appeals for the District of Columbia Circuit ('D.C. Circuit') affirmed the lower US District Court's holding that an AI-generated work was not copyrightable as the author was listed as the 'Creativity Machine' and the work was found to not contain any human authorship. For background, Dr Stephen Thaler[86] created a generative AI system, which he refers to as the 'Creativity Machine.' Dr Thaler asserted that the 'Creativity Machine' authored a picture. Dr Thaler named that picture *A Recent Entrance to Paradise*, and submitted it in an application for a two-dimensional artwork for copyright registration with the US Copyright Office in November 2018. In the application filing,[87] Dr Thaler identified the 'Creativity Machine' as the sole author of the picture, and himself as the owner of the picture with a transfer statement of 'ownership of the machine.'[88]

---

85. In *Urantia Found. v. Kristen Maaherra*, 114 F.3d 955, 957–59 (9th Cir. 1997), the U.S. Court of Appeals for the Ninth Circuit held that 'some element of human creativity must have occurred in order for the Book to be copyrightable' because 'it is not creations of divine beings that the copyright laws were intended to protect'. The Ninth Circuit held that the compilation of the book was copyrightable, but the 'divine messages' were not copyrightable. *Id.* In *Naruto v. Slater*, No. 15-cv-04324, 2016 U.S. Dist. LEXIS 11041, at *10 (N.D. Cal. Jan. 28, 2016), the court held that '[monkey] is not an "author" within the meaning of the Copyright Act'. In the subsequent appeal, the Ninth Circuit held that a monkey cannot sue for copyright infringement. *Naruto v. Slater*, 888 F.3d 418 (9th Cir. 2018).
86. Notably, Dr Stephen Thaler is also known for DABUS ('Device for Autonomous Bootstrapping of Unified Sentience') system which was used to create various inventions, such as a beverage container, which has been litigation in several jurisdictions asserting that a non-human inventor should be allowed to obtain a U.S. patent.
87. U.S. Copyright Application No. 1-7100387071.
88. See, the U.S. Copyright Office Review Board letter dated February 14, 2022. In the filed application, Dr Thaler included a note for the U.S. Copyright Office stating that the artwork 'was autonomously created by a computer algorithm running on a machine.' *Id.*

The US Copyright Office rejected Dr Thaler's application for copyright based on the requirement for human authorship. Dr Thaler filed for a review of the US Copyright Office's decision in the US District Court for the District of Columbia. The District Court agreed with the US Copyright Office, and emphasized that, '[o]n the record designed by plaintiff from the outset of his application for copyright registration,' the case had presented 'only the question of whether a work generated autonomously by a computer system is eligible for copyright.' *Thaler v. Perlmutter*, 687 F. Supp. 3d 140, 142 42 (D.D.C. 2023). Dr Thaler appealed to the D.C. Circuit. The D.C. Circuit held:

> We affirm the denial of Dr. Thaler's copyright application. The Creativity Machine cannot be the recognized author of a copyrighted work because the Copyright Act of 1976 requires all eligible work to be authored in the first instance by a human being. Given that holding, we need not address the Copyright Office's argument that the Constitution itself requires human authorship of all copyrighted material. Nor do we reach Dr. Thaler's argument that he is the work's author by virtue of making and using the Creativity Machine because that argument was waived before the agency.

The D.C. Circuit concluded that the Creativity Machine cannot be the recognized author of a copyrighted work based on the US Constitution, US statutory law, and prior US court decisions. The court stated:

> As a matter of statutory law, the Copyright Act requires all work to be authored in the first instance by a human being. Dr. Thaler's copyright registration application listed the Creativity Machine as the work's sole author, even though the Creativity Machine is not a human being. As a result, the Copyright Office appropriately denied Dr. Thaler's application.[89]

In reaching that conclusion, the D.C. Circuit first looked to the US Copyright Act, stating:

> Authors are at the center of the Copyright Act. A copyright 'vests initially in the author or authors of the work.' 17 U.S.C. § 201(a). And copyright protection only 'subsists ... in original works of authorship[.]' *Id.* § 102(a).
>
> The Copyright Act does not define the word 'author.' But traditional tools of statutory interpretation show that, within the meaning of the Copyright Act, 'author' refers only to human beings. To start, the text of multiple provisions of the statute indicates that authors must be humans, not machines. In addition, the Copyright Office consistently interpreted the word author to mean a human prior to the Copyright Act's passage, and we infer that Congress adopted the agency's longstanding interpretation of the word 'author' when it re-enacted that term in the 1976 Copyright Act.[90]

The D.C. Circuit went into further detail regarding the focus of the Copyright Act on the 'human' requirement for authorship, finding seven distinct reasonings that collectively support this requirement, as follows.

---

89. *Thaler v. Perlmutter*, 130 F.4th 1039 (D.C. Cir. 2025).
90. *Id.*

First, the Copyright Act's ownership provision is premised on the author's legal capacity to hold property. A copyright 'vests initially in the author[.]' 17 U.S.C. § 201(a). This means an 'author gains "exclusive rights" in her work immediately upon the work's creation.' *Fourth Estate Pub. Benefit Corp. v. Wall-Street.com, LLC,* 586 U.S. 296, 300–301, (2019) (quoting 17 U.S.C. § 106). Because a copyright is fundamentally a property right created by Congress, and Congress specified that authors immediately own their copyrights, an entity that cannot own property cannot be an author under the statute.

Second, the Copyright Act limits the duration of a copyright to the author's lifespan or to a period that approximates how long a human might live. A copyright generally 'endures for a term consisting of the life of the author and 70 years after the author's death.' 17 U.S.C. §302(a)

Third, the Copyright Act's inheritance provision states that, when an author dies, that person's 'termination interest is owned, and may be exercised' by their 'widow or widower,' or their 'surviving children or grandchildren,' 17 U.S.C. § 203(a)(2), (A). Machines, needless to say, have no surviving spouses or heirs.

Fourth, copyright transfers require a signature. To transfer copyright ownership, there must be 'an instrument of conveyance' that is 'signed by the owner[.]' 17 U.S.C. § 204(a). Machines lack signatures, as well as the legal capacity to provide an authenticating signature.

Fifth, authors of unpublished works are protected regardless of the author's 'nationality or domicile.' 17 U.S.C. § 104(a). Machines do not have domiciles, nor do they have a national identity.

Sixth, authors have intentions. A joint work is one 'prepared by two or more authors with the intention that their contributions be merged into inseparable or interdependent parts of a unitary whole.' 17 U.S.C. § 101. Machines lack minds and do not intend anything.

Seventh, and by comparison, every time the Copyright Act discusses machines, the context indicates that machines are tools, not authors. For example, the Copyright Act defines a 'computer program' as 'a set of statements or instructions to be used directly or indirectly' to 'bring about a certain result.' 17 U.S.C. § 101. The word 'machine' is given the same definition as the words 'device' and 'process,' *id.*, and those terms are consistently used in the statute as mechanisms that assist authors, rather than as authors themselves, *id.* §§ 102(a); 108(c)(2); 109(b)(1)(B)(i); 116(d)(1); 117(a)(1), (c); 401(a); 1001(2), (3). In addition, when computer programs and machines are referenced in the statute, the statute presumes they have an 'owner,' *id.* § 117(a), (c), who can perform 'maintenance,' 'servic[e],' or 'repair' on them, id. § 117(d).[91]

91. *Id.* The D.C. Circuit further noted that the U.S. Copyright Office updated its regulations to explicitly require that works must 'owe their origin to a human agent[.].' *Id.*, quoting Compendium First Edition § 2.8.3. Further, the D.C. Circuit commented on the U.S. Congress creation of the National Commission on New Technological Uses of Copyrighted Works ('CONTU') in the 1970s, which discussed several aspects of the creation of new works by automatic systems or machine reproduction, but apparently never suggested that authorship would be seen as by a computer or machine. Instead, computers and machines were viewed as tools used by potential authors. See published CONTU meeting notes, including CONTU, Meeting No. 2 at 10–11 (Nov. 19, 1975), https://perma.cc/857K-VRSB;

The D.C. Circuit challenges one to substitute the word 'machine' for 'author' in the Copyright Act in order to see how this is not possible as a machine cannot have a nationality, or children, et al.

Further, the D.C. Circuit addressed the work-for-hire section in the Copyright Act which allows for corporations to be 'considered the author,' but not be the author.[92]

The D.C. Circuit addressed the part-human, part-machine authorship issue, and closed such issue as not relevant to the present case as Dr Thaler had listed the Creativity Machine as the sole author in the application for copyright registration.

> [T]he human authorship requirement does not prohibit copyrighting work that was made by or with the assistance of artificial intelligence. The rule requires only that the author of that work be a human being – the person who created, operated, or used artificial intelligence – and not the machine itself. The Copyright Office, in fact, has allowed the registration of works made by human authors who use artificial intelligence. See Copyright Registration Guidance: Works Containing Material Generated by Artificial Intelligence, 88 Fed. Reg. 16,190, 16,192 (March 16, 2023) (Whether a work made with artificial intelligence is registerable depends 'on the circumstances, particularly how the AI tool operates and how it was used to create the final work.').
>
> To be sure, the Copyright Office has rejected some copyright applications based on the human-authorship requirement even when a human being is listed as the author. See Copyright Office, *Re: Zarya of the Dawn (Registration # VAu001480196)* (Feb. 21, 2023), https://perma.cc/AD86- WGPM (denying copyright registration for a comic book's images made with generative artificial intelligence). Some have disagreed with these decisions. See Motion Picture Association, *Comment Letter on Artificial Intelligence and Copyright* at 5 (Oct. 30, 2023), https://perma.cc/9W9X-3EZE (This 'very broad definition of "generative AI" has the potential to sweep in technologies that are not new and that members use to assist creators in making motion pictures.'); 2 W. PATRY, COPYRIGHT § 3:60.52 (2024); Legal Professors Amicus Br. 36- 37 ('The U.S. Copyright Office guidelines are somewhat paradoxical: human contributions must be demonstrated within the creative works generated by AI.').[93]

The D.C. Circuit emphasized the public policy for having the Copyright Act, stating:

> But the Supreme Court has long held that copyright law is intended to benefit the public, not authors. Copyright law 'makes reward to the owner a secondary consideration. … "[T]he primary object in conferring the monopoly lie[s] in the general benefits derived by the public from the labors of authors."' *United States v. Loew's, Inc.*, 371 U.S. 38, 46–47 (1962) (quoting *Fox Film Co. v. Doyal*, 286 U.S. 123, 127 (1932)).[94]

CONTU, Meeting No. 3 at 1–11 (Dec. 18–19, 1975), https://perma.cc/EB3T-KNR4; CONTU, Meeting No. 4 at 1–8 (Feb. 11–13, 1976), https://perma.cc/NPG6-J8E3; CONTU, Meeting No. 6 (May 6–7, 1976), https://perma.cc/HCX5-6ZYX. *Id.*

92. *Id.* See also, 17 U.S.C. § 201(b).
93. *Id.*
94. *Id.*

The D.C. Circuit did not find that such public policy of encouraging the sharing of creativity with the public would be stymied if a machine could not have authorship rights, and remarked that such consideration of public policy is a matter for Congress, not the judicial system.[95]

In the end, the D.C. Circuit found that the Copyright Act 'provides "a sufficient ground for deciding this case, and the cardinal principle of judicial restraint – if it is not necessary to decide more, it is necessary not to decide more – counsels us to go no further."' quoting *PDK Laboratories Inc. v. United States Drug Enforcement Agency*, 362 F.3d 786, 799 (D.C. Cir. 2004) (Roberts, J., concurring in part and concurring in the judgement).[96]

The US Copyright Office has continued to hold fast to the requirement for human authorship in order for works to be copyrightable. One recent application for copyright registration is *Zarya of the Dawn*, referred to in *Thaler v. Perlmutter*, in which the original copyright registration was canceled and reissued to exclude the AI-generated images. *Zarya of the Dawn* is a comic book authored by Kris Kashtanova for which Copyright Registration No. Vau001480196 was issued. After registration, the US Copyright Office was made aware of statements made on social media that the comic book was produced by Midjourney AI technology,[97] and alerted Ms Kashtanova that the registration was going to be cancelled unless she provided additional information to indicate why the registration should not be cancelled.[98]

In response to a US Copyright Office communication, Ms Kashtanova subsequently informed the US Copyright Office about the extent of Midjourney's AI technology used for certain images in the comic book.[99] Ms Kashtanova put forth that she edited some of the Midjourney AI created images, showing the various stages

95. *Id. See also,* efforts by U.S. Congress in the recently published U.S. House of Rep., *Bipartisan House Task Force Report on Artificial Intelligence* at 111–136 (Dec. 2024), https://perma.cc/Y69R-DM3D, and efforts by the U.S. Copyright Office in the recently published guidance of *Copyright and Artificial Intelligence, Part 1: Digital Replicas at 57 (Jul. 31, 2024),* https://perma.cc/8CUH-DN5A, and *Copyright and Artificial Intelligence, Part 2: Copyrightability* at 32–40 (Jan. 29, 2025), https://perma.cc/W9VR-TLQP.

96. *Id.*

97. According to the U.S. Copyright Office Letter dated February 21, 2023, re 'Zarya of the Dawn' Comic Book, by Kris Kashtanova, 'Midjourney is a subscription service that allows users to pay to generate images, with subscription plans corresponding to the computational time it uses to generate images. *See* Fast and Relax Mode, MIDJOURNEY, https://docs.midjourney.com/docs/fast-relax ("Midjourney uses powerful Graphics Processing Units (GPUs) to interpret and process each prompt. When you purchase a subscription to Midjourney, you are purchasing time on these GPUs."); Subscription Plans, MIDJOURNEY, https://docs.midjourney.com/docs/plans (providing information about different subscription plans).'

98. U.S. Copyright Office Letter dated October 28, 2022, re 'Zarya of the Dawn' Comic Book by Kris Kashtanova, referred to by U.S. Copyright Office Letter dated February 21, 2023, re 'Zarya of the Dawn' Comic Book, by Kris Kashtanova, https://www.copyright.gov/docs/zarya-of-the-dawn.pdf.

99. This case involved a few issues including that Ms Kashtanova did not originally inform the U.S. Copyright Office of the use of AI-generated material in the work, and that the work is an 'adaptation of Kashtanova's original story about Zarya.' *See* Kashtanova Letter dated November 21, 2022. Thus, the work is a derivative of the original story, 'requir[ing] that the Work contain separate textual authorship from the story that is itself sufficiently

of her edits of different aspects of the images, including a modification to the upper lip of the girl in the image.

However, the US Copyright Office determined that such modifications as the changes to the girl image's mouth 'are too minor and imperceptible to supply the necessary creativity for copyright protection.'[100] The US Copyright Office requires that a resulting work from a human author's edits must contain a 'sufficient amount of original authorship' in order to qualify for a copyright registration.[101] In this case, Ms Kashtanova's edits were not concluded to be sufficient.

Further, it was argued that Ms Kashtanova provided 'prompts' to the Midjourney AI technology 'tool' and 'guided' the structure and content of each image. However, the US Copyright Office concluded that the images generated were clearly generated by Midjourney. Rather than a tool that Ms Kashtanova controlled and guided to reach her desired image, 'Midjourney generates images in an unpredictable way.' The US Copyright Office referred to the *Burrow-Giles* case to demonstrate the difference, explaining that the '"author" of a copyrighted work is the one "who has actually formed the picture," the one who acts as "the inventive or master mind."'[102] The US Copyright Office looked to the Midjourney AI technology to determine how it responded to text prompts, explaining that 'a person who provides text prompts to Midjourney does not 'actually form' the generated images and is not the "master mind" behind them.'[103] Instead, the US Copyright Office determined that user prompts 'may 'influence' generated image, but prompt text does not dictate a specific result ... The fact that Midjourney's specific output cannot be predicted by users makes Midjourney different for copyright purposes than other tools used by artists.'[104]

Specifically, in correspondence dated 21 February 2023, the US Copyright Office determined that:

> Ms. Kashtanova is the author of the Work's text as well as the selection, coordination, and arrangement of the Work's written and visual elements. That authorship is protected by copyright. However, as discussed below, the images in the Work that were generated by the Midjourney technology are not the product of human authorship. Because the current registration for the Work does not disclaim its Midjourney-generated content, we intend to cancel the original certificate issued to Ms. Kashtanova and issue a new one covering only the expressive material that she created.[105]

creative for copyright protection.' U.S. Copyright Office Letter dated February 21, 2023, re 'Zarya of the Dawn,' by Kris Kashtanova.

100. *Id.*
101. The U.S. Copyright Office 'will refuse to register a claim if it determines that a human being did not create the work.' U.S. Copyright Office, Compendium of U.S. Copyright Office Practices § 313.2 et seq. (3d ed. 2021) ('COMPENDIUM (THIRD)')
102. *Id.*, quoting *Burrow-Giles*, 111 U.S. at 61.
103. *Id.*
104. *Id. See* COMPENDIUM (THIRD) § 313.2 ('the Office will not register works produced by a machine or mere mechanical process that operates randomly or automatically without any creative input or intervention from a human author').
105. U.S. Copyright Office Letter dated February 21, 2023, re 'Zarya of the Dawn' Comic Book, by Kris Kashtanova, https://www.copyright.gov/docs/zarya-of-the-dawn.pdf.

For Ms Kashtanova, while the US Copyright Office will remove copyright protection for the AI-generated images, the US Copyright Office will not change the effective date of the registration certificate – with the subsequently modified certificate having the same effective date as the original copyright registration certificate of 15 September 2022.[106]

The US Copyright Office has encountered additional applications for copyright registration in which the efforts of AI technology and a human are even more intertwined in creating a work.[107] For example, in Jason M. Allen's artwork, *Théâtre D'opéra Spatial*, the artwork was initially created using Midjourney AI technology, and then modified by Mr Allen using Adobe Photoshop. The US Copyright Office denied the registration for copyright of his edited work because the work 'contain[ed] more than a *de minimis* amount of content generated by artificial intelligence ("AI"), and this content must therefore be disclaimed in an application for registration. Because Mr Allen is unwilling to disclaim the AI-generated material, the Work cannot be registered as submitted.'[108] Like in the previous case, Mr Allen argued that his at least 624 text prompts to Midjourney AI technology and later adjustments using Adobe Photoshop should constitute Mr Allen as the author. The US Copyright Office determined that Mr Allen's text prompts and iterative process 'did not amount to human authorship.'[109]

In its decision, the US Copyright Office stated that 'when an AI technology receives solely a prompt from a human and produces complex written, visual, or musical works in response, the "traditional elements of authorship" are determined and executed by the technology – not the human user.'[110] Mr Allen refused to exclude

106. *Id.* In applications for U.S. copyright registration, there is a 'Limitation of Claim' section where one can list any materials that form part of the work which are not claimed for the copyright registration. For example, if the work is a derivative work, one can identify previously published or registered works in this section. Likewise, this is the section where one can also identify AI-generated material so that it does not thwart copyright registration of the human authored work. *See* Copyright Registration Guidance: Works Containing Material Generated by Artificial Intelligence, 37 C.F.R. Part 202 (March 16, 2023), https://www.federalregister.gov/documents/2023/03/16/2023-05321/copyright-registration-guidance-works-containing-material-generated-by-artificial-intelligence.
107. The U.S. Copyright Office's Copyright and Artificial Intelligence, Part 2, states that '[i]t is axiomatic that ideas or facts themselves are not protectible by copyright law, and the Supreme Court has made clear that originality is required, not just time and effort. In *Feist Publications, Inc. v. Rural Telephone Service Co.*, the U.S. Supreme Court rejected the theory that "sweat of the brow" alone could be sufficient for copyright protection. "To be sure," the Court further explained, "the requisite level of creativity is extremely low; even a slight amount will suffice. The vast majority of works make the grade quite easily, as they possess some creative spark, 'no matter how crude, humble or obvious' it might be."' quoting *Feist Publ'ns, Inc. v. Rural Tel. Serv. Co.*, 499 U.S. 340, 344–45, 352–361 (1991). *See also*, U.S. Copyright Office, Compendium of U.S. Copyright Office Practices § 101 (3d ed. 2021).
108. U.S. Copyright Office Letter dated September 5, 2023, re Théâtre D'opéra Spatial, by Jason M. Allen.
109. *Id.*
110. *Id., quoting* U.S. Copyright Office, *AI Registration Guidance*, 88 Fed. Reg. at 16,192 (March 2023).

'the non-human authorship elements,' and so registration of the copyright was denied.[111] Subsequent filings including AI-generated portions continue to be registered and/or denied in the US Copyright Office.

4.1.1 Copyright Protection of AI Output

As discussed herein, current US Copyright Law does not support protecting AI-generated output with copyright registration. While it is possible that the human author's work is tightly intertwined with the AI-generated output, the US Copyright Office, as well as the courts, have been consistent in requiring a human author and that any AI-generated output be excluded from copyright protection. That being said, if an AI-generated output is actually a human-controlled output where the AI technology is used as a tool or the like, and the requirements for authorship as described above are met, then, yes, it can be said that AI-generated output is protectable by US copyright.

Recently, the US Copyright Office has been issuing registrations to works involving AI-generated outputs. In the *AI Registration Guidance* issued by the US Copyright Office, Part II, as discussed herein:

> [A] human may select or arrange AI-generated material in a sufficiently creative way that 'the resulting work as a whole constitutes an original work of authorship.' A human may also 'modify material originally generated by AI technology to such a degree that the modifications meet the standard for copyright protection.'
>
> Other generative AI systems also offer tools that similarly allow users to exert control over the selection, arrangement, and content of the final output.
>
> Unlike prompts alone, these tools can enable the user to control the selection and placement of individual creative elements. Whether such modifications rise to the minimum standard of originality required under Feist will depend on a case-by-case determination. In those cases where they do, the output should be copyrightable.[112]

For example, the US Copyright Office allowed the copyright registration of *A Single Piece of American Cheese*, US Copyright Registration No. VAU001543942, based on a selection, coordination, or arrangement of AI-generated elements.[113]

In a published article, Kent Keirsey, CEO of Invoke (owner of the work), is quoted as stating that they used 'inpainting' to generate 35 elements within the image. Initially, the work was denied registration, and later allowed after submissions were provided showing the creative process and the control that was exerted. According to the US Copyright Office, 'the resulting collage as a whole contained a sufficient amount of human original authorship in the selection, arrangement, and coordination of the AI-generated material such that the entire image (but not the specific

111. *Id.*
112. U.S. Copyright Office, *Copyright and Artificial Intelligence, Part II* (January 2025).
113. Kendra Chedraoui, *This Company Got a Copyright for an Image Made Entirely With AI. Here's How*, CNET, 10 February 2025, https://www.cnet.com/tech/services-and-software/this-company-got-a-copyright-for-an-image-made-entirely-with-ai-heres-how/. See also, https://publicrecords.copyright.gov/detailed-record/voyager_37990563.

elements) could be copyrighted. Importantly, the applicant appropriately disclaimed the underlying images generated by AI in its application.'[114]

Additional US copyright registrations including AI-generated output have been reported for 2D artwork and AI-generated video with AI-generated music.

4.1.2 Neighbouring Rights Protection of AI Output

While the US copyright law does not fully recognize the concept of 'neighbouring rights' as defined by, for example, European jurisdictions, the US Digital Millennium Copyright Act of 1998 does provide a limited performance right in sound recordings for digital performances, applying to 'noninteractive digital streams.' A noninteractive digital stream is a digital broadcast where a listener cannot choose the order of the music. At this time, it is unclear as to how this limited form of protection will be treated in the context of AI outputs.

4.2 AI-Generated Output Infringes Existing Copyright

Under US Copyright Law, Title 17 of the United States Code, AI-generated output, like any other work, may infringe an existing copyrighted work. In the United States, proving copyright infringement involves demonstrating that (1) the plaintiff owns a valid copyright, and (2) the defendant copied elements of the work that are protected by copyright law.

Under (1), demonstrating that the plaintiff owns a valid copyright involves proving that the work is original and that the plaintiff has registered the copyright with the US Copyright Office. While registration is not required to have a valid copyright, it is necessary to bring a claim for infringement.

Under (2), demonstrating that the defendant copied elements of the work that are protected by copyright law usually involves two sub-elements. The first sub-element is access. The plaintiff must demonstrate that the defendant had access to the copyrighted work. The second sub-element is substantial similarity. The plaintiff must show that the allegedly infringing work is substantially similar to the copyrighted work. This often involves comparing the two works to determine if they share similarities that would not occur by coincidence or through independent creation. If these elements are successfully proven, the court may find in favour of the plaintiff.

In the context of AI-generated output, demonstrating access and evidence of copying is much more difficult than in traditional copyright infringement cases. The data used for training AI models may include copyrighted material, proprietary databases, and/or other intellectual property. In general, providers of AI models do not normally disclose their training data, and extracting the training data set from a model is, under most circumstances, not technically possible. This is due to several reasons including that the data used for training large AI models can be vast and complex, making them difficult to share or distribute effectively. The data often requires substantial preprocessing, which is part of the value that AI providers add.

114. *Id.*

In addition, sharing large datasets requires significant resources for storage, bandwidth, and management, which makes maintaining and distributing these datasets logistically challenging and costly. Furthermore, the specific data and methods used for training AI models can be a significant competitive advantage. Revealing this information could allow competitors to replicate or improve upon the technology. Therefore, plaintiffs alleging copyright infringement by an AI provider have been left to rely on circumstantial evidence to infer access to their copyrighted work.

For example, in the pending case against Stability AI, the Getty Images watermark appears in AI-generated outputs, which Getty Images alleges to strongly suggest direct copying.[115] Other pending cases are grappling with the issues of access to copyrighted works such as books,[116] visual art,[117] music,[118] and news articles.[119] It is possible, however, that litigants may be able to obtain in discovery the inputs into the AI system that produced the allegedly infringing work. These inputs may constitute circumstantial or even direct evidence of copying.

Another challenge is demonstrating that protected elements were indeed copied. The act of copying is not always a violation of copyright law; rather, the output must include protected elements, such as an expression from the original work, rather than just ideas. Additionally, because AI-generated content is probabilistic, the same prompt may yield different outputs each time the prompt is entered by a user, complicating the process of proving that a particular source was copied, rather than a mix of elements from various sources.

In addition, each of these inquiries into access and copying are made increasingly difficult due to the breadth of the types of the AI models presently available, and the mode of operation of the different AI models. For instance, there may be a wide variety of applications depending on whether the AI model generates images, text, music, etc. Each AI model has a unique mode of operation and manner generating output, and the copyrighted works allegedly used for training each AI are different, including books, videos, articles, websites, images, music, and text.

Separately, Section 1202(b) of the Digital Millennium Copyright Act (DMCA) addresses the removal or alteration of copyright management information (CMI) and prohibits the distribution of works with removed or altered CMI knowing it will induce, enable, facilitate, or conceal an infringement. There have been instances where Section 1202(b) claims have been raised, particularly concerning the use

115. *Getty Images, Inc. v. Stability AI Inc.*, No. 1:23-cv-00135 (D. Del.).
116. *Tremblay v. OpenAI, Inc.*, 716 F.Supp 3d 772 (N.D. Cal. 2024).
117. *Andersen v. Stability AI Ltd.*, 700 F.Supp.3d 853 (N.D. Cal. 2023).
118. *Concord Music Grp., Inc. v. Anthropic PBC,* No. 24-cv-03811-EKL, 2025 U.S. Dist. LEXIS 55639 (N.D. Cal. Mar. 25, 2025); *Concord Music Grp., Inc. v. Anthropic PBC,* 738 F. Supp. 3d 973 (M.D. Tenn. 2024).
119. *N.Y. Times Co. v. Microsoft Corp.*, *Daily News LP v. Microsoft Corp.*, and *Center for Investigative Reporting, Inc. v. Microsoft Corp* , Nos. 1:23-cv-11195, 1:24-cv-03285, 1:24-cv-04872 (S.D.N.Y.) consolidated as *N.Y. Times Co. v. Microsoft Corp.*, No. 23-cv-11195 (SHS), 2025 U.S. Dist. LEXIS 64462 (S.D.N.Y. Apr. 4, 2025); *Intercept Media, Inc. v. OpenAI, Inc.*, No. 24-cv-1515 (JSR), 2025 U.S. Dist. LEXIS 30147 (S.D.N.Y. Feb. 20, 2025); *Raw Story Media, Inc. v. OpenAI, Inc.*, 2024 U.S. Dist. LEXIS 204101 (S.D.N.Y. Nov. 7, 2024).

of AI to manipulate or generate content, but in many instances those claims were dismissed.[120]

4.3 Remedies and Enforcement

Copyright remedies are crucial components of copyright law, providing mechanisms to address and rectify the infringement of copyrighted works. When an author's creative expression, protected under copyright law, is unlawfully used, reproduced, or distributed without proper authorization, the copyright holder has several avenues to seek redress. In general, the remedies available are designed not only to compensate the copyright owner for losses suffered due to infringement, but also to deter future violations and uphold the integrity of intellectual property rights. The primary remedies available under copyright law typically include injunctive relief, monetary damages, and, in some cases, statutory damages.

Under 17 U.S.C. § 502, shown below, injunctive relief involves a court order to immediately cease the infringing activities, effectively preventing further unauthorized use of the copyrighted material. This can be particularly important in cases where ongoing infringement could cause irreparable harm to the copyright holder's market or reputation. Courts may issue injunctive relief to halt infringing activity, including restricting access to copyrighted training data, and halting the distribution and provision of AI services training on infringing data.

> § *502. Remedies for infringement: Injunctions*
>
> (a) Any court having jurisdiction of a civil action arising under this title may, subject to the provisions of section 1498 of title 28, grant temporary and final injunctions on such terms as it may deem reasonable to prevent or restrain infringement of a copyright.
>
> (b) Any such injunction may be served anywhere in the United States on the person enjoined; it shall be operative throughout the United States and shall be enforceable, by proceedings in contempt or otherwise, by any United States court having jurisdiction of that person. The clerk of the court granting the injunction shall, when requested by any other court in which enforcement of the injunction is sought, transmit promptly to the other court a certified copy of all the papers in the case on file in such clerk's office.

According to 17 U.S.C. § 503, courts have the authority to mandate the destruction of infringing goods. If an AI model is deemed to be infringing and a more limited remedy, such as removing the unauthorized material from the model, is not practical or achievable, courts may order the destruction or alternative handling of some or all of the AI model itself.

Monetary damages may be awarded, and include actual damages or profits, and statutory damages. The aim of awarding monetary damages is to compensate the copyright owner for financial losses incurred due to the infringement, such as lost

120. *Kadrey et al v. Meta Platforms, Inc.*, Case No. 3:23-cv-03417-VC (N.D. Cal. Mar. 7, 2025); *Andersen v. Stability AI Ltd.*, 700 F.Supp.3d 853 (N.D. Cal. 2023); *Doe v. Github, Inc.*, Case No. 22-cv-06823-JST (N.D. Cal. Sep. 27, 2024); *Raw Story Media, Inc. v. OpenAI, Inc.*, 2024 U.S. Dist. LEXIS 204101 (S.D.N.Y. Nov. 7, 2024)

profits or licensing fees. Under 17 U.S.C. § 504, copyright owners may seek actual damages and disgorgement of the infringer's non-duplicative profits. The copyright owner may alternatively elect, under certain circumstances such as when actual damages are difficult to quantify, statutory damages that range from USD 750 to USD 30,000 per work infringed, and up to USD 150,000 per work infringed if infringement is wilful. Statutory damages provide a predetermined range of compensation that the court can award, as specified in 17 U.S.C. § 504(c), offering a measure of flexibility and deterrence.

It should be noted that statutory damages are not available under all circumstances.

Statutory damages are generally unavailable for works that have not been registered with the US Copyright Office prior to the commencement of the infringement or within three months of the work's first publication. Registration is a prerequisite for pursuing statutory damages and attorney's fees under 17 U.S.C. § 412. Furthermore, statutory damages may not be fully available for cases of 'innocent infringement.' While statutory damages can be awarded, the amount may be significantly reduced if the infringer proves they were not aware and had no reason to believe they were infringing a copyright. However, statutory damages are technically still available, albeit at the lower end of the spectrum. Statutory damages are not available against the US government or its employees acting in an official capacity. Instead, the remedies are limited to actual damages and profits, as outlined in 28 U.S.C. § 1498(b).

It should also be noted that punitive damages are not available as a remedy for copyright infringement under §504.

Additionally, 17 U.S.C. § 505 allows courts to award attorney's fees and costs to the prevailing party, further emphasizing the legal and financial consequences of copyright infringement. Typically, in the US each party is responsible for their own legal fees. Nevertheless, the Copyright Act does vest courts with the discretion to award attorney's feeds in appropriate circumstances under 17 U.S.C. § 505:

> *§505. Remedies for infringement: Costs and attorney›s fees*
>
> In any civil action under this title, the court in its discretion may allow the recovery of full costs by or against any party other than the United States or an officer thereof. Except as otherwise provided by this title, the court may also award a reasonable attorney's fee to the prevailing party as part of the costs.

Under certain circumstances, copyright infringement can be prosecuted as a criminal offence. According to 17 U.S.C. § 506, criminal penalties may apply if the infringement is wilful and conducted for purposes of commercial advantage or private financial gain. Some specific scenarios that can lead to criminal charges include the wilful infringement involving the reproduction or distribution of one or more copies of copyrighted works with a retail value exceeding USD 1,000 in any 180-day period (§ 506(a)(1)(B). The penalties for criminal copyright infringement can include fines and imprisonment, with the severity depending on the nature and extent of the infringement.

Furthermore, 17 U.S.C. § 512 is a provision of the DMCA that outlines the legal framework for limiting the liability of online service providers (OSPs) for copyright infringement occurring through their services. At the present time, several challenges have been brought under the DMCA against AI providers. However, there have been no claims that have survived a motion to dismiss. Nevertheless, if a DMCA claim were to be maintained, the infringer would be subject to the remedies under 17 U.S.C. § 512.

This particular section is commonly known referred to as the 'safe harbour' provision of the DMCA. It covers several key aspects including Transitory Digital Network Communications (§ 512(a)), System Caching (§ 512(b)), Hosting (§ 512(c)), and Information Location Tools (§ 512(d)). Section 512 establishes a notice and takedown process, which allows copyright owners to notify OSPs of infringing content. Upon receiving a proper notice, OSPs must expeditiously remove or disable access to the infringing material to retain safe harbour protection. OSPs must adopt and reasonably implement a policy for terminating accounts of repeat infringers to qualify for safe harbour protection, and they must not interfere with standard technical measures used by copyright owners to protect their works.

Lastly, licensing systems may be applied to resolve disputes over copyright infringement claims related to the public performance of musical works. Again, in the context of AI, it is not yet clear whether such licensing systems may be applicable. However, 17 U.S.C. § 513, shown below, may provide a framework for application. Specifically, § 513 establishes a mechanical licensing system for digital music, which is necessary for the reproduction and distribution of musical works in digital formats. It allows for a compulsory licensing system, meaning that eligible parties can obtain licences without negotiating directly with rights holders, provided certain conditions are met. Section 513 is a response to the digital distribution of music, ensuring that artists and rights holders are fairly compensated in the evolving music industry.

> § *513. Determination of reasonable license fees for individual proprietors*
>
> In the case of any performing rights society subject to a consent decree which provides for the determination of reasonable license rates or fees to be charged by the performing rights society, notwithstanding the provisions of that consent decree, an individual proprietor who owns or operates fewer than 7 non-publicly traded establishments in which nondramatic musical works are performed publicly and who claims that any license agreement offered by that performing rights society is unreasonable in its license rate or fee as to that individual proprietor, shall be entitled to determination of a reasonable license rate or fee as follows:
>
> (1) The individual proprietor may commence such proceeding for determination of a reasonable license rate or fee by filing an application in the applicable district court under paragraph (2) that a rate disagreement exists and by serving a copy of the application on the performing rights society. Such proceeding shall commence in the applicable district court within 90 days after the service of such copy, except that such 90-day requirement shall be subject to the administrative requirements of the court.
>
> (2) The proceeding under paragraph (1) shall be held, at the individual proprietor's election, in the judicial district of the district court with jurisdiction over the applicable consent decree or in that place of holding court of a district court that is the seat of the Federal circuit (other than the Court of Appeals for the Federal Circuit) in which the proprietor's establishment is located.
>
> (3) Such proceeding shall be held before the judge of the court with jurisdiction over the consent decree governing the performing rights society. At the discretion

of the court, the proceeding shall be held before a special master or magistrate judge appointed by such judge. Should that consent decree provide for the appointment of an advisor or advisors to the court for any purpose, any such advisor shall be the special master so named by the court.

(4) In any such proceeding, the industry rate shall be presumed to have been reasonable at the time it was agreed to or determined by the court. Such presumption shall in no way affect a determination of whether the rate is being correctly applied to the individual proprietor.

(5) Pending the completion of such proceeding, the individual proprietor shall have the right to perform publicly the copyrighted musical compositions in the repertoire of the performing rights society by paying an interim license rate or fee into an interest bearing escrow account with the clerk of the court, subject to retroactive adjustment when a final rate or fee has been determined, in an amount equal to the industry rate, or, in the absence of an industry rate, the amount of the most recent license rate or fee agreed to by the parties.

(6) Any decision rendered in such proceeding by a special master or magistrate judge named under paragraph (3) shall be reviewed by the judge of the court with jurisdiction over the consent decree governing the performing rights society. Such proceeding, including such review, shall be concluded within 6 months after its commencement.

(7) Any such final determination shall be binding only as to the individual proprietor commencing the proceeding, and shall not be applicable to any other proprietor or any other performing rights society, and the performing rights society shall be relieved of any obligation of nondiscrimination among similarly situated music users that may be imposed by the consent decree governing its operations.

(8) An individual proprietor may not bring more than one proceeding provided for in this section for the determination of a reasonable license rate or fee under any license agreement with respect to any one performing rights society.

(9) For purposes of this section, the term 'industry rate' means the license fee a performing rights society has agreed to with, or which has been determined by the court for, a significant segment of the music user industry to which the individual proprietor belongs.

Overall, copyright remedies play a vital role in maintaining the balance between encouraging creative endeavours and protecting the rights of creators, ensuring that intellectual property laws remain effective and relevant in an ever-evolving digital landscape. The availability and scope of these remedies can vary based on factors such as the nature of the infringement, the conduct of the infringer, and the specific provisions of national copyright laws.

4.4 Summary

While the US Copyright Office and the courts have provided sufficient clarity that an AI model cannot be an author, there are still questions surrounding the data used to train an AI model, and the outputs of AI systems. There is an absence of explicit statutory guidance on using data to train AI systems, but the US Copyright Office has published reports to address these gaps, with further guidance expected within the next year.

Training AI systems with copyrighted materials is a subject of growing concern and debate at the intersection of law, technology, and ethics. One of the primary issues is the difficulty plaintiffs might face in raising infringement claims against AI developers. The process of training an AI involves using vast amounts of data, often sourced from various places, some of which may include copyrighted material. This data is used to teach AI systems to recognize patterns, generate content, or perform specific tasks. However, because the data is typically processed and transformed into a statistical model, it becomes challenging to pinpoint how specific copyrighted materials have been utilized, if at all, in the final AI output. This transformation complicates the task of demonstrating direct infringement, as the original material is not reproduced in a recognizable form.

Moreover, the applicability of the fair use doctrine to AI training processes remains uncertain. Fair use is a legal doctrine that allows for the use of copyrighted material without the permission of the rights holder primarily for purposes that benefit the public, such as education, commentary, criticism, and research. For AI models trained with copyrighted material, the question of fair use hinges on four factors that courts evaluate to determine whether a particular use qualifies as fair use.

The first factor considers the purpose and character of the use, including whether it is of a commercial nature or for nonprofit educational purposes. AI models developed for commercial gain might find it harder to claim fair use compared to those intended for research or educational purposes. However, even commercial uses can qualify as fair use if they are deemed transformative, meaning that they add new expression, meaning, or message to the original work. The second factor examines the nature of the copyrighted work. Generally, the fair use defence is more readily applied to factual works than to highly creative ones, such as novels or films. The third factor looks at the amount and substantiality of the portion used in relation to the copyrighted work as a whole. In the context of AI, this can be particularly complex, as the training process often involves using large datasets, possibly incorporating small portions of many works. Finally, the fourth factor considers the effect of the use on the market value of the copyrighted work. If the use of copyrighted materials in AI training negatively impacts the market for the original works, it is less likely to be considered fair use. However, if the AI application merely provides a different function that does not replace or suppress demand for the original, it might weigh in favour of fair use.

As AI technology continues to evolve, courts will likely face increasing pressure to provide clarity on these issues, balancing the rights of copyright holders with the innovative potential of AI. This ongoing dialogue will shape the future landscape of intellectual property law in the digital age, affecting stakeholders across creative, technological, and legal sectors.

Lastly, in the United States, remedies for copyright infringement are designed to address violations of the exclusive rights granted to copyright holders under the Copyright Act. When a copyright owner believes their work has been infringed upon, they can seek relief through the courts. The remedies available in US copyright infringement lawsuits are primarily aimed at compensating the copyright owner, preventing further infringement, and deterring future violations. These remedies can be broadly categorized into monetary damages, injunctive relief, and other equitable remedies. Courts aim to balance the interests of protecting intellectual property rights with promoting creativity and innovation.

5. CONCLUSION

The US is navigating uncharted territory at the intersection of AI and copyright as there are no specific laws and few precedents directly regulating the use of copyrighted material for training AI systems. However, this issue is actively being addressed through multiple ongoing cases, where existing statutory copyright laws and exceptions are being applied. This evolving legal framework indicates a critical period as developers of AI and creators of copyrighted material await further guidance and clarification.

The legal framework being developed surrounding AI and copyright demands a flexible, case-specific approach, with fair use as the cornerstone for evaluating unauthorized uses of copyrighted material. Any new legal framework must be carefully crafted to preserve the adaptability inherent in current copyright laws. Prior to the innovations in AI, courts have adeptly managed other disruptive technologies such as the rise of digital music, streaming, video recording, and 3D printing, ensuring the adaptability of US copyright law without the need for immediate legislative intervention. The fair use doctrine is designed to be flexible and adaptive, allowing courts to assess new technologies within the existing copyright framework. Congress has allowed courts to apply fair use and other legal principles before intervening, as judicial decisions may sufficiently resolve and clarify the issues without the need for statutory intervention.

Balancing the interests of fostering creativity, protecting copyright holders' rights, and ensuring public access to information remains crucial. Instead of hastily adopting compulsory licensing or collective management models, it is prudent to allow courts to apply existing copyright doctrines to ascertain the necessity of new legal interventions. As US courts deliberate these issues, the decisions must balance the protection of rights holders with the public interest in technological advancement.

Furthermore, given the rapid evolution of AI systems, premature policymaking may become obsolete before implementation, thus allowing more responsive forces to lead. The legal framework should be cognizant of the rapidly changing nature of AI. Novel technical solutions may soon enable AI systems to better assess the extent to which outputs are derived from specific training data, including copyrighted material. Should these novel technical solutions prove reliable, they could provide substantial evidence for assessing infringement, complementing legal evaluations rather than relying solely on presumptions of access and copying a copyright work. Nonetheless, each case requires a nuanced analysis, as no single framework can universally apply to all AI models and their outputs.

AI systems frequently operate across multiple jurisdictions and are often trained using data from diverse legal and jurisdictional environments. Achieving harmonization of copyright laws concerning the use of such data in AI training could enhance efficiency and predictability for all stakeholders. However, these efforts must align with existing US law and respect the national copyright traditions of each country while balancing competing interests. Rather than imposing a rigid, one-size-fits-all rule, a nuanced approach that accommodates the unique legal landscapes and priorities of different jurisdictions will be essential in effectively navigating the complexities of AI and copyright law.

AIPPI LAW SERIES

1. Sanna Wolk, Kacper Szkalej (eds), *Employees' Intellectual Property Rights*, Second Edition, 2018 (ISBN 978-90-411-9230-1).
2. Jochen Bühling (ed.), *Patent Protection for Second Medical Uses*, Second Edition, 2020 (ISBN 978-94-035-0935-8).
3. Christopher V. Carani (ed.), *Design Rights: Functionality and Scope of Protection*, Second Edition, 2022 (ISBN 978-94-035-3210-3).
4. Eléonore Gaspar (ed.), *Genuine Use of Trademarks*, Second Edition, 2021 (ISBN 978-94-035-2833-5).
5. Jürgen Meier, Oswin Ridderbusch (eds), *Antibody Patenting: A Practitioner's Guide to Drafting, Prosecution and Enforcement*, Second Edition, 2023 (ISBN 978-94-035-3626-2).
6. Christian Czychowski, Jan Bernd Nordemann (eds), *Law of Raw Data*, 2021 (ISBN 978-94-035-3280-6).
7. John C. Todaro, Martin Bensadon, Brigitte Carion-Taravella (eds), *Pharmaceutical Test Data Exclusivity: A Multi-Jurisdictional Survey*, 2022 (ISBN 978-94-035-0106-2).
8. Jonathan P. Osha (ed.), *Artificial Intelligence and Patents: An International Perspective on Patenting AI-Related Inventions*, 2023 (ISBN 978-94-035-2215-9).
9. Christof Augenstein, Johanna Flythström (eds), *Enforcement of Decisions of the Unified Patent Court: A Survey of Participating Member States*, 2023 (ISBN 978-94-035-4846-3).
10. Guillaume Henry, Sanna Wolk (eds), *Artificial Intelligence and Copyright*, 2025 (ISBN 978-94-035-4278-2).

www.ingramcontent.com/pod-product-compliance
Ingram Content Group UK Ltd.
Pitfield, Milton Keynes, MK11 3LW, UK
UKHW020249290926
15470UKWH00002B/823

9 789403 542782